The Challenge of Coleridge

Literature and Philosophy

A. J. Cascardi, General Editor

This series publishes books in a wide range of subjects in philosophy and literature, including studies of the social and historical issues that relate these two fields. Drawing on the resources of the Anglo-American and Continental traditions, the series is open to philosophically informed scholarship covering the entire range of contemporary critical thought.

Already published:

J. M. Bernstein, *The Fate of Art: Aesthetic Alienation from Kant to Derrida and Adorno*
Peter Bürger, *The Decline of Modernism*
Mary E. Finn, *Writing the Incommensurable: Kierkegaard, Rossetti, and Hopkins*
Reed Way Dasenbrock, ed., *Literary Theory After Davidson*
David P. Haney, *William Wordsworth and the Hermeneutics of Incarnation*
David Jacobson, *Emerson's Pragmatic Vision: The Dance of the Eye*
Gray Kochhar-Lindgren, *Narcissus Transformed: The Textual Subject in Psychoanalysis and Literature*
Robert Steiner, *Toward a Grammar of Abstraction: Modernity, Wittgenstein, and the Paintings of Jackson Pollock*
Sylvia Walsh, *Living Poetically: Kierkegaard's Existential Aesthetics*
Michel Meyer, *Rhetoric, Language, and Reason*
Christie McDonald and Gary Wihl, eds., *Transformation in Personhood and Culture After Theory*
Charles Altieri, *Painterly Abstraction in Modernist American Poetry: The Contemporaneity of Modernism*
John C. O'Neal, *The Authority of Experience: Sensationist Theory in the French Enlightenment*
John O'Neill, ed., *Freud and the Passions*
Sheridan Hough, *Nietzsche's Noontide Friend: The Self as Metaphoric Double*
E. M. Dadlez, *What's Hecuba to Him? Fictional Events and Actual Emotions*
Hugh Roberts, *Shelley and the Chaos of History: A New Politics of Poetry*
Charles Altieri, *Postmodernisms Now: Essays on Contemporaneity in the Arts*
Arabella Lyon, *Intentions: Negotiated, Contested, and Ignored*
Jill Gordon, *Turning Toward Philosophy: Literary Device and Dramatic Structure in Plato's Dialogues*
Michel Meyer, *Philosophy and the Passions: Toward a History of Human Nature*. Translated by Robert F. Barsky
Reed Way Dasenbrock, *Truth and Consequences: Intentions, Conventions, and the New Thematics*
David P. Haney, *The Challenge of Coleridge: Ethics and Interpretation in Romanticism and Modern Philosophy*

The Challenge *of* Coleridge

Ethics and Interpretation *in* Romanticism and Modern Philosophy

David P. Haney

The Pennsylvania State University Press
University Park, Pennsylvania

Library of Congress Cataloging-in-Publication Data

Haney, David P., 1952–
The Challenge of Coleridge : Ethics and Interpretation in Romanticism and Modern Philosophy / David P. Haney.

p. cm.—(Literature and philosophy)
Includes bibliographical references and index.
ISBN 0-2710-2786-x (cloth : alk. paper)
1. Coleridge, Samuel Taylor, 1772–1834—Ethics. 2. Romanticism—England. 3. Ethics in literature. 4. Hermeneutics. I. Title. II. Series.

PR4487.E8 H36 2001
821'.7—dc21

99-089047

Printed in the United States of America
Published by The Pennsylvania State University Press,
University Park, PA 16802-1003

It is the policy of The Pennsylvania State University Press to use acid-free paper for the first printing of all clothbound books. Publications on uncoated stock satisfy the minimum requirements of American National Standard for Information Sciences—Permanence of Paper for Printed Library Materials, ANSI Z39.48–1992.

For Lisa and Jim

Contents

Abbreviations

Works by Coleridge:

AR	*Aids to Reflection*
BL	*Biographia Literaria*
C & S	*On the Constitution of the Church and State*
CL	*Collected Letters*
CM	*Marginalia*
CN	*Notebooks*
EOT	*Essays on His Times*
Lects 1808–1819	*Lectures 1808–1819 on Literature*
LS	*Lay Sermons*
P Lects	*Philosophical Lectures*
SW & F	*Shorter Works and Fragments*
TT	*Table Talk*

Other Works:

OB	Levinas, *Otherwise than Being*
TI	Levinas, *Totality and Infinity*
TM	Gadamer, *Truth and Method*

Preface

This study treats the work of Samuel Taylor Coleridge as an important phase in the history of the relationship between ethics and hermeneutics. I use a reading of Coleridge in dialogue with twentieth-century criticism and philosophy to explore the question of how the ethical problems of human interaction are related to the interpretive problems of how selves understand the world and each other. Coleridge is an appropriate focus for this question not only because his synthesis of poetry and philosophy forced him to think deeply about the relationship between interpretation and ethics, but also because he has directly influenced modern theories of both selfhood and interpretation.

My main goal in writing this book is to contribute to the vital discussion of the relationship between ethics and literature now taking place in both literary criticism and philosophy. Given the current interrogation, both inside and outside the academy, of the social usefulness of literary study, as well as the much more pressing social questions of the relationship between the interpretation of works of art (especially popular films and music) and acts of violence, this discussion's importance extends far beyond the academy. While this book, as a specialized academic study, will no doubt be read only by a relatively small number of professors and graduate students, I hope it will be of some help to those who do reach outside the academy as teachers of literature and philosophy in the essential task of thinking through the relationship between real-world ethical questions and the ethical force of imaginative literature.

My purpose is not to compete with those critics who have already done a thorough job of placing Coleridge within the history of ideas. Scholars who have devoted their careers to Coleridge, and to whom I owe a great debt that is, I hope, appropriately acknowledged, may find my explanations of familiar Coleridgean themes somewhat tedious and will, I am sure, have legitimate criticisms of my individual readings. The incredible range of Coleridge's writings makes it easy to fall into the trap of making him say whatever we want him to say, and while I have tried to follow the journalistic principle of verifying any statement with multiple sources, I am sure my own critical agenda has produced some inevitable distortion. But, as Coleridge himself says, "Doubtless, it would ~~be a saying, that~~ visit the Realm of Literature with a plusquam polar Ink-frost, if a man ~~should~~ were bound to write on nothing ~~unless~~ till he understood every thing!" (*SW & F* 1425).

That said, I hope to make some contribution to our developing understanding of Coleridge as a philosopher, building on work such as Laurence Lockridge's study of his ethical philosophy, Raimonda Modiano's work on his natural philosophy, and Mary Perkins's recent study of Coleridge's philosophical interpretation of theology. More importantly, though, I hope to have done something like what Jerome Christensen attempts in his study of Coleridge: "this is a book that does not try to understand Coleridge but to read him" (*Coleridge's Blessed Machine of Language* 27). My goal, however, is not simply to read Coleridge through the theoretical lens of modern philosophy; nor is it simply to see Coleridge as having anticipated modern philosophical positions, which, as Stephen Prickett points out, is "all to easy" to do (*Romanticism and Religion* 57). Rather, my intent is to read both Coleridge and some modern positions in light of each other, within the conversation that Hans-Georg Gadamer sees as the appropriate model for our interpretation of the past.

In that context, I also hope this book will be of interest outside of Coleridge studies as a contribution to the continuing dialogue in studies of Romanticism about the function of history both in Romanticism itself and in our critical relation to the period. As in my previous book, *William Wordsworth and the Hermeneutics of Incarnation*, I draw on Gadamer's notion of a transhistorical conversation that is more comprehensive than the horizon of either the modern interpreter or the historical text, a concept which, in my view, can provide an important alternative to the currently dominant ideological interpretations of history. Reading Gadamer's hermeneutics in concert with the ethical theories of Emmanuel Levinas, Paul Ricoeur, Bernard Williams, and others gives me a way to bring out some important connections between Coleridge's interest in interpretation—as a poet, literary critic, and biblical scholar—and his poetic, philosophical, and personal speculations on ethics. Laurence Lockridge, who has studied Romantic ethics with primary reference to the moral philosophy of the time, deliberately employs a "weak" "grammar of interpretation" that attempts to provide "a grammar of the entire range of possible ethical positions" (*The Ethics of Romanticism* 7), and warns that the interpreter of Romantic thinkers should "think twice before compounding their esoterism with his own" (8). Rushing in where he has wisely feared to tread, I am employing a range of "stronger" grammars from twentieth-century hermeneutic and ethical theory, but I hope that, rather than simply compounding esoterisms, this effort will allow modern and Romantic positions to elucidate, supplement, and critique each other.

In addition, although the specific pedagogical implications of hermeneutic theory are beyond the scope of this book and have been treated by others,[1] I hope to suggest that we can learn from and teach literature in a way that supplements thematic explanation, postmodern deconstruction, historical reconstruction, and ideological identification by placing the texts of the past and the present into a conversation in which the attention of both partners is focused, albeit from different historical horizons, on important issues of mutual concern. This hermeneutic model can provide an important corrective to the increasingly ubiquitous technological model of understanding, a model to be explored in Chapter 2. Such a corrective is particularly important now, as the humanities are increasingly assessed from without according to the criteria of technological production, with resources being allocated according to the production of quantifiable "student credit hours" or job-ready graduates, and as they are dominated from within by a parallel focus on technology, visible not only in our fascination with computers but more fundamentally in the assumption, underlying many recent studies, that imaginative literature is best understood according to a model of technological production.[2]

The Argument

In the first chapter I begin with some theoretical problems faced by an attempt to link ethical and interpretive thought as a context for discussing the connection between ethics and hermeneutics in Gadamer's thought. I argue against the prevailing view that modern historical analysis can contextualize and thereby critique the ideology of an historical text, observing that Romantic new historicism, while it claims to address the hermeneutic problem of how the interpreter is affected by the object of interpretation, largely ignores the long history of that issue in hermeneutics itself. Gadamer's model demonstrates that interpretive activity can go both ways. Even as contemporary philosophers provide insights unavailable to Coleridge's theological and idealistic model, Coleridge, partly *because* he operates from within a horizon no longer available to us, can illuminate some aspects of contemporary thought. This complicates the notion of a poem's addressee, as interpretive questions are posed not only to but also by poems.

Chapter 2 places the relation between ethics and aesthetics into the context of Aristotle's distinction between *phronesis*, or ethical knowledge, and *techne*, or productive knowledge. Gadamer and Levinas provide a way to link phronesis to aesthetic autonomy in terms of the means-end unity of *phronesis* and the ethical claim of the other, although Gadamer overemphasizes the autonomy of the artwork and Levinas underemphasizes the ethical possibilities of the aesthetic. Wordsworth and Coleridge present the ethical encounter with the other as in tension with *techne*, but they also show that tension itself to be ethically significant.

Chapter 3 explores how Coleridge engages the debate, still very much with us, about the role of knowledge in ethical discussion. His theological emphasis on the divine person universalizes the notion of the person without reducing it to an abstract category, which helps to remove the distinction between abstract ethical principles and lived moral life. His blending of the concept of the good into the concept of the person on both the divine and the human level escapes the abstraction of the Kantian morality of "obligation" and thus answers some recent objections to that tradition, such as those voiced in the very different ways by Ricoeur and Williams. At the same time, Coleridge tries to steer a middle course between views that would give too much priority either to the self or to the material world by developing a phenomenological empiricism that places empirical understanding within the dialogic interchange that constitutes human ethical life.

Chapter 4 discusses Coleridge in relation to the "is/ought" question: the problem of whether or how the ethical "ought" can be derived from an understanding of what "is." I argue that Coleridge manages to preserve the value of "ought" without depending on the aspects of the distinction that have come under attack in this century. He both collapses the distinction and reverses the priority of the two terms, deriving the "is" from an ultimately divine ethical command. However, the distinction reappears in the *Rime of the Ancient Mariner* as a necessity of narrative rather than of ethical life: the process of judging past actions demands that we first have a text—something that "is"—before we can pass judgment, or engage the "ought" side of the pair. The Christian conversion narrative's tendency to pass judgment on a rejected past is an exemplary model of this process; I suggest that the Mariner's inability to achieve the closure of the classic conversion narrative reflects the tension between the ethical insufficiency and the narrative necessity of the separation of fact and value for Coleridge. Thus this poem straddles Ricoeur's boundary between the imaginative freedom of narrative and the call to responsibility of ethical life.

Chapter 5 addresses the relationship between literary criticism and moral philosophy by setting up a dialogue between Coleridge and modern philosophers (primarily Williams and Martha Nussbaum) who, like Coleridge, see tragedy as an important vehicle for exploring the relationship between individual agency and external contingency in terms of nonpropositional knowledge. Coleridge is partly within the very tradition of rational autonomy that Nussbaum and Williams critique, but the sense of moral agency that he draws from tragedy, in concert with the complex relationship between rational judgment and submission to illusion in his concept of "poetic faith," cannot be reduced to the conflict between rational autonomy and external contingency that establishes the initial terms for Nussbaum's and Williams's discussions. Drama also contributes to ethical understanding by way of its nonmimetic relation to ethical life, requiring a "sacrifice" on the part of the spectator. This argument has important contemporary implications for both postmodern and conservative assumptions of a continuity between aesthetic representation and ethical action. The productive difference between aesthetic and ethical thought is further illustrated by Coleridge's discussions of the relationships among poetic, novelistic, and philosophical discourse and his place in the complex history of the alienated aesthetic consciousness.

The remainder of the book moves from the ethical issues raised by Coleridge's aesthetics to his theological, philosophical, and personal engagement with the relationship between subjectivity and otherness. The main argument of Chapter 6 is that Coleridge negotiates between what can be called, with many reservatios, a "Christian" and a "Hebraic" sense of the self-other relationship. I situate this Coleridgean tension within the modern debate between Ricoeur and Levinas. I discuss the Christian side of Coleridge's concept of subjectivity by building on Ricoeur's discussion of the ethical self's negotiation between its status as an objectively observable third-person "character" subject to classification within moral systems and its status as a first-person subject who relates to others in terms of "promise" and "attestation." This sense of subjectivity is allied to the side of Coleridge's theology that sees God as self-othering Logos. Coleridge's thought overlaps but complicates both Williams's notion of an "internalized other" and Adam Smith's notion of the "impartial spectator." It is here that Coleridge's hermeneutics and his ethics join most closely: the otherness both inside and outside the self that determines ethical life is also the otherness that grounds understanding as self-consciousness. Coleridge's speculations on the role of the will in original sin and remorse present problems for his notion of a self-othering subjectivity, problems that lead to a consideration of the Levinasian side of his thought. Levinas understands ethical subjectivity as grounded in an absolute sense of the other person, who always exceeds and disrupts the horizons of self-conscious conceptualization. This relation is manifested in Coleridge's mature theology, which argues that the self-othering divinity of the Logos must be grounded in a sense of God as absolutely other. His own reading of the Bible demonstrates the interdependence of an absolute otherness that transcends conceptuality and the conceptuality within which that otherness must be thought.

The confrontation between the Christian and Hebraic forms of the self-other relationship is complicated by the fact that Coleridge, in opposition to the tradition running from Kant to Freud that associates the affective realm with desire, gives love a foundational ethical status as the prime example of moral solicitude. I argue in Chapter 7 that he attempts to make love a ground for a (Ricoeurean) moral solicitude involving a reciprocity between self and other, but runs up against the (Levinasian) absolute otherness of the beloved who does not requite one's love, as well as the tendency of the self to vacillate between the egoistic desire to assimilate the beloved to oneself and the desire to obliterate the self in the face of the beloved's otherness. In this context, Coleridge's personal experiences of ego-annihilation are both ameliorated and complicated by his thoughts about Sara Hutchinson, his inaccessible beloved. His notion of the "absolute self" as both consoling and terrifying also allows a version of Levinasian otherness to assault the self from within. These multiple manifestations of otherness within Coleridge's concept of subjectivity prevent him from enjoying either Ricoeur's confidence in a self-generated solicitude for others or Levinas's hope for an ethical responsibility based on the annihilation of the ego. As a way of specifying Coleridge's relation to the tradition of moral and aesthetic autonomy in which he is often placed, I conclude by considering this model of subjectivity in terms of his discussions of the relationship between individual choice and a higher form of necessary freedom.

Acknowledgments

Portions of Chapters 2 and 5 appeared as "Aesthetics and Ethics in Gadamer, Levinas, and Romanticism: Problems of Phronesis and Techne" in *PMLA* 114, 1 (January 1999), and are reprinted by permission of the copyright owner, Modern Language Association of America. An early version of the argument now in parts of Chapters 4, 6, and 7 appeared as "Understanding and Ethics in Coleridge: Description, Evaluation, and Otherness" in *The Ethics in Literature*, edited by Andrew Hadfield, et al. (London: Macmillan; New York: St. Martin's Press, 1999). The paragraphs remaining from that version are reprinted with the permission of Macmillan Press Ltd. A very early version of part of Chapter 3 appeared as "Coleridge and the Ethics of Particularity" in *Afterimages: A Festschrift in Honor of Irving Massey*, edited by William Kumbier and Ann Colley (Buffalo and Toronto: Shufaloff Press, 1996). I would like to thank Princeton University Press for permission to quote from Coleridge's *Collected Works* and *Notebooks*. I am grateful to Jerome McGann and Alan Liu for permission to quote from their comments posted on the listserv operated by the North American Society for the Study of Romanticism.

At Auburn University, I would like to thank the English Department, headed by Dennis Rygiel, and the Hargis Foundation for supporting the release time needed for completion of this project. Special thanks go to the College of Liberal Arts and Dean John Heilman for a research grant during the summer of 1997 and to the University for a professional improvement leave during winter quarter 1995. Conversations with my colleagues have helped shape the ideas and opinions in this book; I would particularly like to thank Paula Backscheider, Lou Caton, Miriam Marty Clark, Dan Latimer, Marc Silverstein, Miller Solomon, and Don Wehrs. Thanks to Drew Clark for taking over my administrative duties during the summer of my final revisions. My graduate students at Auburn have been insightful, helpful, and patient as the arguments in this book have been developed either explicitly or implicitly in class discussions. Jack Jacobs's incisive and often brilliant comments deserve special mention. I would like to thank Tony Cascardi and Donald Marshall for their generous and extremely helpful readings of the manuscript and for giving me a second opportunity to publish in Penn State Press's Literature and Philosophy series.

Most of all, I would like to thank my wife, Lisa Baldwin, whose critical sympathy (in many late-night talks) realizes Gadamer's model of the authentic conversation and whose love exemplifies Levinas's generosity toward the other. And thanks to my stepson Jim for keeping me sane and in touch with worlds I otherwise would not know.

1

Hermeneutics, Ethics, and Historicism

I. Hermeneutics and Ethics

How closely are ethical and hermeneutic issues related? That is to say, to what extent is ethical action or thought dependent on processes of interpretation, and to what extent does interpretation itself have an ethical component? A comprehensive answer is a topic for another book, but some preliminary considerations of what is at stake in such questions will help set the stage for their relevance to Coleridge. The deep connection in Coleridge's thought between the interpretive activity of self-consciousness and its ethical, ultimately theological underpinnings may justify us in assuming, without much argument, a clear link between ethics and hermeneutics. The many recent explorations of the connections between literature and ethics also assume, by their very existence, that literary criticism in its broad sense can somehow be connected with the ethical, whether by emphasizing the ethics implicit in particular schools of literary criticism, as in Tobin Siebers's *The Ethics of Criticism,* by seeing the process of reading deconstructively as an ethical demand, as in J. Hillis Miller's *The Ethics of Reading,* or by finding in literature a source of thick ethical example, as in Martha Nussbaum's *Love's Knowledge*. It is difficult for most academics to envision an activity that does *not* involve verbal interpretation, so that ethical action becomes a subset of an even broader range of interpretively conditioned action. Although Barbara Herrnstein Smith's *Contingencies of Value* is about interpretive processes of "evaluation" that occupy an area both inside and outside of what most people would call the ethical, she succinctly emphasizes the ubiquity of interpretive evaluation: "for a responsive creature, to exist is to evaluate" (42).

While this close connection between interpretation and ethical activity may be a given for both Coleridge and his interpreters, it is not a necessary connection. To assume too close a link between interpretive, reflexive activity and ethics might lead to the conclusion that the best interpreters are the most ethical people, a conclusion that is not only contrary to experience, but also suspiciously self-serving, if this conclusion comes from an academic who is in the business of interpreting. Charles Altieri, whose work is probably the most ambitious attempt in recent years to find a meeting ground for aesthetics and ethics, is suspicious in this way of both Charles Taylor and Stanley Cavell. Cavell, he says, idealizes philosophy by treating the philosopher, whose main activity is verbal articulation, as the "representative person" (*Subjective Agency* 201). Altieri comments, making an important distinction, that "most people, I suspect, do not, and need not, try to own their lives in the way intellectuals do, that is, by elaborating verbal equivalents for them. Agents live by meanings, but not all agents determine meanings by writing (literally or figuratively)" (202). If "writing" in Altieri's broad sense is close to "interpretation," this comment suggests that the "meanings" essential to the ownership of one's life and the possibility of ethical action are not necessarily *articulate* meanings worked out in a hermeneutic process. To use a loose version of Altieri's Wittgensteinian terminology, we can operate in and construct a perfectly meaningful ethical world by participating in language games that do not necessarily require us to isolate "meaning" in the narrow sense of a concept reached through a process of interpretation. Along the same lines, though with a very different emphasis, Charles Taylor notes that the moral frameworks within which ethical action occurs are, more often than not, inarticulate, but not therefore less important. Restricting ethical terms to "reasons" leads to the "strange cramped theories of modern moral philosophy" limited by procedural reason (*Sources of the Self* 89) and unable to talk about substantial moral goods that do not fit into the context of such reason. Ethical terms such as "brutality" and "courage" can be "indispensable" to the "non-explanatory contexts of living" (58); we necessarily have recourse to strong ethical terms as we live our life whether or not we use those terms in the context of an interpretive discourse that gives reasons for actions. Ethical action is closely related to the meanings we give life, or, more simply, to the ethically-laden terms we use, but that meaning may or may not be an articulated object of a process of interpretation.

This distinction between ethical meaningfulness and hermeneutic meaning is not a distinction between the inarticulate or articulate status of the same meaning, as if ethical meaningfulness were like a repressed memory recoverable in analysis. For example, someone might save me from an attacker, exclaiming, "I've got to show some courage and rescue this guy from such brutality." This is clearly an example of meanings being attached to "courage" and "brutality" and being used in ethical action. The philosopher or critic who analyzes "courage" and "brutality" in terms of *reasons* for actions is not necessarily unpacking meanings that were simply latent in my rescuer's use of the words, but rather is using those words in an entirely different way. The philosopher or critic uses them within a language game in which words describe concepts, while my rescuer used those same words in a language game in which words are part of an immediate responsiveness to a situation. Meaning, and coherent systems of meaning, are present in both cases, but the meaning in the case of the philosopher or critic is a product of the process of interpretation, with its articulation of reasons, while (luckily for me) the meaning in the case of my rescuer resides in a set of attitudes about brutality and courage that are part of his or her immediate responsiveness to a situation. Obviously, the same person can use meaning in both ways; my rescuer might in fact be a philosopher who, one hopes, will not act like one in this situation.

If it is a mistake to see ethical life as dependent on interpretive processes, it is even more clearly a mistake to see interpretive activity as fundamentally ethical. Hans-Georg Gadamer argues, in response to Derrida's accusation that his hermeneutics depends on the Kantian concept of "good will," that hermeneutic understanding is ethically neutral. It has "nothing to do with ethics" because "[e]ven immoral beings try to understand one another" ("Reply to Jacques Derrida" 55). As we shall see below, Gadamer's own position is not as clear-cut as this suggests, because his own theories of interpretation draw heavily on ethical concepts, but it is important to remember that there is nothing necessarily ethical about interpretive processes, particularly those employed in literary criticism. Even if, as Barbara Herrnstein Smith argues, our interpretive existence in a relativistic world forces us to "evaluate" constantly, evaluation (as she is quick to point out [161–62]) is not necessarily ethical, nor does it necessarily lead to ethical positions. We can evaluate a situation in terms of its agreeableness, its shock value, its humor, or its ethical force, and a premeditated murder is heinous precisely because it follows a process of interpretation/evaluation.

The notion that interpretation may or may not be ethical is important to remember when considering the paradoxes of the current ideologically-charged critical climate. As Geoffrey Galt Harpham points out in his brief summary of the fate of ethics in recent theory, ethics has been seen as complicit with everything that literary theory has attempted to "subvert," from logocentrism to autonomous selfhood to totalitarianism to gender bias ("Ethics" 387–89). However, ethics is in this scenario a repressed that inevitably returns in the wake of the 1987 exposure of Paul de Man's pro-Nazi wartime journalism, at which point polite discussions of language "gave way to charges of personal immorality, collaboration in the Holocaust, opportunism, and deception" (389). But we do not need Harpham's Freudian concept of repression to explain this turn, because the revolutionary rhetoric of theory from Derrida (whose links to the ethics of Levinas and the political turmoil of the 1960s in France were lost in his early reception in the United States) to current developments in cultural studies commits itself to an easily romanticized binary ethics. Altieri describes this ethics in his characterization of cultural studies as caught in "a single grounding binary opposition between the symbolic order, linked with paternal power or dominant ideologies, and a locus of possible value in a radical other of representation all too easy to romanticize" (*Subjective Agency* 65–66). If everything one does is ideologically determined, then interpretation will always fall on the "good" or "bad" side of this ethical binary. According to this logic, by a strange twist, all writing becomes autobiographical, and de Man's formerly subversive deconstruction is itself deconstructed and revealed as the expression of totalitarianism.

The error in this kind of thinking is not that the accusations against de Man's character are unfair, but that this argument leaves no room for the fact that acts of interpretation may be ethical or not, and that not every ethical act of criticism carries the same ethical force. Both the extreme of turning de Man's overall critical project into a moral tale, such as "the triumph of falling" that Tobin Siebers finds (98–123), and the opposite extreme of taking at face value de Man's own objections to ethics as merely "a discursive mode among others" (qtd. "Ethics" 389) prevent any discrimination between acts of interpretation that do carry an ethical weight and those that do not, as well as among the kinds and intensities of ethical force in the first category. The lesson here is that it is important to explore this problematic relationship between ethics and interpretation while avoiding the temptation either to align them too closely or to separate them too distinctly. The fact that ethics and hermeneutics are so clearly interconnected while at the same so clearly incommensurable is exactly what makes this topic important.

As Altieri points out, even if interpretation does not cover the entire field of ethical action, such reflexive second-order thought plays an important role in the articulation of ethical responsibility. He cites the example of Mother Theresa, whose "constant acts of charity are not instances of ethical thinking" because they are "more deeply rooted in responsiveness to others than strictly ethical thinking can generate or account for." Ethical reflection would enter the picture only if Mother Theresa were called on to justify her actions: "Then she must engage a discourse about responsibility and justification, and then we have a clear instance of ethical reflection" (*Subjective Agency* 154).

Altieri chooses to restrict his discussion to this second-order realm of responsibility, because it allows him to illuminate the expressive agent's appeals to grammars of responsibility, while at the same time enabling him to evade the discussion of "the good" that he finds so problematic in philosophers such as Taylor. My topic will not allow me to be so strategic: the relation between hermeneutics and ethics in Coleridge will not allow an exclusionary relationship between prereflective direct responsiveness and reflexive "ethical" responsibility. As I will try to show with reference to some links between Coleridge and Emmanuel Levinas, the ethical is deeply imbedded in interpretive processes, but the ethical also stands as a limit to such processes, precisely because those prereflective hypergoods, which Altieri's reflective expressivism hopes to avoid, are in some ways unavoidable, if only in the form of the basic assumptions about human nature that underlie any ethical theory.

Within the realm of reflective thought (as opposed to direct responsiveness) an important link between hermeneutics and ethics can be found in the ethical implications of the "hermeneutic circle," the interpretive concept that Maurizio Ferraris traces back to Flacius Illyricus in the sixteenth century, according to which the parts of a text can be understood only in the context of an evolving foreknowledge of the whole (30–31). Drawing on Heidegger's version of the circle, Gadamer explains it as follows: "A person who is trying to understand a text is always projecting. He projects a meaning for the text as a whole as soon as some initial meaning emerges in the text. Again, the initial meaning emerges only because he is reading the text with particular expectations in regard to a certain meaning. Working out this fore-projection, which is constantly revised in terms of what emerges as he penetrates into the meaning, is understanding what is there" (*TM* 267). Quoting Heidegger, Gadamer stresses that this is not a "vicious" circle from which one would wish to escape, but rather a description, with "an ontologically positive significance," of the way understanding works (266). Gadamer sees a similar process in Aristotle's ethical concept of *phronesis* (to be treated in more detail in the next chapter), which addresses the interdependence between general ethical principles and their application to particular situations. P. Christopher Smith, who has translated Gadamer's major treatises on ethics and written extensively on the ethical implications of Gadamer's thought, summarizes this ethical/hermeneutic circularity with remarkable precision: "One chooses on the basis of what one 'always already' knows to be right, though this knowledge remains indeterminate until one has made a choice that concretizes it" (204). Smith argues persuasively that this notion provides an important mediation between, on one hand, ethical philosophies that argue from abstract principles such as rational rules, individual rights, and even doctrinaire pragmatism, and on the other hand, those that would retreat to a Nietzschean unmasking of such principles as merely the expressions of personal or class-based preferences. Coleridge, who like Gadamer is deeply rooted in both the Protestant tradition of biblical hermeneutics and the German Idealist tradition, sees the circle in theological terms with clear ethical implications: "In order to an efficient belief in Christianity, a man must have been a Christian, and this is the seeming argumentum in circulo, incident to all spiritual Truths" (*BL* 2:244). The foreunderstanding that comes from one's practice of faith and involvement in the historical tradition of Christianity is necessary to the concretization of "spiritual Truths."

As this circularity suggests, ethical understanding is difficult because it must both depend on and differentiate itself from the particularity of concrete ethical decisions. "If man always encounters the good in the form of the particular situation in which he finds himself," says Gadamer in his discussion of Aristotle in *Truth and Method,* then "the task of moral knowledge is to determine what the concrete situation asks of him" (313). Gadamer's careful wording here, which grants authority both to a general concept of "the good" and to the particular situation, suggests the methodological difficulty in determining the appropriate role of philosophical ethics in relation to actual ethical decisions. According to Gadamer, philosophical ethics should not be so tied to the particularity of the individual moral action that it "usurp[s] the place of moral consciousness," but neither should it be so distanced from concrete application that it "seek[s] a purely theoretical and 'historical' knowledge." Rather, it should help "moral consciousness to attain clarity concerning itself" by "outlining phenomena" (*TM* 313). In ethics, this means that one must already *have* a moral consciousness: "through education and practice he must himself already have developed a demeanor that he is constantly concerned to preserve in the concrete situations of his life and prove through right behavior" (313). Similarly in the hermeneutic situation, where "meaning" is always encountered as particular manifestations of meaning, the hermeneutic endeavor can not identify with the text completely as if one could interpret without bringing presuppositions to bear, but neither can it provide a purely theoretical or historical account to be applied to the text after the fact. As Gadamer says with reference to Bultman, "[A]ll understanding presumes a living relationship between the interpreter and the text," a requirement for "*fore-understanding*" (331).

These hermeneutically paradigmatic theological and Aristotelian contexts, to which Gadamer often returns, suggest the deep intertwining of ethical and hermeneutic issues, particularly when we consider an author such as Coleridge, who promoted the constant interpenetration of theology, metaphysics, moral philosophy, and even literary criticism. Gadamer also links ethics and hermeneutics in terms of the relationship between rhetorical understanding and practical philosophy in Aristotle. "[T]he Greek word for the act of understanding and for being habitually understanding toward others, *synesis*," moves from an ethically neutral word to "a kind of intellectual virtue" in Aristotle's practical philosophy: "'[b]eing habitually understanding toward others' means a modification of practical reasonableness, the insightful judgment regarding someone else's practical deliberations," and thus implies "much more than a mere understanding of what was said," because it "entails a kind of communality" (*Reason in the Age of Science* 132–33).[1]

Even though understanding is desired by both the moral and the immoral, there does seem to be an unavoidable ethical element in the hermeneutic act: a demand for a certain generosity toward the other and for the recognition of, in terms of Gadamer's Aristotle, "a kind of communality in virtue of which reciprocal taking of counsel, the giving and taking of advice, is at all meaningful in the first place" (*Reason in the Age of Science* 133).[2] While the content of that "advice" can be moral, immoral, or neither (it could be advice on doing good deeds, robbing a bank, or repairing a car), the context requires a kind of ethical attitude: even evildoers must listen to each other generously if they are to work together. Thus, even before we consider arguments such Tobin Siebers's, that literary-critical positions imply ethical presuppositions, or J. Hillis Miller's, that there is an ethical imperative to read deconstructively, *any* act of interpretation necessarily engages the ethical sphere in some way merely by virtue of its status as an interpersonal exchange. This is not to say that every act of interpretation can be given a particular ethical content, but it is to say that it is as important to see the connections between interpretation and ethical thought as it is to recognize their differences.

II. The Romantics and Us: Problems of Historicizing

These uneasy connections between hermeneutics and ethics are complicated by the problems of historical interpretation. Just as the contemporary reduction of history to ideology totalizes the ethical field by seeing history as a binary struggle between good and bad forces, so too it totalizes the interpretive field by ignoring or merely paying lip service to many of the problems of historical interpretation. To use some Gadamerian language that will be clarified as this study progresses, the "challenge of Coleridge" is first and foremost to read him with an attentiveness both to his horizon and to our own that will enable his texts to "speak" to us in a way that can produce insights into issues of common concern to the Romantics and to us. This kind of approach demands that we eschew the polarities of agreement or critique that have characterized recent Romantic studies. In the politically charged atmosphere of recent literary criticism, studies of Coleridge, particularly when they focus on his movement toward a Trinitarian theological position, tend either to accept his position as coherent and valuable, as in Ronald C. Wendling's *Coleridge's Progress to Christianity*, which is very specifically Christian in orientation, or else to read Coleridge through the lens of twentieth-century theory, unmasking the contradictions and hidden ideological positions in his work. The latter approach is of course much more predominant, ranging from Jerome Christensen's semideconstructive *Coleridge's Blessed Machine of Language* to Nigel Leask's examination of the political implications of Coleridgean imagination, *The Politics of Imagination in Coleridge's Thought*.[3] I share the latter group's faith in the applicability of contemporary theory to Coleridge, but I also share the former group's desire to take seriously Coleridge's position as a challenge to some of that very theory. My hope is to produce a kind of criticism that will see Coleridge's writing, not as embodying a set of concepts (hidden or apparent) to be affirmed or critiqued by modern theory, but as embodying a set of perspectives that can be put into a mutually illuminating and mutually challenging relationship with more recent perspectives.

The negotiation between Coleridge and his critics is further complicated by the fact that the relationship between hermeneutics and ethics in Romanticism is by its very nature an issue both within Romanticism and within our relationship to Romanticism. James Chandler notes that "much of Romantic 'literature' inclines to organize itself around" the very "historical specificity" that is of such interest to modern historical critics (*England in 1819* 78). The same could be said for issues of interpretation and ethics: twentieth-century attempts to articulate how interpretative and ethical issues interact in a postexistential world reflect (and in some ways can be traced back to) efforts such as Coleridge's to give the production and interpretation of imaginative literature a strong ethical basis and purpose. Romanticism has almost never been the object of disinterested study, a body of knowledge that could be detached from an ethically charged relation to a past exerting a strong hold on the present. This is more than obvious in recent criticism, and can be attributed partly to what Pierre Mileur calls the "critical romance," the notion, for example, that the ethical force of reading itself—"reading as the vehicle of humane virtues"—is a Wordsworthian invention that "sets the underlying agenda of the project of criticism as we have inherited it in our Anglo-American tradition" (*The Critical Romance* 48–49). Other citations of Romanticism's historical effect abound: Paul de Man commented in a 1967 lecture on "how powerful a source romanticism still is for our own consciousness"; Geoffrey Hartman's recent work shifts seamlessly from Romantic uses of language to the testimony of Holocaust victims; Jerome Christensen connects the political unrest of the early nineteenth century and the late twentieth century according to a Romantic logic of "willful anachronism"; and Gene Ruoff has collected a series of essays, including testimonials by contemporary poets, stemming from a 1988 conference, entitled *The Romantics and Us*.[4] And of course Jerome McGann's *Romantic Ideology* has made a new generation of critics aware of how deeply our critical attitudes are influenced by Romanticism.

All these works testify to the strong presence of Romanticism in the ethically diverse impulses of modern criticism. At the same time, part of Romanticism's hold on us is the evolution of a historical consciousness that emphasizes the otherness of the past: Romanticism is thus for us both an "other" past and a familiar heritage—but a heritage of meditation on the otherness of its own past. The very horizon that we share with Romanticism necessitates its own transgression: if part of the ethical position that we share with Romanticism is a call to acknowledge otherness, then we must recognize the otherness of Romantic writers even as we share this horizon. This means we should not relate to Romanticism in the symmetry of either agreement or critique, because both of these relations place us and them within a system of differences that denies otherness. As René Girard points out, systematized difference is not otherness, but rather that which we set up to combat and control otherness.[5] The dichotomy between a passive appreciation of the past and an active critique is in any case a false one from the hermeneutic perspective, because interpretation partakes of both. P. Christopher Smith argues that interpretation is both "something that happens to us" and "something that we must 'do'": "It turns out that the two dimensions of interpretation—of opening ourselves to the past and of projecting the past within the present into the future—are in fact indissociable" (193).

The idea that the fundamental values of contemporary criticism are parts of a Romantic heritage that carries with it an immanent self-critique, but that also needs an objective and politically informed recontextualization in terms of historical specifics, is an important ground for the historicist reevaluation of Romanticism of the last two decades. As Jerome McGann, who has played a major role in that revaluation, says, "Aesthetic effect depends upon the distancing of the art work, the estrangement of it, its isolation from our immediacy" ("Keats and the Historical Method" 459). However, one of the paradoxes of the turn to a "new" history is its neglect of the hermeneutic tradition, which, in a direct line from Romanticism to the post-Heideggerian work of Gadamer, is similarly concerned with how the horizon of the present can interact with a past that is both the origin of and irreducibly different from that present. Part of this neglect can be attributed to the "conservative" reputation of Gadamer's emphasis on tradition, which Terry Eagleton dismisses as "a grossly complacent theory of history" (*Literary Theory* 73), and which is seen as opposed to the various levels of Marxist influence on new historicism.[6] Gadamer has also been critiqued by feminist critics such as Julie Ellison for leaving hermeneutics with "a desire for ethical consensus—and an aversion to the [forgotten and highly gendered] history of that desire" (96). As Ellison notes, feminist biblical scholars such as Elisabeth Schüssler Fiorenza have accused Gadamer of preferring "'identification with' . . . the androcentric text" to "critical solidarity with women in biblical history" (97).

More often than not, twentieth-century hermeneutics is simply ignored. Cyrus Hamlin, who has been championing hermeneutics since the 1970s, notes that "[t]heories of interpretation have had relatively little impact on the practice of reading" (59). Despite the advent of "theory" in the 1970s and 1980s, such theory was usually based on a theory of language or culture, bypassing a theory of reading itself by treating literary texts as "instances or examples" of theory (29).[7] One result of the categorical rejection of twentieth-century hermeneutics is that it comes to represent an ideologically motivated concept of reading synonymous with a vaguely defined "idealism." To take an extreme recent example, Terence Hoagwood reduces the "hermeneutic operation" to a psychologizing and conceptualizing program that "makes history, and the actual changes to which it submits things, into an idea, a mental act, available in the same shiny newness now that it had then" such that "[n]othing really important is lost" (*Politics, Philosophy, and the Production of Romantic Texts* 169). This narrow reading of Schleiermacher's specifically Romantic hermeneutics supports Hoagwood's argument that "the production of literary texts was an event in social and historical space whose meanings will be concealed and abstracted by any hermeneutic reading that remains at the level of concepts" (174). His own conceptual leap here ignores twentieth-century hermeneutics' emphasis on the historicity of concept-formation itself, its demonstration that "the level of concepts" and "an event in social and historical space" cannot be so easily separated, because the development of concepts is itself an important historical event tied up with the historicity of language. Gadamer, who sharply critiques exactly the Schleiermachian, intentionalist notion of hermeneutics that Hoagwood invokes, stresses "the *character of language as event:* the *process of concept formation*" (*TM* 427–28).

The irony of Hoagwood's argument is that his "conviction that the word [hermeneutics] needs redefinition in Romantic criticism" (167) ignores the redefinition that has gone on in the hermeneutic tradition itself throughout the nineteenth and twentieth centuries. This makes for some lamentable wheel-reinventing. For example, he sees the fact that "[t]he production and distribution of scripts, poetic and exegetical, does not take place outside the economy of social relations" (173) as a materialist, antihermeneutic statement, when in fact he unwittingly echoes in 1996 what Gadamer said thirty years earlier: "Even in those masterworks of historical scholarship that seem to be the very consummation of the extinguishing of the individual demanded by Ranke . . . we can classify these works with unfailing accuracy in terms of the political tendencies of the time in which they were written" (*Philosophical Hermeneutics* 7). Hoagwood's point is not identical to Gadamer's, of course, but the overlap suggested here could have made for some fruitful dialogue, and even without the overlap it is puzzling that as philosophically astute a critic as Hoagwood could present a program for redefining Romantic hermeneutics without even mentioning as major an effort in that direction as Gadamer's.

Part of the neglect of the philosophical issues raised by hermeneutics can be attributed to the antitheoretical bent of much new historicism (suggested by Hoagwood's dismissal of "concepts"), particularly as it has moved into a straightforward effort to revive forgotten forms of response, for example in McGann's effort to recover the topos of sensibility in *The Poetics of Sensibility*. In much of McGann's work, however, the basic problems of hermeneutics are both brought to the fore and effaced. For example, he says in "The Third World of Criticism," "The *Oresteia* today means both more and less than it meant in 458 because its meaning—which is always localized in the present—carries along the many histories of meaning that were only initiated in the trilogy's first appearance" (93-94). This suggests an acknowledgment of Gadamer's principle of *wirkungsgeschichtliches Bewußtsein* or "historically effected consciousness." According to Gadamer, "[i]f we are trying to understand a historical phenomenon from the historical distance that is characteristic of our hermeneutic situation, we are always already affected by history. It determines in advance both what seems to us worth inquiring about and what will appear as the object of investigation" (*TM* 300). McGann's observation on the *Oresteia* echoes Gadamer's argument that "we are always already affected by history"; for Gadamer, a work from the past means more than it did at the time in the sense that subsequent interpretations of a historical phenomenon form a part of "the web of historical effects" that should prevent us from "tak[ing] its immediate appearance as the whole truth" (300). Conversely, historical knowledge is always less than complete in the sense that "we always find ourselves within a situation, and throwing light on it is a task that is never entirely finished" (301). For Gadamer, this particular "less" is in relation to a conceptual wholeness that can never be achieved, then or now, rather than, as in McGann, the possibility of a historical reconstruction: there is no meaningful sense of an original understanding to be obscured by the history of interpretation.

To Gadamer, this understanding of history is an advance over and a challenge to the Romantic notion, which he attributes to Schleiermacher, that history can simply be reconstructed in its "original" form:

> Reconstructing the original circumstances, like all restoration, is a futile undertaking in view of the historicity of our being. What is reconstructed, a life brought back from the past, is not the original. In its continuance in an estranged state it acquires only a derivative,

> cultural existence. The recent tendency to take works of art out of museums and put them back in the place for which they were originally intended, or to restore architectural monuments to their original form, merely confirms this judgment. Even a painting taken from the museum and replaced in a church or building restored to its original condition are not what they once were—they become simply tourist attractions. Similarly, a hermeneutics that regarded understanding as reconstructing the original would be no more than handing on a dead meaning. . . . [T]he essential nature of the historical spirit consists not in the restoration of the past but in *thoughtful mediation with contemporary life*. . . . Every age has to understand a transmitted text in its own way, for the text belongs to the whole tradition whose content interests the age and in which it seeks to understand itself. (*TM* 166–69, 296)

Although McGann's comment on the *Oresteia* parallels this insight into the "historicity of our being," his work also demonstrates, in the name of a critical approach to Romanticism, a strong faith in at least the attempt at the very historical reconstruction that Gadamer rejects as "Romantic." For Gadamer, the attempt at reconstruction is implicitly an imperialistic gesture, transforming the past into tourist attractions for present-day consumers. For McGann, reconstruction does the opposite. The retrieval of historical specifics combats the imperialism of "tradition": "The works must be raised up from their narrowly imagined totalities, must be seen as part of that larger context that emerges when they are *specifically* situated, when they are delivered over to their historical and social localities" ("The Third World of Criticism" 88). Or as he says much more simply in *The Poetics of Sensibility*, criticism must entertain a "hope of meeting the work on its own terms" (9).

The question that hermeneutics poses to McGann's version of new historicism is this: what is to prevent the reconstruction of, for example, "sentiment," as in McGann's *Poetics of Sensibility*, from becoming, in Gadamer's terms, a mere "tourist attraction"? That is to say, how would McGann answer Gadamer's argument that the task of reconstructing the "original" is exactly what prevents us from understanding the past text as McGann would have us understand the *Oresteia?* I posed this question, accompanied by the some of the foregoing quotations, during a discussion of related issues on the North American Society for the Study of Romanticism internet discussion group, and McGann offered the following response (I've preserved his characteristic lower-case):

> dave haney reminds us of the presence of the hermeneutic circle. its presence affects (afflicts?) as we know any engagement of these kinds—there is never any "presence" in the sense posed by this paradox. part of the paradox is to pose "presence" as a conceptual form. so an historical "reconstruction" is no more or less problematic than any other—reading aeschylus is just as impossible (in the sense posed by the paradox) as reading charles bernstein.
>
> all that seems to me well known by now.
>
> for myself, i don't feel the force of the paradox except as a curiosity of the human mind and its passion for logic. it has the same charming irrelevance as zeno's various paradoxes. i say that by no means to denigrate "irrelevance." things of charm and irrelevance, like decorative moments in art, are human fundamentals. ("Reconstructing Sensibility Again")

It would be unfair to press this spontaneous response too hard, but it does suggest why hermeneutics and new historicism have such trouble hearing each other. McGann insinuates that the hermeneutic circle itself is simply a "well known" paradox that we must accept and move beyond, trusting in our own critical generosity to avoid the problems Gadamer identifies. He argues that the effect of the hermeneutic circle is nullified by the fact that it applies equally to all conceptual structures, whereas Gadamer would argue that this ubiquity is exactly the power of the hermeneutic circle. At the same time, however, even the circle's "irrelevance" is recoverable within a critical field that eschews a hierarchical division between the relevant and the irrelevant.

McGann sees no Gadamerian conflict between the task of historical reconstruction and *wirkungsgeschichtliches Bewußtsein* because to take such a conflict seriously would be to engage what is for him a restrictive conceptual system. He connects the paradox to the problem of "presence as a conceptual form," implicitly distinguishing, as he does elsewhere, between the conceptual problem of the "presence" of the past text and the praxis of reconstructing the past in whatever way we can. In "Rethinking Romanticism" he acknowledges that even the dialectical approach of his own *Romantic Ideology* is restrictive in this way, and that the only way to secure the "freedom" of criticism is for it to accept "the historical limits of its own forms of thought" by imagining theory "not as a conceptual structure but as a set of investigative practices—and a set of practices that play themselves out under a horizon of falsifiability" (740).

McGann thus shares Gadamer's belief in the finitude of historical understanding, but with a nearly opposite valorization of "truth" and "method." Gadamer emphasizes the limitations of method in order to preserve truth; *Truth and Method* concludes with the observation that "what the tool of method does not achieve must—and really can—be achieved by a discipline of questioning and inquiring, a discipline that guarantees truth" (491). McGann appears to have more faith in the method of "a set of investigative practices" as a way to respect the human finitude that is, in his view, denied by "conceptual structures" such as the hermeneutic circle. Thus, as in the playful dialogue that concludes "Rethinking Romanticism," he can embrace both "Romantic" and "anti-Romantic" positions as a gesture of ironic freedom from such conceptual schemes. This gesture is thoroughly Romantic, of course, as McGann would freely acknowledge, whether in the German, Schlegelian sense of contradictory positions held in suspension, or, more relevant for McGann, the very different, because blatantly non-theoretical, Byronic "resistance to theory" ("Rethinking Romanticism" 737): "As I see it, criticism should be seeking a dialectical philology that is not bound by the conceptual forms it studies and generates. The paradox of such a philology is that its freedom would be secured only when it accepts the historical limits of its own forms of thought. It is not bound by its theoretical forms because it holds itself open to the boundary conditions established by other conceptual forms" (740). Finitude is freedom because by recognizing our conceptual limits we are open to "boundary conditions," including, presumably, the paradoxical relationship between freedom and historical limitations. Here McGann sounds something like Richard Rorty's liberal ironist, who pragmatically chooses the best available narrative on the authority of language's and philosophy's own finitude and contingency.[8] According to the Lévi-Straussian categories that form part of James Chandler's recent analysis of the rise of historicism, by which one is always engaged in the tradeoff between theory's "comprehension," gained at the expense of specific information, and anecdotal "information," gained at the expense of theoretical comprehension (*England in 1819* 70), McGann clearly opts for the latter. Gadamer would argue that holding one's position "open to the boundary conditions established by other conceptual forms" does not free one from one's own "theoretical forms," but is instead a function of a historical position by which we are specifically bound by the structures of our own "foreunderstanding," as a necessary corollary of the prejudices that make up our historical horizon, even as we open those structures to other forms.

McGann's position is symptomatic of a political inconsistency evident both inside and outside the American academy. McGann's opposition between restrictive conceptual approaches and the "freedom" of nontheoretical praxis is a variation on the polarization, which Charles Taylor traces back to the Romantics, of instrumental reason and an ideal of "authenticity." According to Taylor, this polarization encourages a contradictory and selective emphasis on "freedom" in the modern notion of the self. For example, American conservatives (the boosters of instrumental reason and technological development) advocate traditional communities in morals and religion, but simultaneously advocate unchecked self-fulfillment in economics. Liberals (the boosters of "authenticity" and opponents of unchecked technological development) advocate personal fulfillment in morals, as in arguments for abortion, but also advocate the preservation of traditional communities in areas such as ecology and ethnicity (*The Ethics of Authenticity* 94-95).[9]

McGann's approach is a literary-critical example of Taylor's "liberal" contradiction: the critic must be authentically "free" from conceptual paradigms, but literature must be returned to and preserved in the (unfree) specificity of its historical context, its real "traditional community," as opposed, for example, to what Stuart Curran calls the poetic tradition whose "chronology has been written wholly, and arbitrarily, along masculine gender lines" ("The I Altered" 187). The McGannian critic gets to invoke or withhold freedom as it suits him: by artificially separating out "investigative practices" from "conceptual structure[s]," the critic grants himself a Urizenic freedom to bind the poet to the historical specificity unearthed by his "investigative practices," as well as to critique the ideology of the very concept of individual autonomy that must underlie the critic's own "free" practice. And while "conceptual structures" are isolated from "investigative practices" on the level of theory, they are reunited when it is Romantic practices and conceptual structures that are investigated: Romantic practice is evidence for the conceptual structures of Romantic ideology.

Gadamer and Taylor show that the acknowledgment of the finitude of our conceptual systems need not entail giving up foundational concepts, or what Taylor calls in *Sources of the Self* the often unarticulated "inescapable frameworks" that underlie ethical and political practice and thought. Such frameworks, such as the increasing philosophical importance of "daily life" that Taylor traces back to the Reformation, underlie the concept of human finitude just as surely as the substantive concept of a universal Good underlies the human connection to an eternal order in the Platonic model.[10] Thus an affirmation of human finitude and contingency can lead in many other directions than that of the critical "freedom" of the Byronic ironist.

Coleridge thought in a more dialectical way than either Taylor's modern liberal or his modern conservative, partly because he saw rational freedom of individual choice not as an absolute political value, but as part of a larger structure of historical forces. Whether or not one wants to accept the politics of this Burkean side of Coleridge, it brings to consciousness some of the contradictions that, according to Taylor, remain hidden in modern American politics, and it also shows how difficult it is to classify Coleridge according to modern political categories. For example, Coleridge's opposition of "progression" and "permanence" in *On the Constitution of the Church and State* directly confronts the contradiction in the confused advocacy of tradition and self-fulfillment that Taylor finds in modern American politics. Self-fulfillment and instrumental reason are on the side of "progression" (he even calls this side "personal interest") and tradition and land are on the side of "permanence" (24–29). Thus he can coherently advocate a national trust and state education (like a modern liberal) and traditional moral values (like a modern conservative), while granting the rights of commercial interests and personal fulfillment as the acknowledged other side.[11] It is we, not Coleridge, who indiscriminately argue for "progression" or "permanence" as it suits our political ends, without noticing the contradiction.

For late-twentieth-century Americans, "conservative" means faith in small government and laissez-faire economics. However, the "Tory" Coleridge despised the laissez-faire economics of Adam Smith and presents in *On the Constitution of the Church and State* what would now be seen as a quasi-socialist argument for state-supported education as a corrective to the excesses of privatization. The fact that this would be accomplished by a national *church* and the "clerisy" is a function of what he saw as theology's historical role as preserving philology, historical understanding, and ethical and social thought;[12] that the Christian church would fulfill this role is "a blessed accident" (55), not a theological necessity.[13] Like most of the Romantics, Coleridge was critical of the emerging structures of capitalism, but the line from Romanticism to Marxism is complicated by the fact that even the radical Shelley preferred the social hierarchy established by inherited land to the new hierarchy of capitalism.[14] Coleridge's critique of capitalism defended both social hierarchy and the state's responsibility for public welfare, values often seen to conflict today.

The danger of being unreflective about the theoretical models we impose on the past and about the past's effect on those models has worried

Marjorie Levinson who, unlike McGann, is very much concerned with issues of theoretical coherence. As one of the foremost critics of new historicism's refusal to take seriously the theoretical issues of the past's effect on the present, she offers an internal challenge to new historicism that parallels Gadamer's in some ways, although she diverges sharply from Gadamer in her Marxist concept of dialectic. As early as 1989, she writes that, although "[*w*]*e* are the ones who, by putting the past to a certain use, put it in a certain order," at the same time "we seem not to consider that this interest of ours in a certain use might also be an *effect* of the past which we study, and that our mode of critical production could be related to that past as to the absent cause which our practice instantiates" ("The New Historicism" 20–21). For Levinson, the Marx-inspired effort to objectify history does not go far enough, because, in our failure to "objectify our own subjectivity" as producers of historical value (20), "[w]e have, in short, and very much against our will, reified the Romantic science" (22).

The desire to take on the impossible task of objectifying history is partly a manisfestation of what David Hiley sees as the tendency of twentieth-century thought to apply Enlightenment standards of rationality while denying the enlightenment telos: "[o]ur problem in the twentieth century is that we have inherited the . . . Enlightenment conceptions of reason, autonomy, and hope for ourselves and the future, yet we have rejected the metaphysical structure and teleological conception of history that made the Enlightenment view plausible" (63). We attempt to give a unified epistemological foundation—such as the universalization of the "material"—to a *critique* of the epistemological foundations of Romantic self-representations, such as the assertion of the origin of knowledge in self-consciousness. Though historicist critics often show a theoretical awareness of their paradoxical position, the incoherence that this paradox produces often remains in practice. For example, Greg Kucich's "Romanticism and Feminist Historiography" concludes with a warning against the historical totalization implicit in "promulgat[ing] a separate 'women's epistemology'," arguing that we should focus "instead on the ways that any single mode of historical understanding must partially include and remain implicated in, sometimes by its very efforts to exclude, the experiences of women and other marginal groups" (138). However, he still invokes uncritically the McGannian notion of "the actual escape from history and elision of women that inform Romantic ideology" (137), a notion that seems to affirm exactly the sort of "single mode of historical understanding" he wishes to critique.

Implicit in such critiques is also an Enlightenment vision of epistemological and ethical progress, a vision certainly shared by most Romantics, as in Keats's "grand march of intellect." We see our versions of Romanticism as more knowledgeable (we've expanded the canon) and more ethically enlightened (we've exposed the ideological foundations of Romantic notions of self-consciousness) than the positions of both the canonical Romantics themselves and the previous generations of Romanticists. Such a one-sidedly critical approach to the Romantic Ideology does exactly what Hans Gadamer claims the Romantics themselves did in adopting a hypercritical relation to the Enlightenment: to reverse the terms of the past, whether by substituting Romantic self-consciousness for Enlightenment universal reason or by substituting critical historicity for ahistorical Romantic self-consciousness, is to remain trapped within the same necessarily polarized binary opposition.[15]

One result of this critical approach, noted by Levinson, is a clearly ethical subtext: "we're forced to interpret these textual binds as ethical matters" as "our criticism is preoccupied with questions of blame and defence" ("The New Historicism" 50). In a later essay, the critique is even sharper, as she sees the emphasis on cultural "practice" as producing unhistorical ethical dramas of competing subjectivities: "At this stage we allow no materials that are not traces of former or competing practices, no alienation that is not rich in countercultural opportunities, no ends that are not 'for' someone or some group . . . and thus prolifically 'against' another such group, and no determining orders that are not also and *essentially* anthologies of human interest stories" ("Romantic Criticism" 271–72). Levinson's solution is to see "critical agency in terms of discontinuous generations, broken lines, and not collectivities bound by interests, however diverse" (280). These "broken lines" involve fully dialectical relations between past and present. Thus, in the earlier essay, she argues that in Wordsworth's sonnet, "The world is too much with us," the speaker's inability to posses the Greek past that he poses as an alternative to the present leads to a set of contradictions that "do not anticipate the Marxian solution, they precipitate it" ("The New Historicism" 47). At the same time, we must recognize the Marxist solution, "*our* fantasy" of "a consciousness produced by its ongoing life activity," which is "not an expressive and not a mechanical activity" (46) *as* a fantasy. In Levinson's adaptation of Raymond Williams, criticism "has no choice but to throw itself into history, not by agonized confessions of its own locatedness but by the embrace of 'the changing materialist content [and, adding to Raymond Williams's phrase, the changing *form*] of materialism'" ("Romantic Criticism" 280).

Levinson recognizes the problem also identified by Gadamer: to "objectify" the past without considering its effect on the present is, in her very apt metaphor, to put us in a situation where "[t]he motor runs but the car doesn't go because we don't operate the dialectic diachronically" ("The New Historicism" 34). However, the limitation of her position from a hermeneutic perspective is that, like McGann's, it is dominated by the trope of irony and conflict, "an ironic view of history as lived and a comic view of history as reproduced by the future" (51). She proposes "the inseparability of the constitutive and the deconstructive" (49), but by circumscribing the field within those alternatives she leaves no room for relations to the past that cannot be characterized within that pair. As in McGann, we are left with a dialogue that has only two oppositional sides, with nothing outside of the dialogue itself.

This limitation is particularly important to notice if our concern is to consider the ethical implications of hermeneutic issues. As Levinson demonstrates, much current historicism retreats to an unproductive ethics of affirmation or critique. But even her historical dialectic does not go far enough ethically in its combination of alienation and identification, construction and deconstruction, because the only available ethical vocabulary is still the limited combination of "for" and "against," however they are combined. As subtle as Levinson's readings are, they still totalize the "Romantic" position as a site of contest between its overt ideology and the contradictions it presents. This prevents the critical interaction from opening out into a conversation that goes beyond the binaries of identification and alienation or affirmation and critique.

For example, according to Levinson, one of Marx's achievements was to "neutralize one idealism (absolute objects) while guarding against another (Mind)" by positing "a Nature which is always already culture" ("The New Historicism" 32). She contrasts this with the Romantic dialectic between essentialized concepts of nature and mind. Her contrast cannot account for the fact that Coleridge did indeed operate within the nature-mind opposition, but also struggled, as Levinson says Romanticism did not, to avoid an essentialized materialism as well as an essentialized idealism. This can be seen in Coleridge's attempt to avoid what he saw as the former extreme of Schelling and the latter extreme of Fichte. He carries on that struggle, of course, by a theological and ethical rather than a materialist route, but he acknowledges the cultural embeddedness of even spiritual history: Christianity "is spiritual yet so as to be historical—and between these two poles there must likewise be a . . . mid-point, in which the Historical & Spiritual meet" (*SW & F* 1119). As I hope to show, this set of ideas interacts in rather subtle ways with some diverse modern ethical positions, such that our interpretive acts need not be reduced to the impoverished ethics of "for" and "against" that Levinson laments but does not fully escape.[16]

I propose to see certain fundamental issues in Coleridge (including the nature of the subject, the role of the other, the ethical implications of interpretive activity, and the ethics of love) as illuminated by a conversation between present and past that is not *simply* dialectical. The potential critical humility in this hermeneutic position is that both present and past perspectives are subordinated to what Gadamer refers to as the "common subject matter" that "binds the two partners" in conversation (*TM* 388), in contrast to the notion that there is nothing beyond the materialist dialectic of alienation and identification. The risk of critical arrogance in this position is that I will de-emphasize the historical dialectic, denying the truth in Levinson's observation that "history moves by its bad side" ("Romantic Criticism" 280), and placing the *Sache* of the hermeneutic conversation outside of history.

To see our relation to the literature of the past as a matter of "us" against "them"—even when that opposition is viewed within the complexity of a Marxist dialectic—suggests, as Paul Ricoeur points out in a slightly different context, "a naive concept of *mimēsis,* the very one that is spotlighted in certain fictions, like the first *Don Quixote* or *Madame Bovary*" (*Oneself* 161). That is to say, if, as cultural studies asserts, and as Romantic new historicism often assumes, literary texts are equivalent to all other acts of cultural expression, we are in danger of tilting at windmills in interpretive and ethical terms either by confusing literary events and lived ethical life or by reducing both to the lowest common denominator of power differentials. I hope to show that by considering issues of ethics and historical understanding in tandem, we can allow Coleridge to engage us in a conversation about ethics that neither reduces the past to a model of edification nor dismisses it as ideologically blind.

For Gadamer, a true conversation is enabled, not simply by the interaction of two subject-positions, but by the fact that both partners in a conversation put their subjectivities at risk by turning toward a common topic that is open to questioning; conversations are always "about" something that is not settled. "To conduct a conversation means to allow oneself to be conducted by the subject matter to which the partners in the dialogue are oriented," and the ideas that result from good conversations always "presuppose an orientation toward an area of openness from which the idea can occur" (*TM* 367, 366). If we accept this premise, then a conversation with Coleridge is enabled by the fact that he, as both a poet and a philosopher, is interested in some of the same ultimately undecided (and undecidable) issues that haunt thinkers in the twentieth century, such as the nature of subjectivity, the ethical relation to otherness, the ethical implications of interpretive acts, and the relationship between imaginative writing and real-world ethical relations.

This conversation is informed by Gadamer's principle of *wirkungsgeschichtliches Bewußtsein* insofar as our interpretations are always implicated in the interpretive history of which we are a part. While McGann and Levinson both acknowlede this principle, Gadamer can help us put it to productive use. In light of this principle, the dialogue with Coleridge is partly a dialogue with the sources of our own questions and interests; not in the sense of a Bloomian *agon,* but in the more flexible sense that the complex mixture of problems, positions, and processes we label "Romanticism" is an important source for many modern philosophical positions, albeit a source that is variously embraced, denied, rejected, ignored, and questioned. One reason there are so many common areas of concern between Coleridge and us is that our thought is so thoroughly conditioned by Romanticism; thus the same factors that make the conversation difficult also make it important. Hermeneutics itself, of course, participates in this historicity, as evidenced by its dual position in this book as both a modern critical approach, exemplified most thoroughly by Gadamer, and a historical phenomenon in which Coleridge participated: the history of interpretive theory that emerged out of eighteenth-century Biblical criticism. Since the former emerged from the latter, the line between them cannot be sharply drawn. Eighteenth-century hermeneutics played an important role in the thought of Romantics such as Coleridge, influenced later nineteenth-century theories of history, was existentialized by Heidegger, and emerged in Gadamer, Ricoeur, and others as an important alternative to the methods of the natural sciences.[17]

The historical consciousness emphasized by hermeneutics suggests a certain humility before the texts we study, but not the servile humility before the "tradition" of which Gadamer is sometimes accused, most famously by Habermas. The past is both a source and an other, a notion that can be radicalized with the help of Levinas. I am suggesting a kind of Levinasian humility before the otherness of the past text: an approach that refuses to assimilate the other into the categories of my ego, that treats this other as "infinite" in the sense that it is incommensurable with my categories and consciousness, but that by the same token refuses agreement. As Simon Critchley points out in his reading of Levinas, Levinasian ethics requires a certain ingratitude toward the other, because gratitude would force me and the other into a relation of other-denying reciprocity.[18] Robert Bernasconi describes Levinas's own seemingly contradictory reading of Buber in similar terms, distinguishing Levinasian hermeneutics from Derridean "double reading": "Levinas in reading Buber is in the first instance concerned . . . with recalling certain necessities which govern thinking, his own thinking as much as that of Buber. But he also encountered Buber in an ethical relation. His readings of Buber exhibited the asymmetry and separation of such a relation" (128). This asymmetry goes beyond a merely "critical" approach that would see the "Romantic Ideology" as something that can be objectively exposed; ideological criticism remains within the reciprocal symmetry of agreement and critique.

The other text's necessary resistance to interpretation it is not so much a sign of its authority over our interpretation as it is an indication of the finitude of our interpretive stance. As Gerald Bruns says of this historical/hermeneutic situation: "the text resists our understanding in such a way as to bring into the foreground the historicality—the limits or finitude—of our hermeneutical situation" (*Hermeneutics Ancient and Modern* 155).[19] The importance of this sense of interpretation as attentiveness to the other goes beyond the practice of literary criticism, as Gadamer suggests in an essay from 1983: "[T]he authentic task of the human future which has truly gained global significance lies in the area of human coexistence." This task demands the "risking of one's own [self] for the understanding and recognition of the other" (*On Education, Poetry, and History* 207) and poses, he argues, an important challenge to the future of the humanities.

The ethical/hermeneutic approach to Coleridge that I am attempting will sometimes look like a "deconstruction" of Coleridge, though I recognize that Coleridge is usually his own best deconstructor. Thus some of my arguments resist the totalization that Coleridge desired, and sometimes claimed, for his philosophical program, but at the same time I affirm the priority of the ethical that he explicitly articulates. I attempt to trace a series of ethical *events* in his work—or in our reading of his work—that are not simply concepts or ethical positions held by a critical or poetic intending ego. The insights I am after depend less on an appraisal of Coleridge's positions than on the observation of what happens when those positions—such as the grounding of Being on a principle of self-consciousness—are placed into the contexts of both his own contradictory, ego-questioning experience and some modern reflections on related issues.

III. The Reader and the Questioning Past

Tilottama Rajan, in *The Supplement of Reading,* argues that "Coleridge's Conversation with Hermeneutics" (the title of her chapter on Coleridge) leads to a "reflexive" reading in which the conversation poems become "paradigms for the way a traditional hermeneutic, when pushed to explore its own interior distances, opens into a kind of dialogical self-reading" (110). Her discussion of the implications of this self-deconstructing hermeneutic, within a history characterized by "a growing emphasis . . . on the reader as co-producer of the text" (19), teaches us a great deal about how Romantic texts function as a challenge to the reader who must "supplement" the text, particularly when, as is often the case with Coleridge, the reader is also figured within the text. I accept the premise that the conflicts within and between Coleridge's theory and practice pose a particular challenge to the reader, but I am both expanding and contracting this notion of the reader. I am expanding it, in the sense that I am concerned not just with a reader, however historically contextualized, and not with the issues of reception theory, but with modern critical and philosophical positions that both read and are read by the past of which Coleridge is a part. (In this hermeneutic conversation, the modern "reader" may or may not have actually read Coleridge.) I am contracting Rajan's notion of the reader in that I want to restrict the conversation to the interaction between hermeneutic and ethical problems in Coleridge as they intersect and challenge selected modern positions.

In a sense this effort entails reversing the direction of the "question" of Coleridge. Questions posed by critics to texts, from "What did Coleridge think?" to "In what kind of ideology does Coleridge implicate himself?" belong to the valuable but limited effort of historical reconstruction, "the reconstruction of the question to which a given text is an answer" (*TM* 373). Gadamer places that effort within the prior horizon of the question posed *by,* not *to* the text: "[T]he relation of question and answer is, in fact, reversed. The voice that speaks to us from the past—whether text, work, trace—itself poses a question and places our meaning in openness. . . . Reconstructing the question to which the text is presumed to be the answer itself takes place within a process of questioning through which we try to answer the question that the text asks us" (374). This reversal of the question by which the critic becomes the questioned before he or she becomes the questioner need not signal a return to the oracular Romanticism that has been the object of ideological critique or to the vagaries of reader-response, although Gadamer's own literary criticism grants a perhaps excessively oracular status to poetry, and Hans-Robert Jauss grounded his "aesthetics of reception" on Gadamerian principles.[20] Rather, I hope to give a hearing to the "voice that speaks to us from the past" by reading Coleridge's position as a challenge to some specific modern positions in the intersection between ethics and hermeneutics. This is not to suggest the superiority of either a Romantic or a modern position, but rather that Coleridge's thought—in its historical difference, its intensity, as well as its often contradictory nature—poses an interrogative challenge to modern thought precisely because he writes/speaks from within a historical, theological, and metaphysical horizon that most of us cannot share, although it is an important part of our past, whether as a direct cultural inheritance or as the result of serious attention to this past irrespective of our own cultural background.

Particularly in lyric poetry, and in Wordsworth's and Coleridge's "conversation" poetry, the notion of the question posed by the poem is related to the poem's self-consciousness about its own manner of address. As Gadamer says of Paul Celan's enigmatically addressed lyrics, in which "'I,' 'you,' and 'we' are pronounced in an utterly direct, shadowy-uncertain and constantly changing way," such a poem's "address has an aim, but it has no object" (*Gadamer on Celan* 69). This uncoupling of "aim" and "object" means that the aim retains a direct specificity even as the object shifts: the relationship between the poem's "I" and "you" can be specified (the poem's "aim") while the "you" or even the "I" (the poem's "object") may change. This helps to show how the poem can speak to us across temporal and cultural boundaries in a way that entails neither transcendental claims for a poem's existence outside of historical temporality nor the artificial narrowing of the poem's "you" to an "original" or "intended" audience. This is not, however, to say that the "sense" of the poem, or what it says, is a self-contained entity that can function independently of the poem's "reference," or what it refers to, to invoke Frege's distinction. As Paul Ricoeur points out, sense and reference are dialectically interdependent (*Interpretation Theory* 19–22), and Gadamer shows how all meaning, including the poetic, exists only in concrete application. The "aim" requires an "object" (you have to aim *at* something, or you're not aiming) but it is not tied to that particular object.

This indeterminacy of the poem's object places the reader in the paradoxical position of both being and not being the poem's addressee. Particularly in a Romantic conversation poem, we know that the poem is written "to" someone inaccessible to our horizon, as we both listen in on that foreign conversation and allow the poem as a whole to speak to us.

For example, as the speaker turns to Dorothy at the end of Wordsworth's "Tintern Abbey," the poem closes down into a "private" conversation even as it is making its final statement to posterity. Dorothy's culturally specific, historically situated memory becomes a kind of reflection of the poem's future reception as it preserves the imagery of the poem's controlling vision ("these steep wood and lofty cliffs, / And this pastoral landscape" [156–67]) as well as the speaker's relationship to the scene: how these elements were to him "More dear, both for themselves and for thy sake" (159). Whether we are reading the poem in 1798 as the anonymous conclusion to the *Lyrical Ballads* or in 2000 in a hypertext edition, we are forced to negotiate (in different ways, of course) between Dorothy's status as as historically specific "object" and her status as the image of the poem's future "aim" at a shifting series of readers. Even the memory she preserves for William vaccilates between the determinacy of a clearly dated autobiographical narrative and the indeterminacy of a philosophical statement.

Coleridge played with this problem of address even more self-consciously than Wordsworth. The most elaborate example is perhaps the evolution of the "Dejection" ode, which began as a verse letter to Sara Hutchinson, full of direct address and references to specific private events, such as Coleridge's unhappy marriage and the experiences he shared with Sara. Even here, before the addressee was explicitly changed to "William," it is implicitly addressed to Wordsworth, since the letter's affirmation that "we receive but what we give / And in *our* Life alone does Nature live" ("A Letter to ——" 295–96)[21] is, as Parrish points out (Introduction to *Coleridge's Dejection* 11), an implicit answer to the questions raised by the beginnings of Wordsworth's "Immortality" ode. In the series of unpublished and published versions of the poem, Parrish notes five changes of address in a single line ("A Letter to ——" 295; "Dejection" [1817] 47) between 1802 and 1817—"Sara," "Wordsworth," "Edmund," "William," and "Lady"—and points out that these changes in address required surprisingly little rewriting (17). This is not simply because, as Parrish says, "the original poem was more about Coleridge than about Sara" (Introduction 18); it is also a function of Coleridge's constancy of "aim" in addressing a shifting series of "objects."[22]

When the poem was first published in the *Morning Post,* the forum was public and the putative addressee was the nonspecific "Edmund," but the date—October 4, 1802—was Wordsworth's wedding day, which makes it a kind of wedding-present with a very specific addressee, even as that addressee is celebrating an event that makes an important link between private and public realms.[23] To add a further complication, the *Morning Post* version claims to omit "the sixth and seventh Stanzas" ([1802] 87). There is no evidence for the existence of these stanzas, which suggests another self-consciously playful complication in the addressee's situation: the *Morning Post* reader must posit another reader—specifically *not* him or herself—who has access to those "missing" stanzas. Even without the notation of these absent stanzas, the poem itself sets up a clear distinction between the reader and its internal addressee. As Cyrus Hamlin argues, discussing the 1817 version addressed to a "Lady," part of the experience of reading a poem such as "Dejection" is the recognition of the sharp difference between our own situation and the idealized, unconscious situation of the addressed "Lady" (223–24).

Thus it is part of the poem's own historical situation that the object of its address self-consciously shifts, even as the aim remains true. The poem questions us, who have access to this evolution through comparative texts such as Parrish's, in a complex way. It asks us to read it in terms of historically and even contemporaneously multiple addressees as we attempt both to understand and to become the addressee. At the same time, it asks us to consider claims that come from an historical horizon specifically different from our own. These kinds of questioning are connected in hermeneutic experience. We become the poem's addressee—we listen to it and learn something about ourselves—by hearing the voices in the poem speak to others, as an example of the Gadamerian principle by which "[s]elf-understanding always occurs through understanding something other than the self and includes the unity and integrity of the other" (*TM* 97). This understanding that connects self and other is not simply a conceptual appropriation of the other or even the self, however, because the process depends on what Gadamer calls "the hermeneutic productivity of temporal distance" (297), by means of which "we must adopt a standpoint in relation to art and the beautiful that does not pretend to immediacy but corresponds to the historical nature of the human condition" (97). We neither treat the poem as something to be appropriated to the immediacy of our own experience, as when literature is trivialized by being made "relevant" to our present concerns,[24] nor encase it in the alien past of its "original" situation, as when we attempt to reconstruct the poem's first production and reception. Despite their differences, both efforts similarly deny the "productivity of temporal distance" (with whose discovery Gadamer credits Heidegger), the first by assuming that the past text can be transported to the present, the second—more contradictorily—by assuming that the present can "objectively" access the past and gauge its otherness to the present. As Fred Dallmayr argues, the "complex interlacing of transparency and nontransparency" in hermeneutic interpretation, which he connects to the productivity of multicultural rather than simply historical distance, enables the interpreter to avoid "the temptations both of complete appropriation and of renunciation" (*Beyond Orientalism* 44). The next chapter will explore how this hermeneutic distance can grant a work of art the otherness both of another person and of a made object, two conflicting kinds of otherness whose interaction has important ethical ramifications.

2

Ethics and Art

Problems of *Phronesis* and *Techne*

I. *Techne* and *Phronesis* in Romanticism

A central problem for the relationship between hermeneutics and ethics is how to connect the kind of knowledge involved in the production of literary texts with the kind of knowledge involved in ethical relations. This is an especially vital question both for the Romantics and for us, from the rarefied atmosphere of theory to the practical realm of public policy, because it goes to the heart of the role of the aesthetic in human relations, the value of art in education, and why it is (or is not) "good" for people to read literature. Do we use the distinction between aesthetics and ethics as grounds for excluding the aesthetic from the ethical? This is what Gadamer calls Kant's "achievement in moral philosophy, which purified ethics from all aesthetics and feeling" (*TM* 40). Or do we emphasize the other side of this separation, and purify aesthetics from ethics? This is what Oscar Wilde did in his famous pronouncement, "[t]here is no such thing as a moral or an immoral book. Books are well written, or badly written. That is all" (Preface, *The Picture of Dorian Gray* ix). Or do we reconnect aesthetics and ethics, following Matthew Arnold's insistence that poetry serve moral life in the broad sense of "how to live" as the "powerful and beautiful application of ideas to life" ("Wordsworth" 339)?[1] Or do we critique the Arnoldian connection of art and ethics, as Geoffrey Galt Harpham suggests we did during the "Theoretical Era" of

1968–87, by subsuming ethics under ideology, viewing "ethics" as an ideologically blind cover for private desire or structures of domination ("Ethics" 388)? The distinction between the knowledge employed in ethical decisions and that which produces artworks goes back at least to Aristotle. In the *Nicomachean Ethics,* he divides knowledge into three categories: theoretical (*episteme*), productive (*techne*), and practical (*phronesis*). Works of art result from *techne*—the creation of tangible objects via the technique of the artist's craft—but ethics falls under the very different domain of *phronesis,* "a state grasping the truth, involving reason, concerned with action about what is good or bad for a human being" (6.5.1140b). Unlike *episteme,* which has to do with necessary truths that cannot be otherwise than they are (6.3.1139b), both *phronesis* and *techne* treat "what admits of being otherwise" (6.5.1140a), but they posit a different relation between means and ends. In *techne* the end produced by art or craft is separated from the "means" of the artist's technique, and both are predetermined, while ethical action is its own end, which cannot be determined in advance: "production has its end beyond it; but action does not, since its end is doing well itself" (6.5.1140b).

Thus, despite Coleridge's claim that it is a fragment of his unconscious, even "Kubla Khan" is a separable "product" resulting from the choice of predetermined poetic conventions. In ethical thought, however, the end—living well as a human being—is inseparable from the means, and neither can be determined in isolation from one's particular situation in life. Although these two kinds of thought are in tension, they are inseparable when it comes to works of art that purport to be "ethical": a literary work whose content concerns the means-ends unity of ethical life must face the fact that it is itself a product of *techne,* in which the written text is separated from the artistic means by which it was produced. As Ricoeur points out, this is an inevitable fact of written discourse: "Language is submitted to the rules of a kind of craftsmanship, which allows us to speak of production and of works of art. . . . The generative devices, which we call literary genres, are the technical rules presiding over their production" (*Interpretation Theory* 33). Invoking Aristotle's distinction, not between *techne* and *phronesis,* but between *techne* and *episteme,* Ricoeur also notes that "only *technê* generates individuals . . . whereas *epistêmê* grasps species" (77), which adds a further complication when we consider that ethical thought, too, at least in its Romantic and postromantic versions, tends to work with individuals rather than species.

Even though, as Lockridge argues, the Romantics' emphasis on imagination allows for "a *homology* of art and ethics because it is the source of both," rather than a mere analogy, as in Kant (*The Ethics of Romanticism* 79), the problems raised by Aristotle's distinction show up in Romantic poets' recognition of some important differences between the aesthetic and the ethical. Coleridge objects in ethical terms to Schelling's exaltation of art above ethics: "Strange morality, to place contemplation & Painting above the most heroic and pure Virtues in Action" (*CM* 4: 421). The specific tension between the *phronesis* of virtuous action and the *techne* of art can be seen when Wordsworth exalts the ethical force of poetry even as he denigrates the poet's work as mechanical *techne*. While arguing that the affective dimension of poetry can heal an ethically impoverished culture, he recognizes that poetry is a matter of technical production, not ethical life: "[h]owever exalted a notion we would wish to cherish of the character of a Poet . . . his situation is altogether slavish and mechanical, compared with the freedom and power of real and substantial action and suffering" (*Prose Works* 1: 138). Coleridge attempts to resolve this tension by keeping "fancy" and "imagination" separate, subordinating *techne* to ethical consciousness in both art and life. For him, the process of poetic production in the "secondary" imagination is not mere *techne*, but rather an addition of "the conscious will" to the life-founding act of self-consciousness, the "repetition in the finite mind of the eternal act of creation in the infinite I AM" (*BL* 1: 304). Laurence Lockridge has demonstrated the ethical grounding of that self-consciousness in "conscience" (*Coleridge the Moralist* 124–26); without "conscience" defined as "my affections & duties toward others," Coleridge says in a notebook entry, "I should have no self" (*CN* 2: 3231). Like Aristotelian *phronesis*, Coleridgean self-consciousness unites means and ends via a dialectic (borrowed from Schelling) in which the end of self-conscious existence is identical to the self-conscious means by which that self is known: "object and subject, being and knowing, are identical, each involving and supposing the other" (*BL* 1: 273). This unity is absent in the *techne* of fancy, in which the self is separated from the means it employs, having "no other counters to play with, but fixities and definites" (1: 305).

For Coleridge, the separation between imagination and fancy is important partly because when ethics becomes mere *techne*—or, to invoke a traditional distinction that has been revived recently, when the more comprehensive category of "ethics" is reduced to systematic "morality"[2]—it impedes the higher imaginative function, which is the ultimately ethical foundation of all consciousness. Frances Ferguson summarizes Coleridge's opposition to ethical *techne* in her discussion of his conversation with Anna Letitia Barbauld about the "moral" of the *Rime of the Ancient Mariner*: "while Mrs. Barbauld could be said to regard the learning of reading and morals as *technical* skills, Coleridge recognizes reading as moral because one's *techné* can never suffice" (256). Wordsworth's pragmatic combination of poetry's *phronesis*-like ethical force with its status as "mechanical" *techne,* implicit in his expansion of imagination to include "aggregation" and "association," comes under fire when Coleridge accuses him of having "mistaken the co-presence of fancy with imagination for the operation of the latter singly (*BL* 1: 294) in his poetic theory and of attempting to combine the disparate functions of the moral essay and the poem in his *Excursion* (2: 130–31). Because its primary end is "pleasure" rather than "truth," says Coleridge, poetry should not usurp the office of didactic prose by expecting to effect a direct translation from poetry to "*real life,*" technically refashioning taste, "making" it into what it "ought" to be. In the current imperfect state of affairs, while there remains a gulf between aesthetic pleasure and philosophical truth, poets should "proceed upon that state of association, which actually exists as *general*; instead of attempting first to *make* it what it ought to be, and then to let the pleasure follow" (2: 130).[3]

But the inappropriate intrusion of moral *techne* into poetry is the very flaw that Coleridge identifies in his own *Rime,* a circumstance that suggests the difficulty of keeping *techne* in a separate, lower realm both aesthetically and ethically. Coleridge sees the "moral" of the *Rime* as an impediment to imagination, claiming that "the fault of the Ancient Mariner consists in making the moral sentiment too apparent and bringing it in too much as a principle or cause in a work of such pure Imagination" (*TT* 1: 149). In response to Barbauld's objection that the poem is "improbable, and ha[s] no moral," he asserts that "the chief fault of the poem [is] that it ha[s] too much moral, and that too openly obtruded on the reader" (1: 272–73). The "moral sentiment" divides means and ends: the Mariner's statement "He prayeth best who loveth best / All things both great and small" (*Rime* 660–61)[4] becomes a means to the separable end of making the Wedding Guest—and presumably the reader, upon whom this "moral" is "too openly obtruded"—arise "sadder and . . . wiser" (670) the following day. Paradoxically, the more the poem tries to impose a technical "moral," the further it moves away from the *phronesis*-like means-end unity of "pure Imagination."

The *Rime*'s history also manifests this tension. As "a work of such pure Imagination" it is related to the *phronesis*-like ethical authority of the "Imagination," but it is also a product of *techne:* a "work." On the one hand, Coleridge and Wordsworth consciously planned the work in the popular Gothic style, with a distinct commercial end: "to defray the expenses" of a walking tour (Moorman, *Early Years* 347). On the other hand, for Coleridge the Mariner shifted from a separate poetic creation to an image of the poet's self, as he consciously identified with his character in notebook entries made on his lonely journey to Malta in 1804. As Coleridge revised the *Rime,* he increased its supposed involvement in the processes of culture and history, de-emphasizing its status as a separate product of an artist's *techne*. McGann shows how the poem's several layers of narrative—tale, ballad narrative, editorial gloss, and Coleridge's own presentation—make for an "imitation of a culturally redacted literary work" ("The Meaning of the Ancient Mariner" 222). The revised poem is presented not as the simple product of art, but as an attempt to "illustrate a significant continuity of meaning between cultural phenomena that seemed as diverse as pagan superstition, Catholic theology, Aristotelian science, and contemporary philological theory" (222). The poem is presented as emerging from a complexly layered and shared cultural experience, rather than from a process of artistic technique. However, those same interpretive layers force the reader to see the poem as a self-conscious work of art; real-life experiences are not usually accompanied by archaic language and scholarly glosses.

Within the poem, the negative consequences of the tension between moral *techne* and the ethically whole imaginative self are evident in the involuntary process that painfully separates the tale from the Mariner's own self-consciousness, but paradoxically this same process reveals the equally negative consequences that follow when the self is deprived of a controllable *techne:*

> Since then, at an uncertain hour,
> That agony returns;
> And till my ghastly tale is told,
> This heart within me burns.
> ([1817] 586–89)

The "ghastly tale" works in explicit opposition to the Mariner's moral being, but it is his own ("my") tale nevertheless. This situation suggests two contradictory possibilities. On the one hand, it demonstrates the alienation of technical production that occurs when the artist loses control over his product because of *techne*'s separation of means and ends: just as the artist has no control over the use to which his product will be put once it is separated from his or her creative process, so the Mariner is alienated even from his own narration of the tale. On the other hand, the same situation presents a tragic proximity of means and ends, in that the Mariner, unlike the poet, cannot separate his work from its means of production and send it into the world. For the Mariner, the end to which the tale is put—the moral education of those who "must hear" him (635)—coexists with the means: the repeated process of recreating the experience. In this sense the Mariner teaches "by his own example" ([1817] marginal gloss to 614–21); as an example of action with the immanent end of "doing well" rather than a separable end product of a technical means, the Mariner's compulsive narrative becomes a nearly unlivable kind of *phronesis* without the relief of *techne*.

In the Mariner's crime and punishment we also see something like what Heidegger finds is the ambiguous "essence" of technology in "The Question Concerning Technology." This active essence (or "essencing") is technology's "way of revealing" (12), which Heidegger differentiates from its "correct" but not "true" definition in terms of instrumentality and the separation of means and ends (6). What is important to Heidegger in modern technology is not an agent's use of separable tools toward a separable end, but rather the sense in which things are transformed from being objects that stand "over against us" (17) into what he calls "standing-reserve" (*Bestand*). The character of standing-reserve is that "the energy concealed in nature is unlocked, what is unlocked is transformed, what is transformed is stored up, what is stored up is, in turn, distributed, and what is distributed is switched about ever anew" (16), as in a hydroelectric plant. A car or an airplane is in this sense not so much an object created by a technological means as it is a repository of stored, regulated, on- or off-switchable energy.[5] The pervasiveness of this sense of the technological world as a repository of stored and regulated energy-reserves is evident in the transference of this vocabulary to the human realm, as in "the current talk about human resources, about the supply of patients for a clinic" (18).

The problem with this situation lies not in the prospect of technology taking over the world in the usual sense, but in its concealing of this very process of its own "essencing." If man is not concerned with "what is unconcealed" even as an object, but simply treats everything as "standing-reserve," with himself as "nothing but the orderer of the standing-reserve," then tragedy is imminent: "he comes to the point where he himself will have to be taken as standing-reserve" even as he "exalts himself to the posture of lord of the earth" (26–27). Heidegger's hope, however, is that man "never is transformed into mere standing-reserve" (18), not because he is in any way in control of the process, but because "he is challenged more originally than are the energies of nature" (18), and that art, by returning us to the Greek unity of *techne* and *poeisis,* will provide a way out of technology's domination and self-concealment as standing-reserve. Coleridge, who, as the foregoing analysis suggests, was perhaps less confident than Heidegger in the possibility of the Greek reunification of *techne* and *poeisis,* presents in the *Rime* a version of the human "fall" into standing-reserve. Violating nature's hospitality by shooting the albatross, the Mariner treats the bird not as a part of a nature that would assist in a process of revealing but as part of a reserve of energy that can be regulated, treating it either simply as something whose life-energy can be cut off, or, in the crew's contradictory interpretations, as something that controls the redistribution of meteorological energy: the Mariner is blamed because he "had kill'd the Bird / That made the Breeze to blow" (91-92), then praised because "'Twas right . . . such birds to slay / That bring the fog and mist" (97-98). Not only does the crew's self-contradiction undercut this interpretation of the bird as a reserve of energy whose power may be redistributed to the ship's advantage, but by the second statement we have moved from "the Bird" to "such birds"; the bird has moved from an object to be encountered to a truly anonymous reserve of energy.

The result is that the Mariner himself becomes a tragic embodiment of standing-reserve: a repository of narrative energy that is repeatedly bottled up and released in the telling of his tale, and one who is therefore unable to see into the life of that process as Heidegger would wish. Heidegger hopes that art, "a realm that is, on the one hand, akin to the essence of technology, and, on the other, fundamentally different from it" ("The Question Concerning Technology" 35) will be able to save us from the blind submission to standing-reserve by confronting the essence of technology. If Coleridge has succeeded in providing a work which, rather than obtruding a moral on its readers, reveals this "essencing" of technology, then perhaps he has fulfilled Heidegger's aim. In Heidegger's terms, the *Rime* might be said to fulfill this mission of art by illustrating the ambiguity of "Enframing" (*Ge-stell*), a process that Heidegger defines as the challenge of technology to man "to reveal the real, in the mode of ordering, as standing-reserve" (20). On the one hand, Enframing blocks the relation to truth in the "frenzied-ness of ordering" presented by standing-reserve, as the Mariner becomes an almost inhuman autobiographical machine. On the other hand, Enframing grants the possibility that man will endure "as the one who is needed and used for the safekeeping of the coming to presence of truth" (33), as the Mariner's tragic self-presentation shows the truth of technological reality as standing-reserve, making us sadder but wiser. In my terms, which invoke a more traditional understanding of *techne* than Heidegger's, the *Rime* also reveals the workings of *techne,* but the irreducible tension between *techne* and *phronesis* offers less optimism about the salvific potential of art than does the Heideggerian version. This tension, as in Heidegger, reveals poetry's kinship with and difference from technology, but it presents problems in the relation between ethics and aesthetics that cannot be resolved by the translation of *techne*'s domination into the revealing of its essence.

II. Ethics and Interpretation: The Rise of *Techne* and the Return of *Phronesis*

The Mariner's submission to an involuntary moral *techne* foreshadows the modern assumption that we have no alternative to *techne* in art or life, an assumption that threatens the autonomy of art, the possibility of a link between imagination and *phronesis,* and the controllability of *techne*. Coleridge himself worried about the modern disappearance of the poet into a "mechanized" linguistic universe, complaining that language had become "mechanized as it were into a barrel-organ," bypassing the self by "suppl[ying] at once both instrument and tune" (*BL* 1: 38). Twelve years later, in "Signs of the Times," Carlyle would characterize his present as "the Mechanical Age," devoted to *techne*'s calculated adaptation of means to ends to the exclusion of the directly human: "[i]t is the age of Machinery . . . the age which, with its whole undivided might, forwards, teaches and practices the great art of adapting means to ends. Nothing is now done directly, or by hand; all is by rule and calculated contrivance" (59).[6] *Techne* extends into the self: "[n]ot the external and physical alone is managed by machinery, but the internal and spiritual also" (60). This felt tension between the human and the "mechanical," as that which is threatening or transforming the human, the linguistic, and the historical is traced by Gadamer back to the Cartesian separation of mind and body, which resulted in the seventeenth-century division of knowledge into "a cosmos of the empirical sciences and a cosmos of the world-orientation based upon linguistic traditions," or the natural sciences and the humanities (*On Education, Poetry, and History* 198).

The attempt to articulate the special character of the "human sciences" in relation to a technological model of knowledge has been a preoccupation of hermeneutic thought at least since the early nineteenth century, and this attempt is tied to the origin of the modern university that now appears so outdated to some. It is no coincidence that Wilhelm von Humboldt both founded the University of Berlin (in 1810), which marked the origin of the modern "research" paradigm for the humanities as well as the natural sciences, and also did important work in hermeneutics.[7] As Charles E. McClelland notes, the Humboldtian concept of the university effected the "sundering of the 'technical' and 'theoretical' education in the nineteenth century" (*State, Society, and University* 125).

In the twentieth century, several strands of thought converge to demonstrate the foundational role of *techne*. Walter Benjamin's widely accepted assertion, "that which withers in the age of mechanical reproduction is the aura of the work of art" (221), suggests the disappearance of any aesthetics that claims to escape the domination of the *techne* of art's production and reproduction in the marketplace. Despite the popular view that technology's empirical basis provides a kind of epistemological certainty unavailable in "softer" forms of interpretation, the real point may be that technology's emphasis on practical results acknowledges the impossibility of epistemological certainty. Following Lyotard, Frances Ferguson notes that the emphasis on technology goes hand in hand with the postmodern denial of such certainty: "the notion of communicable technology becomes the delimited replacement for Kantian transcendental structures of perception; and 'know-how' becomes identical with the impossibility of epistemological certainty" (*Solitude and the Sublime* 15). This structure of replacement helps to explain the antitheoretical bent of many new-historicists, who see even the theoretical coherence of poststructuralist theory as too epistemologically certain, opting instead for the more limited empirical certainty of technological practice.

According to this model, all intellectual activity is seen as cultural "labor," following the production-driven model of *techne*.[8] If all is *techne*, any effort to reserve a special place for the aesthetic outside of the model of production and power will necessarily be seen as bad faith, as in Jerome McGann's critique of Romanticism's ideological "polemic on behalf of the special privilege of poetry and art" (*The Romantic Ideology* 70).[9] Ironically, from the standpoint of the Aristotelian model (which of course these critics would not accept) the very "cultural production" model that is used to critique aesthetic ideology is itself highly "aesthetic" in the sense that it depends on the *techne* of cultural labor by which works of art are produced, rather than the *phronesis* by which a life is "lived well" rather than "made." At its worst, the aesthetic becomes the bad faith of tyranny, as in Benjamin's analysis of the aesthetic foundations of Fascism (241–42).

The domination of *techne* is not just an aesthetic or even a political problem; for Gilles Deleuze and Félix Guattari, even desire is only "production," "the set of *passive syntheses* that engineer partial objects, flows, and bodies, and that function as units of production" (26). If selves are products rather than agents of *techne,* as in Deleuze and Guattari's assertion that "there is no fixed subject" without the psychological mechanism of repression (26), then ethical relations are restricted to alienated structures of production that leave out even Aristotle's technical craftsperson, not to mention the ethical agent of *phronesis*. Like the Ancient Mariner, we "pass, like night, from land to land" with "strange power of speech" (*Rime* 632–33) produced by cultural conditions or mechanisms of desire rather than creative will.

Even a self-consciously "ethical" critic such as Wayne Booth, who certainly does not see the cultural labor of aesthetic creation as alienated, narrows (or perhaps expands) the notion of the ethical "character" to the range of virtues—neutrally defined as "powers"—that one exercises in a manner that is here indistinguishable from *techne:* "If "virtue" covers every kind of genuine strength or power, and if a person's ethos is the total range of his or her virtues, then ethical criticism will be any effort to show how the virtues of narratives relate to the virtues of selves and societies, or how the ethos of any story affects or is affected by the ethos—the collection of virtues—of any given reader" (*The Company We Keep* 11). According to Booth, this sort of logic "exposes the falseness of any sharp divorce of aesthetic and ethical questions" (11), but it does so by tending to reduce *phronesis* to *techne*—the virtuous character becomes indistinguishable from the expert craftsman, exercising a "power"—and by disconnecting ethics from any concept of the Good. Booth's list of the "virtues" exhibited by Milton places "courage" on the same level as "a most impressive proficiency with metaphor and irony" (113).[10]

Perhaps little room is left for *phronesis* because "we are living in a time when the very conditions required for the exercise of *phronesis*—the shared acceptance of universal principles and laws—are themselves breaking down" (Bernstein, "From Hermeneutics to Praxis" 286). For some, the resulting shift to *techne* is an opportunity, as in the ubiquitous self-help literature that offers techniques for remaking our lives or in Richard Rorty's directive to remake ourselves on the open-ended plan of liberal irony (*Contingency* 196).[11] Sharply criticizing Heidegger's attempt to create a final substantive, noninstrumental vocabulary, the attempt "simply to hear the resonances of the words of the metaphysicians rather than to use these words as instruments" (118), Rorty pragmatically embraces the aesthetic as nothing more than a technique, with personal but not universal or metaphysical overtones, that offers a method by which, through an "awareness of the power of redescription," we should literally remake ourselves into liberal ironists, and "*create* a more expansive sense of solidarity than we presently have" rather than "*recognize* such a solidarity, as something that exists antecedently to our recognition of it" (89, 196).

However, the recent revival of Aristotelian *phronesis* by philosophers such as Alasdair MacIntyre and Martha Nussbaum suggests the continuing value of this concept even in a world that no longer shares universal principles. Gadamer returns to Aristotle to emphasize the dangers of acceding to the dominance of *techne:* ethical decisions, in contrast to acts of "production," depend on the immediacy of particular situations, and "there can be no anterior certainty concerning what the good life is directed toward as a whole" (*TM* 321). Gadamer asks, "Does man learn to make himself what he ought to be, in the same way that the craftsman learns to make things according to his plan and will?" (314–15). The problem with an affirmative answer, even if the "plan" is open-ended, is that it removes the need for deliberation, under the assumption that complete knowledge of a self-made product is possible: "if technical knowledge were available, it would always make it unnecessary to deliberate with oneself about the subject" (321). Coleridge glosses this notion in his late satire on the adage "know thyself," suggesting that such self-knowledge would only be possible in the unlikely event that the self could be made as in a technical "trade": "Say, canst thou make thyself?—Learn first that trade;—/ Haply thou mayst know what thyself had made" ("Self-Knowledge" 4–5).[12] For Gadamer, the expansion of *techne* leads to cultural control: "the fields of mastering means to pregiven ends have been rendered even more monological and controllable" in a culture where "the fields of *techne* and art are much more expanded" ("Hermeneutics and Social Science" 313). For literary criticism, the result is to confine ethical discussion within the vocabulary of power, as when Julie Ellison remarks, "The choice of the term 'ethics' or 'ideology' marks the style of critics interested in the question of power (and who is not?)" (108).

The emphasis on culture as a matter of technical "production" is paralleled by an increase in the role of interpretation as a fundamental human activity. What Benjamin identifies as a transition from the "cult value" to the "exhibition value of the work" (224) in an age of increasingly mechanical reproduction, a shift from a work's authenticity and originality to its reproducibility for an audience, is paralleled by the post-Romantic emphasis on interpretive activity as a defining characteristic of human life. If for Aristotle the essential human characteristic is rationality (1.7.1098a), for the post-Romantic tradition it is a life of language and interpretation. Thus what Gadamer calls the "world of signs and indices," which, already in Greek conceptions of the poet, is "subordinate to no particular aims" and is thus higher than other forms of *techne* (*The Idea of the Good* 120–21), has for us expanded from the world of poetic *techne* to the world in which we live. According to Gadamer, Romanticism has taught us that "understanding and interpretation are the same thing," and that "*language is the universal medium in which understanding occurs*" (*TM* 388–89). One can thereby conclude that "[l]anguage is not just one of man's possessions in the world; rather, on it depends the fact that man has a *world* at all" (443). If, in Aristotle's terms, to be a good person means to exercise well the characteristic activity of humans (1.7.1098a), and if that characteristic activity is interpretation in language, then interpretation and ethical thought are inevitably connected. While Gadamer remains confident that the fundamentality of language need not lead to the dominance of *techne,* his mentor Heidegger echoes Coleridge's implicit fear that to live in a linguistic world may be to shift from controlling a technical means to being controlled by the "barrel-organ" of language: "Man acts as though *he* were the shaper and master of language, while in fact *language* remains the master of man" ("Building Dwelling Thinking" 146).

As Alan Liu suggests, the importance of *techne* in modern American literary criticism, along with its clear historical ties to Romanticism, can be seen in the evolution of New Criticism, particularly in the Agrarians who combined a formalist aesthetic with a Wordsworthian agrarian ideal. In discussing "the entire history of changing relations between economics and rich, unaccountable, poetic craft on its way to techne in a modern mode," Liu notes that "we have not only the New Critics as precedents but also the Romantics themselves" ("Formal vs. Historical Value"). Interpretation and *techne* join forces in some recent evolutions of that critical trend, in which literary criticism joins forces with ethics, but at the cost of replacing moral agency with interpretive *techne,* while maintaining a guarded optimism against Heidegger that this interpretive activity can be productively controlled. For example, J. Hillis Miller's discussion of "the law governing the ethics of reading" (*The Ethics of Reading* 11) constrains ethics within the technical exercise of deconstructive interpretation as a programmatic response to the Kantian moral law, a "perpetual deferral of direct confrontation with the law" (25). That is to say, in order to make a virtue out of deconstructive reading Miller has to reduce ethics to the assertion or the undoing of this "moral law." This is a reduction to *techne* in a very specific way: both the means—narrative's deconstructive play—and the end—the confrontation with a narrow Kantian notion of a moral "law"—are laid out in advance, and despite the particularity of Miller's engagements with texts, his ethics of reading remains in this specific sense a "technical" exercise.

Barbara Herrnstein Smith, although she notes that the relativism on which her theory of "evaluation" is founded entails "no particular moral stance" (161), links ethical life with interpretation by arguing that, in a relativistic world, the actions of a moral agent consist in the evaluation of the contingent conditions he or she perceives. For Smith, interpretation is a subset of evaluation: "[t]he relativist's social and political choices and actions are 'compelled' . . . by the specific, contingent *conditions* in which she operates as an agent, as she perceives, interprets, and considers these conditions—or, in short, *evaluates* them" (163-64). The danger in this position, particularly given Smith's use of a literary/aesthetic model of interpretation, is that its reduction of moral agency to a technique of interpretation implies a claim, even stronger than Miller's, that good literary critics will be good moral agents. As Wayne Booth argues, one of the problems with ethical literary criticism is that it moves all too quickly to a mode of evaluation that cannot help but be normative, even if the evaluative criterion is one of "openness"; not only is "openness" an illusory goal within an intelligible, and therefore somewhat "closed" narrative, but it is as monolithic an example of what Booth calls "lumping" criticism as any other (*The Company We Keep* 60-65).

Geoffrey Galt Harpham has carefully considered the relationship between ethics and the interpretive activity of narrative without reducing one to the other, arguing that "narrative and ethics imply each other without being identical" (*Getting it Right* 160). However, by seeing the relation between narrative and ethics as one of "mutual dependency, resistance, and repression," he tends to contain the ethical within the interpretive *techne* of psychoanalysis. Therapy is not necessarily incompatible with *phronesis,* as Martha Nussbaum shows in her carefully qualified endorsement of the medical analogy in Aristotle (*The Therapy of Desire* 58-69). However, by identifying psychoanalysis with the conversion experience and generalizing the whole as ethics itself, Harpham (who gives short shrift both to Aristotle and to his revivers [51-53]) makes it clear that for him ethics, although it is certainly not under the control of instrumental reason, nonetheless follows the *techne* of psychoanalytic conversion (146). This has the effect of seeing ethical life as "made" rather than "lived," the end-product of analytic *techne* rather than the means-ends unity of *phronesis*. It is one thing to claim, as Tobin Siebers does in *The Ethics of Criticism,* that modes of literary interpretation imply ethical positions; it is quite another thing to reverse those terms and subsume ethics under interpretive techniques. To do so is to give in to a rather restricted view of ethical life, whether it is Miller's deconstructed Kant, Smith's relativism, or Harpham's psychological laws. These positions also base an ethical theory on one practice in life—interpretation—that can be ethical, unethical, or neither. In the last chapter I suggested the limitations of Charles Altieri's restrictions of the ethical to reflective thought, leaving out the direct responsiveness of actions that would be considered ethically beneficial; to reduce ethical thought to the technique of instrumental reason is even more restrictive.[13]

If some critics have eliminated *phronesis* by reducing ethics to the *techne* of interpretive activity, ethical philosophers who have turned to literature, often in search of some version of *phronesis,* have tended to underestimate those very interpretive issues. Alasdair MacIntyre integrates *phronesis* and interpretation by discussing our ethical life as embedded in interlocking narratives of which "we are never more (and sometimes less) than the coauthors" (*After Virtue* 213), but he is relatively untroubled by the differences between life and art, the problem of translating the *techne* of the quest-narrative into the *phronesis* of "the life spent in seeking the good life for man" (219). Similarly, for Nussbaum the "adventure of the reader" of a James novel is "like the adventure of the intelligent characters inside it" in that "it involves valuable aspects of human moral experience that are not tapped by traditional books of moral philosophy" (*Love's Knowledge* 143). As Altieri points out, MacIntyre's reduction of life to such a single genre is inevitably a simplification: "the whole idea of a single quest motif providing unity greatly oversimplifies the psychology involved when ethical considerations play roles in our actions" (*Subjective Agency* 187). Although the narrative impulse itself and specific narrative genres certainly play an important role in ethical understanding, Altieri's accusation of oversimplification could easily apply to Nussbaum's novelistic "adventure" as well as MacIntyre's quest romance. From opposite positions, both trends minimize the difference between aesthetic and ethical experience, Miller and Smith by reducing ethics to a fundamentally literary act of interpretation, and MacIntyre and Nussbaum by appropriating literary narratives to ethical experience.

III. Ethical and Aesthetic Autonomy

Coleridge's poetry, and, in a different way, Wordsworth's, suggest a revision of the concept of the "autonomy" of the work of art, involving a complex ethical claim that combines (1) the poetic presentation of the unity of means and ends found in *phronesis,* (2) the poetic text's resemblance to a human other in its resistance to incorporation into subjectively controlled concepts, and (3) the ethical implications of a poem's self-awareness as a product of nonethical *techne*. The theoretical possibilities of this claim can be explored through Gadamer and Levinas.

In arguing against the modern ubiquity of *techne,* Gadamer grants implicit ethical force to the notion of aesthetic autonomy identified and critiqued by Benjamin, who claims that "[w]hen the age of mechanical reproduction separated art from its basis in cult, the semblance of its autonomy disappeared forever" (226). Gadamer's *Truth and Method,* insofar as it is an argument against "method," or interpretation as *techne,* presents Aristotle's account of *phronesis* in the *Nicomachean Ethics* as "a kind of *model of the problems of hermeneutics*" (*TM* 324).[14] Thus Gadamer links aesthetic interpretation and ethics, but he does so within an argument that dissociates moral agency from the exercise of interpretive technique. He also contextualizes the aesthetic socially and historically without reducing literature to one form of cultural production among others and thereby avoids the pervasive modern equation of culture and *techne*.

For Gadamer, the work of art is autonomous, but not because art can be isolated from culture and then reapplied to it as a separable standard, as in the often critiqued Arnoldian tradition or the fascistic aestheticization of politics to which Benjamin objects. On the contrary, what Gadamer calls "aesthetic differentiation," the practice, which he traces back to Schiller, of "dissociating the work of art from its world" so that one can "see everything 'aesthetically'" (*TM* 85–86), is for him the wrong turn that hermeneutics took in the nineteenth century: "through 'aesthetic differentiation' the work loses its place and the world to which it belongs insofar as it belongs instead to aesthetic consciousness" (87). In its extreme form, this results in the identification of the aesthetic with "virtuosity" (89), which leads to the cultural dominance of *techne*. For Gadamer the special character of the work of art lies instead in the fact that art, though a form of *techne,* unlike craft does not separate means from ends: "The intention of the producer is realized not in the fact that the product serves a useful purpose, but clearly only in the fact that it is simply there." Even if art serves a social or religious function, it is in that function that the work "manifests itself in its real nature" (*The Relevance of the Beautiful* 118); it is not subordinated to its external purpose. Gadamer notes that even in the Greek culture in which *poiesis* refers to the "production" of both the artisan's and the poet's *techne,* poetic and technological production cannot simply be identified: "the poet occupied a position alongside the king and the orator, and was the only artist who was not considered a mere artisan" (118). The *techne* of the poet (in Plato) "produces something in perceptible reality," as does the *techne* of the artisan, but with the important difference that what is produced is "a world of signs and indices that directs us to the ideal" and is thus "subordinate to no particular aim" (*The Idea of the Good* 120–21). Thus poetic *techne* deemphasizes the separability of specific means and specific ends that characterizes *techne* in general.[15]

Particularly in linguistic art, another unity of means and ends is manifested in art's special form of *mimesis*. Whereas other kinds of texts, such as historical accounts, are means that point to some original event or utterance, a literary text is the original event. The end of a referential text is "the return to the supposed given" ("Text and Interpretation" 31), but aesthetic *mimesis* is not a representation of something else; rather, "what is represented is itself present in the only way available to it. . . . [T]he work of art does not simply refer to something, because what it refers to is actually there" (*The Relevance of the Beautiful* 35). This notion of a *mimesis* that does not purport to refer to an original (foreign to the post-Saussurean tradition of the binary sign) is exemplified by the "festival," whose reality is determined in an act of repetition that does not refer back to any original. The festival is "not an identity like a historical event, but neither is it determined by its origin so that there once was the 'real' festival—as distinct from the way in which it later came to be celebrated. . . . Thus its own original essence is always to be something different." The "autonomy" of a work of art, then, lies not in its separation from an "original" referent or the temporality of human life but in its own kind of temporality; the festival "is temporal in a more radical sense than everything that belongs to history" (*TM* 123).

Gadamer's critique of "aesthetic differentiation" stems partly from an effort to recover art's pre-Romantic attachment to its cultural context, as in the exemplary status of architecture, which "belongs inalienably to its world" (*TM* 157). However, his own notion of the autonomy of the work of art has decidedly Romantic roots. In a 1982 essay he admits that his confrontation with "the French continuation of Heideggerian thought" has shown him "how deeply rooted" he is "in the romantic tradition of the humanities and its humanistic heritage" ("Text and Interpretation" 24). This may explain why, despite his critique of one kind of Romantic aesthetic autonomy, his claims for the almost hermetic autonomy of the literary text are perhaps too strong to take us very far in terms of ethics, although it is important to keep in mind that Gadamer's own argument is hermeneutic rather than ethical. These claims, in essays published in the 1970s and 1980s, grant more autonomy to the literary text than do those in the earlier *Truth and Method,* where Gadamer states that "the difference between a literary work of art and any other text is not so fundamental" (163). However, a connection can still be made between the unity of means and ends in the special case of the literary text emphasized in the later Gadamer and the unity of means and ends that distinguishes *phronesis* from *techne* in the Aristotelian ethical model for hermeneutics in *Truth and Method*. This connection will enable an important, if limited, parallel between the autonomy of the literary text and the autonomy of the other person in an ethical relationship while showing how the problem of *techne* persists on both sides of the parallel.

In drawing this connection, however, I do not make (or attribute to Gadamer) the assertion that poems are equivalent to persons; to do so would be to forget the difference between the *phronesis* associated with living well and the *techne* of making things, or to subscribe to the notion that ethical life is that which one "authors" (or, in MacIntyre's view,coauthors) as one authors a literary text, a view that reduces ethical life to literary *techne*. As Ricoeur points out, we become the "coauthor" of life "as to its meaning" only by virtue of not being "the author as to existence" (*Oneself* 162). Neither is the autonomy of the work of art, despite its basis in *phronesis,* to be equated with intentionality. As Gadamer says, "It is a hopeless misunderstanding of what literature is, if one wishes to reduce the literary image to an act of intending to which the author gives expression" ("On the Truth of the Word" 145).

My claim is a more restricted one: that the *structure* of the reader's interpretive relationship to a literary text has affinities with a person's ethical relationships to others. The use of words such as "friend" (as in the title of Coleridge's short-lived periodical *The Friend*) to describe the products of artistic *techne* has genuine ethical significance.[16] Gadamer helps to explain this connection when he points out that in ordinary language we use "true," as in the phrase "true friend," as a form of *aletheia* or "openness"—what Heidegger calls "unconcealing"—in describing relationships to friends as well as to poems (The *Relevance of the Beautiful* 108). The point, then, is not exactly that "[p]oems are / Men, if true poems," as Elizabeth Barrett Browning's Aurora Leigh fervently asserts (3.90–91), but rather that the process by which the "truth" of a poem is revealed is instructively similar to the "unconcealing" that goes on in the ethical hermeneutics of being open to (instead of imposing, asserting, or conceptualizing) the truth of another person. This is not epistemic truth, but the truth of authentic relationship. It is also not rule-bound rational truth that can, like *techne,* be taught, but is rather immanent to historical practice. As P. Christopher Smith points out, the kind of "linguistic knowledge" involved in the intricacies of metaphorical thought "is not rule-governed; rather, it is knowledge of how to break the rule or at least reconstrue it given the new occasion. Hence, like ethical knowing this knowing cannot be taught. It is only to be acquired by practice *within* an evolving tradition of speaking that, as Gadamer and MacIntyre both say, is historically constituted and historically constitutive" (56). Terry Eagleton clarifies the Romantic origins of this connection between human subjects and works of art and thus perhaps identifies a peculiarly modern relationship between *phronesis* and *techne*. He argues that the eighteenth century development of the autonomous subject, subsequently problematized by Romanticism, paralleled the development of the concept of aesthetic autonomy, so that, for Shaftesbury, "the morally virtuous individual lives with the grace and symmetry of an artefact" (*The Ideology of the Aesthetic* 35). This parallel suggests both the positive function of the aesthetic as ethically unifying—as in *phronesis,* the symmetry of the artifact involves a coincidence of means and ends—and its negative function as a product of *techne:* to have the symmetry of an artifact is to be less than human.

For Gadamer, one of the most important consequences of the work of art's special form of truth is the kind of claim it makes on the interpreter. Because art cannot be understood in terms of its "use" as a product of *techne* or in relation to an origin to which it simply refers, "we typically encounter art as a unique manifestation of truth whose particularity cannot be surpassed." Art thus "resists pure conceptualization" (*The Relevance of the Beautiful* 37). The autonomy of the work of art and the engagement of the spectator are interdependent; as Gadamer says of drama, "openness toward the spectator is part of the closedness of the play. The audience only completes what the play as such is" (*TM* 109). This claim recalls Gadamer's understanding of Aristotelian *phronesis,* which also involves a particular immediacy that resists conceptualization: moral knowledge involves self-deliberation "in the immediacy of the given situation" (322) rather than *techne*'s application of predetermined means to known ends, and thus a bond to another person involves thinking "along with" him or her rather than conceptualizing (323). This praxis-bound knowledge suggests a mediation between the direct responsiveness of ethical action and the second-order ethical reflection that Altieri sees as separated: the untaught knowledge of *phronesis* that involves "thinking along" with the other could be construed as the kind of "knowledge" that is brought to bear when one sympathetically performs an immediate, nonreflective good deed.

A work of art overpowers us because its autonomy resists our efforts to conceptualize it: "we are always unprepared and defenseless when exposed to the overpowering impact of a compelling work" (*The Relevance of the Beautiful* 37). This is part of Gadamer's overarching premise that our engagement with a historical text can be modeled on a conversation with another person, even though texts are obviously unlike conversational partners: "one partner in the hermeneutical conversation, the text, speaks only through the other partner, the interpreter" (*TM* 387). But the analogy holds in that "the common subject matter is what binds the two partners, the text and the interpreter, to each other" (388), just as in conversation between persons. Subjectivities are subordinated to the "play" of a conversation in which the "truth" that emerges fuses and transcends partners' individual conceptual "horizons" (a term Gadamer borrows from Husserl to indicate the flexible boundaries of understanding [302–7]): this truth "is neither mine nor yours and hence so far transcends the interlocutors' subjective opinions that even the person leading the conversation knows that he does not know" (368).

The dialogue with a literary text, given the kind of autonomy that Gadamer ascribes to such texts, has a kind of ethical intensity that in a way exceeds the implicitly ethical dialogic model that Gadamer applies to all texts.[17] Reflecting that Gadamer's insistence on the absoluteness of art represents a challenge to his own notion of a dialogue of give-and-take, Donald Marshall observes that "we have to do here not only with the absoluteness of art, but with the ethical demands of dialogue itself" (212). Because the artwork unites means and ends, resisting attempts to understand it in reference either to its use or to an origin to which it refers, one's relation to it resembles the ethical relation to another person, who must be thought of under *phronesis,* even more than does the general hermeneutic relation, in which texts and individual subject-positions disappear into the shared meaning of the hermeneutic conversation. That poetic "form" is more than the exercise of poetic *techne* is suggested by a comment on Goethe, quoting "West-East Divan," that Gadamer made in a 1949 radio address, "Goethe and the Moral World": "Man's recovery to a state of health lies in a process of taking form. 'Everyone likes to hear a sound that develops into a tone.' That is not an aesthetic view of life that could be opposed to an ethical one. The poet presents us with what is essentially human" (*Literature and Philosophy in Dialogue* 29). This ethical notion of the literary text can also be understood in terms of Gadamer's critique of the semiotic view of presence. The "unsurpassed particularity" of the work of art that finds one "unprepared and defenseless" can be said to resist conceptualization partly because of the inverse relationship between representational and ethical-hermeneutic presence. In the representational presence enabled by sign-systems, the representing sign's goal is to disappear into the represented meaning.[18] A sign is "foregrounded from the context in which it is encountered" only "in order for its own being as an object to be superseded and for it to dissolve (disappear) into meaning" (*TM* 412). This reduction of language to "its efficient functioning as sign material" is ultimately a reduction of language to the "technical term," the artificial "word whose meaning is univocally defined, inasmuch as it signifies a defined concept" (414). Not surprisingly, given his general critique of *techne,* for Gadamer "a technical term is a word that has become ossified" and "[u]sing a word as a technical term is an act of violence against language" (415).

To this Greek representational notion of language Gadamer opposes the Christian concept of language as "event," based on the analogy of the Incarnation: "The uniqueness of the redemptive event introduces the essence of history into Western thought, brings the phenomenon of language out of its immersion in the ideality of meaning, and offers it to philosophical reflection. For, in contrast to the Greek logos, the word is pure event" (*TM* 419).

To characterize language in this way as communicative "event" rather than "sign"[19] is to shift the discussion of "presence" from the representational fiction of self-presence critiqued by the early Derrida to the very different "presence" of one person to another. For Derrida, the sign is "from its origin and to the core of its sense marked by this will to derivation or effacement" in relation to the self-presence of the "voice," "a medium which both preserves the *presence of the object* before intuition and *self-presence,* the absolute proximity of the acts to themselves" (*"Speech and Phenomena"* 51, 76). Gadamer suggests that the word is not just a sign willing the impossible task of effacing itself before a desired self-presence. Such a sign would have the artificiality of the "technical term," and would deny the historicity and contingency or real language, and to the extent that words do have a "technical" function as signs, they disappear into the things represented, not the speaking subject. Instead, he says (in response to Derrida's reading of Heidegger), "The word is what one person speaks and another understands. How does [Derrida's notion of] presence play a role in this? Who listens at all to his or her own voice?" ("Letter to Dallmayr" 95). Part of human finitude is that "the imperfection of the human mind consists in its never being completely present to itself but in being dispersed into thinking this or that" (*TM* 425), but this deficiency is of the mind, not the word, which is coextensive with knowledge itself: "The word is not formed only after the act of knowledge has been completed . . . it is the act of knowledge itself" (424).

For Gadamer the word is primarily a communicative event within a universally incomplete human understanding, rather than an artificial sign within a fiction of transparent representation, and the infinite "multiplicity of words" in our finite world (*TM* 425) is a function of the same human incompleteness rather than an effect of the paradoxes and inadequacies of language. If this is granted, then texts' immediate "presence" is not the illusion of success in signs' efforts to attain the self-presence of the voice, but rather an indication that communication is incomplete: "only a disruption in communication provides a motive for reaching back to the text as the 'given'" ("Text and Interpretation" 34). For example, we examine the text of a contract closely only when there is a disagreement between the parties. The more successfully "technical" a text becomes—as in a set of instructions or a scientific article—the less we notice the presence of the text itself. In this sense a text is more immediately "present" the further it moves from being such a mere sign of a prior situation, a means to an end, toward its involvement in the necessary ambiguity and multiplicity of nontechnical, historically evolved language—what Wordsworth calls in the Preface to the *Lyrical Ballads* the "real language of men in a state of vivid sensation" (*Prose Works* 1: 118)—in which "disruption of communication" is an inevitable result of human finitude. A text, like a person, is "present" to us, in the sense that he, she, or it must be faced and questioned, to the degree that the person or text maintains its otherness and has *not* been "technically" placed within or behind a representational system desiring to efface itself before a fictional "presence."

A literary text is "text in the highest degree" in which "*language itself* comes to appearance in a very special way" because "the poetic text . . . is something that seems to originate in itself" ("Text and Interpretation" 42). In this essay, Gadamer seems at least implicitly to differentiate the ways in which texts draw attention to their own language in the disruption of communication and in poetic autonomy. However, when viewed from the perspective of the overarching contrast between *techne* and *phronesis,* the two ways join in opposition to the technical ideal of the sign-system. There is also a positive connection between our relation to the "unsurpassed particularity" of the artwork—its resistance to our attempts at conceptualization—and the particularity of human finitude that makes communication difficult. As Wordsworth says, part of the pleasure of poetry is the "sense of difficulty overcome" (*Prose Works* 1: 150), and as Gadamer says in a very Wordsworthian way, "The poet presents us with what is essentially human." The difficulty of human finitude is of course the reason we need to discuss ethics in the first place, and an important part of art's claim on us is its presentation of the gaps and conflicts in human communication. In this context the autonomy of the literary text that results from its "unsurpassed particularity" and the self-referentiality of the nonliterary text that occurs when communication falters intersect in an important way.

This nonrepresentational presence of otherness in Gadamer's hermeneutics helps explain why his statements about the "overpowering impact of a compelling work" that "resists pure conceptualization," as well as his assertion that to interpret a work, as he put it in an interview, is to "allow it to obsess us and lead us beyond our own horizon" (qtd. Foster 16), resemble Emmanuel Levinas's call for an ethical subjectivity based on the overwhelming "proximity" of the other person. This proximity cannot be contained within the structures of rationally controlled "synchrony" but is instead constituted by "the difference between the same and the other in the nonindifference of the obsession exercised by the other over the same" (*OB* 85). For Levinas, the approach of the other is characterized by the disruption of subjectively or rationally controlled representational structures, just as for Gadamer the immediacy and extra-conceptual impact of the work of art is a heightened function of the text's obsessive self-presentation as an other, rather than as a transparent medium of representation. Although it does not address Levinas, James Risser's *Hermeneutics and the Voice of the Other* brings out this important facet of Gadamer's thought, arguing that the "way of experience" followed by philosophical hermeneutics finds, in dialogues with both other people and works of art, an implicitly ethical encounter with a challenging otherness that cannot be assimilated: "Understanding comes not from the subject who thinks, but from that other that addresses me. This other that is a speaking person in every dialogical encounter is also the other in the address of language, the other that speaks when 'language becomes voice.' It is this voice that awakens one to vigilance, to being questioned in the conversation that we are" (208). According to Levinas, as in Gadamer, language in this context is not binary representation, but performative activity: it is "not reducible to a system of signs doubling up beings and relations"; instead, "language seems to be an excrescence of the verb" (*OB* 35).

Like Gadamer's "overpowering" work of art, the ethical in Levinas resists representation; it is incarnated in the irreducibly particular face of another person: "the Good cannot become present or enter into a representation" (*OB* 11), because "The face of the Other at each moment destroys and overflows the plastic image it leaves me, the idea existing to my own measure and to the measure of its *ideatum*—the adequate idea" (*TI* 50–51). In Levinas's ethical relation, as in Gadamer's account of the relation to a work of art, the relation to the other takes the form of a conversation that overflows concepts: "To approach the Other in conversation is to welcome his expression, in which at each instant he overflows the idea a thought would carry from it" (51). Gadamer's statement that a work can "obsess us and lead us beyond our own horizon" is probably a conscious echo of Levinas, who says that "obsession by the other, my neighbor . . . reduces the ego to a self on the hither side of my identity, prior to all self-consciousness, and denudes me absolutely" (*OB* 92).

Donald Marshall has argued for the consistency of Gadamer's and Levinas's notions of dialogue (213), and Gadamer reads Levinas with approval ("Letter to Dallmayr" 97, "Hermeneutics and Logocentrism" 119), although Gadamer and Levinas differ, for example, in that Gadamer sees dialogue as fundamentally reciprocal while Levinas argues against concepts of reciprocity such as Martin Buber's "I-Thou" relationship (*TI* 68). However, because the literary text as Gadamer views it has a kind of autonomy that exerts a claim stronger even than that of an ordinary partner in the hermeneutic conversation, it begins to resemble the nonreciprocal Levinasian other. If the interpreted text is a literary one, exerting an overpowering and normative claim in its autonomy and particularity, then it overflows our conceptual structures in a way that gives the conversation the asymmetry that one finds in the Levinasian encounter, and thus it is at least structurally ethical.[20]

This model brings up an important conflict between the means-end relationship as it obtains in ethics and as it obtains in texts. The ethical demand that other people be treated as ends rather than means is implicit in the unity of means and ends in Aristotelian *phronesis* and explicit in

Kant, while as *techne* the made object is a means to an end. However, in one sense texts work in just the opposite way. In Gadamer's taxonomy, nonaesthetic texts include judicial, religious, and scientific texts, to which we could add ethical treatises. Here text is "a mere intermediate product [Zwischenprodukt], a phase in the event of understanding" ("Text and Interpretation" 31), which ultimately "drops away" (41) in the process of understanding. That is to say, it is a means, not an end. This is also what Booth, following Louise Rosenblatt, calls an "efferent" transaction, "motivated mainly by a search for something to 'carry away'" (*The Company We Keep* 13). "Aesthetic" texts, on the other hand, have for Gadamer (and for Booth and Rosenblatt) the kind of autonomy as ends in themselves that I have been discussing as "ethical," even though that very autonomy distinguishes them from texts about ethics. As Booth points out, however, it is partly in a work of art's nonefferent function—its effect on us while we experience it, rather than its effect in terms of what we "carry away" from it—that a major portion of the ethical effect of a work of art exists: "the actual consequences, the load of values carried away from the experience, can often be most substantial when the reader has been least conscious of anything other than 'aesthetic' involvement" (14).

This problem of a text's ethical reference is further complicated by the fact that, on the one hand, Coleridge is often viewed as one of the founders of an aestheticizing movement that would deny the explicitly didactic value of aesthetic texts. As Charles Taylor says, we have inherited the Romantic portrayal of the "the artist as one who offers epiphanies where something of great moral or spiritual significance becomes manifest," but "what is conveyed . . . is just the possibility that what is revealed lies beyond and against what we normally understand as morality" (*Sources of the Self* 423).[21]

On the other hand, Coleridge assumed, as most authors and critics have until very recently, and as most readers and teachers still do, that literature does have a moral effect.[22] The debates over whether English teachers should or should not advocate a political program, and the extent to which arguments over the expansion of the canon depend on essentially moral attitudes toward the character of the authors or canonizers in question, show that literature's didactic force is implicitly acknowledged now more than ever. In discussing education, Coleridge distinguishes between the early-awakened power of imagination and the later development of specifically moral faculties (*Lects 1808–1819* 2: 192–93). However, throughout such discussions he assumes that imaginative literature is an important "means" to the "end" of a child's moral development, and the critical tradition at least since I. A. Richards and Robert Penn Warren has given the Coleridgean imagination an important role in the creation of values.[23] His expansion of moral development to include the imagination makes imaginative literature in this sense more, not less morally effective, even as he distinguishes the purely imaginative text from the moral. Thus Coleridge can offer the advice to the overly didactic Wordsworth that "the communication of pleasure [the end of poetry, as opposed to philosophy] is the introductory means by which alone the poet must expect to moralize his readers" (*BL* 2: 131).

This paradoxical relationship between a text's function as means to an end (didactic texts and art as *techne*) and an "aesthetic" text's ability to be its own (therefore "ethical") end, is one of the central problems in the relationship between ethics and interpretation in Coleridge. Obviously, texts can be both means for representational or "efferent" functions and "present" as autonomous works that resist conceptualization, and the same texts can be read both ways. Wordsworth's "Tintern Abbey" can be read, as Marjorie Levinson has done, as a representation of an excluded social reality.[24] However, such a reading, while placing the poem in an ethical context by exploring the social implications of the poet's act of representation, precludes a relation to the poem itself that can be structured along ethical lines. Gadamer's claim, with clear Romantic roots, that literary texts resist a clear referential connection to the world will always be seen as a repression of the world if the sole criterion for a text's relation to the world is accurate representation of social reality. If that resistance to representational conceptualization is given a positive value, however, it is possible to have an ethical interpretive relation to the text itself. In its extreme form, this is Coleridge's relation to Wordsworth's *Prelude* in "To William Wordsworth" (inextricable, of course, from his relation to the author) when he exclaims after having heard the poem read, "Into my heart have I received that Lay / More than historic" and finds himself "Scarce conscious" and "in prayer" (2–3, 108, 112). This clearly "obsessive" response sounds very much like the Levinasian encounter with the other, an encounter that "reduces the ego to a self on the hither side of my identity, prior to all self-consciousness, and denudes me absolutely" (*OB* 92).

That Coleridge finds himself "in prayer" suggests the theological roots of this experience. According to Gerald Bruns, part of Luther's contribution to the development of hermeneutics was to characterized the experience of reading scripture as "one in which the reader is exposed to the text, vulnerable to it, yet is also capable of being illuminated and transformed by its light" (*Hermeneutics, Ancient and Modern* 146). For

Coleridge, this experience of involuntary exposure is a test of scriptural authenticity; as he says in *Confessions of an Inquiring Spirit*, "In short, *whatever finds me* . . . bears witness for itself that it had proceeded from a Holy Spirit" (*SW & F* 1121–22). Bruns connects this vulnerability to the text to Levinasian ethics, arguing that this "condition of intimacy in which understanding takes place" can be described as "ethical in the sense in which Emmanuel Levinas uses this term when he speaks of our relation to the other as a condition of proximity and exposure" (148).[25]

Even as aesthetic autonomy presents this ethical potential, it is bound to the demands of *techne* insofar as a poem, like all other kinds of texts, must be a willful product of technique and must be about something, however much it resists a referential connection to the world. These functions of the aesthetic are not merely separate and conflicting but also interdependent. The Ancient Mariner's dual presentation of himself as moral example and detached text highlights the conflict between the *phronesis* of a life well-lived with others, containing its end in itself, as in his desire to "walk together to the Kirk, / And all together pray" (*Rime* 651–52), and the horrible *techne* by which his narrative is both in conflict with its origin, causing the heart to "burn," and put to the separate use of admonishing unsuspecting strangers. In another register, Keats's urn "tease[s] us out of thought" because it is both a "Cold Pastoral" of aesthetic *techne* and in the ethical position of a "friend to man" ("Ode on a Grecian Urn" 44, 45, 48), where the *techne* of art is itself the (heavily ironized) moral admonishment.

This interdependence of *phronesis* and *techne* is perhaps the inevitable conflict between living ethically and talking about ethics: once we produce texts about ethics, we have moved from *phronesis* to *techne*. Shelley followed Coleridge in granting the imagination a moral capacity: "The great instrument of moral good is the imagination; and poetry administers to the effect by acting on the cause" ("A Defence of Poetry," 283). However, as in the famous image of the "fading coal," *techne* gets in the way, making actual poems "a feeble shadow of the original conceptions of the poet" (294). As Levinas says, "Though I live my life, the life I live and the fact of living it nonetheless remain distinct" (*TI* 122).

The ethical immediacy of aesthetic autonomy, as well as the inseparability of that immediacy from the artifice of *techne*, is evident in that the Mariner appears most like a Levinasian other, whose immediacy disrupts the subject's conceptual categories, when the Wedding Guest, hearing a narrative that seems to describe the Mariner's own death, perceives the *conflict* between the tale and the apparently living man before him (Rime

226–32). This conflict makes it difficult even to distinguish between the Mariner's role as a Levinasian other calling the Wedding Guest to responsibility (which is how Adam Newton reads the encounter [4–7]) and his role as the violent imposer of a technical moral concept (which is how Coleridge reads the encounter with the reader in his conversation with Barbauld). The latter is what Levinas denigrates as the violence of "rhetoric," which "manages to apply a category" to freedom instead of calling it into question (*TI* 70).

IV. Ethical Encounters in Coleridge and Wordsworth

Wordsworth's account of the blind beggar in Book 7 of the *Prelude* suggests both the tension between and the interdependence of ethical otherness and *techne*. Seeing the beggar "[w]earing a written paper" of his autobiography, the poet's "mind turn[s] round / As with the might of waters," and the poet gazes "as if admonished from another world" because "[t]his label seem[s] of the utmost we can know / Both of ourselves and of the universe" (*Fourteen-Book Prelude* 7.641, 7.643–44, 7.649, 7.645–46). This comment is a response to the beggar's autonomy as an other by which the poet is "smitten / Abruptly" (7.637–38); the beggar's separation from the flow of life in London shows the limits of the poet's conceptual structures and calls him to responsibility. This call to responsibility occurs not simply because the man is begging, an act that would be, in Levinas's terms, "a phenomenon subject to the action and domination of a freedom" (a freely made request eliciting from the passerby a free response that would in fact be an act of domination) but because he is "presenting himself . . . from the first as an absolute" (*TI* 215) in his role as an otherworldly admonishment. Wordsworth stresses that the beggar is "a sight not rare" (7.638), suggesting that this is not just a unique experience of the sublime, but in fact something like Levinas's universal experience of particular otherness. This notion is consonant with Wordsworth's theory of the sublime. In "The Sublime and the Beautiful" Wordsworth argues, contra Edmund Burke, that sublime impressions are not dependent on novelty, but instead require "a preparatory intercourse with that object or with others of the same kind" (*Prose Works* 2:359).[26] Like the temporality of the "festival" in Gadamer's account, whose "own original essence is always to be something different," such a spectacle's autonomy lies not in its separation from time, despite the emblematic, otherworldly status of the beggar and his paper, but in its unique and human temporality, as "single forms and objects" such as the beggar draw on their embeddedness in the "huge fermenting mass of humankind" (7.623, 7.621). As in the "spots of time" in Book 12, "renovating virtue" (*Fourteen-Book Prelude* 12.210) resides not in the autonomous experience of a moment, but in the healing effect of that moment's incorporation into the temporality of memory and revisitation.

What Wordsworth experiences as an admonishment "from another world" thus closely resembles what Levinas calls the encounter with a "face coming from beyond the world, but committing me to human fraternity," a face whose "destitution cries out for justice" (*TI* 215). At the same time, the conceptual limits the beggar's presence exposes are partly a function of the inevitable translation of a "blindly" lived life into the visual articulation of a text, in this case, a text that is not only an emblem of Levinasian otherness but also, and much more pragmatically, a technical means to the specific end of contributions from passersby (the beggar would no doubt much prefer to be the recipient of alms than the source of ethical admonishment). To complicate matters further, the very discrepancy between the beggar's *techne* and his presentation of this Levinasian version of the ethical is itself an important part of the moral "admonishment": the sublime response to the "utmost we can know" is also the recognition that this "utmost" is reducible to the *techne* of the autobiographical text, an insight with often noted implications for the autobiographical poem in which this scene occurs.

The conflict between poetry's ambivalent relation to ethical otherness and the power of *techne* is presented in "Resolution and Independence."[27] Like the image of the blind beggar, the scarcely heard discourse of the leech-gatherer resembles an "admonishment" by one "from some far region sent" (118–19) rather than a discourse understood in either representational terms—"nor word from word could I divide" (115)—or even dialogic understanding: the poet repeats his questions and does not really listen to what the leech-gatherer says. Like the artwork as described by Gadamer, the old man presents a Levinasian otherness that exceeds the reciprocity of dialogue. Even in memory the man does not speak; he is pictured "[w]andering about alone and silently " (138). It is this nonrepresentational, even nondialogic autonomy and otherness that corrects the self-involved subjectivity of "[w]e Poets" who are "by our own spirits . . . deified" (48, 47).

Poetic subjectivity is complexly situated between the situation of the speaker and that of other, less fortunate poets. The state the speaker finds himself in as a thoughtless "happy Child of earth" (31) resembles what Levinas calls "enjoyment": a condition of "existing . . . without being the individuation of a concept" and "remaining outside the distinction between the individual and the general" (*TI* 118). Like the attitude of Wordsworth's poet, who walks "[f]ar from the world . . . and from all care" (33), this state is a "withdrawal into oneself" (*TI* 118) and hence egoistic, but it is not the egoism of the subject who manipulates or imposes concepts, as in the Mariner's—or the *Rime*'s—obtrusion of moral *techne*. Because "enjoyment" is a "breach of . . . totality" in Levinas, it readies the self for the "critical presence of the Other" who "will call in question this egoism" but "will not destroy its solitude" (119). For Wordsworth, such a critical presence is provided by the leech-gatherer, who corrects the ego and adds the dimension of the ethical to his solitude.

However, Wordsworth complicates Levinas's paradigm by suggesting an alternative scenario, particularly common for poets, in which this same "enjoyment" that invites the correction of the other, precisely because it "take[s] no heed at all" (42) for the self, leads to "despondency and madness." Poetic life becomes a means to the tragically predetermined end of an ultimately destructive self-deification, in which power turns to misery and death in thoughts of "mighty Poets in their misery dead" (123). The life of poetry can thus lead either to a self-sustaining recognition of otherness or to the exercise of an ultimately uncontrollable power that turns back on its source. This power has an ambivalent relation to subjectivity, functioning both as the self-aggrandizing *techne* of the "mighty Poet" and as a lack of care for the self, an ambivalence suggested in the description of the suicidal Chatterton as the self-neglecting "sleepless Soul" that nevertheless "perish'd in its pride" (44).[28]

Coleridge's attempt to maintain a stricter separation between the *techne* of fancy and the *phronesis*-like quality of imagination makes the dual function of art even more explicitly a relationship of conflict. For instance, the possibility of reviving the damsel's song in "Kubla Khan" would result in the estrangement of the demonic poet from those who would "cry, Beware! Beware!" (49). The poet would be feared for two reasons with opposite effects. First, he would be feared because, having "drunk the milk of Paradise" (54), he represents the autonomy of art that resists conceptualization and overwhelms the reader, as in Gadamer's paradigm. Second, he would be feared because, having evolved from a chronicler to an imitator of Khan's accomplishment, he has entered the product of his own creative work, conflating art and life. This conflation is the moral error of fictional narrative, according to Coleridge,[29] and in "Kubla Khan" it makes the poet almost inhuman, deserving of the exorcism implied by "weave a circle round him thrice" (51). The demonic poet's overwhelming autonomy suggests the possibility of an ethical relation to the otherness of the work of art; his entry into the product of his own aesthetic *techne* suggests the tragedy—still ethically important—of art as technique rather than life.[30]

What Gadamer calls the "opacity" of the work of art, its "resistance against any superior presumption that we can make sense of it all" (*The Relevance of the Beautiful* 34), makes the work of art ethical in two contradictory ways. First, as in *phronesis,* the work of art combines means and ends; it cannot be understood under a predetermined conceptual scheme that would reduce it to *techne* by calling it a means to an end (a sign for an intention, the expression of a meaning, or a thing that serves some purpose outside itself). It must be granted the unity of means and ends that would be granted another person.[31] Second, the work of art is ethical because it *is techne,* and is clearly *not* a person. Like the blind beggar's paper, poetry proclaims the inevitable reduction of ethical life to technical means separated from ends. But to point out the limits of "the utmost we can know" through a *techne* that acknowledges its necessity as well as its limits is itself an ethical gesture. This gesture is an acknowledgment that *phronesis* must express itself in *techne,* or in Levinas's terms, that the "saying" of ethical experience is inevitably reduced to the "said" of discursive and conceptual structures (*OB* 5–8).

Autobiography is a medium in which this combination of conflict and interdependence between *phronesis* and *techne* is particularly evident. Paul Ricoeur, who picks up Alasdair MacIntyre's notion of ethical life as constituted by narrative, but with a greater awareness of the differences between fictional and real-life narratives, suggests that it is precisely the "entanglement of the history of each person in the histories of numerous others" that makes "life histories differ from literary ones," but that we must borrow always provisional "figure[s] of emplotment" from fiction or history in order to "stabilize the real beginnings formed by the initiatives . . . we take" (*Oneself* 161–62). This "borrowing" is acknowledged in literature itself, particularly in someone like Wordsworth who sees the writing of poetry as a calling that will define, for him, a life well-lived. Thus in the first book of the *Prelude,* various fictional and historical possibilities for narrative are considered, as part of an ultimately autobiographical process that has served, he says, to "fix the wavering balance of my mind" (*Fourteen-Book Prelude* 1.623). This reminds us that, even though poetic *techne* must acknowledge its difference from the *phronesis* by which one thinks about ethical life in general, the decision to undertake such *techne*—to pursue the "honorable toil" of writing poetry (1: 625)—is very much an ethical life-decision. Even Gadamer, in introducing the fundamental difference between *phronesis* and *techne* that is his main emphasis, admits that "There is, no doubt, a real analogy between the fully developed moral consciousness and the capacity to make something—i.e., a techne" although "they are certainly not the same" (*TM* 316).

Insofar as *techne* is seen as an unavoidable, even welcome complement to *phronesis,* the more appropriate contemporary analogue can be found in Ricoeur, a more openly dialectical thinker than either Gadamer or Levinas, who differs from both in his willingness to grant a positive role to *techne* in ethics. As Gary Aylesworth notes, Ricoeur's emphasis on "identity" rather than "character" allows him to argue, contra Gadamer, that "the moment of individuation does not follow from moral reason, but from productive reason (*poiesis, techne*)" (72). In his attempt to find a middle ground between Habermas, well known for his objection to Gadamer's sharp division between technological and hermeneutic knowledge, and Gadamer,[32] Ricoeur criticizes Gadamer's extension of Dilthey's "ruinous dichotomy . . . between 'explanation' and 'understanding'," which restricts the former to the methodology of the natural sciences, and points out that the "objectification" necessary in all understanding means that "truth and method do not constitute a disjunction but rather a dialectical process" ("Hermeneutics and the Critique of Ideology" 92–93). This is also a critique of Gadamer's Romanticism: "The question, once again, is whether Gadamer's hermeneutics has really surpassed the Romantic point of departure of hermeneutics" (67).

For me (and this is admittedly a Gadamerian position), that is a less appropriate question than the question of what we can learn from observing the tension between the *techne* that Gadamer denigrates and the *phronesis* on which he founds hermeneutics as that tension operates within the differing horizons of both Romantic and contemporary thought. Wordsworth and Coleridge, because they are practicing poets and because they operate from within a different historical understanding of the relation between technology and ethical life, both acknowledge, like Ricoeur, the necessary role of *techne* in moral life and feel, like Gadamer, the sharp tension between *phronesis* and *techne*.[33] These English Romantics would not share Heidegger's Hölderlinian nostalgia for a time when *techne* and *poiesis* were gloriously united as "a single, manifold revealing" (*"The Question Concerning Technology"* 34), because they were too conscious of the fundamental tension between life as it is lived and aesthetic objects as they are made, even in a life dedicated to such making.

I depart from both Gadamer and Levinas in combining their insights, which are in many ways opposed. In an effort to release hermeneutics from the hold of *techne*, Gadamer downplays the role of *techne* in art by distinguishing aesthetic autonomy from the separable means and ends of the artisan's craft. Levinas is suspicious of art precisely because of its autonomy, which for him is not the autonomy of the ethical other but, rather, an autonomy that prevents the ethical relationship. He argues in "Reality and its Shadow" that art is a disengaged act of production, stopping time in fixed images. Even in narrative, art "constitutes . . . a dimension of evasion" (141) and "does not give itself out as the beginning of a dialogue" (131). As he puts it in *Otherwise than Being,* "Art is the preeminent exhibition in which the said is reduced to a pure theme. . . . The said is reduced to the Beautiful, which supports Western ontology" (40).

Levinas will thus not grant, as Gadamer does, that the constantly changing interpretations of a work of art are in fact part of the essence of the work itself.[34] However, he does acknowledge the value of art when "the indelible seal of artistic production" ("Reality and its Shadow" 131) is revealed by criticism, which is thus able to integrate "the inhuman work of the artist into the human world" (142), and when we recognize the "misfortune" of aesthetic temporality's tragic difference from the "living instant which is open to the salvation of becoming" (141). By acknowledging the "mechanical" aspect of poetic *techne* and by freezing the poet within the artificial world of "Kubla Khan," Wordsworth and Coleridge share this tragic recognition of the potential inhumanity of art. What Levinas's position does not allow, however, except perhaps indirectly in his frequent use of literary images,[35] is the way in which our relation to art can partake of Levinas's own account of the ethical relation to another.

On the one hand, Levinas gives art too little credit and criticism too much. On the other hand, Gadamer places too much value on the work of art, both in his respect for its autonomy and in the high status he gives aesthetics in his hermeneutics as a whole. As Gianni Vattimo points out, Gadamer's somewhat dogmatic opposition between the aesthetic methods of the human sciences and the technological methods of the natural sciences leans toward an ahistoricity that is in conflict with Gadamer's own emphasis on the historicity of understanding. Once that opposition is itself historicized, *techne* assumes a much larger role, because we see that hermeneutics itself is historically conditioned by its response to technology. Thus Vattimo calls for hermeneutics' "recognition of itself as corresponding to a historical situation determined essentially by the experimental natural sciences," a recognition that would lead to an awareness that "the history of Being in modernity is, above all, a history of techno-science" (*Beyond Interpretation* 22–24). Although I have difficulty accepting Vattimo's radical conclusion that we should find an appropriately Nietzschean nihilism in technology itself, "where this movement to the extremes of calculability leads to a general incalculability" (25), his critique of Gadamer suggests that Wordsworth and Coleridge were right in perceiving the mechanical activity of the poet and the "barrel-organ" of language as historically constitutive aspects of interpretation rather than simply necessary evils or correctable extremes.

By acknowledging both the possibility of a Levinasian encounter with a poem's *phronesis*-like autonomy and the ethical importance of a poem's self-consciousness as *techne*, I have tried to suggest an alternative to Benjamin's argument that an age characterized by mechanical reproduction must reject the notion of aesthetic autonomy. Despite various attempts, particularly by Blake and Coleridge, to restore the vatic status of the poet, the Romantics were well aware that the "Orphic song" Coleridge heard in Wordsworth's *Prelude* and described in "To William Wordsworth" (45) was at odds with an increasingly "mechanized" language and a literary world organized (in Benjamin's terms) around the technical reproducibility of artworks in the marketplace rather than around prophetic utterance. Kubla Khan could build his miraculous, autonomous pleasure dome with a simple decree and no concern for presenting his work to an audience. However, the poet's revival of that effort must confront not only the technical difficulty of reviving the damsel's song, but also an audience that reacts with "holy dread" even to a modern version of such Khan-like aesthetic tyranny. Benjamin and Levinas, for similar good reasons arising from traumatic personal experience, associate aesthetic autonomy with the tyranny of Fascism. However, both Levinas's own conception of ethical otherness and Gadamer's argument for the strong claim made on the interpreter by the work of art suggest that the concept of aesthetic autonomy need not signal either a return to the ethically disengaged cult of "art" or a concession to the ubiquity of *techne*. Wordsworth and Coleridge show that poetry's ethical function combines its self-awareness as *techne* with just such an "ethical" autonomy, whose *phronesis*-like presentation of a definitively human otherness is irreducible to the *techne* of conceptual structures or cultural production.

V. The Historicity of Techne and the Moral Law

The ethical encounter with a poem's otherness is not an ahistorical relation, because part of a past text's resistance to conceptual appropriation by its reader is its *historical* otherness, unless, of course, one is in Coleridge's unusual situation, portrayed in "To William Wordsworth," of being present both as the contemporary auditor and as the addressee of a spoken poem. Even there, Coleridge is responding to the past life portrayed in the *Prelude* as well as to the poem itself. The Aristotelian categories I have been using do not address this historicity in themselves, but Gadamer's hermeneutic adaptation of *phronesis* does. Gadamer's model of interpretation differs from Aristotelian *phronesis* in a way that makes it more amenable to our culturally diverse and historically conscious world, which would have been unimaginable to Aristotle. As Günter Figal argues, Aristotelian *phronesis* does not do justice to "the foreignness that is involved in the accessibility of tradition," but Gadamer's hermeneutics "is able to situate the presently inherited in the play between foreignness and accessibility" (247).

Somewhat like the ethical other in Levinas (although Figal himself does not make this connection), tradition itself manifests an "indestructible independence" (245), which allows hermeneutics to contribute to a "phenomenology of freedom" (247), because, in its attentiveness to tradition, hermeneutics "is experienced as what is utterly not reachable in the completions of understanding" (246). Gadamer writes approvingly of Droysen's notion that the unfathomability of the past, related to "the study of conscience," has a strong ethical element, which, as in Levinas, combines otherness and proximity in a way that is opposed to the technical methods of natural science: "The world of history depends on freedom, and this on the mystery of the person that is unfathomable by research. . . . But on the other hand this distance is also proximity. This historian does not investigate his 'object' by establishing it univocally in an experiment; rather, through the intelligibility and familiarity of the moral world, he is integrated with his object in a way completely different from the way a natural scientist is bound to his" (*TM* 216–17). Although this takes the notion of the ethical "other" in a direction very different from the intent of Levinas, who would not give so much credit either to "freedom" or to "intelligibility," it does suggest how the ethical situation described by Levinas can be transposed to the other of tradition.

Levinas's own sense of a text's historical and ethical otherness comes out in his Talmudic readings. Although his view of the uniqueness of

Talmudic commentary will not allow us to extrapolate this into a general theory of reading, particularly a theory of reading aesthetic texts, his comments on the "signs" of the Talmud are instructive. Calling for a hermeneutic rather than a structuralist reading (his particular references are to Ricoeur and Lévi-Strauss), he demands an engagement with Talmudic texts that recognizes signs as "concrete realities," "realities and often concrete forms and people" that must be confronted and not turned into the binary referential structure of structuralism: "Concrete realities, these signs are this or that according to the context of the life lived" (*Nine Talmudic Readings* 8). This view of the Talmud echoes the nonstructural "signification" in the ethical relation discussed in his philosophical works. In *Totality and Infinity,* Levinas argues that language presents a paradigm for ethical signification, which is about the manifestation of the other person rather than the structural establishment of meaning-systems: "This way the object is posited as a theme offered envelops the instance of signifying—not the referring of the thinker who fixes it to what is signified (and is a part of the same system), but the manifesting of the signifier, the issuer of the sign, an absolute alterity which nonetheless speaks to him and thereby thematizes, that is, proposes a world" (*TI* 96). This human "signifier" does not refer to *himself* in this relation, however; we have not returned to the realm of intention: "the Other, the signifier, manifests himself by speaking of the world and not of himself; he manifests himself by proposing a world, by *thematizing* it" (96).

This takes us back to Gadamer, because for him, as he argues in his critique of the subjectivity of Romantic hermeneutics, the understanding that occurs between people is not a matter of mutual self-reference but always points to the world that encompasses the conversation; it "is always understanding each other with respect to something" (*TM* 180). If the relation to a historical work of art has something of the structure of an ethical relation to another person, then, the extrasubjective *Sache* toward which understanding is directed, both in Levinas's signification and in Gadamer's conversation, is an integral part of both our relationship to other people and our relation to the past.

It is in this sense that the independence of a historical work is not the independence of a subject or author, but the independence of "play," one of Gadamer's favorite analogues for the hermeneutic experience of art, in which the subject puts him or herself at risk in order to participate in the larger process of a "game's" to and fro movement that is not directed toward any purpose outside the game itself. (Gadamer's word is *Spiel,* which connotes "game" and "drama" as well as "play" [*TM* 105].) The independence of the game is achieved through what Gadamer calls "transformation into structure":[36] whereas "'[r]eality' always stands in a horizon of desired or feared, or, at any rate, still undecided future possibilities" (112), when reality is transformed into "structure"—as in the performance of a drama—the full truth of the *Spiel* (in all of its senses) emerges in a truth-recognition: "what we experience in a work of art and what invites our attention is how true it is—i.e., to what extent one knows and recognizes something and oneself" (114). The "something" recognized is the truth of this situation of hermeneutic play: "the being of all play is always self-realization, sheer fulfillment, energeia which has its telos within itself" (113). Such recognition enables us to "resist the temptation to think in terms of purposes, which conceals the game that is played with us" (112). In other words, the "transformation into structure" that occurs in a historically situated work of art is in this sense not a matter of the subject being subordinated to the conventions of *techne*, the rules of artistic production that would suggest that this or that work of art is produced for this or that external purpose, as in the production of craft. Rather, it is a matter of the subject (both author and audience) being subordinated to the independent claim of the *Spiel*'s transformation of reality, which imposes a "bond" on the interpreter that "can have no fixed criterion" (119), even though it is a bond "to the work's own possibilities of being" rather than a situation open to "a mere subjective variety of conceptions" (118).[37]

This is the interpretive situation Coleridge desired for the *Rime*, against Barbauld's suggestion that the work be subordinated to an external moral purpose. The poem "ought to have had no more moral than the story of the merchant sitting down to eat dates by the side of a well and throwing the shells aside, and the Genii starting up and saying he must kill the merchant, because a date shell had put out the eye of the Genii's son" (*TT* 1:273). This *Arabian Nights* tale ("The Merchant and the Genius") is provided as an example of a tale that has no "moral" in Barbauld's sense. It illustrates a scene lacking in moral content because punishment is threatened for an action (eating dates and tossing the shells aside) that specifically lacks a moral or even conscious intention. What the tale does illustrate—the "moral" for Coleridge—is, first, its foreignness to Coleridge's moral horizon, which would have assumed the continuity of intention and moral responsibility, a connection absent in the Genii's strict economy of exchange: "and is it not just, that he who has inflicted death should suffer it?" (*The Arabian Nights Entertainments* 1:57). Second, the tale illustrates what one finds also in the *Rime* and in Gadamer's understanding of "play." The Mariner and the merchant both find themselves participating in serious "games" with an open-ended absence of fixed criteria and purposes: as in any game worth playing, no one knows how the game will end, because in these cases the expected moral rules do not apply or do not produce predictable results. At the same time, such games have the independence and otherness of a self-complete structure, emphasized in both the *Rime* and the *Arabian Nights* tale by an exotic setting and a narrative frame. Participation in the game is also a subordination of the willing ego to the context of the game. The *Arabian Nights* tale is a deadly game of narrative that, like the Mariner's story, is not a simple voluntary act. Scheherezade is telling the story to delay her own execution, and the Merchant's life is spared in exchange for the three tales told by the old men who join him at his appointment with the Genii.

The historicization of *phronesis* that Figal notes suggests the ethical implications of this very serious play. On the one hand, like Gadamer's "structure," the other of the "game" is an independent whole, a transformation of unformed reality into a human meaning that is not simply a particular instance of a universal: every baseball game is a unique event, not simply an instance of the rules the game. As Levinas says, "the individual and the personal count and act independently of the universal, which would mould them" (*TI* 218).[38] On the other hand, the determinate, particular other of the game-player must be granted his or her openendedness, not as a "free" subject, but as one whose freedom is put at risk (as the Merchant's and Scheherezade's are) in the larger context of the *Spiel* and as one who cannot be reduced to what Figal calls "the completions of understanding" (246) or what Levinas would call conceptual "totality" rather than ethical "infinity" (*TI* 83). In both these senses, it is their very resistance to appropriation by contemporary moral codes, a resistance allegorized in the narratives themselves, that grants the story of the Merchant and the Genii, and by analogy the *Rime* as Coleridge wished it had been written, an ethical import far greater than that of Barbauld's desired subjection of the work to an external moral purpose.

Poetry's necessary status as *techne*—the actual *Rime* whose moral was "too openly obtruded on the reader"—is also deeply involved in the self-conscious historicity of Romantic thought. In fact, despite the different conclusions they wish to draw about the value of *techne,* what Gadamer calls the "transformation into structure" of a past work of art, by him differentiated from the technical process of composition by an individual for a purpose, is not too far removed in its effects from what Ricoeur discusses as the necessary *techne* of "the rules of a kind of craftsmanship" (*Interpretation Theory* 33). These rules similarly contribute to the autonomy of the work of art through "the paradox of the intentional exteriorization of discourse" (38), the sense in which a linguistic work is both intentionally crafted by an author and separated from that source by being fixed in a medium, a genre, and a past. Both Gadamer's "structure," which is connected to an historicized version of *phronesis,* and Ricoeur's "exteriorization" need to be taken into account if we are to understand Coleridge's position.

Liu points out that *techne* is deeply involved with history, however much it pretends to escape historical contingency through the supposed atemporal coherence of systematic thought, and that, conversely, there is no access to history unmediated by something like *techne:* "[T]here is no universal formal value that is not contingent upon *historical* determinants of the very value of 'universal' or 'timeless' form. Just so, reciprocally, there are no historical determinants that are not so culturally complex and ambiguous that we can know them 'direct' without the intervention of such ambivalent discourses as the critique of form" ("Formal vs. Historical Value"). Thus the early Agrarian New Critics were interested in "form" in a technical way because of their historical condition, informed partly by the need to negotiate between a rural ideal and a technological reality: "these critics were deeply, powerfully, passionately involved with 'form' *because* they were deeply, powerfully, passionately involved with the historical conditions of their time." They were "'involved' not just because they were incipient professionals punching the clock of the new industrial world order but because they were working out the possibility of being 'critics' within such a world order."

Similarly for Coleridge, whose speculations on form were of great interest to those critics, the potentially tyrannical "mechanization" of language is not simply a philosophical and aesthetic problem, but also an issue tied to the historicity of both poetry and morality, as the full context of his "barrel-organ" image suggests:

> In the days of Chaucer and Gower, our language might (with due allowance for the imperfections of a simile) be compared to a wilderness of vocal reeds, from which the favorites only of Pan or Apollo could construct even the rude Syrinx, and from this the *constructors* alone could elicit strains of music. But now, partly by the labours of successive poets, and in part by the more artificial state of society and social intercourse, language, mechanized as it were into a barrel-organ, supplies at once both instrument and tune. Thus even the deaf may play, so as to delight the many. (*BL* 1:38–39)[39]

The fact that this simile, which Coleridge has already apologized for, takes on a life of its own—"for it is with similes, as it is with jests at a wine table, one is sure to suggest another" (*BL* 1:39)—makes the obvious point that Coleridge himself is far from immune to the "barrel-organ" effect by which the language's own *techne* takes over. Language's automation, by which the "instrument" of language automatically produces the "tune" it plays out of the mass of poetic fragments and artificial expressions that language has become, eliminates the creative subject,[40] but it also reveals language's historicity: the "labours of successive poets" join the artificiality of society to cause this condition. The desired alternative is not to return to the "original" poetry of Chaucer and Gower, which Coleridge pushes back to mythical Greece as the simile proliferates. If today "even the deaf may play," then almost no one could play: language was a "wilderness," not a civilized instrument, and only a very few inventors of a "rude" poetic language (who depended on Pan and Apollo, not the Coleridgean imagination) could produce music. Heidegger's myth of an original Greek union of *techne* and *poesis*, "that revealing that brings forth truth into the splendor of radiant appearing" ("*The Question Concerning Technology*" 34) is not something to be mourned, because it never existed. In Coleridge's terms this is not even a particularly useful myth, partly because his Judeo-Christian heritage prevented him from entertaining the mythical view of an original Greek art held by Heidegger and his German Romantic predecessors. That English and Greek past was a time, at least in this simile, of a language with no tradition; now is a time when a history of poetic *techne* has overautomated the language. This history has threatened to turn poetry into "the manufacturing of poems" (*BL* 1:39), but it is not a history that can be avoided, since without it we would not have Chaucer and Gower (or even Pan and Apollo), whose very examples of original genius have helped stock the "barrel-organ" of language with self-proliferating similes. This history does not result in a Bloomian agon of belatedness with particular previous poets so much as it highlights a struggle with the unavoidable historicity of poetic language itself.

This paradoxical history is also evident in the *Rime*, whose "originality" is partly tied to its involvement in the same allusive history that has produced the "barrel organ" of automated language. As Susan Eilenberg presents the case in *Strange Power of Speech*, "Coleridge himself may have been uneasy about the unnaturalness of his imitation-antique language" (42–43), given his objections to archaisms in others' poems and his revisions of his own archaisms in the *Rime*. The problem with imitating archaic language is not just that, as Eilenberg says, "it acts out of awareness of that which must be unconscious" (43) by bringing the original and primitive to consciousness, but also that it engages one in the inevitable Catch-22 of the "barrel-organ" phenomenon: to engage the history of poetic language as explicitly as the *Rime* does is to risk letting the technical force of that historical language take over. As Eilenberg points out, in repetitive lines such as "Alone, alone, all all alone, / Alone on a wide wide sea," "the mere mechanism or materiality of language seems almost—but not quite—to deny the possibility of sense" (51).

This linguistic paradox has important implications for our understanding of the Mariner as an ethical subject, who in Eilenberg's reading is torn between self-origination and secondariness. Events such as the appearance of the spectre-ship have a strange "lack of antecedent," and "are greeted like sudden recognitions, as if successful interpretation had called them into being" (54). The drinking of his own blood, which enables the Mariner's speech-freeing cry, "A sail! a sail!" (*Rime* 153) (what Eilenberg calls "a Hadean inversion of divine inspiration" echoing the blood-sacrifices of Odysseus that enabled the dead to speak) suggests that "the source of his inspiration is not a higher being but himself" (55).

But the same closed, self-referential, semiautomated world of borrowed language that seems to have no source outside itself puts the speaking subject in a position of secondariness. Thus the Mariner's tale is not told by an autonomous subject, but forced from him, initially as a response to the hermit's question, "'What manner of man art thou?'" (*Rime* 623). As Eilenberg puts it, "he does not choose his words, he suffers them" (34). The poem's frame, with its layers of interpretation precluding an original utterance (for example, we don't know how many times the tale has been told before we and the Wedding Guest hear it), makes the tale self-originating at the same time as it "calls into question the very notion of character upon which considerations of psychology and ethics . . . depend" (38). The zombie-like aura of the Mariner "forces the reader to confront a radical split between speaker and speech" (37), and we are placed "[i]n a world where identity fails to coincide with character" (59).

I suggest that this has to do with the problem of *techne* versus *phronesis*. An artisan, insofar as he or she is solely implementing a technique that could be carried out by anyone with the appropriate skill, technical knowledge, and tools (including the "technique" established by the poetic tradition), drops out of the picture as a subject to the extent the "technique" has been perfectly and transparently rendered. However, the very self-referentiality of this enclosed world of poetic technique (negatively, the "barrel-organ" effect), which on one level excludes the subject, also underlies the analogy that Eagleton discusses between the autonomy of the artwork and the subject, which on another level enables an excess of subjectivity.

Just as the autonomy of *phronesis*' autoteleology and the separation of means and end in *techne* necessarily coexist in poems such as the Rime, the "barrel-organ" problem of a "mechanized" language suggests that this aspect of *techne,* which robs the subject of originary authenticity on one level while it makes him self-originating on another, is not just a necessary evil, but a fundamental aspect of poetry's historicity. For Gadamer, who, though he shares Coleridge's suspicion of *techne* is more optimistic about the consequences of severing a poetic utterance from its creative source, "only the path through its downfall into writing gives the word its radiance, which can be termed its truth," partly because it is in that "downfall" that we see "the disappearance of the author or his transformation into the ideal figure of a speaker" ("On the Truth of the Word" 144). That is to say (to suggest a paradox that Gadamer does not directly address), the process by which the author is effaced when his or her utterance enters the technology of written reproduction is also the process by which the poetic word, freed from the bonds of authorial intention, is presented in its true otherness, such that we can engage it according to the ethical structure of a conversation with an other. Gadamer escapes this paradox through the reader: what is lost in the "downfall into writing" is regained by defining the "ideal speaker" as the "ideal reader," for whom silent reading "is not the reproduction of the original, but rather directly shares the ideality of the original, since reading does not require a move into the contingency of reproduction" (145).

Someone as concerned as Coleridge was with the problems of publication could of course not dismiss the "contingency of reproduction" so easily. Eilenberg's reading suggests that Coleridge's engagement of the history of poetic *techne* enables a kind of self-origination by beating that history at its own game: if the origins of one's linguistic borrowings are sufficiently obscured, originality reverts to the self, and the Mariner can "teach by his own example," in the words of the 1817 gloss to lines 614–21, as an example of means-end unity. But this same allusive web highlights the way in which the history of poetic *techne* robs the self of its autonomy, as the Mariner becomes a talking head transmitting a language not his own.

Philosophically, the later Coleridge struggled with a "higher" form of the opposition between *phronesis* and *techne* in the relationship between, on the one hand, the autonomy of "idea," or that which precedes concrete manifestation, including the definiteness of "conception,"[41] and, on the other hand, the "product" that is realized in the process of "law." In *On the Constitution of the Church and State* the relationship is put straightforwardly: the "idea" is the anterior, subjective, a priori principle, but also the ultimate aim of something, while "law" is the external manifestation or product: "That which, contemplated *objectively* (i.e. as existing externally to the mind) we call a LAW; the same contemplated *subjectively* (i.e. as existing in a subject or mind), is an idea" (13).[42] In his reading of Aeschylus's *Prometheus Bound,* the relation is more complex; he wants to see "Idea and Law, as correlatives that mutually interpret each the other" ("On the Prometheus of Aeschylus," *SW & F* 1277), but as applied to self-consciousness, a tension remains between the concepts, with strong echoes of Kant and Schelling:

> Idea is so far co-essential with nomos [law], that by its co-existence (N. B. not *confluence*) with the nomos . . . it becomes itself a nomos. But (observe) a nomos autonomos, or containing its law in itself. Likewise, even as the nomos produces for its highest product the Understanding, so the idea, in its opposition, and, of course, its correspondence to the nomos, begets in itself an analogon to product; and this is self-consciousness. But as the product can never become Idea, so neither can the idea (if it is to remain idea) become or generate a distinct product. This analogon of product is to be itself; but were it indeed substantially a product, it would cease to be self. It would be an object for a subject, not (as it is and must be) an object that is its own subject, and *vice versâ;* a conception which, if the uncombining and infusile genius of our language allowed it, might be expressed by the term subject-object. Now, Idea, taken in indissoluble connection with this analogon of product, is Mind, that which knows itself, and the existence of which may be inferred, but cannot appear or become a phenomenon. (1276)

To the extent that "idea" produces a product, that product is self-consciousness, but Coleridge must resort to calling that realization of idea an "analogon" to product, since a product is categorically separate from idea, and idea ceases to be such if it is realized in "law's" productive process.

This is the conflict that he sees as played out in Aeschylus's drama: "Jove is the impersonated representative or symbol of the nomos" or law, while "Prometheus . . . is the impersonated representative of IDEA, or of the same power as Jove, but contemplated as independent, and not immersed in the product as Law *minus* the productive energy" (*SW & F*

1278–79). Prometheus' theft is thus not, for Coleridge, the origin of technology; in stealing "a portion . . . from the living *spirit* of law" Prometheus "gave that which, according to the whole analogy of things, should have existed either as pure divinity . . . or was conceded to inferior beings as a *substans in substantiato* [substance in the thing substantiated]." In this separation of idea from law, Prometheus is "*powerless*; for, all power, *i.e.*, productivity, or productive energy, is in LAW" (1280–81). Unable to transform idea into law, *nous* into *nomos,* Prometheus is chained: "The Nous is bound to a rock, the immovable firmness of which is indissolubly connected with its barrenness, its non-productivity. Were it *productive* it would be Nomos; but it is Nous, because it is *not* Nomos" (1282). It is not until (in Aeschylus's lost play) he is released by Heracles, a more lawful descendent of Jove-as-law, that Prometheus will be unbound as "the Nous, or divine principle in man" (1285).

Coleridge's reading of *Prometheus Bound* (which my summary has simplified) to some extent presents "idea" as the hero and "law" as the villain. As in the "barrel-organ" analogy, where the productive powers of language restrict the expressions of individual genius, here the productive power of "law" chains pure "idea" to a rock. But at the same time, that restriction demonstrates the impotence of idea without law, just as poetry without the (however restrictive) history of poetic production exists only in the primitive wilderness of a few inspired players who had to make their own instruments from scratch. The ethical autonomy of the artwork considered in terms of *phronesis*' unity of means and ends, or what Coleridge calls an idea that is manifested as law only insofar as it can be seen as "containing its law in itself" (*SW & F* 1276), is in a relation of both conflict and interdependence with the need for the productive power of law or *techne,* which can chain the idea to a rock or turn language into a barrel organ, but which also produces poetry.

Seen in the larger context of "idea" and "law," this is not just a problem in how to read poetry but is also a major issue in ethics itself, particularly in terms of the traditional relationship, as Harpham defines it, between "ethics" as "a general imperative to 'act on principle'" and "morality" as the concrete application of ethics: "a particular moment of ethics, when all but one of the available alternatives are excluded, chosen against, regardless of their claims" ("Ethics" 397).[43] The relationship as Harpham presents it is similar to the paradoxical interdependence of "Idea" and "Law" in Coleridge's reading of *Prometheus Bound:* "It is morality that realizes ethics, making it ethical. At the same time, however, morality negates ethics, and needs ethics in order to be moral" (397). In Coleridge's terms, this resembles the confrontation between Prometheus as the autonomous "idea" and Jupiter as the productive "law" who both chains "idea" to a rock, denying its autonomous function, and provides it with its necessary and only possible manifestation, without which "idea" is necessarily bound and powerless. For Harpham the need for moral "law" that is this kind of a necessary "other" to ethics prevents ethics from sinking into cultural relativism: "Unless it contains a 'moral' image of the law as a resistant other to society, history, or to the uncritical beliefs and prejudices of the individual, ethics can only be an apology for interests even more ignoble than interest itself" (*Getting it Right* 53). Harpham points out that "Western ethical thought since Kant has witnessed a steady erosion in the status of the ethical law" (49), and that now, without a solid theological or metaphysical ground for ethics, "law" returns somewhat like a repressed other rather than a Kantian dictate of reason. For Coleridge, Jupiter as law has something of this function in relation to Prometheus as idea. However, Jupiter and Prometheus can have this relationship partly because, although Prometheus does anticipate the Christian notion of "the divine principle in man," he is still operating within the Greek pantheistic tradition in which "the corporeal was supposed co-essential with the antecedent of its corporeity" (*SW & F* 1272), a world which, like the postmodern world Harpham describes but unlike Coleridge's Christian universe, does not operate according to faith in an absolute antecedent cause.[44] Hence there is "war, schism, or division, *i. e.* a polarization into thesis and antithesis" of law and idea (2: 1273), because, Coleridge implies, the dialectic is not grounded in the Hebrew concept of "an unbeginning creative One who neither *became* the world; nor is the world eternally; nor made the world out of himself by emanation or evolution; but who *willed* it, and it *was*!" (1271).

The later Coleridge reconciles the autonomy of Idea and the productive force of Law in terms of the mystery of the Trinity by positing a God who is at the same time absolutely autonomous, productively incarnated, and the power of love that connects them. The next two chapters will address some ethical and hermeneutic implications of that mystery: first, the interdependence of epistemology and ontology in Coleridge's speculations on "being," and second, the priority of God's act of will as an ethical command—the primary "ought"—as it relates to the world created by that command: what "is." Both issues will be treated in the context of how some contemporary voices in philosophy and literary criticism engage the distinctions between being and knowing as well as fact and value.

3

Knowledge, Being, and Hermeneutics

I. Knowing and Being

The relationship between "knowledge" and "being" is a familiar topic in Coleridge studies,[1] but I bring it up once more because of its relevance to both Romantic and contemporary questions about the relationship between understanding the world and living ethically within it. Despite recent attempts to reject conceptual structures in favor of "investigative practices" or to reduce conceptual structures to ideological functions, it remains important from both an ethical and a hermeneutic standpoint to consider how conceptual knowledge and practical experience are interconnected and which, if either, should have the upper hand.

The extent to which lived ethical and political life could be based on theoretical knowledge was a vital question for those who faced the French experiment of grounding political life in autonomous rationality and Burke's response that "The science of constructing a commonwealth . . . is . . . not to be taught *a priori*" because metaphysical truth is opposed to moral and political truth: the abstract "rights" advocated by revolutionary theorists in both England and France "are all extremes; and in proportion as they are metaphysically true, they are morally and politically false" (*Reflections on the Revolution in France* 69–71). The later Coleridge was a great admirer of Burke, not only because of Burke's defense of English tradition against French rationality, but also for his engagement in the hermeneutic circle of whole and part: Coleridge praised his "habit of foreseeing, in each integral part, or (more plainly) in every sentence, the whole that he then intends to communicate" (*The Friend* 1: 449).[2] The ethical force of theoretical knowledge was also a question for those who struggled, directly or indirectly, with the consequences of Kant's attempt to ground morality in axioms of practical reason.

The debate about the role of knowledge in ethical life is still very much with us, as evidenced by, on the one hand, rationalist and realist responses to the orthodoxy and subjectivism of ethical "noncognitivism"[3] and Habermas's theory of communicative rationality, and, on the other hand, Lyotard and other postmodernists, who argue that the failure of rational ethical grounds leads us to an ethics and politics characterized by something like the *differend* that sees grounding ethics in knowledge as a sign of bad-faith ideology.

In between, and more relevant to my concerns, are those who want to preserve a role for both local praxis and rational argument in ethics without succumbing either to Lyotard's relativism or Habermas's rational foundationalism. Alasdair MacIntyre, Charles Taylor, Stanley Cavell, Martha Nussbaum, and Bernard Williams often concern themselves with how the relationship between knowledge and ethical judgment is complicated by the problem of what counts as "knowledge." For example, Williams strongly believes in the possibility of "ethical knowledge," but sharply distinguishes the "thick" and "inhabited" concepts within which local ethical judgments are made from reflective conceptual knowledge, which tends to simplify that "thick" knowledge, going as far as the provocative statement that "reflection can destroy knowledge" (*Ethics* 147–49). Martha Nussbaum's *The Therapy of Desire* uses Aristotle to argue that rational argument is not as easily separated from therapeutic practice and desire as our post-Enlightenment assumptions would have us believe. Charles Taylor's central argument in *Sources of the Self* is that epistemological questions develop in relation to the "inescapable moral frameworks" within which we live, and which may or may not be consciously articulated.

Romantic reflections on the relation between conceptual structures and ethical life cannot be reduced to questions of the priority of one side or another, questions such as whether, as Kant believed, a regulative system of ethics could be based on universal concepts such as the categorical imperative, or whether, as Shaftesbury believed, sentiment is prior to reason in ethical issues, or whether, as Hume believed, "*reason* and *sentiment* concur in almost all moral determinations and conclusions" (*Hume's Ethical Writings* 26). Coleridge and his contemporaries have been placed on both sides of the debate as well as in this complex middle. For Keith Thomas, "[i]n their insistence on the primacy of epistemology Coleridge and Wordsworth followed the lead of Enlightenment philosophers . . . for whom epistemology is 'first philosophy'" (*Wordsworth and Philosophy* 9–10). For David Simpson and James Chandler, however, the English Romantics as a group followed the lead of Burke (and we are following their lead) in refusing to grant priority to such French notions as the primacy of an epistemological theory.[4]

For Coleridge, the question of the relationship between knowledge and being was situated within the hermeneutic circle of the relation between whole and part, universal and particular. This is of both ethical and hermeneutic significance for the obvious reason that the relationship between understanding and ethical action is partly a question of how what can be universally known affects particular actions and judgments. On the one hand, Coleridge decried as "pernicious" the tendency for "general Rules to supersede all particular Thought" (*CN* 2: 2124). On the other hand, Coleridge also insisted that the Ideas supporting our moral and physical world are constitutive, not merely regulative: "An Idea is not simply knowledge or perception as distinguished from the thing perceived: it is a realizing knowledge, a knowledge causative of its own reality" ("On the Divine Ideas," qtd. Perkins 157). This exaltation of the Idea may suggest at first a simple idealism—that Coleridge privileges epistemology even more than Kant, following Schelling's revision of Kant in restoring "intuition" from the lowest to the highest form of cognition, such that "everything that is an object, a thing, or an entity has become an object, etc., only through an original synthesis of intuition" ("Treatise Explicatory of the Idealism in the *Science of Knowledge*" 71). However, the theological basis for the constitutive status of ideas (the creativity of the divine Logos) allows Coleridge to make a more fundamental claim for the unity of knowledge and being, preventing any simple hierarchical relationship between what we know and what we are in the world of being. Though "to us the self-consciousness is not a kind of *being,* but a kind of *knowing,*" the principle of being and the principle of knowing are united indivisibly "in a self consciousness in which the principium essendi does not stand to the principium cognescendi in the relation of cause to effect, but both the one and the other are co-inherent and identical" (*BL* 1: 285).

In a process that humans are privileged to repeat on a finite level, Being originates in the willed self-consciousness of God's act of self-affirmation, manifested in the incarnation, so that ideas are constitutive because they are also acts, and not simply general principles. On the one hand, this concept prevents a simple dichotomy between the mental and the sensory. According to a note on Fichte, the "idea" of a thing, as in Spinoza's assertion that "the Body is the Mind's Idea of itself, as an active power," is in that context "used in its primitive material sense of a *total aspect* of any thing, when the whole is seen without any distinct consciousness of attending to the Parts," and only later came to mean a mental construct "in opposition to all image, or sensual impression" (*CM* 2:631–32). On the other hand, the notion of idea as "act" also liberates us from the material: "Now I do not hesitate to assert, that it was one of the great purposes of Christianity, and included in the process of our Redemption, to rouse and emancipate the Soul from this debasing Slavery to the outward Senses, to awaken the mind to the true Criteria of Reality, viz. Permanence, Power, Will manifested in Act, and Truth operating as Life" (*AR* 406–7). The important tension here is not between the mental and the material, but rather between the enslaving passivity of the material as presented through the "outward Senses" and the active principle, irreducible to a mental concept, that grounds the "true Criteria of Reality."

Despite the amalgamation of being and knowing in self-consciousness, Coleridge allows neither the particular to be completely absorbed in the absolute nor the absolute to be grounded in the particular. On the one hand, neither a Hegelian absolute nor a Kantian universal principle can substitute for the particular, despite the importance to Coleridge of both universal principles and an absolute notion of God as the Will behind the Logos. As noted in the previous chapter, the absoluteness of Idea is inseparable from its concrete manifestation in law. On the other hand, as Perkins notes, Coleridge refuses Schelling's view of God as born out of the chaos of the "ground" in a process of self-differentiation (245–47).[5] God is an absolute who *willed*, as Logos, a redemptive process of particular creation; he does not emerge from that creation. This dual perspective enables a continuity between God's foundational creative act and the particularity of human interaction without, however, denying the priority of the divine Will to finite human choice. Life, from the mineral to the moral, is grounded in a principle, not in atomism, but it is a principle of "individuation," a process, as described in *The Theory of Life,* that is itself a combination of separation and unification (*SW & F* 510–14). Coleridge thus directly engages the particular and the empirical without subsuming them into an absolute, but also without placing them at the origin.

Coleridge's balance between the particular and the universal has significant ethical implications. As Lockridge points out, Coleridge sees "conscience" both as a Kantian guide to principles and as "the total act of moral self-awareness, which registers universal principles less than it registers one's participation in a concrete and protean moral world" (*Coleridge the Moralist* 122). In distinguishing conscience from reason, Coleridge presents conscience as that which unites the particularity of the act with the universality of reason: "*The Reaso[n] is not the Conscience* the latter is a *sensation* sui generis, the spiritual feeling ~~of~~ that results from the perceived Consonance or inconsonance of an Act or Purpose with the Universal Will or Reason" (*CM* 4: 263). In *The Friend,* Coleridge does not separate discussion of universal principles from the concrete moral life that is lived at a distance from (or, in Coleridge's tortured life, often in opposition to) organized systems of knowledge. According to Lockridge, "he does not really separate metaethical from normative discussion; that is, he does not see much point in separating talk *about* morality from moral recommendation" (*Coleridge the Moralist* 252).

Coleridge's nondistinction between metaethical and normative discussion creates a potential terminological confusion in the terms "ethical" and "moral," which in both Coleridge and in modern ethical theory are sometimes sharply distinguished and sometimes not. Coleridge seems to follow a spiritualized version of the traditional distinction between "ethics" as referring to the theories that underlie right action and "morals" as referring to the practical application of principles to right action, as when he states that "Ethics, or the *Science* of Morality, does indeed in no wise exclude the consideration of *Action;* but it contemplates the same in its originating spiritual *Source,* without reference to Space or Time or Sensible Existence" (*AR* 293). However, for Coleridge, "moral" generally has more weight than "ethical"—as in his frequent references to our "moral sense"[6]—perhaps because of his suspicion of the many ethical "systems" that were being promoted at the time. Some modern theorists reverse this emphasis, elevating "ethical" over "moral," but this reversal stems from a similar distaste for systematic moral philosophy. For Paul Ricoeur, "moral" connotes a systematic "norm," important but subordinate to "ethical aim" (*Oneself* 169–239). More radically, Bernard Williams, for whom ethics engages the Socratic question of "how one should live," calls "morality" "a particular variety of ethical thought" that "we would be better off without" (*Ethics* 1, 174). In Williams's view, morality reduces ethical questions to questions of obligation and rigidly pure "insistence on abstracting the moral consciousness from other kinds of emotional reaction or social influence" (195). Charles Taylor, though he says "a moral reaction is an assent to, an affirmation of, a given ontology of the human" (*Sources of the Self* 5), also approves of Williams's designation of the "ethical" as, in

Taylor's paraphrase, "the undivided category of considerations which we employ to answer questions about how we should live"(53). In Levinas, "ethics" refers not to a system that would guide moral action, but to a concrete human contact that is precisely the breakup of any such system. One explanation for this terminological reversal is that in both Coleridge and the moderns the ethical is the larger and prior category: Coleridge was enough of an idealist to see the prior category of the ethical as an essentialist conceptual system; for the postexistential tradition, the prior ethical category is of course existence, to which the conceptual systems of morality are subordinate. Despite these important variations and many inconsistencies, then, there is a continuity in the ethics/morality distinction between Romantic and modern efforts to broaden moral considerations beyond the narrowness of systematic rules to a consideration of the question of "how we should live" that has obsessed poetry from the beginning.

It is important to sort out the role of particularity in Coleridge's ethics because, as Bernard Williams has shown, philosophy's continuing difficulty with ethics is the tendency of reflective thought to "impose on ethical life some immensely simple model, whether it be of the concepts we actually use or of moral rules by which we should be guided" (*Ethics* 127) by, for example, universalizing the particular human agent. In a complaint about Kant with which Coleridge would have sympathized, Williams notes that arguments such as Kant's about "rational agents" need "to tell us what it is about rational agents that requires them to form this conception of themselves as, so to speak, abstract citizens" (63). Despite his admiration for Kant, Coleridge is similarly critical of Kant's ability to deal with the particular application of general principles, as in this note of December 6, 1803: "Kant, & all his School, are miserable Reasoners, in Psychology & particular Morals—bad analysts of aught but Notions, equally clumsy in the illustration & application of their Principles—so much indeed as often to shake my Faith in their general System" (*CM* 3: 253). He also criticizes the adequacy of Kant's account of experience in the *Critique of Pure Reason* (3: 248–49).

Coleridge thus mixes a number of approaches that have been taken in recent ethical discussion, just as he mixed, according to Lockridge, many of the traditional categories of ethical discussion.[7] His combination of universal and particular aligns him in some ways with Martha Nussbaum's call for a return to the particularity of Aristotelian *phronesis,* and his emphasis on the particularity of the "person" can be linked to Alasdair MacIntyre's (similarly Aristotelian) call for a character- rather than reason-centered account of ethics, but at the same time he preserves a sense of the "Good" as an absolute focus of orientation for ethical life that provides what Charles Taylor calls "inescapable moral frameworks."[8] He follows Kant by grounding ethics in a moral command from the unconditioned ("Let the Will obey the pure Reason *exclusively & unconditionally*" [*CN* 3: 3293]), an ethical philosophy Bernard Williams objects to because it restricts ethical life to a narrow concept of "obligation" and denies non-ethical factors (such as desire) any role in the unconditionally necessary, or what we "must" do (*Ethics* 184–96). Despite his strong Kantian sense of an unconditioned moral imperative, however, Coleridge implicitly answers some of Williams's objections by having that imperative come, not from a formal law of reason, but from a Person who not only commands humanity, but also creates and loves it. This gives us a much thicker description of the unconditionally necessary than Kantian ethics allows, broadening the divine command from mere obligation to a mandate for creative existence (we are obligated to God, but we are also able to repeat, on a finite level, his creative act) and allowing non- or para-ethical factors such as "love" to join ethical considerations in determining what we "must" do.

Coleridge's hermeneutic emphasis places understanding within the cultural interaction that constitutes ethical life. Knowledge is hermeneutically constituted in the ethical particularity of human dialogue, as Coleridge suggests when he posits "conscience," defined in terms of relations to others, as the reason for the continuity of consciousness. "*From* what reasons do I believe a *continuous* <& ever continuable> *Consciousness?* From *Conscience!* Not for myself but for my conscience—i.e. my affections & duties toward others, I should have no Self" (*CN* 2: 3231). A similar point is made in *Aids to Reflection:* "a Consciousness properly human (i. e. *Self*-consciousness), with the sense of moral responsibility, presupposes the Conscience, as its antecedent Condition and Ground" (125). Knowledge is dependent upon an ethical context, since self-consciousness, which is "for *us* the source and principle of all *our* possible knowledge" (*BL* 1: 284)," depends on the ethical relation to others.[9]

In his annotations of Eschenmayer and Fichte, Coleridge makes it clear that self-consciousness is not merely or even primarily epistemological; it is an error to confuse "Self-Consciousness with the consciousness of Self" (*CM* 2: 552). To restrict self-consciousness to "a mere consciousness of self-modification" (2: 603) is to deny the ethical grounding of self-consciousness in conscience. According to *Aids to Reflection,* spiritual growth, not knowledge, is the goal of Christianity: "the highest knowledge . . .

severed from the growth here mentioned, misses the true end of the word" (131). As discussed in the previous chapter, the very plan of *The Friend* suggests this hermeneutic interplay between ethics and knowledge: the text is to function as a "friend," suggesting a moral relation with that which is a source of knowledge, and its object is both "to refer men's opinions to their absolute principles," or give opinion a basis in knowledge, and "to apply the principles thus ascertained" in the concrete moral, political, and theological realm (1: 16).[10]

Lockridge associates Coleridge with "cognitive non-definism," the school of metaethical thought that "believes we have moral knowledge" but also believes that "moral judgments cannot be translated into expressions having the same meaning yet containing no moral terms" and notes that thinkers in this school "are apt to speak of special moral faculties of knowing, such as 'moral sense,' or 'conscience,' or 'imagination'" (*The Ethics of Romanticism* 151). Coleridge grants ethical intuitions a more primary cognitive status, however, by insisting that cognition itself is morally grounded: even knowledge of facts is ultimately dependent on the conscience. Perkins explains Coleridge's view: "Since, in his opinion, a fact unrelated to the antecedent unity of a self was as impossible as knowledge without an initial *act* of faith, to attempt to divorce facts from conscience and principle was to betray history itself" (266). There remains a fundamental unity between moral and rational knowledge, because Reason is, as Logos, God's word, which is the ground of *all* knowledge. As noted above, Coleridge separates knowledge and being in his discussion of self-consciousness only to reunite them almost in the same breath. He follows Kant in distinguishing between the "*Theoric* or intellective, and the Moral or Practical" manifestations of both Reason and Understanding (*SW & F* 1497), but he complains about those who put "the intellectual & moral . . . faculties at strife with each other," and says that instead they ought to "act with an equal eye to all, to feel that all is involved in the perfection of each" (*CN* 3: 3564). His objections to atomism bring the empirical reality of the created world closer to the sense of willed process involved in ethical action: he asserts that "Life itself is not a *Thing*—a self-subsistent *Hypostasis*—but an *Act* and *Process*" (*Theory of Life*, *SW & F* 557), and "nature" is defined as "the Law or Constructive Powers excited in Matter by the influence of God's Spirit and Logos" (*CM* 3: 943–44).

Coleridge's distinction between the interpretive, ethical, knowledge-grounding act of "self-consciousness" and the merely epistemological "consciousness of self" suggests that he eschews the kind of thinking that would derive knowledge, ethical or otherwise, from what Christopher

Norris, following Saul Kripke, calls "descriptivism." Descriptivism assumes "that the act of reference—of picking out an object—is a matter of applying the appropriate criteria as given by some current conceptual scheme or system of intralinguistic representation," the kind of thinking that would begin with "the *sense* of the referring expression," or "the various descriptions, criteria, or identifying attributes standardly imputed to the referent in question" (*New Idols of the Cave* 166). This concept was used by Frege and Russell in the service of a linguistic analysis that was seen as "fully compatible with a realist epistemology." However, its exaltation of linguistic representation also led, Norris argues, to the relativism of postmoderns such as Lyotard and Foucault, who used the priority of linguistic "sense," defined in Saussurean terms as arbitrary, to argue for the incommensurability and fictionality of discourses. Norris endorses Kripke's proposal "to halt that drift by treating *reference* (not sense) as the primary term and thereby securing a stable—or at any rate logically accountable—order of relationship between word and object" (166), thus adopting a "causal realist" approach in which scientific theory's "measure of success . . . is *not* the extent to which empirical observation can be tested against (or subsumed under) . . . higher-level statements of scientific truth," but rather "the way that such theories succeed in first identifying then actually *explaining* those objects, processes, and events in the physical world that had hitherto lacked any adequate account" (178).[11]

In *The Friend,* Coleridge makes a somewhat analogous distinction between mere "verbal truth," by which "we mean no more than the correspondence of a given fact to given words" and the higher "moral truth," in which "we involve likewise the intention of the speaker that his words should correspond to his thoughts in the sense in which he expects" (1: 42). The former, lesser kind of truth is "merely" descriptive; the stakes are not very high in its demand for adequate correspondence between words and facts, signs and the world.[12] Coleridge was not at all skeptical about science, as *The Theory of Life* and other works attest. But in order to encompass natural science he needed to reject both the descriptivism inherent in merely "verbal" truth that would pretend to describe the world adequately and the atomism of a world that would lend itself to such description. He approaches Norris's (and Kant's) position in arguing that "[t]o explain a power" such as life,—"to unfold or spread it out"—is not the same as "[t]o account" for Life, or "state something prior . . . as the ground or cause of that thing" (*Theory of Life, SW & F* 504, 503). The error of descriptivism is to assume that what Coleridge calls explaining will also be an accounting, that an explanation of how life works must parallel a metaphysically coherent sufficient cause for life. Life cannot be accounted for by demanding that it agree with a general theory, whether atoms or ether. This is not to say that Coleridge did not believe in such a metaphysical foundation or sufficient cause for life. On the contrary, for him (and of course not for Norris) the sufficient cause of both life and our perception of it is God, as the source of life and as the model for human imagination. But such a foundational theory need not parallel a descriptive representation.

To use one of Norris's contemporary examples, our inability to describe adequately the wave/particle within the conventions currently available to us is a mere failure of what Coleridge would call "verbal truth," and therefore no warrant for skepticism or ontological relativism: as Coleridge puts it, "distinct *notions* do not suppose different *things* (*The Friend* 1: 177n). Norris argues that the limits of our observation-language lead to ontological relativism only by narrowly descriptive criteria, and Coleridge would agree that the inadequacies of descriptivism do not supply a very strong argument against knowledge of even the natural world. This perhaps explains why, despite his objections to a descriptive account of the world, Coleridge is almost absurdly empirical, as he traces the principle of "individuation" in *The Theory of Life* through a detailed evolutionary scenario leading from the mineral right up to the ethically-grounded human self-consciousness (*SW & F* 550–51).[13]

Coleridge's objections to descriptivism do not lead, as in Norris, to causal realism. He takes the argument against descriptivism in an almost opposite direction by denigrating descriptivism in favor of a higher, internal principle rather than in favor of a principle of empirical reference. Definition requires a "law," not an always insufficient empirical cause (*Theory of Life, SW & F* 492–93), and his alternative to the descriptive sense of mere "verbal truth" is not real-world reference, but an attentiveness to the "intention of the speaker." His objections to descriptivism come from what would now be called the phenomenological, rather than the causal-realist camp, given the origin of those fundamental laws in the act of self-consciousness. Hence the distinction he locates in Shakespeare between descriptive "observation," which "might be able to produce an accurate copy of a thing" but only in ideas that are "in parts and fragments," and the higher truth of "meditation," which "look[s] at every character with interest—only as it contains something generally true as such as might be expressed in a philosophical Problem" (*Lects 1808–1819* 1: 289).

Despite the subjective implications of "meditation," Coleridge remains (as Husserlian phenomenology claimed to be) empirical in his own way, and he points in the direction of Gadamer's philosophical hermeneutics by translating metaphysical disputes into historical effects,[14] specifically the degeneration of "idea" to a sensory, descriptive concept. This is suggested as early as 1801, when he makes the claim in a series of letters to Josiah Wedgwood that Locke repeated rather than refuted Descartes on the notion of innate ideas. Coleridge is able to perform this denial of the classic difference between French rationalism and British empiricism by pointing to an historical, metonymic degeneration of Plato's notion that "*Ideas* . . . meant what Mr. Locke calls the original Faculties & Tendencies of the mind, the internal Organs, as it were, and *Laws* of Human Thinking," adding that "the word should be translated '*Moulds*' and not '*Forms*'":[15] "By the usual Process of language Ideas came to signify not only these original *moulds* of the mind, but likewise all that was cast in these moulds, as in our language the Seal & the Impression it leaves are both called Seals. Latterly, it wholly lost it's original meaning, and became synonimous sometimes with *Images* simply (whether Impressions or Ideas) and sometimes with Images in the memory; and by Des Cartes it is used for whatever is immediately perceived by the mind" (*CL* 2: 682–83). This reduction of "Ideas" to a "descriptive" content—to images with the which the world may or may not conform—meant that the fault of British empiricism is not its empiricism, but its narrowing of the object of its empiricism from "the internal Organs . . . and *Laws* of Human Thinking" to systems of sense-impressions. He lodges a similar complaint against Schelling, insisting that the real and the ideal present a false opposition: "I avoid the false opposition of Real and Ideal which embarrasses Schelling.—Idea with me is contra-distinguished only from Conception, Notion, Construction, impression, Sensation—" (*CM* 4: 401). In 1815 he extends an almost Blakean call for empiricism to reverse its causal priorities by asking Wordsworth to assert that "the Senses were living growths and developments of the Mind & Spirit in a much juster as well as higher sense, than that the mind can be said to be formed by the Senses" (*CL* 4: 574).

II. Coleridge and the Hermeneutic Tradition

Even without subscribing to the particular principles Coleridge claims to have found, we can see that his ability to deny a descriptive accounting of life without abandoning empirical explanation suggests that knowledge, even empirical knowledge, need not be limited to adequate description: there are other ways to know than by attempting the impossible task of describing Locke's insensible atoms. For Coleridge this way of knowing is firmly within the hermeneutic tradition. Since for Coleridge the Logos is God's Word—"a Light at once intelligent and intelligible, and the communicative medium" ("On the Divine Ideas," qtd. Perkins 157)—and human language is a finite repetition of the Logos, this union of idea and expression foregrounds the importance of interpretation and allows language itself to share in the constitutive status of ideas.[16] Despite his affinity for Kantian metaphysics, this emphasis on language and interpretation places Coleridge within the hermeneutic tradition that, from Schleiermacher to Gadamer, emphasizes the dialogic and historically embedded status of understanding. In 1803, Coleridge planned to write a "History of Metaphysics in England" that will be "not, strictly speaking, metaphysical, but historical" (*CL* 2: 927), and the aforementioned critique of Locke is argued in historical, and even political terms: Locke's specious rebuttal of Descartes is accepted not on its metaphysical merits but as the result of the unthinking Francophobia that Coleridge could critique even as he supported the English cause against France; Locke represented "a Complete triumph of the English over the French" (2: 702). Coleridge would agree with the historical/hermeneutic view that Sabina Lovibond finds in Wittgenstein and traces back to the Romantics: "the practice of talking about an objective world rests, according to Wittgenstein, not upon an alleged rational foundation in our sensory experience but upon certain material facts—facts about the "natural history" of language-users" (39).

Language's fundamental and historical participation in constitutive ideas, the inseparability of rational (or even spiritual) and historical truth, and the theological importance of the divine Word as a world-creating linguistic act, all point to a connection between Coleridge's involvement in biblical hermeneutics and the continuation of that hermeneutic tradition in this century with Gadamer, for whom, following Heidegger, "[l]anguage is not just one of man's possessions in the world; rather, on it depends the fact that man has a *world* at all" (*TM* 443). Coleridge not only objects to the distinction between the "moulds" of ideas and the "images" they are said to contain but also denies the distinction between images of nature and the words that the Lockean would see as superadded to those images: "Words therefore become a sort of Nature to us, & Nature is a sort of Words" (*CL* 2: 698). Language's constitutive role in Coleridge should not be confused with the Derridean position that exalts the materiality of the signifier over logocentrism; Coleridge's philosophy is explicitly logocentric, and the equation of words with "nature" must be considered in light of the fact that, as his objections to both Schelling and Wordsworth show, "nature" is not foundational, at least in its material sense. However, his position does link up with Gadamer, who, like Coleridge, traces the fundamentality of language back to the Christian incarnation.

Perkins briefly notes this connection to Gadamer (104), and I have argued elsewhere for the relevance of Gadamer's insights to Romantic concerns about interpretation and theology.[17] Coleridge sees Plotinus's concept of understanding (*συνιέναι*) as meaning "to go along with me" and finds this an apt expression for philosophical intuition[18] (*BL* 1: 240). Gadamer's conversational model similarly emphasizes the Aristotelian "sympathetic understanding" exercised when one "thinks along with the other" (*TM* 323). In a late (1826) notebook entry, Coleridge's explanation of how the scriptural texts are adapted to the contingent situations of their readers turns on a model of adaptation that applies to conversation as a whole, and that overlaps Gadamer's model at some crucial points:

> [W]hoever speaks, adapts his language to the known or supposed experience & capacity of the persons spoken to. For he speaks to be understood: and as soon as his words reach the ear of his Auditors, it is *their* mind that is to stand *under*, i.e. give the *substance* of thought to the sounds, not his own except as far as it can be identified with *theirs*. The mind of the Hearer may indeed be afterwards modified and enlarged ~~to~~ in consequence of the Words heard; but they must have already been *words*, and not mere *Sounds*, in order to produce this Effect: and ~~they~~ Sounds become *Words* only by exciting in the mind of the Hearer images, thoughts, or apprehensions already existing. (*CN* 4: 5418)

Similarly for Gadamer, words come into being only in a communicative context; he notes that a child's first word, always celebrated by the parents, is really what Coleridge would call a mere sound, a "word that does not exist" because it is not yet grounded in the conversational context of "being-able-to-talk" (*Praise of Theory* 7). In Gadamer's conversational model, the linguistic "substance of thought" is not the speaker's "own except as far as it can be identified with" the auditor, and thus depends on the conversational situation rather than subjective intention. For Gadamer, who describes this situation from the "hearer's" point of view, "we do not relate the other's opinion to him but to our own opinions and views" (*TM* 385). For Coleridge, the Bible is the paradigmatic occasion for a communicative hermeneutic that is not solely dependent on authorial intention. After imposing his own post-Kantian theology on the Bible,

Coleridge asks himself rhetorically, "Do I believe that the Writers of the old Testament were conscious of any such Ideas?—What if they were not?—the Bible *is* that which it is capable of reflecting—It is the Mirror of Faith" (*CM* 2: 423). The intentions of the biblical authors are less important than the process of reflection that occurs when the Bible is read in a spirit of faith that connects the historically alien horizons of the biblical authors with the modern reader's interpretive energy.

Despite his substantial investment in subjectivity and intention, Coleridge argues that speakers and hearers must depend on words that refer to "images, thoughts, or apprehensions already existing," and that the words of biblical authors mirror the faith of the interpreter who submits himself to those words. Intention is thus subject to a loss of ownership. As Gadamer explains this process, when subject-positions are put "at risk" in the hermeneutic conversation, the result is the expression of "something . . . that is not only mine or the author's, but common" (*TM* 388). Understanding what a person says is extra- rather than merely inter-subjective: "To understand what a person says is . . . to come to an understanding about the subject matter, not to get inside another person and relive his experiences (Erlebnisse)" (383). Gadamer emphasizes language as an "event" in the world rather than a structure of "signs," sharing Coleridge's desire to close the gap between the ideality of signification and the reality of experience. Coleridge wants to elevate "words into Things, and living Things too" (*CL* 1: 625–26), and Gadamer calls language "event" rather than sign: "in contrast to the Greek logos, the word is pure event" (*TM* 419). He also shares Coleridge's recognition of our entanglement in a linguistically constituted history, suggested by the "barrel organ" analogy discussed in Chapter 2: "the object of knowledge and statements is always already enclosed within the world horizon of language" (450), which is the "record" of "*the finitude of our historical experience*" (457).

Coleridge's relation to Gadamer's position is complex, partly because both are critical heirs of the same German tradition. On the one hand, particularly in his Shakespeare criticism, Coleridge partakes of Schleiermacher's subjective orientation to interpretation—the "Romantic" notion that one should "reconstruct" the subjectivity of the author—to which Gadamer objects. On the other hand, Coleridge's emphasis on language's role in the constitutive status of ideas, the historicity and cultural embeddedness of understanding, the hermeneutic circle as a structure of interaction between individual will and an inaccessible whole, the conversational nature of interpretation, and the importance of human others, all grant him affinities with Gadamer's hermeneutics, which has its own highly conflicted relation to its Romantic and pre-Romantic origins.

In *Truth and Method,* Gadamer identifies, as an important source of hermeneutic thought, the conflict between the Roman church's emphasis that the interpretation of scripture be mediated by the authority of tradition and Luther's attempt to replace this with a method of reading by which "the whole of Scripture guides the understanding of individual passages: and again this whole can be reached only through the cumulative understanding of individual passages" (*TM* 175), a method that does not require the mediation of the Church's authority. As John M. Connolly and Thomas Keutner note, Gadamer is ambivalent towards Luther; while he positively "takes Luther to claim that a text is understood only in its *application* by the reader to him/herself," he also sees Luther "as the source of the (ultimately misleading) notion of the text's own unique intention" (Introduction, *Hermeneutics Versus Science?* 7). Gadamer points out, following Dilthey, that the Reformation itself soon reinstated the authority of tradition with its own "credal formulae" (*TM* 176), and that Luther was enlisted by the Enlightenment on the side of reason in the "mutually exclusive antithesis between authority and reason" (277).[19]

Coleridge follows a form of Luther's interpretive method in seeing the whole as guiding the interpretation of parts. As he says in *Confessions of an Inquiring Spirit,* "each part of Scripture must be interpreted by the Spirit of the Whole" (*SW & F* 1156). But he also, like Gadamer, sees the sole emphasis on the Bible, such that "we need no Rule, Help or Guide, Spiritual or historical," as leading to the errors of "the so called Rationalists" whose emphasis on the self-sufficiency of human reason "diluted and explained away" important aspects of faith (1144–45), and he grants a good deal of importance to the history of interpretation itself as informing an individual's interpretation of Scripture (1154–55). The importance of tradition as a corrective to radically subjective interpretation was also buttressed, of course, by his firm Burkean belief in the superiority of the historically evolved English constitution over French self-sufficient reason. Thus, by a somewhat different route, he comes to a position that in many ways resembles Gadamer's historical mediation of the Lutheran hermeneutics of part and whole.

Coleridge's historical analysis of reason is linked to his involvement in the biblical hermeneutics that emerged in Germany in the late eighteenth century, particularly his engagement with the work of Johann Gottfried Eichhorn, one of the founders of the German Higher Criticism, whom

Coleridge met in 1799 and whose works he annotated between 1810 and 1819.[20] Coleridge followed closely and approvingly the efforts of Herder and Eichhorn to read the Bible as a syncretic mythology that could be reconstructed through rational historical scholarship. Although this work deeply influenced Coleridge's own poetic mythology, as Shaffer demonstrates in *Kubla Khan* and *The Fall of Jerusalem*, it was impossible for Coleridge to accept the replacement of "the eternal message of the Gospels" with a historical analysis that would produce "a general view of the conditions of religious experience," as Shaffer characterizes the general drift of historical biblical criticism (32). Thus M. H. Abrams's characterization of Coleridge's effort to preserve "the irreducible minimum of the Christian creed within an essentially secular metaphysical system" (*Natural Supernaturalism* 67) is perhaps somewhat misleading. The Bible retains its foundational authority: as Pierre Mileur puts it, "The experience of the biblical text, and the assumption of method that we bring to it, provides the paradigm for the experience of the world as an order, and not vice-versa" (*Vision and Revision* 167). The prophets could not be treated simply as poets, as Eichhorn argued. Coleridge objects that "[t]he~~y~~ Prophets do *not* describe their inspiration as Poets; but relate sudden changes produced without any conscious act of their own will. . . . [T]his state was used instrumentally by the Divine Spirit, as the congruous Base or Suscipient of his ~~immediate~~ spiritual Agency" (*CM* 2: 402).

Coleridge's thought mediates between and responds to (at least) two strands of German biblical scholarship: On the one hand is the rationalist hermeneutics' secularizing critique of religion: the tradition that led from the historical research into biblical texts by scholars such as Eichhorn and Paulus to Feuerbach's assertion "that theology is anthropology" (xvii). On the other hand is the aesthetic sense of history espoused by Herder, and in a different way Schleiermacher, who saw the Bible is a human document, but one that portrays poetically a history in which can be seen, as William Baird says of Herder and Lessing, "the disclosure of God's progressive revelation for evolving humanity" (*History of New Testament Research* 183). Coleridge is critical in his assessment of both traditions as he shares their common objections to the idea that the Bible is in effect the infallible manuscript of a divine author. Coleridge in fact tends to lump all of these authors together in "the German School" (*CN* 4: 5322), which is not surprising since he was primarily familiar with their biblical criticism, which shared the grammatico-historical method. For example, Schleiermacher's specifically hermeneutic thought, little of which was published by Schleiermacher himself, would probably have been unavailable to Coleridge.

In 1817, Coleridge approves the rejection of Eichhorn's and Paulus's extension of Spinoza's reduction of scripture to chronological history by "our learned English Theologians, and by the soundest Divines" as well as "within the last ten or twelve years, by the Philosophers of their own country" (*SW & F* 615–16), presumably referring in the last phrase to the post-Kantian idealists. In the same essay, however, he praises Eichhorn's "masterly method of establishing the authenticity of the books of Moses, of the Gospel and Apocalypse of St John, and the venerable antiquity of the Book of Job" (616). In his annotations to Schleiermacher's *Critical Essay on the Gospel of St. Luke,* Coleridge is sharply and rationally critical of Schleiermacher's abuse of historical evidence, as he defends Eichhorn's theory of an ur-Gospel against Schleiermacher's theory that the Gospels were built from written fragments of an originally oral tradition (*CM* 4: 469–84).

Coleridge is suspicious of any attempt to confuse fact and fiction, which is his objection to the modern novel, as will be discussed in Chapter 5. In response to what he sees as Schleiermacher's suggestion that the evangelists were "men capable of blending Facts & Fictions, without leaving any clue to the Labyrinth," Coleridge responds, "One or the other of three cases must be supposed. Either all is fiction; or all is fact; or the former is not apostolic" (*CM* 4: 479). He objects to Herder's faith in "history" because it is such an allegorized history that it denies a literal faith in Christ's death and resurrection (2: 1079–80). The point is not that fact is always to be preferred to fiction; he ends a note on Schleiermacher with the assertion that "facts, of which Paul probably was, and certainly wished to be, ignorant, have but little claim to rank as articles of faith at the present day" (4: 477). The point is rather that a bad mixture of the two produces a morally offensive contrast between the foundational events of religious faith—"facts, incidents, and discourses which we had received as truths with a ~~more~~ deeper and more passionate Faith, than mere History, even the most authentic, can inspire"—and the "poetic fictions" that "by the violence of the contrast" assume "the character & quality of a Lie" (4: 479). Coleridge will allow no compromise between fact and fiction: he objects to reducing "the detailed account of the Delivery of the Law from Mount Sinai" to "figurative language & poetic drapery," insisting that it must be either "*literal* mater-of-fact Truth, or intentional and deliberate Fiction meant to be received as truth" (4: 47–48).

Coleridge's position is well-illustrated by a comment on Eichhorn's *Einleitung ins Alte Testament*. He argues on Eichhorn's own turf in the spirit of rational biblical criticism, presenting his own historical evidence and logic in opposition to Eichhorn's. Occasionally, however, fundamental differences in theological premises emerge. For example, in his comment on Eichhorn's argument for the purity and superiority of the Mosaic account of the origins of things, Coleridge agrees with Eichhorn's conclusions, but for different reasons:

> So *I* think, who take Gen. I literally and geologically: and so *did* I think, when I interpreted the Chapter as a Morning Hymn, in which the Creation is represented under the analogy of the daily emergence of visible Nature out of Night thro' all the successive appearances till full Sun rise/ ~~a se~~ and hence <explained> the posteriority of the Sun = the visible Orb, to the Light, its far earlier Harbinger. But would not *Eichhorn* deem *this* too refined, and the former visionary? — If so, in what *third* can he find the Dignity, Truth, & freedom from all chimerical notions? *I* have deduced the same process from grounds wholly independent of the Mosaic Cosmogony; in fact, without thinking of the latter and unconsci~~en~~ous of the coincidence. (*CM* 2: 393)

For Coleridge, the dignity, truth, and freedom of the Mosaic philosophy does not need historical or rational arguments when one has either the resources of literal faith in *Genesis* I or the resources of a poetic interpretation that understands both the power of metaphor and its distinction from the truth. These methods are not of equal standing, of course; the metaphorical interpretation of this chapter as a "Morning Hymn" is probably part of Coleridge's rejected Unitarian past. However, that they are given somewhat equivalent interpretive value in opposition to Eichhorn's rational-historical method, even as that method is respected, suggests how Coleridge manages to mediate between a rationalist and a poetic hermeneutics. Coleridge decries the metaphorical insensitivity of the "Neologic Divines,"[21] who "take the *metaphor* as if it were the proper sense" in order to accommodate the biblical text to "the miserable Psilosophy[22] and sparrow-throated capacity of these Innovators" (*CN* 3: 4401).

The important thing is not the identification of specific influences, or even specific determinations of what is factual and what is allegorical, but rather the whole spirit in which the Bible is read, which means the taking of the Bible as a whole. "The original sin of the German School," according to Coleridge, is to focus on the part rather than the whole. In a note on Eichhorn's nonmiraculous interpretation of St. Paul's conversion, Coleridge objects to "the comparing of this or that extraordinary ~~a~~ narrative in the Gospel with some other analogous fact in recent or profane

History—instead of taking the complexus of the New Testament Story & seeking for an analogy to *this,* in any other series of events allowed not to be miraculous" (*CN* 4: 5322). In other words, whether or not Paul's conversion was a miracle, the connection between the New Testament and the world is to be found in its story as a whole, not in the determination of historical specifics.

One way to understand Coleridge's divided attitude toward the biblical hermeneutics of his contemporaries, an attitude that allows historical criticism of the Bible to lead toward, rather than away from, a biblically-grounded faith, is to see him as calling for a less radical version of the deeply historicized hermeneutics presented in Gianni Vattimo's *Beyond Interpretation*. Like Coleridge, who says of the Bible, "I take up this Work with the purpose to read it for the first time, as I should read any other works" (*SW & F* 1120), Vattimo sees "[t]he link between hermeneutics and the emancipation from dogma" as closely tied to "the step towards a consideration of the sacred text as a text among others" (43). Like Coleridge, who combines the secularizing methods of Higher Criticism with a deep faith in the Christian incarnation, Vattimo sees hermeneutics' secularization of scripture as coming full circle to an incarnational faith. Vattimo's argument, somewhat simplified, goes like this: if hermeneutics' Nietzschean call for a world of multiple interpretations rather than facts is not to be deluded into reducing interpretations to a truth that will halt the interpretive process, it must look to its own historical conditions rather than to some ahistorical truth. Hermeneutics finds its own historicity, and that of modernity as a whole, to be linked to the Christian notion of incarnation as *kenosis* (a depletion of God), which Vattimo understands in Heideggerian terms as the weakening of Being. Part of this *kenosis* is, paradoxically, secularization, in that the sense of God as an interpretation-halting absolute is replaced by a notion of charity toward multiple interpretations in the Christian doctrine of love.[23]

Coleridge implicitly affirms the doctrine of *kenosis* when he writes in *Aids to Reflection,* "If [Christ] emptied himself of glory to become Sin for thy salvation, must not thou be emptied of thy sinful Self to become Righteousness in and through his agony and the effective merits of his Cross?" (310). Part of his argument for the primacy of scripture rests on its historical effect, or what Vattimo calls hermeneutics' "theorizing its own constitutive historicity" (47). For Coleridge, the Bible's "very presence, as a believed Book, ~~in~~ has rendered the nations emphatically a chosen race" and this historical process has enabled human participation in the incarnational process of "the eternal I AM, the <ever-living WORD,>" (*SW & F* 1155).

As I shall discuss in more detail in Chapter 6, Coleridge would not place either this historicity or even incarnational *kenosis* at the foundational level where Vattimo locates it, because Coleridge believed, increasingly throughout his life, in a principle of the divine absolute prior to the incarnation. Thus he sees the kind of incarnational history that Vattimo traces, with its emphasis on interpretation, as the absolute's adaptation to human immaturity and apostacy, a position that, according to Vattimo, the incarnation itself denies: "that the transcendent is given in this way and not only by virtue of the immaturity of the human faculties is something that we learn from the incarnation of God in Jesus Christ" (55). For Coleridge (as for Gadamer), the incarnation inaugurates history; for Vattimo, the incarnation represents the irreducibility of historicity.

Despite these differences, Vattimo's argument can show how Coleridge is not simply establishing a forced compromise between the two traditions of literal faith in and historical critique of the Bible. It is the universalization and humanization of this incarnational process of self-emptying (Christ did it, and so should we) that allows for the kind of secularization that Vattimo describes. This is a secularization that *restores* religion, according to Vattimo, by freeing it from dependence on a metaphysical absolute that would halt the process of interpretation. In Coleridge's less radical version of this argument, the deep historicity of language itself, produced by the divinely-originated imaginative power that underlies all perception, coupled with the history of the effect of the Bible, allows for a continuity between the historical process of textual critique inaugurated, if overly rationalized, by the Higher Criticism and a literal, even "geological" faith in *Genesis*. Coleridge always returns to the foundational principle of the logos as the creative expression of God's word, so that the process of creation—in the literal sense of the earth's geologic history—in which Coleridge is expressing faith is the antitype of the creative human process of perception and interpretation that produced, among other things, *Genesis* I. Historicizing the Bible does not for Coleridge lead away from faith, but towards it; thus he can say of Heinrich Eberhard Gottlob Paulus, one of the most rationalistic of the Higher Critics, "As to Pr. Paulus, I differ perhaps as having more nearly completed the Circle than he seems to me to have done" (*CM* 4:46).

Coleridge's hermeneutic is a secularization in the sense that it is premised on God's translation into the human and the historical, and it also includes the religious infinity of interpretation that Vattimo sees as stemming from this secularization. For Coleridge the imaginative basis of perception, and therefore interpretation, refuses to terminate in a concept of the Bible as a merely historical text, as a poetic allegory, or as an act of ventriloquism on the part of the divine mind. The words of the Bible are divinely inspired, but humanly recorded: "But tho' the ~~words~~ origin of the words, even as of the miraculous Acts, be supernatural, yet the former once uttered, the latter once having taken their place among the phenomena of the Senses, the faithful *Recording* of the same does not of itself imply or seem to require any supernatural Working—other than as all Truth and Goodness is such" (*SW & F* 1124).

Although Coleridge happily engages in Higher Criticism's arguments about the biblical canon, to quibble about the canonicity of individual books or parts of books according to the criteria of rational history is to deny the effect of the whole experienced, he says, in "the moment I had been pouring out the love and gladness of my own soul" (*SW & F* 1129) in the process of reading the Bible. To see each word of the Bible as divinely dictated "petrifies at once the whole Body of Holy Writ," turning it into "a hollow Passage for a Voice" when rightly read it is a "breathing Organismus" (1134). If David is merely transmitting divinely-written psalms, he becomes an "*automaton*" and loses his human effect in terms of "sympathy" and "example" (1136). To compromise by seeing scripture as a mixture of fact and allegorical fiction does justice to neither. To adapt Vattimo's terms, the senses of Being that would be characterized either as objective history (Eichhorn) a poetic mixture of fact and fiction (Herder and Schleiermacher) or unmediated communication with the divine (the fundamentalism to which both traditions object) are weakened in order to make way for a hermeneutics that depends on an essentially ethical act of charitable interpretation, founded on God's act of love in the incarnation. Coleridge insists that if one reads the Bible "as he would any other Body of Ancient Writings, the livelier and steadier will be his impressions of its superiority to all other books, till at length all other Books and all other Knowledge will be ~~chiefly~~ valuable in his eyes ~~as~~ in proportion as they help him to a better understanding of his Bible" (1164). For Coleridge the Bible is like other books in the sense that it allows the historicity of language to engage the reader in an endless act of interpretation by providing a reception history of the Word of God. It is unlike other books because it is the paradigmatic example of the incarnational process that Coleridge—and, in post-Nietzschean way, Vattimo—see as underlying authentic interpretation. The next two chapters will explore how this Coleridgean hermeneutic engages some specific problems of literary interpretation in which hermeneutics and ethics converge.

4

Is and Ought in Literature and Life

I. The Is / Ought Problem

The "is/ought" distinction is at the heart of the question, as W. D. Hudson phrases it in introducing a collection of essays on this subject, "How is what *is* the case related to what *ought* to be the case—statements of fact to moral judgments?" (11). The is/ought, fact/value relationship—the question of how and whether what one "ought" to do is a function of facts about what "is"—has a long self-conscious tradition in moral philosophy and a less consciously acknowledged history in literary theory. The usefulness of the is/ought distinction itself was brought into question as early as Hume.[1] As Wayne Booth argues, a strict adherence to the incommensurability of fact and value leads to the mirror-image dogmatisms of "scientism" or "irrationalism": either one assumes that only facts exist and that values are thus illusory, prejudicial, or all equivalent, or one takes the equal and opposite position that the inaccessibility or inadequacy of "mere" facts should liberate us into the emotive sphere of "value" (*Modern Dogma* 13-21). Writing in 1974, Booth presents a long list of citations in support of the "fusionist" trend away from such a sharp split between fact and value (207-11) and points out that even supposed adherents of the split, such as Locke and Kant, did not see it as an impediment to reasoning about values (15).

For literary theory and its philosophical sources, the distinction is very deeply entrenched, perhaps because the "fact" of the text (for New

Criticism), of the structure of language (for structuralism and poststructuralism), of material history (for cultural studies) and of gender (for gender studies) is so often in an unacknowledged tension with the "value" manifested by interpretive and evaluative acts of criticism. The results are often surprising when the fact/value relationship is brought to consciousness. For example, Lyotard, for whom "[r]eality . . . is a state of the referent (that about which one speaks) which results from the effectuation of establishment procedures defined by a unanimously agreed-upon protocol" (*The Differend* 4), a matter of "phrases in dispute," would seem to be an ideal candidate for Booth's "irrationalist" club, opting for value independent of fact. However, when it comes to language, Lyotard's faith in the separability of genres produces a very traditional duality of fact and value, in which Levinas's "prescriptive" or value-laden message is inevitably reduced to the "denotative" language associated with the "fact" side of the split: "But when the initial message is prescriptive, it seems inevitable that the commentary, being denotative, displaces the message's own genre. . . . How does Levinas's commentary on this situation, a situation incommensurable with denotations, escape the trap of denotative metalanguage?" ("Levinas's Logic" 282, 308).

The dialectical procedure of a Marxist critic such as Terry Eagleton takes the derivation of value from fact as an article of faith—values are always grounded somehow in material practices—but at the same time it is the inevitable function of ideology to obscure that relation. As he says in his discussion of Kant's rational ethics, "[v]alues do not flow from facts, in the sense that ideologies are intended not simply to reflect existing social behavior, but to mystify and legitimate it" (*The Ideology of the Aesthetic* 82). Despite the inescapability of ideology in its universal, Althusserian form, the demystifying critic often grants himself an exceptional access to what Jameson calls the "fact" of the "repressed and buried reality of" a "fundamental history" (20).

Perhaps the most common variant of the fact/value derivation or split in literary criticism appears in the vexed relationship between the description of literary facts and various evaluations of their value. In the early part of this century the distinction between description and evaluation showed up in the division of labor between "scholars" who described texts and "critics" who evaluated them.[2] What counts as a "fact" to be described has changed with successive generations of critics, and texts have been evaluated accordingly, based on how well they could be described within a formalist, and later a deconstructive or psychoanalytic paradigm. Lately history has returned, descriptions have become "thick" and anecdotal—

but just as authoritative—and evaluation has moved from the aesthetic to the political. A good example of how the relationship between description and evaluation is used to maintain fact and value in distinct but hierarchically related spheres (even as the objectivist version of the distinction is critiqued) is Barbara Herrnstein Smith's characterization of the relativist as a moral agent. Her view suggests that as moral agents we "evaluate" conditions that we can describe (or at least "perceive" and "interpret" [164]), but that we already recognize as contingent, and that are therefore subject to no higher law than our own act of evaluation. Smith is careful to dissociate this act from autonomous subjectivity (11, 30–32), seeing it instead as operating within an economic model of social interaction. She elides the fact/value distinction in one sense by equating perception, interpretation, and evaluation, discussing "the specific, contingent *conditions* in which [one] operates as an agent, as she perceives, interprets, and considers those conditions—or, in short, *evaluates* them (164). However, it is hard to see how her model can work without a clear separation between the fact of the "contingent *conditions*" and the value of the agent's—even the socially constructed agent's—act of evaluation. Booth, arguing from the opposite, positivist corner, makes a much stronger argument for the synthesis of fact and value, arguing that description always entails evaluation: "even the simplest story cannot be *described* without employing the language of value, the value of its realizing or failing to realize itself: minimally, to become *this story*" (*The Company We Keep* 92).

The problem with this emphasis on "evaluation," whether in Smith's relativist or Booth's positivist version, is that, although it may reflect a literary critic's view of moral life, it is a narrow one. As I argued in Chapter 2, "evaluation" tends, even in Booth's argument, to be the evaluation of technique, thus restricting ethical criticism to the realm of *techne* and denying the claims of *phronesis*. To reduce moral agency to evaluation—particularly aesthetic evaluation—is to miss Julius Kovesi's point that "evaluation," in which we make judgments based on the description of an "is," (as when we call someone a good liar) "is quite neutral to morals. We can and do evaluate both what we value and what we detest" (14). Because evaluation can adopt any criteria, moral, immoral, or amoral, it preempts discussion of the Good, allowing the inescapable moral frameworks that Taylor discusses to remain unacknowledged as we go about our evaluative business. Even the inescapable literary-critical frameworks remain unacknowledged, as evidenced by the rapid shifts in such frameworks, with a corresponding rise and fall in the critical stock of authors. The

New Critics exalted Donne and Keats over Milton and Wordsworth according to the criteria of complexity and ambiguity, until phenomenology, deconstruction, and psychoanalysis rediscovered unconscious subtexts in the latter poets. More recently, ideological and feminist criticisms of the canon make strong, explicitly ethical evaluative claims, refashioning the canon to fit contemporary values, while changing the status of the literary "fact" from an intentional or linguistic object to a cultural artifact. Little attention is paid to the tension between the move toward cultural empiricism on the fact side of the split and toward cultural relativism on the value side.

The concept of evaluation, as inevitable as it is, particularly in the process of reading that forms an essential part of both the authoring and the reception of a text, thus provides only a relatively thin account of moral life, and consequently an incomplete picture of the ethical relations both within a literary text and in our relation to it. In Booth's argument, for example, the price of identifying ethical criticism with evaluation is that "character" is identified with "craft" in the act of reading: "[a]s we stretch our own poetic character to meet the implied character of the maker, we do not say that his craft is one thing and his character another; instead we feel that we are meeting the character as we take in the craft" (*The Company We Keep* 107). Bernard Williams argues rightly that ethical theorists, particularly those who see ethics as embedded in language, import distinctions such as that between "fact" and "value," "is" and "ought," when what they should be finding are "thicker" notions of both reflective and nonreflective ethical "knowledge" (*Ethics* 129–52).

The fact-value debate is further complicated by the historical conditions in which it has occurred. Not only do moral choices and debates about them occur within Taylor's inescapable moral frameworks that change over time and often remain unacknowledged, but, as G. E. M. Anscombe, Alasdair MacIntyre, and others have argued, the terms we use often depend for their meaning on contexts that we no longer consider viable. Anscombe argues, for example, that the very term "ought" is bound to be incoherent in ethical debate since Hume because it is meaningful only in the context of divine law issuing an unquestionable imperative (180–81). MacIntyre cites Anscombe approvingly and adds that we have impoverished our sense of agency by discarding, in addition to divine law, the moral psychology that would ground a theory of virtues and the good as we embrace a scientific empiricism. The result has been an incoherent division between reductive notions of fact and choice—we establish the "facts," then make "choices"—when in fact moral choices are not independent of how we see the facts ("Moral Philosophy: What Next?" 11–12).[3]

How facts are seen is itself problematic, as Norris's objections to descriptivism, discussed in the previous chapter, suggest. Norris is not arguing against the fact/value distinction—in fact, part of his project is to reinforce Kant's distinction between "truths of experience" and aesthetic or ethical judgments (*What's Wrong With Postmodernism* 275)—but his critique of descriptivism's insistence on a homology between experience and conceptual structures nonetheless suggests a problem with the way the "fact" side of the fact/value distinction is presented in some recent theory.

Sabina Lovibond suggests that "it is really the segregation of 'reason' and 'sentiment', or 'reason' and 'passion', in the faculty psychology of the eighteenth century which has been perpetuated in the 'fact/value distinction' of modern analytical philosophy" (22). Coleridge worked to bridge the gap between the sentimental ethics of Shaftesbury and the rational ethics of Kant, and those efforts speak to the twentieth-century effects of the fact/value distinction. The same kind of reasoning that enabled Coleridge to critique descriptivism while preserving a kind of empiricism allows him to preserve a strong sense of "ought" without depending on the fact/value distinction or falling into Lyotardian paradox.

II. "Is" Derived from "Ought"

If Being is the expression of God's willed ethical act, and if our activity is a finite repetition of the divine, then it looks as if, far from deriving ethical "oughts" from statements about how the world "is," Coleridge sees the "is" as an expression of a super-"ought." This follows Coleridge's Kantian/Christian respect for the fundamentality of the moral law coming from the unconditioned. It is in this spirit, however, that Coleridge sees a contradiction in Kant's argument for a self-originating concept of duty, a concept based on the assumption that, since law assumes that the obligating subject can release the obligated subject from duty, the self could release the self. Coleridge counters: "This seems a confusion of juridical general Law ~~of M~~ with the Moral Law—For in the latter how & in what instance can the Auctor Obligationis release the Subjectum Obligationis from the Obligation? Can the Law of Conscience release the Mind from obeying ~~its~~ a Law of conscience? Can God release a creature from the Obligation of obeying his Laws—i.e. infinite Wisdom permit Folly, Holiness Impurity?" (*CM* 3: 267).

This distinction between the subjective contingency of juridical law and the absolute, other-originating command of moral law enables him to escape Anscombe's critique of Hume. Unlike twentieth-century analytical philosophers, Coleridge embraces the concept of absolute divine law that gives "ought" its intelligibility. If one version of our finite repetition of divine creativity is that conscience, defined as the relation to particular others, is the ground of consciousness, then the particular "oughts" of human ethical relations cannot be viewed as dependent on consciousness of an "is," but rather the reverse: the self-consciousness that is the source of all knowledge, including that of the "is," stems from the moral relations to others that we "ought" to have. This position gives universal scope to the "ought." Countering Schelling's implicit distinction between morality and religion, Coleridge asks rhetorically, "Can any thing be right and lovely, and not included in the Ich soll [I ought]?" (*CM* 4: 349). In this sense "fact" and "value" are not homologous with "material" and "rational," so it is not simply a matter of exalting rational value in order to obscure or legitimate a particular relation to material practice, as in Eagleton's reading of Kant (*The Ideology of the Aesthetic* 82–84). If "value" is put in terms of the commanded "ought," both the material and the rational are subservient to that command. The "law of reason" must serve our "moral being," because "the duties which we owe to our own moral being, are the ground and condition of all other duties" (*The Friend* 1: 38). This reversal of priority also expands the moral far beyond the notion of "ought" to include, for Coleridge, God's redemptive act of creating everything that "is."

Coleridge's sense that the world is not to be "known" but interpreted by an imaginative process that repeats the very act of the world's creation, combined with his sense that Being itself is the result of a divine, compensatory act of creation, supports this notion that the "is" is fundamentally derivative in relation to a moral act, and therefore that Being itself is closer to an "act" than a "thing." One effect of this perception of the "is" as an expression of "ought" (as creation is the expression of the Logos) is to deny a difference in kind between "is" and "ought," without denying the priority of "ought." This denial is supported by Coleridge's ethical and hermeneutic (as opposed to atomistic and descriptivist) view of the world; if language, defined on the finite level in terms of cultural dialogue, shares in the constitutive status of ideas, on the analogy of the creative force of God's Word, then to understand what "is" by engaging in that creative language shares in the "ought" of both language's ethical/cultural constitution and God's creative decree.[4]

The notion that the "is" is derived from a command from the unconditioned can easily flip over into a postmodern view of the world, as when Derrida argues that the notion that "nothing *exists* outside context" depends on "an injunction, a law, a responsibility that transcends this or that determination of a given context," adding that "[t]his unconditionality also defines the injunction that prescribes deconstruction" (*Limited Inc* 152–53). Coleridge does not take this route because the anti-atomistic vitalism of his characterization of the natural world allows that world to retain its autonomy (including its dialectical opposition to moral life in its lack of self-consciousness[5]) while sharing in the same forces of polarity and individuation that help to make up human consciousness. This combination of autonomy and sharing makes the natural world look more like a participant in hermeneutic interaction than an object of potentially adequate or inadequate description.

Despite his early admiration for Berkeley, the world does exist for Coleridge outside the context of linguistic or social constructs. The natural world does not need to be a creation of human language because Nature utters "the language of God himself" (*Theory of Life, SW & F* 486), a point made much earlier in "Frost at Midnight," where the forms of nature are described as "that eternal language, which thy God / Utters" (58–59). This complex relation between nature and culture is one reason that, as Karl Kroeber says, "The romantics would not wish to contradict the current critical banality that 'nature' is a social construct (an idea that was already a commonplace to Buffon in the eighteenth century). They would regard the assertion as question-begging, however, because they believed that human consciousness (and the social constructs made possible by it) is a result of natural processes" (*Ecological Literary Criticism* 17). Coleridge, of course, would change these terms slightly to say that human consciousness and its attendant social constructs share in the same process of creation that produced nature, a process that, as *natura naturans* ("nature naturing") rather than *natura naturata* ("nature natured"),[6] looks more like human consciousness than unconscious nature.

Although Coleridge's theories of the relation between the "is" and the divine command were not worked out in detail until well after 1797–98, when Coleridge was working on the *Rime of the Ancient Mariner,* some of the basic elements can be found even in the famously obtrusive "moral" of the Rime:

> He prayeth best who loveth best,
> All things both great and small:
> For the dear God, who loveth us,
> He made and loveth all.
>
> (660–63)

For God to have "made" the "is" of the world is inseparable from his ethical act of love, since creation itself is the ethical, redemptive act of will. Prayer to the Absolute is inseparable from the particular love of the entire range of particular creation, and that particular love repeats the divine act of love. The moral is simultaneously a particular "ought"-laden command to the Wedding Guest—"Farewell, farewell! but this I tell / To thee, thou wedding guest!" (656–57)—and a description of what good prayer-life "is."

If the world is derived from a divine ethical act ultimately indivisible from the "is" of the world, it follows for Coleridge that ethical life is learned by the imitation of particular moral example; ultimately, for Coleridge, this is the "repetition in the finite mind" of the absolute example of the "infinite I AM": one approaches divinity by means of such moral example, and especially not by means of the separated "is" of the physical world: "The voice both of philosophy and religion teaches us man can become like his Maker only by imitation of his goodness, only morally, but these men [those who combined philosophy with magic] taught that there were modes by which physically man could be taken into the Godhead, and the consequence was the most fearful superstition that can be imagined" (*P Lects* 250–51).[7]

Such "modes" of physical incorporation into God would reduce moral and spiritual life to teachable technique, as in the promise held out by various modern cults that the observance of particular teachable practices will lead directly to spritual fulfillment. The teachability of *techne* as opposed to the necessity of example in ethics is a distinction that goes back to Plato; as Gadamer puts it, "In a certain sense the problem at the core of all education is, after all, the fact that unlike the technai, arete is not teachable. Traditional ethical and moral customs are based not so much on teaching and learning as on taking someone as an example and emulating that example" (*The Idea of the Good* 46). In the marginal gloss to the Mariner's "moral" (added in the 1817 version, when Coleridge's logos-philosophy was much more fully developed) the Mariner is said to "teach, by his own example" (gloss to 614–21). In Coleridge's notes on Kant's *Die Religion innerhalb der Grenzen der blössen Vernunft,* he speaks of the "influence of Example, of Education, in short of all the administrants and auxiliaries of the will" (*CM* 3:311) as an analogy for the possibility, contra Kant, of both phenomenal and noumenal supernatural influence on the will. This example-knowledge is not subject to Kant's rules of access that would allow phenomenal knowledge but deny noumenal knowledge: we can follow even God's example (and thus have real *phronesis*) without claiming the knowledge of *techne* or *episteme* that gets us into Kantian trouble, just as the Wedding Guest can follow the Mariner's example without claiming to "know" the inaccessible world he has described. In referential terms, the example follows the logic of the Coleridgean symbol, which "always partakes of the Reality which it renders intelligible" (*LS* 30). As Altieri points out, following Nelson Goodman, "an example is any sign that involves in its signification the properties it can be said to possess" (*Subjective Agency* 119). Thus this notion of "example" effects a continuity between noumenal and phenomenal and makes ethical effect coequal with ethical existence. The fact or "is" of the Mariner's example is inseparable from the "ought" or value he teaches; the latter is not derived from the former.

III. The Ethical Demand of Narrative

Paradoxically, the very denial of the is/ought distinction effected by Coleridge's hermeneutic theory of the world, a theory that unites knowing, interpretation, and creation as a fundamentally moral act prior to the "is," forces the distinction to reappear as a function of the interpretive narrative necessarily privileged by that hermeneutic view.[8] God's act of self-expression and self-othering, expressed in the Logos of John's gospel, is the ground of our ethical being, because that divine act is God's response to human apostacy and the beginning of salvation history. That act is also a model for our self-understanding, and that self-understanding involves an ethical version of the hermeneutic circle in which we understand ourselves and become ethically self-conscious beings (which for Coleridge is more or less the same thing) by means of interacting with both internal and external others. Understanding is thus always existentially historical, and never rationally autonomous in the Cartesian sense, because it depends on a world of others—both God and other humans—who are always already there. Coleridge suggests in a notebook entry that our "Being"—our self-consciousness—is posterior to our existence. While comparing "the human Soul to a . . . Ship's Crew cast on an unknown Island," after which the "shipwrecked man" is "stunned, & for many weeks in a State of Ideotcy or utter loss of Thought & Memory—& then gradually awakened," he observes, "The moment, when the Soul begins to be sufficiently self-conscious, to ask concerning itself, & its relations, is the first moment of its *intellectual* arrival into the World—Its *Being*—enigmatic as it must seem—is posterior to its *Existence*" (*CN* 3: 3593).[9] Our "intellectual" arrival coincides with the soul's recognition of "itself, & its relations" as matters for self-conscious questioning. As Gadamer phrases this existential insight, "There is always a world already interpreted, already organized in its basic relations, into which experience steps as something new" (*Philosophical Hermeneutics* 15).

For Coleridge, the historical others who populate the world of relations to which we "awaken" cannot be sharply distinguished from others in fictional narratives. Historical understanding is partly a matter of imagining or re-imagining others rather than reconstructing them. As Coleridge says of Milton's expansion of a few lines of *Genesis,* in Collier's account of Lecture 9 of the 1811-12 *Lectures on Shakespeare and Milton,* "It is idle to say then that this or that is improbable because history says that the fact is so. The story on which Milton has founded his Paradise Lost is comprized in the Bible in four or five lines & the Poet has substituted the faith of the mind to regard as true what would otherwise have appeared absurdity" (*Lects 1808-1819* 1: 363). Also, part of task of ethical understanding is to speculate on potential rather than real others, and to imagine ourselves *as* others, as past and future selves. In connecting selfishness with the despotism of the present, Coleridge argues for an ethical link, via the concept of self, between the relation to one's neighbor and to one's imagined future self: "My Neighbor is my *other* Self, *othered* by Space—my old age is to my youth an other Self, *othered* by Time" (*CN* 3: 4017).

Because Coleridge sees this hermeneutic, historical engagement in the world of others as ethically defined—it is the other-directed "conscience" that sustains self-consciousness—acts of understanding are ethical all the way down, and the "is" cannot be isolated as a neutral Archimedean point from which an ethical "ought" can be derived. But if this hermeneutic understanding of the world is for Coleridge in some respects ethical, the converse is also true: we become ethical beings not by simply following a moral law, but by engaging in this hermeneutic relationship, by orienting ourselves toward historical others. And that hermeneutic relationship is pursued partly through narratives, because it is the kind of understanding that works by telling the story of our engagement with others. But, as Coleridge believed (much more strongly than most of us do, given his suspicions of fiction and the centrality of the novel in later nineteenth- and twentieth-century critical discourse), telling a story is not the same as living a life. As Ricoeur points out, the fact that "in our experience the life history of each of us is caught up in the histories of others" is one of the ways in which "life histories differ from literary ones" (*Oneself* 161). The ethical demands of narrative are different from the ethical demand of life in general, even if ethical life is deeply sustained by narrative understanding.

If evaluation is "quite neutral to morals" in general, it is not at all neutral to the ethics of autobiographical narratives, particularly narratives of conversion, of which the Mariner's tale is a strange kind of example. Precisely because ethical thought refers to a life that is constituted by a host of ethical and nonethical thoughts, expressions, and decisions, in which evaluations, descriptions, and other forms of expression are not separated, autobiography has traditionally had to do the work of providing an "evaluation" of that life in ethical terms. In their classic form, such conversion-autobiographies present one's past life as an "is" that is evaluated over the course of the narrative in order to serve as an exemplary "ought" for the reader. Augustine evaluates his past to say that we ought not to live a life like that he had lived before his conversion, and Wordsworth's self-evaluation in the *Prelude* presents as exemplary his conversion from a political to an imaginative concept of liberty. Such a layer of evaluation is usually necessary to justify the existence of the autobiographical narrative. In the 1805 version of the *Prelude* Wordsworth worried whether his post-*Prelude* work would be, as he says, "Sufficient to excuse me in men's sight / For having given this record of myself" (*Thirteen-Book Prelude* [A-B Stage Reading Text] 13: 388–89); it can be justified only as a "gift" (*Fourteen-Book Prelude* 14: 417) to Coleridge, a gift whose preservation of mutual exemplary memories, including the memory of the *Rime*'s composition (14: 401–2), offers the possibility that "the history of a Poet's mind / Is labour not unworthy of regard" (414–15).

Earlier I suggested that Coleridge's ethical thought resists a hard and fast distinction between "is" and "ought." However, a version of the is/ought distinction reappears in interpretive moral narratives such as the *Rime* in a way that shows the inevitability of the distinction in a conversion narrative. This may help explain why, despite all the reasons I have discussed for the merging of "is" and "ought," Coleridge nonetheless argues in his *Opus Maximum*, as Lockridge points out, for a sharp distinction between the language of "ought" and "is," because moral judgments require an act of assent not required by empirical judgments, and empirical judgments may be revised by reconsideration of evidence while authentic moral judgments "can be denied only by an 'act of mind' that separates us from the entire grammar of morality" (*The Ethics of Romanticism* 150).

Harpham argues that the analytical or interpretive process by which "ought" is derived from "is"—a process of repression and evaluation in which one text drives another down to a secondary level—is not easily avoided, at least where a certain kind of narrative is concerned: "[T]he production of the *ought* out of the *is* entails the imposition of a repressive force that . . . drives the primary text down to a position of secondary dependence: the truth of the primary can only be delivered by a secondary text that represses the "evaluation" that constituted the primary text" (*Getting it Right* 142). Such narratives, according to Harpham, derive some sort of "ought" from the evaluation of an "is," an evaluation that must repressively reconstruct the evaluated text *as* an "is" rather than as a prior layer of evaluation. Thus a "moral" narrative like the Mariner's seems inevitably to encounter problems of evaluation associated with the move from "is" to "ought," if only because the narrative needs to distinguish between the experience (the "is") and the telling (which in a moral tale produces the "ought"). This suggests both the inevitability and the undesirability of the evaluative "ought" proceeding from the "is" of what should be a "work of . . . pure Imagination" (*TT* 1: 149), but Coleridge cannot even object to this situation without saying "ought": the *Rime* "ought to have had no more moral" than the tale from *The Arabian Nights* (1:273). This gives an ethical cast to the difference that Benveniste presented semiotically as the tension between *histoire* and *discours,* between the past otherness of the narrated tale (the supposedly neutral given of the "is") and the dialogic present of the act of narrating (the "ought," whose utterance requires the presence of an auditor, in this case the Wedding Guest).[10]

The layers of interpretive texts surrounding the Ancient Mariner's autobiographical tale demonstrate a compulsive tendency to "evaluate" experience as an "is" separated from a posterior "ought." The Mariner underwent an experience that redefined the "is" of his life into a constant repetition of the narrative evaluation performed by the conversion narrative. However, the very compulsiveness of his lifelong repetition of the tale itself prevents him from translating the is-ought structure into real ethical life: he imagines a stroll "to the Kirk / With a goodly company" (*Rime* 649–50), but the Mariner tells his story *instead* of living a life. He also pulls the Wedding Guest out of the world of marriage-feasts to redefine his "is"—he becomes "A sadder and a wiser man" (670)—based on the emphatic "ought" of the Mariner's story. In Harpham's terms, the secondary text of the Mariner's moral injunction to the Wedding Guest represses the moral ambiguity of the experience at sea (turning it into an "is" available for moral evaluation), and the marginal gloss repeats the process of repression in an even more overt process of analysis.[11] This process is in a radical tension with the fact that the narrative's "is"—the "content" of the story—is a world of strange and unpredictable "oughts" wildly disconnected from any known "is." This world, directed by powers appearing from nowhere, in which the empirical causality assumed by the crew's contradictory interpretations of the Mariner's act (91–102) is exposed as absurdly inappropriate, is a world in which "ought"-related acts, be they acts of killing birds, propelling ships, dicing for a human life, or blessing snakes, take priority over any describable reality. It is such a frightening world to visit and such a difficult world to return from partly because the Mariner must speak a narrative language in which the autobiographical narrative progression from "is" to "ought" is forcibly contradicted by an experience that denies such a progression.

Harpham suggests that the narrative construction of the is/ought split always follows a logic of conversion: "In the scene of analysis, there is nothing but conversion. If a general commandment governing every element in this scene—perhaps the general commandment of 'ethics itself'—were to be formulated, it could be stated thus: Become what you are (not)" (*Getting it Right* 146). On the one hand, as M. H. Abrams has shown, the conversion experience is essential to Coleridge ("Coleridge and the Romantic Vision of the World" 108–16). As Stephen Knapp points out, Coleridge parallels his own experience of "my final reconversion to the whole truth in Christ" with Augustine's in the *Biographia* (*BL* 1:205, qtd. Knapp 45), and Tilottama Rajan asserts that "[t]he *Biographia* is . . . a conversion narrative" (*The Supplement of Reading* 105). However, Coleridge also protests in the same work that his "principles of *politics*" and his "principles of *taste*" had not changed (*BL* 2:208), arguing instead for their continuity in the face of charges of apostacy, conversion's evil twin. In this sense, Coleridge self-consciously avoids the kind of conversion narrative associated with Augustine or even Wordsworth, in which past experience tends to become a series of facts correctly evaluated by one who has been converted from that experience.[12] Perhaps it is just this ambivalence toward the structure Harpham identifies that produces such strange, truncated versions of the repression/conversion process in Coleridge. In *Christabel* the only correct interpreter of dreams and potential vehicle for conversion (the poet Bracy) is ignored, and the Law of the Father replaces/represses all other experiential narratives with an "ought" (we ought to help Geraldine) composed of a distorted mix of lust, nostalgia, and the fatherly anger analyzed so ambiguously in the "Conclusion to Part II." For the poet of "Kubla Khan" to "revive" the damsel's song is not to figure it as a past "is," but hubristically to repeat the process of creation, and therefore to become the demonic poet at the poem's end. Coleridge's poetry is of course full of self-recrimination, but instead of the retrospective evaluation of the convert (as in Wordsworth's judgments of his youthful desires in the *Prelude*), we find either an external reproof of dubious credibility, as in Sarah's sudden appearance at the end of "The Eolian Harp," or a present self-accusation with only a dim hope for conversion, as in "The Pains of Sleep."

The *Rime* is perhaps as close as Coleridge ever gets to a true conversion narrative, and were the Mariner's conversion experience like that of Augustine, the poet of the *Prelude,* or even Blake's Milton, all of whom evaluate past experience from a "converted" standpoint, Coleridge would be open to the critique of Christian hermeneutics brought by Jill Robbins. She argues that the hermeneutically fundamental Christian conversion narrative acts as a totalizing suppression of Hebrew alterity, on the model of the New Testament's figuring of the Hebrew Bible as the "Old" Testament: "the partial view of the experiencing subject, blinded by sin, is contrasted with the totalizing viewpoint of the converted narrator, for whom every sinful moment prior to conversion can be understood *as* sin prior to grace" (*Prodigal Son* 24). However, as Knapp points out, the converted point of view for Coleridge is not simply a totalizing subjectivity, because conversion is "a movement from the empirical individuality of subjective error to the collective identity of suprapersonal reason or truth" (45), a movement away from subjectivity itself.

The *Rime* fits Robbins's critique even less than Knapp's general characterization of Coleridge suggests, because there is no resting place in "suprapersonal reason or truth."[13] The "converted" narrator is doomed to repeat not just the narrative of his conversion, but the unpredictable process of agony and liberation:

> Since then, at an uncertain hour,
> That agony returns;
> And till my ghastly tale is told,
> This heart within me burns.
> ([1817] 586–89)

As has often been noted, the Mariner tells a story about agonized suffering and release, including thirst followed by self-sacrificial release and hope (149–53) and the work of Death and Life-In-Death followed by the blessing of the water-snakes (201–93), and the telling itself is a similar experience of repeated agony and freedom. Thus the "converted" Mariner is less like the smug Christian of Robbins's model, who builds a new

Testament by suppressing and reconstructing the old, than he is (to use an analogy perhaps not inappropriate to the addicted Coleridge) like a recovering alcoholic who, though "converted" to sobriety, must painfully reenact that conversion daily, and often in narrative form. To invoke a distinction that Irving Massey makes in another context, Robbins's Christian hermeneutics of conversion is always "retrospective," implying a totalizing vision, whereas the *Rime*'s conversion, despite the Mariner's retrospectively summary moral, is equally "prospective," unpredictably subject to repetition at any time (11–12). Even if the poem's layers of repetition and interpretation impose the retrospective "ought" of Christian conversion, when "the agony returns" only "at an uncertain hour" the repetition is just the opposite, anticipated with the uncertainty of a "prospective" temporality.

The possibility of the kind of salvation recorded in Christian conversion stories is of course part of the *Rime*'s structure, particularly in the gloss, and Coleridge was solidly Christian in his interpretation of the Hebrew Bible as fulfilled by the New Testament. However, we become sadder as we become wiser because conversion is also repetition, not just retelling, of particular experience: the "repetition in the finite mind of the eternal act of creation in the infinite I AM" (*BL* 1:304) can lead, in our finite realm, to a repetition compulsion: Mariners compulsively grabbing Wedding Guests, or poets repeating damsels' tales only to become demons, or good and prayerful Christabels imitating snake-eyed Geraldines. The reader is not merely "deluded" by the poem's epistemological and ethical uncertainty, as Frances Ferguson argues in "Coleridge and the Deluded Reader," but rather forced to confront *both* the retrospective, Christian hermeneutics of conversion and the prospective, experiential, particular repetition of agony and release.

IV. Narrative and Freedom

The inevitability of narrative's engagement with the is/ought distinction is problematic for Coleridge. On the one hand, as Ricoeur points out, narrative presents a "concept of dynamic identity which reconciles the same categories that Locke took as contraries: identity and diversity" (*Oneself* 143). This is also an important Coleridgean principle, since, according to *The Theory of Life*, this is the story told by life itself, in its dialectic of "individuation" and "attachment," and the narrative side of his poetry directly confronts the complex relationship between the narratives that help to structure ethical life and the narratives of art. However, unlike our contemporaries, he saw narrative as a lesser literary genre. Narrative, the aspect of imaginative literature valued so highly by Ricoeur, Nussbaum, MacIntyre and others, is for Coleridge only the necessary background, not the primary means, of art: "the great men of former times . . . seemed to have regarded the *story* in a not much higher light, than the painter regards his canvass: as that *on,* not *by,* which they were to display their appropriate excellence" (*BL* 2: 187). Coleridge would perhaps have viewed our post-Freudian assumption that the self is structured along narrative lines as a self-deceptive universalization of a minor aesthetic principle, which makes for a relationship between narrative and freedom that complicates and challenges some aspects of modern narrative theory.

The *Rime* straddles Ricoeur's categories of narrative's imaginative freedom and life's demand for ethical responsibility, which may help explain both Coleridge's addition of the gloss's interpretive layers, as an attempt to grant the poem a narrative self-sufficiency, and his own identification with the Mariner's plight as an analogue to his own life-history. For Ricoeur, narrative mediates between what he calls "*idem-*" and "*ipse*-identity." These terms will be important later, once we begin to address more directly the problem of subjectivity in Coleridge; for now it is sufficient to understand *ipse*-identity as the first-person intending or phenomenological self, whose goal is self-constancy, and *idem*-identity as third-person "character," or the self seen from the outside as objective and permanent. According to Ricoeur, narrative translates *ipse* to *idem,* as the self's aims are given the objectivity of narrative form: "In narrativizing the aim [self-constancy or *ipse*-identity] of the true life, narrative identity gives it the recognizable features [permanence in time or *idem*-identity] of characters loved or respected" (*Oneself* 166).[14]

However, Ricoeur also notes that the artificial narratives of literature present their own difficulties. These stem partly from narrative's freedom to swing either to the *idem*-pole of science fiction, in which identity is typecast as "of a piece with the impersonal treatment of identity on the conceptual level" (*Oneself* 150) or, at the opposite extreme, the "unsettling" modern narratives in which the objective support of "character" is removed, "exposing selfhood by taking away the support of sameness" (149). Focusing on the latter kind of narrative, Ricoeur translates the gap between "narrative identity and moral identity" into a "fruitful tension" (167) by setting up a new version of the *ipse-idem* dialectic between the imaginative freedom of narrative to say "I can try anything" (including trying to dissolve the self) and the subject's moral fixity as one "who has been made responsible by the expectation of the other" (168).

Ricoeur's terms suggest a certain ethical freedom in narrative, but one that comes with a price. Wayne Booth suggests a reader's version of Ricoeur's "I can try anything," seeing one of the ethical functions of fiction as the opportunity to try on various roles: "I should be able to embrace the unquestioned ethical power of narratives, in order to try on for size the character roles offered me" (*The Company We Keep* 268). But the freedom of narrative to avoid the causality that operates outside of narrative, a causality that severely limits our ability to "try on for size" various roles, can become tyrannical as narrative imposes its own rules while mimicking the causality of life outside of narrative. In the *Rime,* for example, the question of whether the Mariner must speak his agonizing tale because of his trauma or whether this trauma results from the evaluative drive of narrative itself is unanswerable, partly because of narrative's freedom to avoid that extraliterary notion of causality while seeming to imitate it. This blurring of the line between fact and fiction is Coleridge's main objection to the genre of the novel, as I will discuss in more detail in the next chapter: for him this kind of narrative freedom approaches morally suspicious license.

The freedom of narrative is also difficult simply because freedom is difficult. Levinas discusses the easily forgotten "arbitrariness of freedom, which is precisely what has to be grounded. . . . To welcome the Other is to put in question my freedom" (*TI* 85).[15] The British Romantics saw in the French Revolution and its aftermath how easily freedom, particularly if grounded in an Enlightenment concept of the free use of instrumental reason, can become arbitrary tyranny. Even Wordsworth, who is perhaps closest to the Kantian sublime in affirming the freedom of self-consciousness, as in the "Imagination" passage in Book 6 of the *Prelude,* was clearly aware of the potential tyranny of ungrounded liberty, as I have discussed elsewhere in the context of his suspicion of the tyranny of the eye and associated rationalist conceptual systems.[16] For Coleridge, who was much less confident than Wordsworth in individual selves, however much he promoted the idea of self-consciousness, the sublime meant, as Raimonda Modiano puts it, "not the attainment of personal power but the absorption into a higher unity" (122). Similarly, Shelley's idea of liberty was grounded on a denial of the always tyrannical individual, creative will, and Blake's Fourfold Man rejected the tyranny of a singular conceptual position.

Coleridge was aware that to ground freedom in otherness—to ground self-consciousness in "conscience"—involves giving up the autonomy of the individual self. The "freedom" to rebuild Kubla's dome and its environs leads to a recognition of that freedom's violence, which, when contained by the frightened spectators who cry "beware!," becomes alienation. The intending, creating poet who wants to revive the damsel's song ("freely" "trying on" the song of another person and another gender) becomes an extremely "other" third-person "character" whose flashing eyes and floating hair mark his isolation within the thrice-woven circle. Thus it is not simply, as in Ricoeur, a tension between the freedom to "try anything" and the expectations of others. As in the paradox of language's "barrel-organ" function, where poetic freedom is thwarted by its own history, narrative freedom from the start requires the appropriation of both events and narratives that belong to someone else, in this case, Kubla's actions and the damsel's "symphony and song." The damsel's music is borrowed from the poet's own vision, of course, but that vision is paradoxically characterized in the poem's introduction as having been received, interrupted, and even published due to forces outside of the poet's control. All this suggests both the illusoriness of a "pure" concept of freedom and the potential for violence in the individual will: one of Coleridge's definitions of evil is "Will that would manifest itself as Will, not in Being," with "Being" here defined as *Ετερότης* or "otherness." By denying the claims of that otherness the evil will "shrink[s] inward, if so it might itself remain the One, by recoiling from the One" (*CN* 4: 5076), engaging in the contradictory effort to usurp the absolute freedom of the divine will.

Turning to the other narrative extreme identified by Ricoeur—science fiction's "technological dream" that treats identity impersonally as "sameness"—we see that Coleridge complicates this side of the picture as well. One of Coleridge's arguments *against* narrative, at least in its modern emphasis on contingency and specificity, is that literature should deal with the ideal, not the individual: "the *persons* of poetry must be clothed with *generic* attributes" (*BL* 2: 46). Coleridge, unlike Wordsworth, thus wants to engage the side of narrative of which Ricoeur disapproves, in which individual *ipse*-identity is de-emphasized in favor of the generic, publicly defined "character" of *idem*-identity. We tend to think of subjectivity in novelistic terms as the *individual* subject, while for Coleridge subjectivity is a *generic* attribute of human self-consciousness. Thus the Mariner is a "Mariner," not a named individual, constituted by layers of publicly defined literary convention, and he functions as an example, not as one individual speaking to another.

However, the difficulty of preserving this ideal sense of third-person character makes the *Rime* swing to the opposite extreme, resembling one of Ricoeur's limit cases of first-person or *ipse*-identity. In the *Rime,* as in Musil's *The Man Without Qualities,* and as in "the nights of personal identity" in many conversion narratives, "The self refigured . . . here by the narrative is in reality confronted with the hypothesis of its own nothingness" (*Oneself* 166). In Ricoeur's terms, this is "a self deprived of the help of sameness" (*Oneself* 166), or the stability of identifiable "character." Coleridge emphasizes this deprivation by having the Hermit ask a question whose answer should be a statement of one's "character": "What manner man art thou?" (*Rime* 623). The "answer" of course, is nothing of the kind:

> Forthwith this frame of mine was wrench'd
>   With a woeful agony,
> Which forc'd me to begin my tale
>   And then it left me free.
>
> (624–27)

Instead of identifying what kind of character he is by invoking a category that would give him an identifiable sameness, the Mariner's "frame" is "wrench'd." His very body, the outward manifestation of character, is taken from his control, and he tells his tale of how his identity was reduced to practically nothing. He is left "free" not in the positive sense of a free rational agent who can adopt the retrospective point of view of the Christian convert, but only in the negative sense of being temporarily released from the external control of his traumatic past.

In complaining to Coleridge that his poem lacked a moral, Mrs. Barbauld wanted him to produce an aesthetic ideology, by means of which ethical life could be given an aesthetic form. Coleridge, who knew, tragically, that art could not structure life, refused, complaining that the poem had too much of a moral. The poem itself suggests both the narrative inevitability and the experiential insufficiency of the description/evaluation, is/ought pair, as well as the difficulties that attend the narrative "freedom" advocated by Booth and Ricoeur, and thus the real moral for us may be to suggest the complexity of the relationship between lived experience and its transformation into literary structure. I will explore this issue in the next chapter in terms of Coleridge's own literary and dramatic criticism.

5

Literary Criticism and Moral Philosophy

Despite Coleridge's reputation as a progenitor of both Romantic aestheticism and modern formalism, his literary criticism is a prime example of the kind of "ethical" criticism called for by Booth and others. His concern for what Booth calls "the ethical powers of form" (*The Company We Keep* 7) resembles many of the ethical concerns about both popular and "serious" art voiced today, more often outside of the academy than within. He was concerned with the effect of imaginative literature on the young, the effect on the populace of works presented to large crowds in public spaces, and the role of the media in shaping public ethics. His concerns for the ethical dimensions of art and art's interpretation stem from at least three sources: his place in a tradition that had never stopped granting an ethical role to the aesthetic; his participation, with Wordsworth, in a post-Revolutionary aesthetic program that would humanize an increasingly rationalized and technological world order; and his effort to establish a connection between art and religion at the deepest level of human consciousness and culture. Precisely because the aesthetic had for him such a self-evident ethical role, he avoided the twin twentieth-century temptations either to free art from the ethical entirely—the position that sees potential censorship in the suggestion of any link between art and ethical effect[1]—or to identify the aesthetic and the ethical: the position that blames violence in works of art for real violence. His speculations on aesthetic effect show that, as Altieri says in a different theoretical context, "[a]rt is not life, but it does modify what we can take life to be" (*Subjective Agency* 34). Coleridge has a good deal to contribute to the academic discussions that would either engage or deny the connection between ethical and aesthetic thought. This is not to say that he offers a coherent alternative to modern views—his positions certainly have their own well-known incoherencies—but rather that he affords the occasion for a productive dialogue with some more recent reflections on the relation between aesthetic and ethical experience.

Coleridge's literary criticism is particularly important for the present study because of his constant association of ethical issues with the interpretive issues raised by imaginative engagement with works of art. As Julie Ellison notes, "*Biographia Literaria,* in addition to everything else it intends and desires, is a discourse on the ethics of criticism" (133). For Ellison, this means that Coleridge's criticism, concerned with and operating out of complex assumptions about gender and genre, displays his "anxieties about intellectual violence" (134). I am less interested in ascertaining what Coleridge's criticism reveals about him than I am in exploring the ethical and hermeneutic implications of his criticism for us, in an age in which moral philosophy often turns to literature and in which literary criticism is a site of ethical contest. For Coleridge the imagination is both ethically grounded and ethically foundational, so that ethical issues and the processes of imaginative understanding are deeply intertwined.

I. Necessity and Freedom in Drama

Coleridge associates the origins of drama with ethical and religious instruction, comparing ancient Greek drama to the Bible, his touchstone for both ethical and hermeneutic history and practice: "Tragedies formed a sort of Bible or biblical Instruction for the People" (*Lects 1808–1819* 1: 46), and "the *Drama* re-commenced in England as it first began in Greece—in religion" (1: 49), the Christian religion that "in its worst and most corrupted form . . . cannot wholly separate itself from Morality" (1: 53). Hence Shakespeare is seen as a source of ethical knowledge; at least part of his effect, as both "a profound metaphysician & a great poet," is to give the spectator "a deeper knowledge of his own heart, & the actions of his fellow creatures" (1: 229).

Recent efforts to use Greek tragedy as a source of nonpropositional ethical knowledge, particularly in Nussbaum's *The Fragility of Goodness* and Williams's *Shame and Necessity*, share Coleridge's sense of the deep connection between drama and ethics. For Nussbaum, tragedy demonstrates the "fragility" of human goodness and its dependence on, as well as its tension with, the full complexity of life's contingencies. Similarly, Coleridge sees Shakespeare as ethically valuable because he engages the whole of life—"he availed himself of his psycological genius to develope all the minutiae of the human heart" (*Lects 1808-1819* 1: 306)—in contrast to what Coleridge saw as the facile moral positions presented in early nineteenth-century drama. However, unlike Williams and Nussbaum, Coleridge locates the ethical impact of drama not so much in its presentation of alternative ethical stances as in the hermeneutic interaction between the differing horizons of the play and the spectator. These horizons differ both in their historical separation and in the difference between aesthetic understanding and ethical life.

For both Williams and Nussbaum, Greek tragedy's engagement of a world whose contingency is not under the control of reason provides grounds for a critique of the post-Kantian (or, for Williams, post-Platonic) rationally self-sufficient moral agent, as well as of the accompanying historical bias according to which, Nussbaum writes, "the way the Greeks pose the problem of agency and contingency is primitive or misguided" (*Fragility* 4). For Nussbaum, Greek tragedy and philosophy present a fruitful combination of "the aspiration to rational self-sufficiency" and "the special beauty of the contingent and the mutable," or "luck" (3). Very differently, Williams sees Greek tragedy as providing an account of ethical responsibility and action that does without the misguided tradition of rational moral autonomy instituted by Platonic philosophy and Christianity.

Both accounts draw an important line (though they draw it in different places) between, to put it very simply, an ancient world that does not make sense and a modern world that we mistakenly think does makes sense. According to Williams, "Plato, Aristotle, Kant, Hegel are all on the same side, all believing in one way or another that the universe or history or the structure of human reason can, when properly understood, yield a pattern that makes sense of human life and human aspirations. Sophocles and Thucydides, by contrast, are alike in leaving us with no such sense" (*Shame* 163). This contrast engages the problem, very important to Coleridge, of the relationship between Greek tragedy and modern (post-Platonic and Christian) tragedy, the latter of which for Coleridge is exemplified by Shakespeare. Both Coleridge and these more recent thinkers are interested in the question of whether and how there can be a viable concept of tragedy in a modern world that "makes sense," or that makes a kind of sense different from that found in the world of Greek tragedy. Gadamer, who finds less discontinuity between ancient and modern thought than Williams, Nussbaum, or Coleridge, nonetheless raises the issue that "the idea of Christian tragedy raises a special problem, since in the light of divine salvation the values of happiness and haplessness that constitute tragic action no longer determine human destiny" (*TM* 132).

Coleridge deals with this discontinuity by distinguishing between the polytheistic multiplicity of Greek tragedy and the monotheistic "wholeness" of Shakespeare, clearly preferring the latter. However, he does not make sharp distinctions between ancient and modern treatments of free agency and external destiny. That is to say, there is no qualitative distinction (though there is a quantitative one) between a modern world that makes sense and an ancient one that does not: he does not see the understanding of the relationship between the individual will and external contingent forces as having radically changed. This is partly necessitated by his faith in the biblical assertion of the originality of monotheism and the relative continuity of salvation history; for example, in his essay on Aeschylus's *Prometheus Bound* he discusses Greek polytheism and pantheism as a degeneration of biblical monotheism (*SW & F* 1261).

Unlike Williams and Nussbaum, he sees Greek understanding of ethical agency as clearly inferior and even primitive in comparison to modern understanding. For example, he says of Sophocles' Oedipus, "There we see a man oppressed by fate for an action of [which] he was not morally guilty: the crime is taken from the moral act and given to the action; we are obliged to say to ourselves that in those days they considered things without reference to the real guilt of the persons" (*Lects 1808–1819* 1: 317). In Williams's terms, this would suggest an uncritical universalization of the modern notion of guilt, but unlike Williams's misguided moderns he does not see the "real guilt of the persons" as an exercise of autonomous rational will. The ethical issues raised by Coleridge's dramatic criticism are not reducible to the conflict between rational autonomy and external contingency that establishes the initial terms for Nussbaum's and Williams's discussions of the historical distinction between ancient and modern tragedy. Instead, Coleridge places freedom and necessity into a larger context that he finds applicable to both ancients and moderns. This larger context comes from his theology and his German Idealist borrowings, which enable a sublation of the relation between freedom and necessity into an absolute sense of freedom that is indistinguishable from necessity, but along the way he usefully complicates both terms.

Coleridge asserts that "Necessity and absolute freedom are one," although necessity is not compulsion (*Zwang*) and freedom is not individual choice (*Willkühr*) (*CM* 2:641). Absolute submission to God's law—the only "necessity" that matters ultimately—is equivalent to absolute freedom and is to be sharply distinguished from natural contingency. "Natural" necessity is something the submission to which only corrupts the will: if the will "has subjected itself to the determination of Nature (in the language of St. Paul, to the Law of the Flesh), it receives a nature into itself, and so far it becomes a Nature: and this is a corruption of the Will and a corrupt Nature" (*AR* 285). Thus, although he adopts A. W. Schlegel's formulation that "Freedom within, & Necessity from without, these are the both Poles of the Tragic World" (*Lects 1808–1819* 1:448), "fate" is not natural necessity: "like the Freedom that opposes it, it must lie beyond the world of the Senses, in the depth of the invisible & the illimitable" (1: 448). This distinction between natural necessity and fate is central to his Christian understanding of Greek tragedy. The Greek tragic conflict is not between mortal agency and divine compulsion, because "the Gods of the Greeks were mere Powers of Nature, and tho' immeasurably higher than Mortality, yet in relation to the true Infinite in the same step with her" (1: 448). This means that freedom, as Coleridge defines it, always wins in the end, because Greek fate remains subject to a higher law of freedom: "The Fate must conquer, as far as the event is concerned; but the free determination remains unconquered, & preserves itself either by voluntary chosen Submission, or by voluntary Death" (1:448).

Coleridge's assimilation of all tragedy to a theory of freedom may suggest that he turns a deaf ear to the ethical insights that Williams and Nussbaum find in Greek tragedy, and he certainly has strong roots in both the Kantian and Christian ethical philosophies that they critique, philosophies that negotiate a relationship between autonomous freedom and categorically commanded moral law. However, this does not simply place him on the modern, sense-making side of Williams's division. By defining free will in terms that distinguish it from mere rational autonomy and choice and by seeing a continuity between human freedom and the (however inaccessible) divine freedom that is also necessity, Coleridge frees his thought from some of the Kantianism that Williams critiques. In particular, he does not reduce ethical agency to the rational intentions of individual agents in relation to a moral law. Coleridge achieves this, however, by going Kant one better. For Kant, freedom and necessity are connected in the fact that our freedom is the freedom to prescribe universal laws, and Kant distinguishes absolute moral necessity from natural necessity:

the need "to present moral laws as commands" arises precisely because "the action that morally is absolutely necessary is regarded as quite contingent physically (i. e. [we see] that what *ought* necessarily to happen still fails to happen on occasion)" (*Critique of Judgment* 286). However, for Kant this situation means that freedom (at least in the phenomenal realm) is a regulative, rather than a constitutive principle, and a function of subjective rational agency: we need to act *as if* freedom were universal even though, in the sensible world, it is not.[2] Coleridge, who objected to Kant's sharp division between noumenal and phenomenal realms,[3] grants a higher, constitutive rather than merely regulative status to both freedom and the ethical command by deriving them from God's creative act. Therefore human freedom is not merely rational agency and the "moral law" is more than the universalization of that agency asserted by Kant's statement that man "is subject only to *laws which are made by himself* and yet are *universal*" (*Groundwork of the Metaphysic of Morals* 100).

Even though Coleridge's theological premises may be foreign to us, his very position within that theological tradition allows him to avoid a rigid dichotomization of free moral agency and necessity. At the same time, Coleridge is Kantian enough to see that a regulative system of morality based on rational agency is of some use, avoiding Williams's somewhat ahistorical assumption that "we would be better off without" such a system (*Ethics* 174). Whether we see his flexible account of freedom and necessity as a symptom of synthetic, ambivalent, or even confused thought, it forms part of a constellation worth attending to in light of continuing debates about the relationship between interpretive and ethical agency in aesthetic experience, as I hope to show in the remainder of this chapter.

II. Poetic Faith

Coleridge does not live in a world that "makes sense" in the way Williams sees the post-Platonic world as making sense; that is why we need "poetic faith," a concept with complex links to both rational agency and its limitations. In his 1811 lecture on *The Tempest*, Coleridge claims that the engagement of the reader's sympathy through "the moral feeling called forth by the sweet words of Miranda 'Alack what trouble was I then to you'" prepares him to "wish that if supernatural agency were employed it should be used for a being so lovely." This enables the leap of "Poetic Faith before which our common notions of philosophy give way" (*Lects*

1808–1819 1:362). The poetic use of the supernatural, as it is formulated more famously in chapter 14 of the *Biographia,* is an effort to "transfer from our inward nature a human interest and a semblance of truth sufficient to procure for these shadows of imagination that willing suspension of disbelief for the moment, which constitutes poetic faith" (2: 6). The notion of supernatural agency is phenomenologically real "to every human being who, from whatever source of delusion, has at any time believed himself under supernatural agency" (2: 6); what we admit to be irrational has an ethical force because of its experiential reality. As Paul Magnuson points out, this is a poetically conscious version of what ignorance does, "i.e., mistake a *Subjective* product . . . for an objective fact" (*CN* 43, qtd. Magnuson 72). For Cyrus Hamlin (although he draws his terms from Hegel more than from Coleridge), such a conscious acceptance of fictionality is part of the "hermeneutics of form" played out, for example, in the reader's engagement with the "Dejection" ode. The "conscious fiction" by which "the poetic doctrine of Joy expressed in the central stanzas" is associated with the voice of the lost child of Wordsworth or (later) Otway. Displaced from the speaking poet, this fiction becomes important as a model of hermeneutic reflexivity: "*For us* as readers of the ode, however, this interpretation by analogy may also be seen as a component in the formal design of the poem as a whole, a strategy of the plot, which signifies the kind of reflexivity that we ourselves must achieve in order to understand the hermeneutics of Coleridge's ode" (234). "Our common notions of philosophy give way" before poetic faith because in philosophical terms this is error: a willed category mistake that is acknowledged as such. But, as Hamlin shows in his reading of "Dejection," in hermeneutic terms the "fictionality" of poetic idealization is a kind of "negative norm, against which we measure our understanding of the poem" (235), and thus is put to "real" hermeneutic effect.

Poetic faith also produces real ethical knowledge because it allows the coexistence, at least on the level of moral feeling, of subjective action and supernatural agency; one does not cancel the other out, as would be inevitable if the freedom of rational autonomy were placed in symmetrical opposition to a concept of necessity. As always, Coleridge is trying to find a place for the subject that is between the mind and the external world; he will accept neither a theory of complete subjective awareness, in which the spectator remains immune to delusion, nor a theory of complete delusion, in which the spectator gives in to the external experience completely.[4] The English Enlightenment, as represented by Samuel Johnson, is blamed for the former error, and the French are blamed for the latter error, which "now needs no fresh confutation" (*Lects 1808–1819* 2: 265) in 1818, three years after the defeat of Napoleonic "delusion."

In his discussion of Agamemnon's sacrifice of Iphigenia in Aeschylus's play, Williams says that the correct translation of Agamemnon's decision is that he "put on the harness of necessity," not that he "submitted to necessity" (*Shame* 132–33). Williams's point is that Agamemnon was not operating under a Greek ethics of "fate" that is foreign to modern concerns, but rather was acting in a way that is incomprehensible only if we ask inappropriate questions framed in terms of a theory of an autonomous, rational moral will. Williams promotes a theory of agency that involves a more complex relation among "cause, intention, state, and response," which are "the basic elements of any concept of responsibility" (55). In "putting on the harness of necessity," Agamemnon "takes something that is a necessity, and makes it his own. What must happen in virtue of a long-term design [the need for him to sacrifice his daughter so that the fleet can sail] becomes, in Agamemnon's decision, something that he must do." In other words, "necessity" becomes part of "the character's motivations" that "shape the life he is fated to have: the way his life is shaped by fate is through his motivations" (136).

Coleridge's combination of free will and the willed suspension of judgment that one could call "putting on the harness" of supernatural agency certainly cannot be too closely aligned with Williams's theory of agency, which would emphatically reject Coleridge's Christian understanding of the will. However, Coleridge does present an analog to Williams's insight that elements out of the individual agent's control, which do not fit into the rational order of the universe, still form part of even a modern moral agent's will and "character"—not just as errors to be corrected or external forces to be opposed by the will, but as parts of the moral agent's basic makeup.

This extrasubjective determination is perhaps partly a consequence of what Gadamer says occurs in the hermeneutically fundamental experience of "play," of which drama is a paradigmatic example. In that experience, the identity of the "players" becomes subordinated to the presentation of the play itself: "play itself is a transformation of such a kind that the identity of the player does not continue to exist for anybody. Everybody asks instead what is supposed to represented, what is 'meant'" (*TM* 112). For Gadamer, this "transformation into structure" means a rejection of the criteria of verisimilitude, as the play "no longer permits of any comparison with reality as the secret measure of all verisimilitude" (112), but the very "closedness" of the world of the play has a transforming effect on reality: "The being of all play is always self-realization, sheer fulfillment, energeia which has its telos within itself. The world of the work of art, in which play expresses itself fully in the unity of its course, is in fact a wholly transformed world. In and through it everyone recognizes that that is how things are. . . . From this viewpoint 'reality' is defined as what is untransformed, and art as the raising up (Aufhebung) of this reality into its truth" (113).

Coleridgean "poetic faith" suggests a similar transforming sublation of "reality" beyond both subjective control and the criteria of verisimilitude. Thus Terence Hoagwood is correct when, in his "Prolegomenon for a Theory of Romantic Drama," he argues against the temptation to "sever the drama's *meanings* from the public domain, by resituating their *medium* in the (apparently) private realm of mentality" (53). Coleridge's theory suggests that "poetic faith," although it involves a "private" choice to suspend disbelief, in fact engages forces beyond the subjective. However, it is not simply, as Hoagwood argues, that "the plays' ideological content and political importance are customarily displaced symbolically" (51). This "displacement," at least in Coleridge's theory, engages an area of ethical determination that is not available to the subjective activity of conscious rational choice. This is not Schiller's argument, as paraphrased by Julie Carlson, that "spectators take themselves out of the world temporarily in order to return to it with fuller effect" ("Command Performances" 122), but rather the notion that taking oneself "out of the world" in this way engages a kind of experience not available in what Gadamer would call the "untransformed" world of reality.

Thus the displacement of "ideological content" is by no means a displacement away from ethical experience in a simple substitution of private for public experience. It is part of human character that we can be fooled, if only temporarily, and this is an experience with positive ethical significance. In our understanding of Shakespeare's Miranda, our willingness to accept the supernatural Ariel is not the result of any belief in sprites but is rather an extension of the "moral feeling" resulting from our sympathy for Miranda's self-effacing character, an extension of sympathy that suspends our subjective act of judgment. The trauma resulting from the Mariner's confrontation with supernatural forces is real and affecting, whether or not we (or even the Wedding Guest) believe the factual details of his story. In this context, Booth usefully differentiates the "'nonce beliefs' . . . that the narrator and the reader embrace only for the duration" of a tale (such as the faith that geese can lay golden eggs in the Aesop fable) from the "fixed norms" or "beliefs on which the narrative depends for its effect but which also are by implication applicable in the 'real world'," such as the fable's moral about human greed (*The Company We Keep* 142–43). The consequence of this distinction, according to Booth's adaptation of Coleridge, is that "we willingly suspend disbelief about some matters but not about all" (151). In fact, Coleridge presents a more complex situation: it is not just a matter of believing in the *Rime*'s "fixed norms" while only pretending to believe in the Mariner's adventures; rather, the very "nonce beliefs" demanded by poetic faith have their own moral force, partly by virtue of their very irrationality.

Precisely because Coleridge accepts the world of post-Platonic and post-Kantian rational moral judgment, as well as a Christian understanding of free will—categories that Williams would like to wean us from—it is more difficult for him than for Williams to think outside the opposition between individual agency and external contingency. He does not have the option of simply trying to clear away some of the biases of modernity and recover the insights of the Greeks, as Williams does, and as Alasdair MacIntyre does in *After Virtue*. Though for Coleridge this is a matter of religious and intellectual faith, it also suggests a more subtle sense of the hermeneutics of historical understanding than is sometimes shown by our contemporaries who, in their eagerness to critique the failed "enlightenment project," as MacIntyre calls it, even when their critique is directed at "a deep lack of historical consciousness" (59), show a residue of that lack in suggesting that the "enlightenment project" can be simply rejected. Coleridge suggests a version of Gadamer's notion of *wirkungsgeschichtliches Bewusstsein:* the idea that we are inescapably products of the past we are examining, and that this necessarily prejudicial position needs to be taken into account in our understanding of history, and not rejected as a dispensable ideology.

For Coleridge, who rejects neither the rational will nor the reality of the supernatural, there is a particularly delicate relationship between the supernatural invoked by poetic faith and the copresence of autonomous rational judgment on one side and religious faith on the other. On the first side, we have the paradox of the inclusion within the rational will's repertoire of judgments the judgment to suspend itself. On the one hand this paradox is enabled by the will's own power to construct the self dialectically, its ability to see itself as an object upon which logical operations such as this suspension of judgment can be performed. As Paul Magnuson says of the *Rime,* "both in the writing and in the reading of 'The Ancient Mariner' the initial act is disbelief in the supernatural to realize poetic faith in its fictions" (73). According to Coleridge, the will remains, but behind the curtain, or operating in "background mode" we might say in terms of modern computer technology: "The poet does not require us to be awake and believe; he solicits us only to yield ourselves to a dream; and this too with our eyes open, and with our judgement *perdue* [hidden away] behind the curtain, ready to awaken us at the first motion of our will" (*BL* 2: 218). As Burwick points out, Coleridge's theory of aesthetic illusion evolved toward the position that "volitional participation becomes a necessary condition in all aesthetic illusion" (210). This entails the simple truth that the power of rational judgment extends to the point that it can exercise power over itself. For Coleridge, true rational freedom is not a monolithic force that necessarily subjects everything to its judgment; the union of freedom and necessity occurs on a much higher level. Thus rational freedom is not an ideological force in disguise; rather, it has the power of "deciding" to adopt other criteria than its own. This power parallels what Nussbaum calls literature's ability to indicate the limits of its own questions: for her, the novel's ability to "include, or at least indicate, the silence into which its own responsive prose has no entry" (*Love's Knowledge* 190).

At the same time, the suspension of judgment is enabled by the nonfoundational status of rational judgment itself. The experiential reality of the power of supernatural agency, even as we recognize its fictionality, gives poetic figures (in both senses of poetic characters and figural constructions) the kind of power and "otherness" that I discussed in Chapter 2. As Magnuson points out, while in Wordsworth "the context can transform the figure" as, for example, the figure of the discharged soldier is domesticated by affection and social restoration, in Coleridge, as exemplified by the figure of the Mariner, "the figure can dominate and determine the context" (95). Even more centrally for Coleridge, although "supernatural agency" in this context is a poetic, rather than a theological idea, it demonstrates the subservience of rational judgment to the more fundamental category of faith. In the *Biographia,* he states this subservience as a general principle: "Credidi, ideóque intellexi [I believed, and therefore I understood], appears to me the dictate equally of Philosophy and Religion" (2: 244).

On the one hand, poetic faith and religious faith are not to be confused; insofar as theatrical "illusion" is a version of poetic faith, a condition, as opposed to "delusion," in which "[we] *chuse* to be deceived," it places the mind "[i]n this state in which Images have a negative reality" (*Lects 1808–1819* 2: 266). On the other hand, this "negative reality" is not to be understood as "unreality," but as self-conscious idealization—the "negative faith in the existence of such a being, which we willingly give to productions *professedly ideal*" (*BL* 2: 214)—and is thus related to religious faith in at least two ways. First, "the true Criteria of Reality" are not sensory images, but the "Permanence, Power, Will manifested in Act, and Truth operating as Life" (*AR* 406–7), so that the theatrical images' "reality" is not a judgment on their correspondence to the empirical world, but on the power of their operation. Second, their reality is "negative" not because their reality is negated, but because their reality is produced by the "negative" process of the rational will's suspension, a process that enables one to move beyond the sensory, albeit into the realm of fiction. Poetic faith produced *Paradise Lost* (*Lects 1808–1819* 1: 363), and poetry shares with religion the ability to carry one "beyond the narrow sphere which his hand can touch or even his eye can reach" (1: 325). As Pierre Mileur summarizes Coleridge's concept, "Coleridge's supernatural serves as an important instance of the willed discontinuity which yields a definition of the undefined continuity" (*Vision and Revision* 141).

The rational will's power to suspend itself is thus both a power of its own and a manifestation of its relation to the unconditioned, the noumenal. To "put on the harness" of the supernatural in willingly suspending disbelief is, as in Williams, a recognition that external necessity and volition do not exclude each other, but Coleridge achieves this insight without rejecting either the "real" basis of the unreal supernatural—poetic faith is a part of our divinely creative nature—or the power of the rational will: we can choose to suspend our judgment.

Geoffrey Hartman illustrates the nature and importance of the psychological truth entailed by Coleridgean suspension of disbelief by associating it with what modern psychology has identified as "the non-experienced experience" of recovered traumatic knowledge. Traumatic knowledge, like poetic faith, is defined by imaginative testimony rather than representation of fact: "Emphasis falls on the imaginative use of language rather than on an ideal transparency of meaning" ("On Traumatic Knowledge" 544). This is real knowledge, in the sense that it is knowledge of a psychologically foundational experience, but "poetic" in that it comes from the "literary" attestation of trauma, rather than from a correspondence theory of factual reality. For Hartman, the *Rime* demands to be read as just such traumatic testimony, such that the poem's fantastic elements "are invested with a phenomenality meaningful in itself." In the traumatic experience recorded in the *Rime*, both in the Mariner's testimony and in its reception by the wedding guest, fantasy has the therapeutic role of reorganizing the individual's relation to the culturally sanctioned symbolic order: "Fantasy has entered to repair a breach—not so much a breach *of* the symbolic as *between* the symbolic and the individual. . . . Coleridge suggests the creation of a new, communalized self, much wiser about its relation to symbols" (543). The self is "communalized," or relieved of its limited status as an individual confronting a putatively objective reality, partly in recognition that this traumatic, fantastic knowledge, not under the self's control, has the effectual, phenomenal reality possessed by the object of poetic faith, a kind of reality organized figurally rather than empirically.

As in Williams, such a self maintains both a sense of responsible human agency—an agent becomes wiser about symbols as he attests to their power—and a sense that many aspects of ethical life are incompatible with a notion of rationally autonomous selfhood. Traumatic knowledge obviously does not proceed from an autonomous self; the very definition of trauma is for the psyche to be thrown into disorder. In the *Rime,* as Hartman notes, "[t]he very absence of an intuitable psyche, or the speechless deed itself, sets up the possibility that here there is no motive based on selfhood" ("On Traumatic Knowledge" 542). This is not poetic mystification; in fact Hartman goes so far as to suggest that the current obsession to *de*mystify the "poetic" "may itself be an effect of traumatic dissociation" (545).[5] Acknowledgement of the "traumatic" knowledge that Hartman associates with Coleridge's suspension of disbelief leads not to an "explanation" of trauma as a psychological symptom, but rather to an acknowledgement of its power, "to an unsentimental acknowledgment of the human condition, and a view of art as at once testimony and representation." The "reality" of the supernatural is thus not an empirical matter of the existence of Greek fate or an aesthetic matter of the symbolization of external contingency, but rather a matter of the power of the symbols to which we choose to attest. For Coleridge, to ask whether those symbols are symbols of an empirical reality or if they are human creations is to imply a false dichotomy, since "reality" is as much a matter of creative power as of empirical fact.

According to Coleridge's December 17, 1818 lecture on Shakespeare, the suspension of judgment in poetic faith is like that in dreams, except that in dreams there is no choice to suspend disbelief (*Lects 1808–1819* 2: 266). According to the 1825 *Aids to Reflection,* even in real dreams, without the intervention of rational choice, the unconscious workings of fantasy have a moral effect. The moral effect of dreams reinforces the notion that morality is not a matter of rationally fixed principles, but rather a process of our dual nature's growth and adaptation to the contingency of earthly existence: "Morality is the body, of which the faith in

Christ is the soul—so far indeed an earthly body, as it is adapted to our state of warfare on earth . . . yet not 'terrestrial,' nor of the world, but a celestial body, and capable of being transfigured from glory to glory, in accordance with the varying circumstances and outward relations of its moving and informing spirit" (*AR* 31–32). Dreams play a significant role in this process: in the early stages of spiritual growth, "in the morning twilight, while yet the truth . . . is below the horizon," the "pilgrim's" dreams "become a *mould* for the objects in the distance; and these again give an outwardness and a sensation of reality to the Shapings of the Dream" (35–36), and the dreams of the lowest order of mystic "transfer their forms to real Objects; and these lend a substance and an *outness* to his Dreams (391–92). By providing a "mould" for the experience of external reality, and by themselves gaining exteriority or "outness" from that encounter, dreams enable a prerational engagement in the process of the human spirit's development in relation to "the varying circumstances and outward relations of its moving and informing spirit."

If it is legitimate to combine Coleridge's comments in the *Aids to Reflection* and the 1818 lecture on Shakespeare, it appears that the *rational* choice to enter the dream-state of poetic faith allows one to reenter that productive pre-rational engagement with the external world, acknowledging the ethical significance of (1) rational choice, (2) the active suspension of that choice in giving way to the dream, and (3) the prerational, twilit, but developmentally important process of dreams' engagement with reality. This suggests that the dilemma between self-sufficient rationality and external contingency is a false one, because part of rationality's task is to use its power to negotiate with the irrational. For Coleridge, the willed category-mistake of poetic faith demonstrates the power of our judgment and the subordination of our judgment to our divinity, as it shows how human agency is informed rather than negated by "putting on the harness" of supernatural agency.

In asserting the priority of belief to understanding, Coleridge demonstrates the importance of the "thick" ethical concepts surrounding religious experience that are irreducible to rational reflection and that provide an experiential, historical context for that reflection, as in the experience of the dreaming "pilgrim." Of the four "evidences of Christianity" that form its "temple," discussed in chapter 24 of the *Biographia,* the "arched ROOF" is "the experience derived from a practical conformity to the conditions of the Gospel" (2: 244), or the necessity for belief and hence understanding to be grounded in character formed by experience: "In order to an efficient belief in Christianity, a man must have been a

Christian" (2: 244). In terms of ethical life, this statement is not, contrary to some views of Romanticism, a discrediting of reason by faith, tradition, and experience;[6] Christianity's "consistency with right Reason" is "the outer Court of the Temple—the common area, within which it stands" (2: 243). Rather, it acknowledges that such an opposition is a false dichotomy because reason, though a ubiquitous "common area" (and ultimately grounded for Coleridge in Kant's transcendental "pure" Reason) exists in the context of one's existence within personal and historical traditions of experience, just as morality is the "earthly body, as it is adapted to our state of warfare on earth," to the soul of faith.

Gadamer argues that because we are formed by tradition, by effective-history, our reason proceeds by operating from the initial standpoint of "prejudice." He rehabilitates this term from the negative connotations attached to it by the Enlightenment, connotations stemming from the assumption that reason could remove all prejudices.[7] Placing the term in the context of Heideggerian "fore-understanding" and the legal context of provisional verdicts (*TM* 269–70), Gadamer defines prejudice as the necessary provisional understanding we bring to any situation. The prejudices we bring to a situation, which may or may not be changed in the interpretive situation, are "brought into play by being put at risk" (299); thus there is a productive interplay rather than an antithesis between the prejudices that stem from our situation within a particular tradition and the reflection and discussion by which those prejudices are tested and reshaped. This rehabilitation of prejudice emphasizes the extent to which we are not autonomous subjects, in that our historically formed prejudices define us much more than our self-awareness: "The self-awareness of the individual is only a flickering in the closed circuits of historical life. *That is why the prejudices of the individual, far more than his judgments, constitute the historical reality of his being*" (276–77). Although for Coleridge the "prejudice" of Christian faith is not at all provisional, Coleridge's assertion of the priority of belief to understanding, which parallels the priority of conscience to self-consciousness, allows him to suggest, like Gadamer, that the active, practical grounding in belief and tradition—"the experience derived from a practical conformity to the conditions of the Gospel"—is a way of putting our prejudices/beliefs to the test. It is a necessary part of the process that leads to understanding: the "actual *Trial* of the Faith in Christ" (*BL* 2: 244) by which one acts *as* a Christian in a nonreflective way is itself the path to reflective belief. To pursue God's word for the sake of knowledge alone is "not the true end of the word," because to sever knowledge from spiritual growth is to create a monster: "If any one's head or tongue should grow apace, and all the rest stand at a stay, it would certainly make him a monster" (*AR* 106).

In Coleridge's dramatic theory, the interplay between the illusion of poetic faith and the reintroduction of the judgment also suggests the hermeneutic circle of a foreunderstanding that is subject to revision in the process of reflection. As Gadamer describes this process, "[w]orking out this fore-projection, which is constantly revised in terms of what emerges as [a person] penetrates into the meaning, is understanding what is there" (*TM* 267). Poetic faith is a conscious decision to suspend the rational judgment that would deny the prerational engagement with the poet's dream, but that "fore-projection" is subject to the revisionary power of the interplay between our entry into the poet's dream and the judgment waiting behind the curtain, which produces a kind of knowledge unavailable to reflection alone.

Although he would no doubt resent the comparison to Coleridge's essentially theological model, Williams suggests a secular version of this insight when he points out that there are many kinds of authentically cognitive ethical knowledge, such as "unreflective" beliefs and practices (often reflected in the public sphere of drama) that successfully dictate ethical relations between people, but that are not helped, and in fact are hurt, by reflection: "reflection might destroy knowledge, because thick ethical concepts that were used in a less reflective state might be driven from use by reflection, while the more abstract and general ethical thoughts that would probably take their place would not satisfy the conditions of propositional knowledge" (*Ethics* 167).[8]

As noted in Chapter 1, Coleridge acknowledges the historicity of even the spiritual knowledge that is contained in such "spiritual Truths, to every subject not presentable under the forms of Time and Space, as long as we attempt to master by the reflex acts of the Understanding what we can only *know* by the act of *becoming*" (*BL* 2: 244). As he says in *Confessions of an Inquiring Spirit,* synthesizing the historical critique of the Bible undertaken by the German Higher Criticism with his own spiritual belief, history's providential character does not deny its historicity. Playing on the etymology of "providence" (*pro + videre,* "to look forward"), he calls providential history "a Providence, a Preparation and a Looking-forward to Christ." Christianity "is spiritual yet so as to be historical—and between these two poles there must likewise be a . . . mid-point, in which the Historical and Spiritual meet" (*SW & F* 1119).[9] Thus even in the case of spiritual knowledge, the "reflex acts of the Understanding" can, in Williams's terms, destroy "thick" ethical knowledge when employed alone.

Williams tends to treat the conflict between nonpropositional and propositional knowledge as an opposition that is simply played out in history's move from the former toward the latter. Gadamer's notion of the historicity of all understanding can help articulate Coleridge's insight that this conflict must be supplemented by the historicity of propositional knowledge itself, in the sense that understanding depends on, and is not merely in conflict with, the prejudgment of belief. Insofar as all knowledge, even spiritual knowledge, is part of a historically conditioned process of beliefs being tested against the contingency of external existence, the experience of poetic faith—the rational decision to "put on the harness" of a prejudice in favor of irrational supernatural necessity—is an active engagement with the concrete reality of that process.

III. Imitation and Copy

Poetic faith's ability to cause "our common notions of philosophy" to "give way" and belief's priority to understanding in both philosophy and religion come together in Coleridge's speculations on the history and nature of drama, showing how drama contributes to, but is not simply to be identified with, ethical understanding in general. If ethical knowledge is not translatable into the metalanguage of ethical philosophy, according to the doctrine of "cognitive non-definism" that Lockridge associates with Coleridge (*The Ethics of Romanticism* 151), then the very differences between dramatic and philosophical understanding permit drama to be a resource for such nonpropositional ethical knowledge. This is of course an important reason that contemporary ethical philosophers such as Williams and Nussbaum often turn to drama for insights into ethics.

Many of Coleridge's statements on how art is produced and understood apply equally to narrative and drama; terms such as "poetic faith" that originated in his dramatic criticism were subsequently applied to aesthetic experience in general. It is also true, as Carlson and others have argued, that Romantic writing on and even for the theater tended to assimilate and subordinate the publicly dramatic to the privately poetic.[10] However, drama retains something of a unique role in the arts because, as Coleridge says, "Instead of simply narrating the actions of men, it represents men acting; or if it narrates, it is narrative in representation" (*Lects 1808–1819* 1:43). "Narrating the actions of men," especially one's own actions, as I argued in the previous chapter is the case with the

Rime, sets up an inescapable is-ought relationship by virtue of the separation between the past "is" of the story and the present moral force of the tale, which, at least for Coleridge, is in tension with the very problematic nature of that distinction in ethical life. "Representing men acting" closes that particular gap somewhat, since the action and the telling are for the most part simultaneous, and even when narrative occurs, it is in the context of represented action and the retrospective evaluation characteristic of narrative is disabled. The actor "takes us by storm" so that "[w]hat would appear mad or ludicrous in a book, presented to the senses under the form of reality & with the truth of Nature, supplies a species of actual Experience. . . . There is no time given to ask questions, or pass judgments" (1:429). But drama is not simply experience, because as the narrative gap between "is" and "ought" closes, the gap between "men acting" and drama's "representation" opens, foregrounding the interlocking issues of the nature of that representation and the nature of the audience's understanding of that relationship.

For Coleridge the experiences of the artist and the spectator are parallel in many ways, because his basic hermeneutic position was solidly Romantic and Schleiermachian in that he believed that the spectator's goal was to reconstruct the creative process of the artist, "the imaginative reconstruction of the alien or other mind in its historical context," as E. S. Shaffer summarizes Schleiermacher's position ("The Hermeneutic Community" 202). In Coleridge, however, this model of understanding does not result in the subjective aestheticism of which Gadamer accuses Schleiermacher, and Romantic hermeneutics in general, when he complains that in seeing "the act of understanding as the reconstruction of the [author's act of] production" (*TM* 192), and in raising this aesthetic principle to encompass all understanding, Schleiermacher "views the statement a text makes as a free production, and disregards its content as knowledge" (196).[11]

Just as the audience's understanding is framed in terms of the distinction between the "illusion" that constitutes poetic faith and "delusion," the mechanism of artistic representation is framed in terms of the relationship between "copy and "imitation." An exact copy leads only to a confusion between the original and the copy, but imitation involves a productive combination of identity and difference. For Coleridge, the spectator's imitation of the author's experience is not a copy but involves very real knowledge of the world, according to art's function as a medium between mind and nature, subject and object. In his account of Coleridge's fifth lecture in the 1811–12 series, J. Tomalin presents Coleridge's notion of "living words" or "*Verba Viventia*": "words are the living products of the living mind & could not be a due medium between the thing and the mind unless they partook of both. The word was not to convey merely what a certain thing is, but the very passion & all the circumstances which were conceived as constituting the perception of the thing by the person who used the word" (*Lects 1808–1819* 1: 273). Thus understanding is reconstruction of the word's use, as determined by the original speaker's psychological state, circumstances, and intention, rather than merely the word's reference. That reconstruction is neither a denial of words' relation to the world in the name of expressivism nor a copy-like representation, but rather an affirmation, akin to Gadamer's, of language's "living" function as a "medium between the thing and the mind."

Coleridge's position can be illuminated by Ricoeur's dialectical adaptation of Frege's distinction between "sense" ("the 'what' of discourse") and "reference" ("the 'about what' of discourse"): "the sense, so to speak, is traversed by the referring intention of the speaker" (*Interpretation Theory* 19, 20). For Coleridge, however, the terms must be reversed: one might say that it is the "reference" that is traversed by the intentional "sense" of the speaker. For him the important distinction is not between "sense" defined within a closed linguistic realm and "reference" as the relation to an extralinguistic world, but between the higher "sense" of the self-conscious subject—"the intention of the speaker that his words should correspond to his thoughts in the sense in which he expects"—and the lower "reference" to the world in which that subject lives: the realm of "verbal truth," by which "we mean no more than the correspondence of a given fact to given words" (*Friend* 1: 42).

Because, as in the famous definition of Imagination in chapter 13 of the *Biographia*, perception of both the world and the self is a "power" that involves much more than "reference" as a correspondence between fact and word, words must be considered in their expressive function in order to do justice, not merely to the expressing subject, but also to the world mediated by language. Art's role in mediating between the self and that world is of ethical interest because the world is human in two ways. First, aesthetic ideas, like all ideas, participate in both objective and subjective processes; they "are essentially one with the germinal causes in Nature," the artist's "Consciousness being the focus and mirror of both" (*Lects 1808–1819* 2: 222). Second, the world contains other people, making imitation an intersubjective endeavor. Both ideas are suggested in Coleridge's analogy for authentic imitation: "To that within the thing, active thro' Form and Figure as by symbols [?discoursing/discovering/discerning]

Natur-geist must the Artist imitate, as we unconsciously imitate those we love—So only can he produce any work truly *natural,* in the Object, and truly *human* in the Effect" (2: 223). Before we dismiss this as idealistic spiritualization of nature, it is worth noticing Coleridge's analogy, which is not in the Schelling from which he borrows much of this passage: the imitation of the "spirit of nature" is analogous to the unconscious imitation of "those we love." As is often the case in Coleridge, the concrete ethical relation to others provides a means of avoiding both idealism's assimilation of the world to the self—the "belief that everything around us is but a phantom, or that the Life which is in us is in them likewise"—and materialism's assimilation of the self to the world: "that to know is to *resemble*" (2: 222). Both the naturalness of the work's "object" and the humanity of its "effect," as it actively mediates between the human and the natural, going over to neither side completely, is based on the unconscious but nonetheless very active and, as I will discuss in Chapter 7, ethically foundational process of imitating a loved one.

An exact copy that deludes us into confusing it with the real is of no interest, but an imitation combines "Identity & Contrariety—the least degree of which constitutes *Likeness*—the greatest, absolute Difference—but the infinite gradations from [form?][12] all the Play & all the Interest of our Intellectual and Moral Being, till it lead us to a Feeling and an Object more aweful, than it seems to me compatible with even the present Subject to utter aloud." The "Feeling" and "Object" stem from an ultimately divine "principle which probably is the condition of all consciousness" (*Lects 1808–1819* 1: 84). The combination of likeness and difference in imitation keeps subjectivity and otherness, as well as art and life, in a living relationship that prevents the will from either turning in on itself or being absorbed in nature. An important example of this relationship is provided by the interaction between the natural and the artificial in nature or in art in Coleridge's acknowledgment of the force of the picturesque: "Whenever in Mountains, or Cataracts, we discover a likeness to anything artificial which we yet know was not artificial, what pleasure!—so in appearances known to be artificial that appear natural" (1: 84).

Coleridge's notion of imitation suggests that the artifice of drama imitates life in a way that exposes the interaction between its artificiality and its naturalness: just as narratives such as the *Rime* present narrative's intrusion of the is-ought mechanism into a life that does not always work that way, and just as part of a poem's ethical effect resides in its self-consciousness as *techne* rather than *phronesis,* drama presents a constructed universe that operates differently from our lived experience, and whose moral effect plays on our sense of that very difference.[13] The interaction of unity and difference in imitation is the "reflex act" of self-consciousness that distinguishes humans as morally responsible beings from the simultaneity of "plan and execution" in nature: "The wisdom in Nature [is] distinguished from Man by the coinstantaneity of the Plan & the Execution, the Thought and the Production—In nature there is no reflex act, but the same powers without reflection, and consequently without Morality" (*Lects 1808–1819* 2: 221).

This "reflex act," associated with imitation and enabling self-conscious moral life, is also associated with the temporality of human, hearing-oriented consciousness as opposed to the simultaneous visuality of nature. Coleridge's notes for this lecture begin, "Man communicates by articulation of Sounds, and paramountly by the memory in the Ear—Nature by the impression of Surfaces and Bounds on the Eye" (*Lects 1808–1819* 2: 217). Art mediates between these two realms, which makes writing the primary form of art, because it is a "use of the visible in place of the Audible," that is to say "a *translation,* as it were, of Man into Nature" (2: 217). Recent criticism, still under the (not always acknowledged) influence of the early Derrida's association of the voice with logocentric presence, tends to read this kind of distinction in terms of the repression of the contingency of the visible,[14] or, especially in the case of drama, a politically conservative anxiety about the revolutionary implications of the visible, for example, what Carlson calls the "doubts about vision" expressed in Coleridge's *Remorse* (*In the Theatre of Romanticism* 113). Coleridge's critique of Charles Maturin's *Bertram* as an example of theatrical "jacobinism" (*BL* 2: 221) does indeed downgrade the merely visible in relation to hearing and associate spectacle with the ignorance of the (potentially revolutionary) mob: he sarcastically remarks that the unmotivated movement of "mute dramatis personae" is justified by the fact that "they afford something to be *seen,* by that very large part of a Drury Lane audience who have small chance of *hearing* a word" (2: 232).[15]

However, as I have argued elsewhere in relation to Wordsworth,[16] our attempt to recover the repressed "visible"—whether of writing or of revolutionary theatricality—should be balanced by the acknowledgement of another, much older tradition of the relationship between hearing and vision. This tradition leads from the Hebrew emphasis on the hearing of God's always-invisible command to the Pauline and Augustinian inner hearing of God's word as a balance to the potentially excessive visuality of a God who had been visibly incarnated, an iconoclastic position revived by the Protestant tradition that emphasizes the hearing of the "inner word" in opposition to the perceived idolatry of Catholic visual images. The association of human moral life with auditory temporality, in opposition to the eye's association with that which is merely natural or bodily—as when Wordsworth refers to the "bodily eye" as the "most despotic of our senses" (*Fourteen-Book Prelude* 12.128–29)—is part of a tradition that for Coleridge goes directly back to Paul: according to *Confessions of an Inquiring Spirit,* to make the written Bible, isolated from religious experience, "the subject of a special article of faith" can have "the effect of substituting a barren acquiescence in the *letter* for the lively faith that cometh out of Hearing: even as the Hearing is productive of this faith, because it is the Word of God that is heard and preached (*Rom.* X. v. 8. 17)" (*SW & F* 1151).

That elevation of hearing reappears in the post-Heideggerian, anti-Enlightenment versions of Protestantism and Judaism represented by Gadamer and Levinas, respectively. For Gadamer, hearing is preferable, not because it leads to the aural self-presence critiqued by Derrida or the repression of the contingently visible by the egoistic imagination, but for the opposite reason: hearing is more hermeneutically authentic because it is *not* under the control of the subject: "When you look at something, you can also look away from it by looking in another direction, but you cannot 'hear away'" (*TM* 462). Speaking does not lead to "self-presence"; as Gadamer pointed out in reference to his 1981 exchange with Derrida, "who listens at all to his or her own voice?" ("Letter to Dallmayr" 95). Gadamer's position here resembles Coleridge's. According to Coleridge, we must avoid the static, purely visual and therefore inhuman falsehood of the wax-figure "copy," the egotistical "idle rivalry" with the passivity of "*natura naturata*" ["nature natured"], and instead embrace the active temporality of nature in process, or "*natura naturans*" ["nature naturing"], which "presupposes *a bond* between *Nature* in this higher sense and the soul of Man" (*Lects 1808–1819* 2:220–221).

Our ability to communicate by "articulation of sounds"—sound become language—distinguishes man from mere nature but at the same time de-emphasizes the individual will, or at least grounds it in something bigger; the "reflex" that accompanies human linguistic temporality in contrast to nature's visual spatiality does indeed exalt the human, but not the self, because that temporality is also an insertion of the self into contexts of difference larger than the self, such as religious tradition: the "lively faith that cometh out of Hearing" is an example of what Gadamer refers to as the linguistic dimension in which "tradition comes down to those now living," which "has always been the true essence of hearing, even before the invention of writing" (*TM* 463).

The connection of hearing's role in this temporality to the "Morality" of human reflexivity is suggested by Heidegger's more Hebraic heir, Emmanuel Levinas, according to whom sound disrupts vision's adequation of form and content: "In sound, and in the consciousness termed hearing, there is in fact a break with the self-complete world of vision and art. In its entirety, sound is a ringing, clanging scandal. Whereas, in vision, form is wedded to content in such a way as to appease it, in sound the perceptible quality overflows so that form can no longer contain its content" ("The Transcendence of Words" 147). Sound interrupts the "self-complete" world of sight, and for Levinas this interruption is a manifestation of how absolute otherness calls us to responsibility. Similarly for Coleridge, the self-complete natural world associated with sight, characterized by "the coinstantaneity of the Plan & the Execution" is differentiated from the ethically prior, radically human world of sound. Aesthetic "imitation," in the paradigmatic case of linguistic art, mediates between the human, reflexive world of sound and the visual immediacy of nature by translating the human into the natural, the audible into the visible.

For Levinas this translation of sound's ethical scandal into sight's self-completion is exactly the problem with art, as I pointed out in Chapter 2: he claims that even narrative art freezes ethical temporality into the space of narrative form. Coleridge suggests a similar move away from the ethical in art's translation of human, aural reflexivity into nature's visual terms, but for him the situation is more complex. First, even nature's visuality is not in fact static, as his emphasis on the bond between human life and *natura naturans* or the active side of nature suggests. Second, just as part of art's ethical force is its self-conscious relation to the *techne* that is opposed to *phronesis*, art's human, ethical reflexivity resides partly in its own recognition of its intermediate status between the ethical world of human self-consciousness and the amoral world of *natura naturata*.

IV. The Sacrificial Spectator

This intermediate status of art for Coleridge suggests why it is with only apparent inconsistency that he can insist on the moral force of aesthetic "imitation" while following Kant in sharply distinguishing aesthetic judgments of the beautiful from ethical judgments of the good. Beauty "is characterized by . . . being always *disinterested*" (*SW & F* 280), and so distinguished "from the AGREEABLE, which is beneath it, and from the GOOD which is above it: for both these have an interest necessarily attached to them; both act on the WILL, and excite a desire for the actual existence of the image or idea contemplated, while the sense of beauty rests satisfied in the mere contemplation or intuition, regardless whether it be a fictitious Apollo, or a real Antinous" ("The Principles of Genial Criticism," *SW & F* 380). This Kantian distinction between ethical and aesthetic judgment separates Coleridge from the post-Kantian aestheticization of the ethical while it complicates, but in no way denies, the ethical significance of the aesthetic. According to Emile Fackenheim, Schelling's solution to the problem of the need for true religion to negotiate between moral freedom and the otherness of God (a problem in Coleridge that I will take up in Chapter 6) is found in artistic creation: "The aspect of free moral activity is preserved, in the conscious aspect of artistic creation. Preserved also is providential order in its aspect of otherness, for in artistic creation 'another, as it were, is experienced as acting through us'" (72, quoting from Schelling's *System of Transcendental Idealism*). Similarly, for many of the German Romantics, Kant provided, as Rodolphe Gasché explains in his foreword to Friedrich Schlegel's *Philosophical Fragments,* a rationale for turning the problems of philosophy in general, and of epistemology in particular, into aesthetic issues. By denying that noumena can be known, but by offering in compensation the presentation of regulatory ideas in the realm of understanding, Kant changed the issue from one of representation (*Vorstellung*) to one of presentation (*Darstellung*): "The issue is no longer how to depict, articulate, or illustrate something already present yet resisting adequate discursive or figural expression, but of how something acquires presence—reality, actuality, effectiveness—in the first place" (xx).

Coleridge was deeply committed to negotiating between moral freedom and divine otherness, and his emphasis on the performative, rather than simply representational efficacy of the "living words" of language is certainly an example of the move from *Vorstellung* to *Darstellung*. However, although his involvement with these issues can be seen in both the aesthetic and the philosophical spheres, in fact he objected strenuously to the assimilation of life to art, refusing to follow the lead of Schelling in resolving either theology or ethical reality into art, or in subordinating them to art.[17] His sensitivity to the problematic relation between ethical life and the *techne* of art, exacerbated by his mixed attitude toward his own role as a poet, prevented him from providing a purely aesthetic solution to theological or ethical problems. For example, it is precisely the tension between moral freedom and divine otherness discussed by Fackenheim that provides, for Coleridge, not an aestheticized theology, but a *distinction* between poetry, which partakes of the conscious will in the work of the secondary imagination, and prophecy, which is different precisely because God speaks through the (passive) prophet, preserving Schelling's "providential order in its aspect of otherness" by its very difference from art: "They Prophets do *not* describe their inspiration as Poets; but relate sudden changes produced without any conscious act of their own will, both on their bodies and their minds" (*CM* 2: 402). And as the earlier discussion of *techne* and *phronesis* implies, language's function as *Vorstellung* rather than *Darstellung*—Coleridge's "living words"—while it does grant the artwork an autonomy that enables a structurally ethical relationship, also unleashes a powerful *techne* that warns against the aestheticization of life. His surprised response to Barbauld's complaint about the *Rime*'s "moral" suggests that for him the difference between literature and life, as well as the clear effect of literature on life, was too obvious to need stating.

Oddly enough, this makes Gadamer more traditionally "Romantic" than this side of Coleridge, if we see the "Romantic" as an aestheticization of the good. For Gadamer, following Plato, "the beautiful is distinguished from the absolutely intangible good in that it can be grasped" (*TM* 481), which means that beauty is a kind of concretion of the good: "[t]he beautiful reveals itself in the search for the good" in that "[i]t is the mark distinguishing the good for the human soul" (481). Coming down on the Platonic side of Kant's assertion that "the beautiful is the symbol of the morally good" (*Critique of Judgment* 228), Gadamer's emphasis is the opposite of Coleridge's. Coleridge emphasizes not beauty's symbolic relation to the good but Kant's distinction between the disinterestedness attached to beauty and the interestedness attached to the good. In the passage quoted above, Coleridge is paraphrasing Kant's argument that the good is determined by "the presentation of the subject's connection with the existence of the object" as opposed to the "merely *contemplative*" status of "a judgment of taste" (51). For Coleridge, it is the interested striving after the good that entails "desire for the actual existence of the image or idea contemplated," whereas the disinterested "sense of beauty rests satisfied in the mere contemplation or intuition."

Like many Coleridgean oppositions, of course, this one is more complex than it appears on the surface. The argument for the separation between the beautiful and the good in "The Principles of Genial Criticism," written in 1814, closes with the essential caveat, "I have confined myself to the Beauty of the Senses, and by the Good have chiefly referred to the relatively good," deferring a discussion of "the supersensual Beauty, the Beauty of Virtue and Holiness," which is "distinguishable" but "not separable" from the "ABSOLUTELY GOOD" (*SW & F* 385). This higher form of beauty is discussed in 1826 in terms much closer to Gadamer's. Here "the intuition of the *Beautiful*" is in fact "*spiritual*" and is "the short-hand, Hieroglyphic of Truth—the mediator between Truth and Feeling, the Head & the Heart—<The Sense> Beauty is *implicit* knowledge" (*CN* 4: 5428). This reflects the side of Kant emphasized by Gadamer, that the beautiful has a symbolic relation to the realm of "truth" in which the good resides.

In Coleridge's discussion of sensory beauty and the relatively good, "interest" is on the side of the good, and the good is "always discursive" as "the congruity of a thing with the laws of the reason and the nature of the will" whereas "disinterested" perception of beauty "arises from the perceived harmony of an object . . . with the inborn and constitutive rules of the judgment and imagination" and is therefore "always intuitive" (*SW & F* 382–83). This comparison associates beauty with passivity and the good with action, which is consistent with the higher form of the good, "the Reason as one with the *absolute* Will," as he puts it in the 1820 "Essay on Faith" (*SW & F* 841). But in the latter case the role of "interest" is very different, for the "absolute will" stands above and against "all mere individual interests" as well as the "Discursive Faculty" of the merely finite "Understanding" (840–41), becoming a continuously exerted "*energy*" of "the Whole Moral Man" (844).

This higher form of the good that transcends both the individual interest and the discursiveness associated with the relatively good suggests, in a less radical form, Levinas's point that the ethical relation, considered absolutely, entails a "disinterestedness" that is also "non-indifference": to rise above the "interest" attached to the merely "relatively good" is not to fall into the passive disinterestedness of aesthetic contemplation, but to rise to the higher disinterestedness of this moral energy. Like the Coleridge of the "Essay on Faith," Levinas sees "interest" as egoistic self-interest: "Being's interest takes dramatic form in egoisms struggling with one another" (*OB* 4). The "disinterestedness" or "ontological indifference" that opposes such "interest" is also "non-indifference to another, to the other" (178). Similarly for Coleridge, the absolute good that transcends personal interest is, in the "Essay on Faith," intimately tied to a "non-indifference" both to the individual human other and to the absolute other of God.[18]

This notion of otherness will be explored in more detail in the next chapter; my point here is to warn against taking Coleridge's Kantian distinction between the "interest" attached to the good and the "disinterested" perception of beauty too absolutely. It is also important to note that the appreciation of art involves more than judgments about beauty, especially in the case of poetry, to which Coleridge grants a philosophical fundamentality. Conversely, as the applicability of beauty to "a fictious Apollo, or a real Antinous" suggests, judgments about beauty are not restricted to art. Nevertheless, the tension between philosophical (including ethical) and aesthetic judgment remains a significant factor, because "creative power" and "intellectual energy" are at odds, finally to be reconciled but not identified in Shakespeare's drama, where they "fought each with his shield before the breast of the other" or, like two antagonistic streams, ultimately joined in "a wider channel" so as to "blend, and dilate, and flow on in one current and with one voice" (*BL* 2: 26).

The distinction between philosophy and aesthetic creations remains insofar as the former "proposes *truth* for its immediate object, instead of *pleasure*" (*BL* 2: 130), and "[a] poem is that species of composition, which is opposed to works of science, by proposing for its *immediate* object pleasure, not truth" (1: 13). The "intellectual energy" that struggles with "creative power" in Shakespeare is of course not necessarily ethical—in fact, as we shall see, in Coleridge's Shakespeare the very opposite can be the case—but the tension between poetry/pleasure and philosophy/truth repeats on a more general level the specific tension between aesthetic judgment and ethical judgment, because both tensions have to do with art's translation of the truth of the human temporality of consciousness into the static but pleasurable world of *natura naturata*.

"Pleasure" is of course a term with complex links to philosophy in general and moral philosophy in particular for Coleridge. Coleridge's emphasis on pleasure as the end of poetry bears traces of the "moral sense" philosophers such as Shaftesbury and Hutcheson in which, as Eagleton puts it, "ethics, aesthetics and politics are drawn harmoniously together" in the unity of the aesthetic and the sensuous (*The Ideology of the Aesthetic* 37), a tradition that would lead Wordsworth, in the "Preface" to the *Lyrical Ballads,* to state that "[w]e have no knowledge, that is, no general principles drawn from the contemplation of particular facts, but what has been built up by pleasure, and exists in us by pleasure alone" (*Prose Works* 1: 140). This is too extreme for Coleridge, at least by 1817, when he argues against the notion "that our *Feelings* are to be the ground and guide of our Actions." For him, feelings are not the ground, but rather "among the things that are to be grounded" (*SW & F* 570). Thus he praised Wordsworth for his *combination* of "deep feeling" and "profound thought" (*BL* 1: 80). But earlier, as Christensen points out, part of Coleridge's 1803 "rebuttal" of Hartley's associationism (which Christensen believes was never entirely successful), was to substitute "states of Feeling" for Hartley's "Trains of Ideas" (*CL* 2: 961, qtd. in *Coleridge's Blessed Machine of Language* 82). Mileur argues for the temporal complementarity of pleasure and truth for Coleridge: pleasure is "the anticipation of a realized intelligibility," and truth "answers to a realized intelligibility which precedes its objects" (*Vision and Revision* 138). As Altieri points out in his sketch of the development of the "aesthetic ideology" in the eighteenth century, the concept of pleasure provided a crucial link among aesthetics, psychology, and philosophy: "Theorizing about pleasure proved crucial to isolating aesthetic experience as a subject about which one could philosophize—in part because the theme of pleasure helped secure the psychologizing of aesthetic discourse that took place during the eighteenth century" ("The Values of Articulation" 67).[19]

Despite his own contributions to the psychology of aesthetic pleasure, Coleridge resisted the identification of pleasure and ethical principle. In a notebook entry from his journey to Malta, Coleridge struggles to avoid the conclusion that the "twin Despotism of Pain & Pleasure" comprises the "Main Springs" of "human conduct," including the (for him) ethically foundational experience of love: "And Love too—No! That too is no Creature of Pain & Pleasure—say rather the Parent *nursed* & sustained by its Children" (*CN* 2: 2058). In response to Kant's argument that self-love cannot be a universal maxim because it can be used to justify the morally contradictory act of suicide, Coleridge implies that this kind of self-love (as opposed to a higher version, to be discussed in Chapter 7 below) should be thought of within the context of pleasure and pain, as *opposed* to ethical principle; it is merely "the sum or instrument of pleasurable Feeling; & of course, with perfect consistency may impel a man to the destruction of Life, when Life is believed to be the Sum & Instrument of Pain & Evil" (*CM* 3: 253).

Coleridge distinguishes the disinterested play of art and the "pleasure" of poetry from moral action so as to avoid reducing ethics to aesthetics, but at the same time he sees our aesthetic and our ethical responses to the world as stemming from the same source in an ultimately ethical self-conscious reflexivity. On the one hand, judgments of beauty work according to a process unconnected with the agreeable or the good, but on the other hand the aesthetic activity of "imitation" operates according to the "truth" of reflexivity's temporal difference, in tension with the amorality of *natura naturata*. That reflexivity is what connects aesthetics and ethics, but because it is "a *translation,* as it were, of Man into Nature" (*Lects 1808–1819* 2: 217), it can also pit art's mediation between man and nature against ethics' strictly human, reflexive orientation. Art is at least partly irresponsible in the sense that it mediates between the moral world of humanity and the amoral world of nature, the reflexive, temporal world of hearing and the simultaneity of sight. But even in its difference from the good, aesthetic judgment can have an ethical *function* by entering and complicating the world of moral reflexivity rather than by offering a metadiscourse on that reflexivity in the way that moral philosophy does.

One way tragedy carries out this ethical function while retaining a generic tendency toward the amoral is by presenting a productively incomplete picture of ethical life that allows power to operate in special ways. For example, Ariel in *The Tempest* is interpreted by Coleridge as reason abstracted from morality: "while the Poet gives him all the advantages all the faculties of reason he divests him of all moral character not positively but negatively" whose "last and only reward" is "simple liberty" (*Lects 1808–1819* 1:363–64). Moral character is not removed from Ariel by some positive act; it is simply "negatively" not there. Bernard Williams also sees the incompleteness, in comparison to ethical life, of the closed world of a play as an indication of the difference between the fictional and the ethical. For him, the authorial power to create a world, unlike our own, with no alternatives, is translated into the power of supernatural necessity:

> The general condition with fiction is that, beyond a certain point, there are no interesting or realistic questions about alternatives *to* the action; a special art of Sophoclean tragedy (and the same no doubt applies elsewhere) is to convert this into the sense that there are, at certain points, no alternatives *within* the action. . . . Our sense of supernatural power in a play such as the *Oedipus* is a product of authorial power, nothing but authorial power could give us an idea of it that was so strong or so apparently clear. (*Shame* 146)

In one sense, this is close to Coleridge's notion of "poetic faith": the reader's or spectator's suspension of judgment is a submission to the total power and internal necessity of the author's supernatural fictions, and the power to which we submit (a submission that is total as long as our judgment remains behind the curtain) is translated into the absolute supernatural power that drives the Mariner's ship or that keeps Christabel from speaking. The connection between authorial power and dramatic necessity is compatible with Coleridge's Christian reconciliation of freedom and necessity, and it echoes his emphasis on the priority in Shakespeare of "the inward eye of meditation on his own nature" to external "observation" (*Lects 1808–1819* 1:310).

However, this notion of authorial power (surprising to find in Williams's discussion of Sophocles, given its connotations of the autonomous subjectivity Williams takes such pains to critique) has a very ambivalent role in Coleridge, and as Tilottama Rajan points out, the power Coleridge ascribes to authors such as Shakespeare and Wordsworth is much less secure when the author in question is Coleridge himself, whose poem "This Lime-Tree Bower," for example, "conflates and exchanges author and reader functions" (*The Supplement of Reading* 115). The typically conditional self-depiction of the author in "Kubla Khan" ("*Could* I revive within me / Her symphony and song" [42–43; emphasis added]) openly acknowledges the fragility as well as the potential danger of this authorial power. The poet may *not* have the power to translate Khan's authority (itself threatened by "[a]ncestral voices prophecying war" [30]) into a supernatural verbal creation, and in case he does execute this powerful creative act, spectators are warned to "Beware! Beware! / His flashing eyes, his floating hair!" (49–50). The attempt to repeat Khan's act of creative power may provoke an alienating judgment of horror rather than a suspension of judgment and submission to the author's fictions.[20]

Thus Coleridge, more interested in Shakespeare than Sophocles, and with more faith in both the supernatural and the will than Williams evinces, but with a more nuanced and skeptical sense of authorial power, presents a kind of converse of Williams's insight. Tragedy, at least modern, Shakespearean tragedy works, not by *emplotting* authorial power as supernatural necessity, but by *exposing* power on its own, and thus exploring its relation to the ethical considerations with which it is usually entangled. Shakespearean tragedy presents an incomplete ethical universe, but by separating human—specifically intellectual—power from its proper ethical foundation, so that it can be contemplated in isolation.

Power is an essential vehicle for the revelation of virtue—"[w]ithout power, virtue would be insufficient and incapable of revealing its being" —and Shakespeare's villains "are all cast in the mould of Shakespeare's own gigantic intellect." But, in contrast to Booth's discussion of virtue as "cover[ing] every kind of genuine strength or power" (*The Company We Keep* 11), power is for Coleridge a necessary but not a sufficient condition for virtue, because intellectual power is necessary for virtue but is also "the grand desideratum of human ambition" (*BL* 2: 217). As Gadamer points out in regard to Plato's attempt to mediate between power and knowledge as forces in the Greek polis, "power never aims at anything but the increase of itself" (*The Idea of the Good* 72). Similarly for Levinas, "freedom" that is not grounded in the ethical relation is mere arbitrary power, the "impetuosity of the current to which everything is permitted, even murder" (*TI* 303). Such positions are not critiques of freedom so much as they are attempts to give it an ethical grounding; as Levinas says, "One is not against freedom if one seeks for it a justification" (302). The value of dramatic representation of "the coexistence of great intellectual lordship with guilt" and the power of "superiority to the fear of the invisible world" is that the necessary ethical ground of the free power of the intellect is emphasized by its absence: "in this bad and heterogeneous co-ordination we can contemplate the intellect of man more exclusively as a separate self-subsistence, than in its proper state of subordination to his own conscience, or to the will of an infinitely superior being" (*BL* 2: 217). Coleridge's discussion of Shakespeare's selective exercise of authorial power, his transfer of his own intellectual power (isolated from its ethical ground) to his villains, roughly parallels Williams's discussion of how the authorial power to dictate dramatic events is transferred to a sense of necessity within the play. However, he does not, as in Williams's Sophoclean model, simply suggest that drama presents a universe that operates with stricter necessity than our own, but rather that drama does something more interesting and productively disturbing: it presents the willed power of mind in isolation from its ethical context, forcing a split recognition of power's necessity, its attraction, and its danger in isolation.[21]

This is an instance of Coleridge's recognition of an insight that both Williams and Levinas approach in very different ways: that the conceptual, intending power of the free ego needs to be grounded in a larger human context. For Levinas this ungrounded freedom is the "violence of the choice" (*OB* 57); for Williams the post-Enlightenment moral system conceals "the dimension in which ethical life lies outside the individual" (*Ethics* 191). Coleridge recognizes, however, that what Williams calls the modern "rationalistic metaphysics of morality," related to what Coleridge calls the "self-subsistence" of the intellect, separated in Shakespeare from its ethical ground, cannot simply be split off from other parts of our Enlightenment heritage as inessential, as Williams seems to think it can, but must be confronted in its full force in order to integrate it back into the context of ethical life.

According to Ricoeur, tragedy is of interest to moral philosophy precisely because it does *not* offer philosophical conclusions, but instead challenges and disorients the spectator, so that the "practical wisdom" of ethical thought is generated as a *response* to "tragic wisdom" that gains energy from the difference between the two kinds of thought: "[O]ne of the functions of tragedy in relation to ethics is to create a gap between tragic wisdom and practical wisdom. By refusing to contribute a 'solution' to the conflicts made insoluble by fiction, tragedy, after having disoriented the gaze, condemns the person of praxis to reorient action, at his or her own risk, in the sense of a practical wisdom in situation that best *responds* to tragic wisdom" (*Oneself* 247). Coleridge's version of this disorientation of the gaze leading to reorientation of action is expressed in terms of the need for spectators of drama to undergo a "sacrifice," a heavily loaded term for both Coleridge and the tradition of drama. His objections to contemporary drama revolve around the absence of sacrifice on the part of the audience, as he has the "Plaintiff" say in this dialogue from the dramatic criticism, dating back to 1798, appended to *Biographia Literaria* as "Satyrane's Letters":

> DEFENDANT. Hold! are not our modern sentimental plays filled with the best Christian morality?
> PLAINTIFF. Yes! just as much of it, and just that part of it which you can exercise without a single Christian virtue—without a single sacrifice that is really painful to you! (2: 186)

Here the challenge is placed in Christian terms: rather than enabling us to "seek and find on the present stage our own wants and passions, our own vexations, losses, and embarrassments," as Coleridge has the "Defendant" plea (2: 189), or representing even the "Christian morality" that we already know, tragedy should occasion the painful Christian virtue of self-sacrifice. The ethical effect is not in the play's reflection of virtue, but in its supplying an occasion for the interpretive exercise of virtue.

In the "epilogue" to his own tragedy *Remorse,* printed in the *Morning Chronicle* January 28, 1813, during the play's successful run at Drury Lane, Coleridge has the prudence not to ask for an active sacrifice on the part of his paying audience, but he presents a more palatable version of the same idea. The epilogue is spoken by Teresa, and begins with a tongue-in-cheek defense of her six-year wait for her lover Alvar, based on the distance between her uneducated upbringing and that of the *Morning Post* (and, Coleridge hopes, Drury Lane) audience. Then she reads from the poet's manuscript, which, in typically Coleridgean fashion, arrives late and in an illegible hand:

> Our Poet bids me say,
> That he has woo'd your feelings in this Play
> By no too real woes, that make you groan,

Recalling kindred griefs, perhaps your own,
Yet with no image compensate the mind,
Nor leave one joy for memory behind.
(36–41)

Rather than asking the audience to sacrifice their received notions, he offers an experience that, by presenting "no too real woes," will not cause the audience to identify the characters' woes with their own griefs, but will instead give an "image" to compensate the mind. This is a sugar-coated version of the idea in "Satyrane's Letters," in the sense that it is an argument against mimetic identification as an interpretive mode. Both here and in "Satyrane's Letters" Coleridge implicitly criticizes what Paula Backscheider argues in *Spectacular Politics* is the tendency of late eighteenth-century drama to become "a hegemonic apparatus, a mechanism for the negotiation of a system of knowing and believing—an ideology" by appealing "to emotion through unmediated sensation, a strategy that made the plays theater of identification" (229). As usual, Coleridge's political position here is complex; in criticizing the "jacobinism" of modern drama and exhibiting the fear of the revolutionary masses he participates in the "hegemony" Backscheider describes, even as he objects to the "theater of identification"—the stage's reflection of popular morality—that is the form of such hegemony.

The "Christian virtue" of self-sacrifice to be undergone by the spectator of drama is part of the working of imagination. Instead of "distinct form," the imagination produces "a strong working of the mind still producing what it still repels & again calling forth what it again negatives and the result is what the Poet wishes to impress, to substitute a grand feeling of the unimaginable for a mere image" (*Lects 1808–1819* 1:311). This is an example of the Coleridgean sublime: the mind is thrown into contradiction toward the end of substituting "a grand feeling of the unimaginable for a mere image." The coherence of the "mere image" available to the Understanding is sacrificed for the sake of a sublime intuition of the "unimaginable." But, as is usually the case in Coleridge's (as opposed to Wordsworth's) articulation of the sublime, this is also a *self*-sacrifice, a sacrifice of the coherent world-view that the "Defendant" in "Satyrane's Letters" wants to see simply reflected in drama. The mind combines the production and repulsion of subjective elements with the summoning and negation of objective elements, in a sort of interiorization of the process in a sacrificial offering by which one must destroy ("repel" or "negative") something of value one has "produced" or "called forth" for the sake of a larger good.[22]

The self-sacrifice with which one should approach drama, like "imitation" itself, involves a combination of identification and alienation; here Coleridge would agree with Booth that "the fictions that . . . invite conversation that might prove ethically educational—are naturally those that present mixtures of value" (*The Company We Keep* 207). What Coleridge calls "the ideal"—"the happy balance of the generic and the individual" (BL 2: 214)—can in drama produce an effect independent of the "negative belief" of poetic faith (2: 216), but ethically instructive in a different, more consciously divided way. In the case of the many version of *Don Juan* that were staged during Coleridge's time, spectators negotiate between alienation—"there is no danger . . . of my becoming such a monster of iniquity as Don Juan"—and a complex potential identification:

> But to possess such power of captivating and enchanting the affections of the other sex! to be capable of inspiring in a charming and even a virtuous woman, a love so deep, and so entirely personal to *me*! that even my worst vices (if I *were* vicious) even my cruelty and perfidy (if I *were* cruel and perfidious) could not eradicate the passion! To be so loved for my own self, that even with a distinct knowledge of my character, she yet died to save me! this, sir, takes hold of two sides of our nature, the better and the worse. (*BL* 2: 216)

For Coleridge the ethical force of this kind of drama consists in what Booth, following Kenneth Burke, calls "the total patterning of the reader's desires and satisfactions" (*The Company We Keep* 206), rather than in a simple identification with or rejection of the work's content. The "otherness" of dramatic characters is not simply to be embraced or rejected, but *engaged,* in this case forcing us to confront both "heroic disinterestedness" and the craving for an "outward confirmation of that *something* within us, which is our *very self*" (*BL* 2: 216–17).[23]

As this quote suggests, Coleridge's sacrificial spectator engages in a process of self-interpretation that differs from conceptual representation and that involves both loss and recovery. Stanley Cavell finds in Thoreau that "reading" is "a process of *being read,* as finding your fate in your capacity for interpretation of yourself" (16). For Coleridge, drama also enables self-interpretation: "In the plays of Shakespeare every man sees himself without knowing that he sees himself as in the phenomena of nature, in the mist of the mountain a traveller beholds his own figure but the glory round the head distinguishes it from a mere vulgar copy" (*Lects*

1808-1819 1:352). What we see is not a "copy" of ourselves—that would be the error of asking drama simply to represent our moral preconceptions—but rather an idealized projection of ourselves at our *interpretive* best. In the act of poetic faith we willingly submit to "being read" by that other self, an other self that is "better" not because it is more virtuous, or because it simply recognizes the evil of an Iago, but because it is the self that appears as a result of the "painful" "sacrifice" undergone by the smugly self-contained ego.

Gerald Bruns argues that tragedy's challenge to moral philosophy can be seen in terms of Cavell's argument, in that the reader is implicated in and "exposed" to the tragic events, and hence "tragic knowledge is closer to what Cavell calls acknowledgment and what Gadamer calls hermeneutical experience than it is to what we normally think of as knowledge, namely, knowledge as conceptual representation" (*Hermeneutics Ancient and Modern* (189). Cavell argues in *In Quest of the Ordinary* that "tragedy is a projection or an enactment of a skeptical problematic" by which "the loss of presentness (to and of the world) is something that the violence of skepticism deepens exactly in its desperation to correct it" (173-74). Cavell's example is how Lear "forgoes the world for just the reason that the world is important . . . he finds that it vanishes exactly with the effort to *make* it present" (173).

For Coleridge, tragedy depicts the loss of the *ethical* world that is then recovered by the spectator's interpretative activity. That activity engages the "two sides of our nature, the better and the worse," or our attraction to and repulsion by a world of amoral intellect, as Cavell's skeptic is divided between the drives toward skepticism and certainty. On the surface, Coleridge is more optimistic than Cavell about the possibility of recovering from the moral skepticism portrayed by Shakespeare's Iagos. However, that ethical recovery can only be accomplished by a "sacrifice" of the spectator's moral certainty, by an acknowledgment of the pull toward moral skepticism represented by the attraction and value of isolated intellectual power. As Cavell says in his reading of Coleridge's *Rime of the Ancient Mariner,* "it is natural to the human to wish to escape the human, if not from above then from below, toward the inhuman" (59). The recovery of the human, according to Cavell, entails the "acknowledgment" (as opposed to the "knowledge") that knowledge itself is predicated on both its necessity and its precariousness, as for Coleridge ethical knowledge depends on both the need for ethical certainty (Iago *is* a villain) and the dramatic attraction of amoral power as a real potential alternative. For Coleridge, this is a conflict between reflective knowledge itself and "thick" ethical understanding, between reflective knowledge taken alone—which is antiethical, as in Shakespeare's villains—and the ethical understanding gleaned from interpreting Shakespeare's villains of intellectual power. This is part of what Cavell calls the "struggle of philosophy and poetry for and against one another, for and against their own continued existence" (145).

If, as Gadamer says, tragedy "deepen[s]" the spectator's "*continuity with himself*" because "what he encounters is his own story, familiar to him from religious or historical tradition" (*TM* 133), even as "[the] spectator recognizes himself and his own finiteness in the face of the power of fate" (132), Coleridge presents a very modern version of this notion. The spectator's "own story" is not only the isolated power of intellect in an Iago, or the intensity of Romeo's love (though these are certainly important themes in Coleridge's own personal story), but also the story of the imagination itself as "the distinguishing characteristic of man as a progressive being" according to which we "live by" a prospective "hope and faith" (*Lects 1808–1819* 2: 193),[24] which sacrificially binds itself to the possibility of self-interpretation.

As Ricoeur argues, part of the complementarity of literary narratives and life histories is that narratives combine retrospective unity with protagonists who "are oriented toward their mortal future," and thus literary narratives "teach us how to articulate narratively retrospection and prospection" (*Oneself* 163). For Coleridge, the prospective aspect of literature inheres not so much in the narrative itself as in the imaginative act of reading. This is both a free act of the imagination and a submission of the self to a larger history and truth, consonant with Coleridge's union of freedom and necessity, which holds for the writer as well. The reader of Shakespeare submits himself to the prospect of self-interpretation, and the writer of *Kubla Khan* submits himself to the potential consequences, both positive and negative, of either failing or succeeding in an act of imaginative imitation. Reader and writer experience both the freedom to imagine an alternative life and at the same time an imaginative structure that offers no alternatives to itself. "[E]ven today," says Gadamer, "[t]he writer's free invention is also the presentation of a common truth that is binding on the writer also" (*TM* 133).

But Coleridge is not just advocating self-interpretation; he is also calling for a sacrifice of the self. Other contexts in which Coleridge discusses sacrifice engage the importance of this concept in the history of modern notions of subjectivity and indicate his complex relation to this history. Sacrifice figures importantly in Coleridge's discussion of the origins of

Greek tragedy in the lectures of 1808 and 1813 and in his concern, expressed most fully in the 1825 *Aids to Reflection,* to redefine the Christian concept of Christ's sacrificial death. He takes great pains in Lecture 2 of the 1808 *Lectures on Principles of Poetry* to locate the origins of Greek tragedy in the goat-offering to Bacchus, whom Coleridge associates not simply with festivity, but with "the <organic> energies of the Universe, that work by passion and Joy without apparent distinct consciousness" (*Lects 1808–1819* 1:45). In the first of the 1813 *Lectures on Shakespeare & Education* the same history is repeated, with Bacchus as "the symbol of that power which acts without our consciousness from the vital energies of nature, as Apollo was the symbol of our intellectual consciousness" (1:518).

The move from a sacrifice offered to the unconscious forces of nature at the origin of Greek drama to the notion of self-sacrifice as a Christian virtue to be exercised while experiencing good modern drama suggests the history discussed by Jean Luc Nancy in "The Unsacrificeable." According to Nancy, sacrifice becomes a strangely ambivalent concept in the Greco-Christian tradition; on the model of the self-sacrifice of Socrates and Christ, Christianity conceives of sacrifice as a willed sacrifice of the subject, a kind of sublation of the singular subject into a universal, "a uniqueness of the life and substance in which or to which all singularity is sacrificed" (23). At the same time, sacrifice itself must be "sacrificed" to a spiritual, mimetic, figurative sense of sacrifice: "Western sacrifice is already infinite in being self-sacrifice, in being universal, and in revealing the spiritual truth of all sacrifice. But it is—and must be—infinite also insofar as it reabsorbs the finite moment of sacrifice itself and thus insofar as it must, logically, sacrifice itself as sacrifice in order to accede to its truth. . . . spiritual sacrifice will be sacrifice only in a figurative sense" (24). In Coleridge, pre-Christian notions of sacrifice are "sacrificed" to the Christian sense of sacrifice, a sense which it is important to keep figurative rather than literal, and sacrifice in the contexts of both reading and theology is reinterpreted positively as *self*-sacrifice.

In *Aids to Reflection,* Coleridge calls "[s]in-offerings, sacrificial expiation" one of "the four principal Metaphors" used by Paul to illustrate "the blessed *Consequences* of Christ's Redemption of Mankind" (320). His point is to warn against the illegitimate transfer of meaning from consequence to cause and to argue that we should see this notion of sacrifice as merely allegorical rather than deeply symbolic. That the consequence of Christ's death—redemption—is equivalent to the supposed *consequence* of sacrifice does not justify seeing sacrifice as the *cause* of redemption, particularly if sacrifice is seen as the satisfaction of a debt. Paul used sacrifice as a metaphor (320–34) or "likeness," to which we should prefer John's nonmetaphorical, "symbolic" explanation of redemption as "a re-*generation,* a *birth,* a spiritual seed impregnated and evolved, the germinal principle of a higher and enduring Life, of a *spiritual* Life—that is, a Life, the actuality of which is not dependent on the material body" (322). (This is also the example used in the famous distinction between symbol and allegory [205–6].) In Nancy's terms, the role of sacrifice in the process of redemption is here reduced to the figurative level; this "metaphorical" or "allegorical" concept of sacrifice is thus translated into—or sacrificed to—the "symbolic" or "tautegorical" concept of the subject's spiritual rebirth.

Although Coleridge does not make this link explicitly, the sacrifice to Bacchus, the god of nonconscious nature, is, one could argue, similarly replaced by the notion of the self-sacrifice of the spectator's consciousness. This sacrifice of the spectator is consonant with Coleridge's general sense of the need for the individual self to be sacrificed or sublated into a higher entity, which is of course ultimately a unity with the divine will. In both his discussion of Christian redemption and his discussion of the spectator of drama, sacrifice is a concept that is on one level rejected, as a metaphor not to be taken literally or as a condition for primitive pagan drama, but on another level sacrifice is incorporated into the dialectical development of a "post-sacrificial" concept of *self*-sacrifice. This is for Nancy a problematic gesture because it institutes an ideology of absolute subjectivity: "Sacrifice as self-sacrifice, universal sacrifice, truth, and sublation of sacrifice, is itself the institution of the absolute economy of absolute subjectivity." This sublation also sets up the "old" notion of sacrifice as a "figure . . . which it pretends to know and which in reality it fabricates for its own purposes" (27). Thus for Nancy the "[d]enunciations of economism and simulation" that "run throughout the dialectical understanding of sacrifice" (26) are sublated into an economy of absolute subjectivity and a fiction about the past. In one sense, Coleridge's comments bear out Nancy's model: he denounces the economy of sacrificial atonement in order to support a theology of rebirth and he creates a myth of Greek sacrifice to unconscious nature as a foil for a modern sense of self-sacrifice.

On this reading, we have entered the familiar territory of the Romantic ideology. But it may not be the ideology we have come to expect. Nancy objects to the "problematic anthropology" suggested by René Girard's understanding of sacrifice on the basis of *mimesis,* but Sandor Goodhart, in *Sacrificing Commentary,* uses a Girardian reading of sacrifice to reach a similar conclusion to Nancy's: that the logic of sacrifice has run its course. Nancy takes the existential approach: the language of sacrifice ultimately comes down to saying that "existence is in essence sacrificed, and that rather than sacrifice existence "in" or "to" essence, we should adopt the language of "offering," which preserves the finitude of "existence" because it "is an attempt to mark that, if we have to say that existence is sacrificed, it is not in any case sacrificed by anyone, nor is it sacrificed to anything. 'Existence is offered' means the finitude of existence" (36).

Sacrifice has a deeper hold on culture for Goodhart, because he holds to René Girard's argument in *Violence and the Sacred* that sacrifice is the hidden means by which cultures control violence: the ritual killing of an "other" is an act of violence, but it preserves the cultural distinctions that threaten to collapse into the violence of undifferentiation that would arise if rivalry and the resulting vengeance were allowed to go unchecked: "the sacrificial process prevents the spread of violence by keeping vengeance in check" (Girard 18). The function of "myth" is to disguise this function, for example by giving other, external reasons for sacrifice: "Myths are the retrospective transfiguration of sacrificial crises, the reinterpretation of these crises in the light of the cultural order that has arisen from them" (64).

Goodhart has forcefully applied Girard's theory to the relations between literature and criticism, arguing that literary works, particularly tragedy, tend to "uncover behind the mythic structures from which they are born the violence of their own genesis" (40), while criticism tends to defeat that process by reinstating the myth that obscures this originary violence. For Goodhart, criticism is "sacrificial"—that is to say, it engages in the sacrificial process without recognizing it—both in its cultural domestication of literature and in its repetition of philosophy's domestication of literature. Criticism "is sacrificial with regard to the cultural institutions in which such monstrous writing is to be read (the university, for example) and that it serves by domesticating and safely replaying its distinctions. But it is also sacrificial or protective of the tradition in so far as it repeats the philosophical mechanisms by which Aristotle would already domesticate and safely replay the violence that Plato identifies with the mimetic in general (and tragedy in particular)" (255). For Goodhart, Coleridge's Shakespeare criticism is an important phase in this "sacrificial" act of mythological domestication, by which "we have built our criticism out of the same mythic materials of which the play itself [*Richard II*] is constructed, and about which, ironically, the play is profoundly critical" (44). Seeing the play as "a grand expression of Renaissance humanism" (44) is to remytholigize Shakespeare's source materials and deny the play's critique of these materials.

Goodhart's version of an ethical hermeneutic is that we should read "anti-sacrificially" by becoming aware of such criticism's mythologizing of its own sacrificial act, thereby engaging in "the sacrificial that is aware of the arbitrariness of [its] retrospective reading and names it in advance in order that we might give it up" as opposed to "the sacrificial that rereads itself from the perspective of its own ending" (261). The ethical stakes are high here—the alertness of such "anti-sacrificial" reading, or "Reading After Auschwitz," as Goodhart entitles his final chapter, will, he hopes, give us the opportunity to avoid a repetition of the Holocaust as we mourn and understand that maximization of sacrificial violence (242-43).[25]

The question for us, then, is this: is Coleridge, as Goodhart argues, the original mythologizer of Shakespeare, or does his method of reading place him higher on Goodhart's scale of ethical alertness, either implicitly or explicitly? It is clear that, in Nancy's terms, Coleridge partakes in the dialectic of sacrifice's sublation into self-sacrifice, but Nancy's existential alternative, the preservation of finitude through "offering," would deny the element of idealization that is so important to Coleridge (and about which Nancy is perhaps being too optimistic and ahistorical in his suggestion that that we can move beyond it to a "pure" finitude). Goodhart suggests with more historical acumen that the Girardian logic of sacrifice can be transcended only by a recognition of its inevitability, as we work through and mourn the horror of the Holocaust.

Coleridge's position is ambivalent, but definitely more complex than Goodhart's analysis suggests. I have argued elsewhere that Wordsworth is ambivalent about the role of sacrifice in culture;[26] the same could be said of Coleridge. Like Wordsworth's Wanderer, who objects in the *Excursion* to a sacrificial economy because "wherever man is made / An offering, a sacrifice" he is "employed / As a brute mean, without acknowledgement / Of common right or interest in the end" (9.115-18), Coleridge argues against seeing the sacrifice of Jesus' redemptive act within an economy of debt and atonement. In Goodhart's terms, Coleridge's rejection of the sacrificial mechanism could be read as a mythologization that refuses to acknowledge the social function of sacrifice, as Goodhart himself argues is the case with Coleridge's Shakespeare criticism. Or Coleridge can be read as presenting a Girardian recognition of sacrifice's preservation of an economy of differentiation, but a recognition that desires to move beyond the economy of sacrifice.

It is perhaps both. On the one hand, his rejection of the sacrificial metaphor for redemption, as well as his rejection of Greek sacrifice to unconscious "nature" in favor of Shakespeare's conscious mind, suggests an "anti-sacrificial" desire to expose the mechanism of sacrifice. On the other hand, the "sacrificial" mechanism that he sees as fundamental is not Girard's objective, sociological originary violence, but a sacrifice of the subject. He objects to the association of sacrifice with an economy of the objective, whether it be the fitting of Jesus' death into an allegorical economy of atonement or the Greek sacrifice to unconscious nature. In place of such concepts as the sacrifice to Bacchus or the logic of debt he puts the dramatic spectator's sacrifice of self and the believer's faith in God's incarnation and death, which must remain a mystery: "[m]ore than this, the mode, the possibility, we are not competent to know" (*AR* 324). Thus, even as Coleridge's position argues against Goodhart's notion of the critic as mythologizer, it still operates within a logic of sacrifice—in effect, perhaps, it becomes a mythologization of the critical act of self-sacrifice.

The self-sufficient ego is sacrificially split, and can be reconciled only by the conditional "If I were"—the imagining of an alternative but potentially real self. The imagination of an alternative self is not a simple rational choice, except insofar as poetic faith is a matter of "choosing" to suspend rational choice. Coleridge's imaginative assumption of Don Juan's character suggests Booth's rehabilitation of "hypocrisy," which is in turn reminiscent of Gadamer's rehabilitation of "prejudice"; both are terms whose wholly pejorative connotations stem from the Enlightenment ideal of autonomous subjects capable of free and unlimited rational choice. Booth points out that

> [t]he word "hypocrisy" originally meant simply the playing of a role *on the stage;* dramatic acting, *hypocrises,* from *hypo* ("under") plus *critein* ("to decide, determine, judge"). To give the signs of choosing in a certain way, on stage or off, was to convey a character of a certain kind, in "hypocrisy." . . . What is forgotten in our universal condemnation of hypocrisy is that a kind of play-acting with characters, or characteristics, a kind of *faking* of characters, is one of the main ways that we build what becomes our character. (*The Company We Keep* 252)

Similarly, Gerald Bruns suggests, with direct reference to the Romantic hermeneutic tradition, that the entire process of understanding is a matter of adopting the position of an "other" that exists within each of us:

"Understanding, whether of oneself or another, is just the wearing of masks" (*Hermeneutics Ancient and Modern* 161). The value of such a procedure for the development of personal identity is suggested by Altieri's comments on the importance of "style" as a means of connecting the intending, first-person self with the third-person self that is observable in the world: "where style is concerned there are not selves and worlds, nor even first- and third-persons, but rather endless and irreducible modes for weaving the two together so that substance is inseparable from the shapes intentionality takes" (*Subjective Agency* 87).[27] Coleridge, of course, gives ontological and ethical priority to "inner" conceptions such as will over "outer" conceptions such as masks or style, but the *temporal* priority of the external to the internal in natural history, moral life, and religious history gives it an important kind of necessary anteriority, as in this notebook entry on the relation between "will" and "deed": "The will to the deed, the inward principle to the outward Act, is as the ~~Shell to the~~ Kernal to the Shell; but yet, 1. The Shell is necessary for the Kernal, & that by which it is commonly known; & 2. As the Shell ~~grows~~ comes first, & the Kernal grows gradually & hardens within it, so is it with the Moral principle in man—Legality precedes Morality in every Individual, even as the Jewish Dispensation precedes the Christian in the Education of the world at large" (*CN* 3: 4003).

The trying on of roles was even more a part of Coleridge's life than of most lives, as he shifted uncomfortably among the roles of Pantisocrat, husband, father, poet, dejected lover, journalist, critic, dramatist, philosopher, Sage of Highgate, etc. As the example of drama shows, the "if I were" (though I know I am not) of "hypocritically" identifying with Don Juan is of ethical value not just because we may in fact end up becoming that which we pretend to be, as in many of Booth's examples. Coleridge also ascribes a value to the trying on of characters we know we will *not* become, but not in any simple sense of being warned away from such characters. This giving in to illusion is also not simply the "relatively cost free offer of trial runs" that Booth finds in the ethical experience of fictions (*The Company We Keep* 485), because the imaginative identification with a Don Juan exacts the very real cost of a division within the subject.

For Coleridge, as this suggests, tragedy works somewhat as a "thought experiment," which Ricoeur says is one of the functions of literature in general (*Oneself* 159), but Coleridge finds a different purpose than that ascribed to such experiments by Ricoeur. We perform the "thought experiment" of identifying with Don Juan or Iago, willing ourselves into an acknowledged illusion. The purpose, however, is not to request "the help of fiction to organize life retrospectively" because of "the elusive character of real life," as Ricoeur puts it (162), nor is it Nussbaum's "incompleteness" of the novelist insofar as he "stands apart from some of the confusing complexity of the human scene" (*Love's Knowledge* 188). For Coleridge, aesthetic apprehension has its own elusiveness and confusion, and his biography provides a strong counterargument to the idea that art helps to organize one's life. His thought does not allow for any simple comparison, in terms of relative comprehensiveness or cohesion, between fictional and real worlds, whether it be Ricoeur's "retrospective" fiction or Williams's alternativeless world of dramatic necessity. Criteria such as relative "completeness" still see aesthetic experience as simply *part* of experience in general. For Coleridge, poetry and drama are more than subsets of general experience, because they offer an ethical challenge that arises partly from their ability to "idealize" in a way that differs from both the contingency of everyday life and the conclusions of moral philosophy.

Thus, even though for Coleridge drama presents an "incomplete" ethical universe in the isolation of "power" from ethical context, this should not be confused with the assumption that the universe of the play is in all senses narrower than the real-life universe of the spectator. The narrowing of options that Williams finds in drama should not be confused with "closure"; in fact, philosophers such as Williams and Nussbaum are attracted to literature precisely because of its lack of closure; as Anthony Cascardi notes, "[w]here philosophy is seen as aspiring to 'closure' . . . literature will be defined as that which is disruptive of closure" (xi). Although Williams may be right that fiction presents a universe in which "there are no interesting or realistic questions about alternatives *to* the action," or, in the case of dramatic necessity, "no alternatives *within* the action," at the same time, for Coleridge, a dramatist such as Shakespeare presents a world that is in another sense more comprehensive than that of the spectator, because it is a world of potentiality that exists "out of time": "So it was with Shakespeare he was as much out of time as Spencer out of space, yet we felt that tho' we never knew that such characters existed we felt conscious that they might exist" (*Lects 1808–1819* 1:289). But the natural and potentially objective comprehensiveness of Shakespeare's "vast multiplicity of characters" is a product of subjective "meditation" rather than lower-order "observation," so that (with Coleridge's typical avoidance of the extremes of idealism and materialism) there is at least in theory no conflict between the (limited) subjectivity of authorial power and the (more comprehensive) objectivity of nature: "He had only to imitate such parts of his character, or to exaggerate such as existed in possibility and they were at once nature and fragments of Shakespeare" (1: 289).

In the appropriate experience of Shakespearean tragedy, which entails poetic faith and sacrifice, the philosophical ego, in which judgment is always actively awake, is put on hold so that we can experience the ego—particularly the intellectually ambitious ego—in isolation from the judgment that nevertheless remains "behind the curtain," hidden off-stage, but still part of the play. This is seeing the self at its worst—intellectually ambitious Iagos isolated from conscience and faith—but through an experience of sacrificial self-denial and suspension of judgment that presents the understanding self at its self-denying best. Our suspension of judgment aligns us with Iago in the dream of identification, but separates us from him in that we are sacrificing our egos as he promotes his. Thus, appropriate understanding of drama is both an active engagement of the will and a challenge *to* the will: by actively resisting bad drama's efforts merely to reflect and gratify our desires, we exert this "sacrificial" will in order to hold the isolated will of the ego (the will to self-gratification) in check. This role of the will is consonant with Coleridge's definitions of evil as "Will that would manifest itself as Will, not in Being" (*CN* 4: 5076). The active engagement of the will in realizing the transaction of authentic dramatic understanding—a will that *is* realized in the conflicted Being portrayed by tragedy—confronts and challenges the solipsistic will that is actualized only in itself, in the search for self-reflection and self-gratification.[28]

As Tilottama Rajan suggests, Coleridge's double hermeneutic is not without its problems. Adopting Ricoeur's well-known distinction, she argues that the biblical hermeneutics on which Coleridge's theory of reading is based attempts an uneasy combination of a "hermeneutics of faith" regarding the truth of the spirit and a "hermeneutics of suspicion" regarding the letter (*The Supplement of Reading* 102). Reading the *Biographia* as a conversion narrative that entails "distrust of both a selfhood that must be overwhelmed by 'truth,' and of a truth that needs to short-circuit rational persuasion" (103), she sees Coleridge as promoting "a submissive act that perilously wrests a positive hermeneutic from an act of self-negation" (104). In discussing what she sees as Coleridge's willful misreading of Kant in the *Biographia*—a reading both "Romantic" in its idealization of Kant's skepticism and "deconstructive" in its reading of Kant against the grain—Rajan asks the important question of "whether there is a form of deconstruction compatible with sympathy" (107). Her ultimate answer to this question is a qualified "no" for Coleridge. The conversation poems narrate a struggle with both the problem "of understanding someone the structure of whose experience is radically different from one's own" (114), as in "This Lime-Tree Bower," and the problem of "an otherness within himself" (125), as in Coleridge's ambivalence toward Wordsworth in "To William Wordsworth." The turn to allegory in later poems such as "The Pang More Sharp than All," "Time Real and Imaginary" and others, in which stationary figures replace narrative, makes "these poems renunciations of the hermeneutic project" (134).

Even if—or perhaps because—the tension in Coleridge's double hermeneutic cannot be resolved, the combination of engagement and alienation that it demands of the spectator speaks to some deadly serious and very modern problems of interpretation, as I hope to show with a contemporary cinematic example. Given the current highly publicized questioning of the relation between fictional and real-world violence, the ethical position of the spectator is now far more than a literary-critical issue. My example is Oliver Stone's *Natural Born Killers,* a film that has been held at lest partly responsible for a number of acts of "copy-cat" violence, including the fatal shootings at Columbine High School in Littleton, Colorado, on April 20, 1999. Coleridge can help us see that, if there is indeed a link between the film and acts of violence, the problem may lie not in the film but in our unquestioningly mimetic modes of interpretation.

Assuming some adaptation to the contingent "manners" of the time, not to be confused, Coleridge says, with the permanence of "morals" (*Lects 1808–1819* 1:295),[29] Coleridge might in fact see a film such as Stone's as more "moral" than one such as Roland Emmerich's *Independence Day* (or almost any other recent Hollywood action film) despite the latter film's portrayal of "the best Christian morality." *Natural Born Killers* puts the audience in the uncomfortable but interpretively "ethical" position of identifying with the morally alien consciousness of a pair of nonetheless sympathetic murderers. The spectator is denied any easy self-gratification and forced to experience "power" in isolation from the spectator's own ethical context, and the film emphasizes through cartoon sequences and parody that this experience is a willed "illusion." *Independence Day,* though not without the obligatory postmodern reflexivity of self-parody, reinforces and quickly gratifies the audience's sense of how vaguely defined moral values would come to the fore in the comfortingly unlikely event of an attack by alien creatures who are much too easy to hate; they are not only ugly but also antienvironment.[30]

On the one hand, if Coleridge's approach is not possible, it may be partly because his appreciation for the divided, ethically challenging response elicited by *Don Juan* requires an already developed ethical sense that can no longer be assumed. One cannot benefit from the conflict in appeals to the best and the worst parts of our natures unless one already knows what those parts are. The sacrificial subject must already be a subject, just as "[i]n order to an efficient belief in Christianity, a man must have been a Christian" (*BL* 2: 244). Films and plays can challenge and refine our ethical sense, but they cannot create it. If in fact the movies are the main source of ethical knowledge for children,[31] then Coleridge's sacrificial spectator cannot exist and the critics of media violence have a point. Coleridge himself was less than sanguine about the public's ability to become the kind of spectator he advocated.

On the other hand, Coleridge's argument enables a distinction that is not made often enough today: copy-cat violence may have less to do with the movies than with our modes of interpretation, because even the arguments against copy-cat violence fail to see it as the result of an aberrant mode of interpretation. The conservative argument that controlling the media will control behavior is based on one interpretive mode disdained by Coleridge: the idea that art should reflect and reinforce our values. This position does not argue against imitating films; it just replaces one object of imitation with another, urging us to imitate heroes rather than villains. The postmodern argument that the distinction has dissolved between the virtual reality of films and the "real" reality of human behavior (which has trickled down from Baudrillard to the popular press and is now a cliché of media commentary) has a similar effect and reflects a closely related mode to which Coleridge objects: the confusion between art and life—"delusion" rather than "illusion"—that should be countered by the *willed* suspension of disbelief. This position suggests that we have no choice but to do what is on the screen, because there is no real difference between what is on the screen and what is not. While many commentators deplore and fear this development, it tends to be seen as the inevitable result of an increasingly technological world. Thomas de Zengotita's "The Gunfire Dialogues," published in *Harper's* magazine, provides a good example of this position. He compares the "post-literate fusion of fact and fiction in multimedia narratives of our day" to the "paradigms of behavior and evaluation in an essentially tribal society" that Plato feared in preliterate Greece (57).

As Zengotita's comparison suggests, the potential confusion between the virtual reality of the mind and the ethical reality of social interactions has been with us at least since Plato's worries about the poet "who [is] capable by his cunning of assuming every kind of shape and imitating all things" to be excluded from the republic (*Republic* 3.398, 642). Putting them into an ethically workable relationship is a matter for interpretive responsibility, not legislative responses to a technological or postmodern fate. Ironically, the very Enlightenment schema of representation that worked to promote scientific empiricism is now partly responsible for the virtualization of reality. Just as the binary code of computer language, one of the crowning achievements of that schema, has enabled increasingly realistic technological simulacra, representational theories have dominated theories of interpretation. If an image does nothing but succeed or fail as an instrument of representation, then of course, especially after Derrida and Lacan, the signified can become just another signifier and virtual violence can become real killing.

There is an apparent, but only apparent, sophistication in the assumption that we have thus deconstructed a naive separation between art and life, as when images of "theatricality" are made to proliferate indiscriminately in both theater and history. To take a somewhat random example, Stephen Bretzius argues that "influential critiques of performative discourse and its ritualistic origins in post-subjective (post-Lacanian) sacrifice are generated not only by the postmodern university, but also, in *Romeo and Juliet,* by the early modern theater" (75), in an article that see-saws between the autobiography of Shakespeare and the autobiographies of Shakespearean critics Stephen Greenblatt and Joel Fineman. This is done in the name of a project that looks hermeneutically responsible, in that it acknowledges, as Louis Montrose says, "that the critic's own text is as fully implicated in such an interplay [of history and representation] as are the texts under study" (Montrose 305 qtd. Bretzius 75). It is an important part of the hermeneutic argument that such implication occurs, of course, but by not acknowledging the equally important differences between the horizons of critic and text in engaging the historicity of criticism, this kind of postmodern argument locks itself into a *mise en abyme* that, for all its leftist caché, mirrors the fundamentalist argument in important ways. Like the postmodern deconstruction of the difference between the subject and object of criticism, what Coleridge decries as "bibliolatry" in theology and "delusion" in art refuses to acknowledge the difference between culturally-specific textual expression and either real spirituality or the interpreter's position outside the text.

Just as the postmodern unity of subjective (virtual) reality and objective reality disables any interpretive mediation between them, conservative media critics elide the difference between life and art by assuming that films should provide good rather than bad examples to be imitated in life. This unexamined representational continuity between art and life, found at both ends of the political spectrum, is further enabled, in more general terms, by new-historical arguments that refuse to differentiate between works of art and other cultural artifacts, by political criticism that sees artworks simply as representations of ideology, and by revisions of the canon from either the left or the right that privilege the value of ideological content over the value of interpretive engagement. As Coleridge shows, "sacrificial" reading often puts interpretive engagement in direct conflict with ideological content. If the image, text, or film is more importantly part of a hermeneutic and ethical transaction like that which Coleridge describes, then it is up to us to integrate the seduction of virtual reality into our interactions with others by focusing on the work's hermeneutic challenge rather than its representational function. Thus, if *Natural Born Killers* has "caused" violence, it is at least partly because we have refused to teach or engage modes of interpretation in which an ethically active engagement of imagination allows works of art to challenge the spectator from a position of otherness, rather than simply to represent an ideological, virtual, or even ethical "reality." By "otherness" here, I do not mean a foreignness that comfortably reinforces values such as cultural diversity, which places us back into the representational model, but the foreignness of the sympathetic murderer who challenges our values.

V. The Problem of Narrative

Coleridge's discussions of genre illuminate the difference between his horizon and that of many of our contemporaries. This difference can be philosophically productive despite very reasonable modern objections both to the motivations for some of his distinctions and to some of the conclusions he draws from them.[32] For example, his denigration of the novel in favor of drama and poetry differentiates his approach from those modern critics—Booth, Nussbaum, Ricoeur, and others—who focus on the ethical and hermeneutic implications of narrative. Although, as I argued in the previous chapter, Coleridge inevitably confronts narrative problems, particularly in poems such as the *Rime,* his critical focus explicitly avoids Nussbaum's premise that "ethical" reading entails a parallelism between literary and real-life narratives.

To Coleridge, the novel is a lesser art form than poetry, and potentially "injurious to the growth of . . . the morals" (*Lects 1808–1819* 2: 193) for almost the same reason that it is given ethical value today: because it blurs the line between fact and fiction. In Coleridge, this generic hierarchy is reinforced by gender, but the sexism of his position[33] should not prevent a dialogue with his insights: "Women are good novelists, but indifferent poets; and this because they rarely or never thoroughly distinguish between fact and fiction. In the jumble of the two lies the secret of the modern novel, which is the *medium aliquid* between them, having just so much of fiction as to obscure the fact, and so much of fact as to render the fiction insipid" (2: 193). Coleridge's immediate object of attack, as he lectures in 1818, is the "common modern novel" or the "fashionable lady's novel" (2: 193), well before the fusion of philosophy and realism had produced the great realistic novels of the later nineteenth century; had he been able to read *Middlemarch,* his opinion of the novel (and women novelists) might have changed. This is not simply an issue of gender; despite his admiration for Sir Walter Scott's novels, Coleridge is sharply critical of his inappropriate confusion of the supernatural and the realistic in *Waverly* (*CM* 4: 581).[34] This problem is also not restricted to the novel. The blending of fact and fiction that Coleridge finds in Klopstock's *Messiah,* Schleiermacher's interpretation of the gospels, and even Milton's *Paradise Regained* presents a more extreme version of the same problem with theological implications, as poetic faith is short-circuited by the attempt to mix religious truths that are more than merely historical with fictions that are less than historical: "The more than historic faith in the one prevents us from yielding even a poetic faith to the other" (4: 479).

The higher moral claims made for poetry, coupled with the denigration of the novel's "jumbling" of fact and fiction, distances him from those who, like Nussbaum, connect the novel to moral philosophy by means of its purported engagement with the contingency of life. Against Nussbaum's suggestion that "novels share certain ethical commitments (to particularity, to the moral relevance of surprise) just in virtue of their form" (*Love's Knowledge* 190) we should place Coleridge's statement (borrowed, ironically, from Aristotle, Nussbaum's favorite source) that "poetry as poetry is essentially *ideal,* that it avoids and excludes all *accident;* that its apparent individualities of rank, character, or occupation must be *representative* of a class; and that the *persons* of poetry must be clothed with *generic* attributes" (*BL* 2: 45–46).

That Coleridge's attitude toward narrative is ambivalent is suggested by his reading of the Hebrew Bible. The narrativity of the Hebrew tradition, as opposed to the philosophical myth of the Greeks, is attributed partly to the "personal" ground of faith in the enunciation of "the eternal I AM," which "must be in part historic, and must assume the historic form" of narrative, but it is also attributed to "an accommodation to the then childhood of the human race." Only by this argument can the implicitly lower-order form of narrative be raised to the status of "a synthesis of poetry and philosophy" ("On the Prometheus of Aeschylus," *SW & F* 1267). On the one hand, as Stephen Prickett suspects, Coleridge's reading is "much more shaped by the tradition of the English novel than he knows," and his emphasis on the creation as an act of will suggests what Prickett discusses as the eighteenth-century movement toward a reading of the Bible as both dramatic and narrative (*The Origins of Narrative* 128, 155–59). On the other hand, that very same narrative is an accommodation of the ideal to primitive humanity, just as God's "narrative side"—his existence as a self-othering Logos—is an accommodation to an original apostacy. Narrative is a kind of "fallen" form, which makes it both foundational for our existence and subordinate to more ideal forms.

In implicitly rejecting the narratological link between ethics and literature, Coleridge is forced into the difficult position of arguing that a sharp difference between the work of art and ethical life is morally significant even as aesthetic and ethical practices are united in the foundational self-consciousness that defines "Imagination." Whether he is right or wrong, rejecting the narratological argument usefully forces Coleridge—and us—to confront the ethical function of the work of art without relying either on the comforting sense of narrative's mediation between art and life or on the discomforting postmodern fusion of art and life.[35] Coleridge's emphasis on the *Rime* as a work of pure imagination rather than a moral tale to be applied to life suggests that poetry, like Shakespearean drama, is for Coleridge partly defined in terms of its difference from everyday life. Thus he objects to Wordsworth's poetic claims for "a language taken . . . from the mouths of men in real life" (*BL* 2:42) as well as to Wordsworth's theoretical and practical conflation of the languages of poetry and prose (2:60–63).

As Rajan points out in her discussion of this part of the *Biographia*, Coleridge's position betrays a good deal of anxiety. He "protects the poetry in the text" only by "short-circuiting the grammatical reading of what the poem actually says in favor of a psychological reading of what it meant to say," deliberately misreading Wordsworth's possible critique of the Coleridgean idealization of poetry as a failure to achieve such idealization (*The Supplement of Reading* 107). As Rajan suggests, however, it is the very "displacement" of Coleridge's misreadings that raise the important hermeneutic issues (108). For my purposes, the correctness of Coleridge's reading of Wordsworth and the anxieties revealed by his exaltation of poetry over the novel are less important than the challenge posed by the ethical implications of the position that his reading forces him to take. For Nussbaum, the "adventure of the reader" of a novel such as Henry James's *The Golden Bowl* is "like the adventure of the intelligent characters inside it" in that "it involves valuable aspects of human moral experience that are not tapped by traditional books of moral philosophy" (*Love's Knowledge* 143). Coleridge would probably see this identification of literary and real-life experience as an example of passive "delusion" rather than productive "illusion" in its neglect of the otherness of aesthetic experience. For him, poetry is distinguished from "novels and romances" (with which genres it shares the "*immediate* object" of "pleasure, not truth") by "proposing to itself such delight from the *whole,* as is compatible with a distinct gratification from each component *part*" (*BL* 2: 12–13). Thus the poem's moral challenge is not the presentation of an "adventure" that the reader can share, as in Nussbaum's novelistic model, but rather its ability to bring "the whole soul of man into activity" through the imagination's power to reveal "itself in the balance or reconciliation of discordant qualities" (2: 15–16). Although, as I suggested above, the *Rime* is intertwined with biography and culture, neither the reader nor the Wedding Guest "shares" the Mariner's otherworldly "adventure," as the reader shares the characters' adventures in Nussbaum's Jamesian paradigm, and the shared experience the Mariner desires—"To walk together to the Kirk / With a goodly company!" (649–50)—is conspicuously absent in the poem.[36]

Adam Newton's recent *Narrative Ethics* also assumes a strong connection between literary narrative and ethical experience, but unlike MacIntyre, Nussbaum, Booth, and others, he sees that connection in terms of Levinas's notion of ethical alterity and Stanley Cavell's notion of an "acknowledgment" of otherness that is prior to conceptual "knowledge." This enables Newton to argue that fiction does not simply reflect life, but both enacts and confronts the reader with a call to responsibility based on the irreducible otherness of the ethical relation: "narrative situations create an immediacy and force, framing relations of provocation, call, and response that bind narrator and listener, author and character, or reader and text" (13). His conclusions complement my own, here and elsewhere,[37] in advocating the importance of Levinas's thought to an understanding of hermeneutics and ethics in literature. However, Newton's narratological perspective on the *Rime* contrasts sharply with Coleridge's suspicion of the ethical effects of fictional narrative. Newton comments that "[a]s a communicative act . . . the Mariner's narrating could be said ultimately to repudiate more than revivify" (6). Although Newton makes a strong narratological case that this repudiation, manifested in the halting and suspension of the Wedding Guest's life, suggests narrative's transformative ethical power, the chilling effect of the Mariner's story may also reflect Coleridge's suspicion of narrative itself, or at least of the exigencies that differentiate the ethics of narrative from the ethics of lived experience.

Our aesthetic horizon is so conditioned by "realistic" forms such as the novel and film that Nussbaum's novelistic use of literature in moral philosophy, as well as Booth's use of moral philosophy in his program for reading the novel, may seem inevitable and even natural. It is also undeniable, as Carlson and others have pointed out, that the Romantic preference for the manly art of poetry is objectionably gendered. However, the very difference between Coleridge's "poetic" horizon and the modern "novelistic" horizon brings to light a worthwhile aspect of the ethical experience of art that is not available to Nussbaum's model, while at the same time there are important affinities between the two models. The moral force of the poem as Coleridge sees it is related to the *phronesis* that Nussbaum champions in that the successful poem brings the "whole soul of man" into a dialectical activity, uniting means and ends. In this way the poem differs from what Nussbaum calls "the plainness of traditional moral philosophy" (*Love's Knowledge* 142) and from what Coleridge denigrates as moral injunctions that are "too openly intruded on the reader." However, it is poetic, rather than novelistic, in its refusal to "jumble" fact and fiction and, as I argued in Chapter 2, in its self-presentation both as aesthetic *techne* and as a "whole" experience valuable for its very otherness to the everyday life of the reader. Thus Shakespeare's "vast multiplicity" of characters is not exactly the novelistic complexity that Nussbaum finds in Henry James or that Booth finds in D. H. Lawrence, who provides "a broader *range* of irresolutions, and a deeper engagement with manifold possibilities, than life itself is ever likely to present to any one of us unassisted" (*The Company We Keep* 451). Because Coleridge's poetic rather than novelistic approach demands that poetry's "apparent individualities of rank, character, or occupation must be *representative* of a class," it is no contradiction for him to follow his comment about the "vast multiplicity" of Shakespeare's characters with the statement that "Shakespeare's characters might be reduced to a few, that is to say to a few classes of characters" (*Lects 1808–1819*: 1:290).

The relationship between the ethics of poetry and the ethics of discursive prose is more complex and more explicitly a Coleridgean concern than the relationship between poetry and narrative. On the one hand, dramatic art is *a*moral in that its mind-world mediation is freed from the "proper" human "state of subordination" to the "conscience" (hence the unhinging of beauty from the good), but in that state it can offer an ultimately ethical challenge to the coherence of our ethical life and force us into a "sacrificial" mode of ethical self-questioning. On the other hand, dramatic art is *im*moral if it pretends to "copy"—in Coleridge's sense—ethical philosophy by presenting our own philosophical prejudices without reflecting on them, thus sidestepping the important conflict between philosophy's discursive "truth" (which demands the latter sort of reflection) and poetry's intuitive "pleasure" (which does not). Seeking a passive "copy" of our own preconceptions involves succumbing to the dramatist who "gratifies us by representing those as hateful or contemptible whom we hate and wish to despise" (*BL* 2: 189). That kind of "jacobin" art merely mimics moral philosophy, offers conclusions, and wrongly calls for a direct transfer from text to life. The copy fails to "carr[y] practical wisdom back to the test of moral judgment in situation alone," as Ricoeur says tragedy should do (*Oneself* 241). Such art would deny the necessity of active "sacrifice" by which we accept tragedy's challenge and would ask drama merely to "copy" moral conclusions (not even moral reflections) in an other, inherently less moral medium.

Even though Wordsworth is said by Coleridge to be "capable of producing" "the FIRST GENUINE PHILOSOPHIC POEM" (*BL* 2: 156), unifying the disparate aims of prose and poetry, he is critiqued a few pages earlier for implicitly proposing a continuity between the ethical position within his poems and the ethics of real life: "The feelings with which, as christians, we contemplate a mixed congregation rising or kneeling before their common maker: Mr. Wordsworth would have us entertain at *all* times as men, and as readers; and by the excitement of this lofty, yet prideless impartiality in *poetry,* he might hope to have encouraged its continuance in *real life*" (2: 130). Although this goal of direct moral transfer between text and life is a worthy one, it mistakenly has poetry doing the work of philosophical prose. Wordsworth's didactic "object," according to Coleridge, "belongs to the moral philosopher, and would be pursued, not only more appropriately, but in my opinion with far greater probability of success, in sermons or moral essays, than in an elevated poem" (2: 130).

As Ellison has demonstrated, Coleridge's criticism in the *Biographia* negotiates in a complexly gendered way between "understanding as an aggressive mode" and "understanding as a sympathetic mode" (145). For Coleridge, however, power can be negatively aggressive or positively active, just as its opposite can be negatively passive or positively sympathetic. As we have seen, "power" can be a positive term: the world is to be seen as the result of an act of power, reflected in *natura naturans* and in the activity of imitation versus the passivity of the copy. But it can also be a negative term, as when nature's "powers without reflection, and consequently without Morality" (*Lects 1808–1819* 2: 221) are contrasted with the reflective power of imagination and when Shakespeare's villains demonstrate intellectual power in isolation from ethical context. Similarly, the negation of power can be positively self-effacing sympathy, what Ellison sees as Coleridge's appropriation of the feminine and maternal, or the negative passivity of the copy.

In terms of the continuity or discontinuity between art and life, the negative sides of both oppositions join: the passive copy can be a negatively aggressive force. The problem with the copy is that it posits too close a continuity between art and life. This is also, for Coleridge, the problem with the Wordsworthian poetry that attempts to copy real-life language and that posits too direct a continuity between the ethics of the poem and the ethics of the reader. It is also the problem with poems such as the *Rime* that obtrude their morals on the reader. From the author's point of view, according to Coleridge's critique of Wordsworth, at least until poetry and philosophy can be united, "it will remain the poet's office to proceed upon that state of association, which actually exists as *general;* instead of attempting first to *make* it what it ought to be, and then to let the pleasure follow" (*BL* 2: 130). Poetry should not attempt aggressively to change the world directly, as moral philosophy or literary criticism does; rather, in being receptive to "that state of association, which actually exists as *general,*" it will engage "the whole soul of man" in a positively active sacrificial response rather than the passive response of the "Defendant" in the *Biographia*'s dramatic criticism. As noted above, that ethically productive sacrificial response depends on a subjectivity that already exists. To put didactic truth before poetic pleasure is to get things backward in "a small *Hysteron-Proteron*"; it distorts, but in no way denies the moral effect of poetry, "[f]or the communication of pleasure is the introductory means by which alone the poet must expect to moralize his readers" (2: 131). From the reader's point of view, it is the passive spectator who refuses sacrifice in favor of a reflection of his own ethics who is subject to the aggression of the modern playwright (or, in our time, the Hollywood director), an author whose own passive acquiescence to conventional morality is coupled with an aggressive assault on the senses.

VI. Aesthetic Consciousness

Coleridge's insistence on the alienation of the spectator from the work, as opposed to the various modern views that connect aesthetic and lived experience, aligns him with what Gadamer calls the alienation of "aesthetic consciousness" but also permits some revision of Gadamer's concept. Aesthetic consciousness is the subjectification and dehistoritization of art, which Gadamer, in his early (1934) essay "Plato and the Poets," sees as the object of Plato's ethical critique in the *Republic* (*Dialogue and Dialectic* 64–65) and which he discusses in *Truth and Method* as the positive accomplishment but also the fundamental flaw of the Romantic program articulated by Schiller in his *Letters on the Aesthetic Education of Mankind*. Aesthetic consciousness "consists precisely in precluding any criterion of content and dissociating the work of art from the world" (*TM* 85) by appealing to abstracted inner experience (*Erlebnis*) rather than historically conditioned experience (*Erfahrung*). J. M. Bernstein argues, following Weber and Habermas in an analysis of the categorical separation among truth, morality, and art from Kant through Derrida, that this separation identified by Gadamer is "constitutive of modernity" (2). Gadamer's concept has obvious affinities with what historical literary criticism, after McGann, has labeled the "Romantic Ideology," and what Eagleton, with specific reference to Schiller's *Letters on the Aesthetic Education of Mankind*, analyzes as the ideological fundamentality of the aesthetic (*The Ideology of the Aesthetic* 103–19). Gadamer, whose promotion of the Western aesthetic tradition is criticized elsewhere by Eagleton as "the projection on to the world at large of a viewpoint for which 'art' means chiefly the classical monuments of the high German tradition" (*Literary Theory* 73), is actually much harsher on Schiller than Eagleton is, though the critique is in some ways similar. Like Gadamer, Eagleton sees a danger in Schiller's contentless realm of the aesthetic, which can be "sheer emptiness, a deep and dazzling darkness in which all determinations are grey, and infinity of nothingness" (*The Ideology of the Aesthetic* 108). However, he also sees in Schiller a strong awareness of "[t]he dangers of aestheticizing the law to nothing" (115), ultimately claiming that "Schiller's aesthetic thought provides some of the vital constituents of a new theory of bourgeois hegemony; but it also protests with magnificent passion against the spiritual devastation which that emergent social order is wreaking" (118).

Coleridge's theory of willing suspension of disbelief acknowledges both the power and the provisionality of aesthetic consciousness much as, in

Eagleton's reading, Schiller does. Giving in to dramatic illusion is indeed a disengagement from the world (one that, as I have suggested, has its own ethical force *as* disengagement), but as an act of will that acknowledges the imminent return of "judgment" it remains connected to the world. The self-sacrifice of the spectator presents a more complex relation to aesthetic consciousness, because self-sacrifice can be taken either as a subjectification of tradition (as in Nancy's reading) or as a sacrifice of self *to* something outside the self, an act that attempts to escape subjectivity. Gadamer suggests this paradox in the very different ways he critiques "aesthetic consciousness" in the 1934 "Plato and the Poets" and the 1960 *Truth and Method*. In the earlier essay, the "alienation" of aesthetic consciousness is a result of self-forgetfulness in the process of "imitation" critiqued by Plato in the *Republic,* affecting both actor and spectator:

> Here imitation has become self-exteriorization, self-estrangement. Thus the actor does not merely act out someone else's gestures. On the contrary, all his expressions are the display of an inner nature which is nevertheless not his own human nature. All forgetfulness of self in imitation fulfills itself, therefore, in self-alienation. And even he who merely watches such imitation without acting himself yields to the thing imitated in sympathy, which is to say that he forgets himself in vicariously experiencing through the other whom he sees before him. Thus even looking on, to the extent that it is the self-forgetful yielding of oneself to the vibrations of an alien emotion, always implies at least some self-alienation. (*Dialogue and Dialectic* 64)

Here Gadamer identifies this "imitation" that "implies a split in the self" (64) with the subjectivization and cultural disengagement of "aesthetic consciousness" because "aesthetic self-forgetfulness opens the way for the sophists' game with the passions to infiltrate the human heart" (65). However, in *Truth and Method,* self-forgetfulness, again with reference to Plato and Greek drama, has a positive function as an *antidote* to excessive subjectivity: "In fact, being outside oneself is the positive possibility of being wholly with something else. This kind of being present is a self-forgetfulness, and to be a spectator consists in giving oneself in self-forgetfulness to what one is watching. Here self-forgetfulness is anything but a privative condition, for it arises from devoting one's full attention to the matter at hand, and this is the spectator's own positive accomplishment" (126). Leaving aside the question, which I am not competent to address, of the extent to which this represents a change in Gadamer's thinking between 1934 and 1960,[38] the important question for our understanding of Coleridge is whether the self-forgetfulness implied in his notion of the sacrificial spectator is a retreat into the magical world of art, and thus into an alienated aesthetic subjectivity, as the traditional interpretation of "willing suspension of disbelief" and Gadamer's critique of Romantic aesthetic consciousness would have it, or the opposite: a self-forgetfulness that gets one out of the self into "the matter at hand," in which "[a] spectator's ecstatic self-forgetfulness corresponds to his continuity with himself" and in which "[w]hat rends him from himself at the same time gives him back the whole of his being" not as a disengaged self but in the historical context of "the truth of our own world—the religious and moral world in which we live" (128).[39]

The relatively easy answer to this question, and one to which Coleridge had recourse under the influence of Schelling in chapter 12 of the *Biographia* (but which he later qualified), is simply to define the self dialectically: self-alienation is both true alienation and part of the process that leads to the unity of self-consciousness. In this sense, the tragic spectator's (or actor's) self-forgetful "imitation" of another becomes, in Gadamer's 1934 language, "self-exteriorization, self-estrangement" (*Dialogue and Dialectic* 64). For the Coleridge of the *Biographia* this becomes a dialectical route to coherent subjectivity, expressed in the "I AM," as the "subject becomes a subject by the act of constructing itself objectively to itself; but . . . never is an object except for itself, and only so far as by the very same act it becomes a subject" (1: 273). The more difficult answer, but one that is truer to the range of Coleridge's thought, is in part that his position is indeed vulnerable to the accusation of alienated "aesthetic consciousness" in his separation of the aesthetic from the continuity of life. However, as I have tried to show, this alienation, aware of the artificiality and complex ethical force of its willed giving-in to illusion, also becomes a means of reconnection to the world. This reconnection occurs not through a dialectical sublation of alienation, but through the double hermeneutic of poetic faith, which both preserves and lets go of the rational will, and the sacrifice of the spectator, which demands both an already-developed ethical consciousness and the willingness to have it challenged. In this way Coleridge's complex version of the very alienation of aesthetic consciousness that Gadamer critiques becomes a route to the kind of aesthetic reengagement with the world called for by Gadamer's own hermeneutics.

6

Oneself as Another: Coleridgean Subjectivity

I. The Problems of Selves and Others

The "self" in Coleridge has always been discussed in dialectical terms, from the Schellingesque notion of self-objectification that Coleridge himself sometimes promoted to the various "betweens" that scholars have used to characterize the Coleridgean self: between symbol and allegory (de Man), between the "I am" and the "It is" (McFarland), between self and nature (Modiano), between visionary poet and revisionary reader (Mileur), between Hartlean associationism and free will (Christensen), between Miltonic egotism and Shakespearean proteanism (Bygrave), between deontological and teleological ethics (Lockridge); between "metaphysical monism" and a "dualistic epistemology" (Vallins); between radical egalitarianism and Tory apostacy (Leask), between himself and Wordsworth (Magnuson).[1] Many such studies, particularly the more recent ones, assume that we know, or that our theoretical framework knows, what a "self" is, or that because selves are cultural constructs, philosophical discussions of subjectivity are superseded by historical discussions of ideological function. However, subjectivity is a category that cannot be disarmed simply by historicizing it because, as Manfred Frank argues, "self-consciousness is absolutely not analyzable in expressions that do not already presuppose it" (185). Frank asks, "who but a subject is to be assaulted and repressed by the regimentations of discourse or the 'dispositions of power' expressed by Foucault's powerful incantations?" (178).[2] Thus the subject won't go away, but at the same time it need not become an essentialized concept to be simply textualized, decentered, gendered, historicized, or uncritically defended.

The Coleridge critics who have thoroughly studied his philosophy, such as Coburn, McFarland, Modiano, Lockridge, and most recently Perkins, have given full accounts of the complexity of the Coleridgean subject, but they have often (and perhaps wisely) found the resources of recent theory to be more limiting than helpful. One reason that modern terms are often unhelpful is that Coleridge's notion of subjectivity does not easily fit the terms that usually shape the modern debate: his view does not correspond either to the Enlightenment and Romantic tradition of the autonomous subject or to the post-Marxist tradition that returns the autonomous subject to the status of an historical or discursive effect. As I pointed out in Chapter 1, twentieth-century categories of political subjectivity do not accommodate Coleridge easily: his "conservatism" does not resemble anything that goes by that name today. The difficulty is not just that politics and philosophies of the subject have changed, however. Because subjectivity has been so heavily theorized in this century, opposing models tend to resemble each other in their monolithic and inflexible accounts of the mechanisms that organize the subject, whether they be linguistic, sociological, psychoanalytical, or ideological. As Christopher Norris points out, there is less difference than may appear between the account of subjectivity in the "conservative" notion of the autonomous agent operating in a world of free market forces and the "radical" historicization of that notion: "there is a close resemblance between talk of 'market forces' as an all-purposive regulative mechanism . . . and that strain of quasi-radical thought which likewise sees nothing but error and delusion in the 'discourse' of emancipatory critique" (*Truth and the Ethics of Criticism* 91). Coleridge was suspicious of any attempt to erect a social or economic theory on a single principle that would simplify or ignore the complexity and wisdom of history, as evidenced by his objections to Malthus and Smith. In a note from 1809, he laments the fact that politicians "disregard the opinion of wise & learned men," and "become so ignorant, that when they do appeal to a *book*, it is a Malthus, or an Adam Smith" (*CN* 3:3590).

If anything, Coleridge's brand of political conservatism argues against the kind of uncontrolled pursuit of individual agency that we now associate, at least in economic terms, with a conservative ideology of the subject. Worry about the subjugating power of the self as an autonomous agent—the extreme form in which Romantic subjectivity is usually critiqued by Marxist-inspired historical criticism—is not a recent phenomenon. As Habermas points out, this aspect of subjectivity was the aim of Hegel's critique of German Romanticism's aesthetic. Hegel was concerned "that in the modern world emancipation became transformed into unfreedom because the unshackling power of reflection had become autonomous and now achieved unification only through the violence of a subjugating subjectivity" (*The Philosophical Discourse of Modernity* 32–33). Much of the German philosophy between Kant and Hegel that Coleridge read so avidly "combined perspectives that construct and criticize the standpoint of subjectivity," as Sturma and Ameriks point out in their introduction to *The Modern Subject: Conceptions of the Self in Classical German Philosophy* (1). While the categories of recent literary theory fail to account for Coleridge's notion of ethical subjectivity, philosophers such as Charles Taylor who have studied the genesis of the modern self tend to see Coleridge as representative of a monolithic Romantic tradition of organic expressivism or autonomy.[3] What is missing is an effort to use recent thought on ethics and subjectivity to engage Coleridge in a conversation with the present that neither restricts his thought solely to its own categories nor forces him into the foreign categories of contemporary theory, while recognizing the historicity of both.

To do justice to Coleridge's notion of ethical subjectivity, we should follow Rawls in substituting the notion of the "person"—"a human being capable of taking full part in social cooperation, honoring its ties and relationships over a full life" for that of the "self as knower . . . or the concept of the self as the continuant character of psychological states: the self as substance or soul" ("Justice as Fairness 233," qtd. Norris, *Truth and the Ethics of Criticism* 95). Although Rawls's ethical theory is very different from Coleridge's, this terminology is consistent with Coleridge's subordination of the "self" to a notion of "person"—ultimately, the divine personëity—that is larger than the autonomous self and that joins the public and the private.

The central Coleridgean category of "personëity" addresses the related and still problematic issue, in ethical philosophy as well as cultural studies, of the inevitable conflict between "person" as an abstract, universal category and as a designation for unique individuals.[4] Despite the status of the "Will of Man" as a "representative of the Will of God" that "is above all particulars," Coleridge refuses to abstract the individual into a universal agent. He distinguishes the human from the animal partly according to human particularity: "Unlike a multitude of Tygers, a million of men is far other from a million times one man" ("Essay on Faith," *SW & F* 841–42).

Protestantism is amenable to representative government, he argues, because of its emphasis on the individualizing quality of the "Understanding, or Discursive Intellect," midway between the universality of "Reason" and the animality of "Sense": "Every man has his own understanding. . . . Hence it strives after the Individual, the definably *distinct:* for its proper function is to *comprehend,* and we can only comprehend an object by separating it" (*CN* 4: 5374).

Coleridge rescues the notion of "person" from the universal/individual conflict partly by making it precede the entire conflict theologically and ontologically; as I pointed out in Chapter 4, this is what makes the commanding "ought" prior to the "is."[5] He praises the evangelist John's effort "to emancipate the idea of personëity from the phenomenal notion of Outline, and (generally) from the sensuous Definite in space and time" (*CM* 2: 456). However, this emancipation from definite form is not an abstract universalization because it places the "person" (ultimately the divine person) above and before the rational principles that would effect such abstraction. On both the theological and the human level, persons are prior to and generative of laws and principles:

> in the *first* Man, even as in all is descendents 'born of woman,' the knowledge of the *Legislator* and the conviction of his Right to be obeyed must have been antecedent to the sense and conviction of the rightfulness of the *Law,* and the *Conditio sine qua non* of the latter. And in this case Religion must have been the Basis of Morality, and Morality of sciental Insight: In other words, the Light from God (i.e. God's revelation of his Being and attributes generally, and of his Will relative to Man) must have been introductory to the Light of Reason in the Conscience, and the Light of Reason in the Conscience to the Light of Reason in the Understanding. (Notebook 26, fol. 40v, qtd. Perkins 74)

God appears first as a person, with a will relative to man, as a force to be obeyed, and it is the light of that personal revelation of his Being that later produces the Light of Reason in the Conscience and then the Understanding. "Reason" is here Coleridge's theologization of Kant's term for what, in its highest form, pertains to the noumenal; a region cordoned off as inaccessible by Kant but made at least partially accessible by Coleridge via a concept of God that includes a communicative Logos and a human community capable of using the symbol. As Perkins explains, Reason is "not a divine attribute, but the divine *Person,* both transcendent and incarnate by around 1806" (146). This personification of Reason is demonstrated by Coleridge's rewriting of the Ten Commandments in Kantian terms; the first commandment is "Unconditional Obedience of the Will to the pure Reason, or Conscience/~~as~~ the *Reality* of which is *God—I* am the Lord thy God, thou shalt have no other god but me/Here the *Unity* of God is founded upon & proved by, its best, if ~~it~~ not its only *sure,* foundation & argument/viz.—the unity of the pure Reason.—Let the Will obey the pure Reason *exclusively* & *unconditionally*. Hence, it is a *command*—not an inducement" (*CN* 3: 3293). Reason's connection to the commanding will of a divine Person at its origin partly explains why it is conscience, not knowledge, that first receives the "Light of Reason," and it is conscience that is here equated with Pure Reason. This priority of the "person" not only makes Coleridge's metaphysics fundamentally ethical,[6] but it also prevents, as I pointed out in Chapter 3, a division between universal and particular in the ethical conception of the person. Neither the universal nor the particular is reducible to the other, because a "person" is the source of both universalizing rationality (obedience to the legislator precedes reasoning about laws) and the ethical aspect of particular human persons (the "reality" or noumenal version of human conscience is God).

Most importantly for my purposes, Coleridge's notion of the person contains a rich though divided concept of the "other" that cannot be contained within the notion of the self as an autonomous agent, a concept I will explore with the help of Paul Ricoeur, Emmanuel Levinas and Bernard Williams. The concept of the "other," however, is in contemporary theory as problematic a category as that of "self." For one thing, the word is used to mean two very different things, either the other of feminism and historicist criticism who is unrecognized and illegitimately assimilated to culturally dominant categories, or the patriarchal Lacanian Other that dominates the processes of desire. Norris observes that in a postmodern doctrine that sees other cultures as incommensurably alien, the first kind of otherness can become the other: "For it is no great distance, whether in philosophic or in psychological terms, from the attitude that on principle renounces all claims to know or comprehend the other to the attitude that views otherness as a threat—an absolute since radically alien threat—to its own very being and life-world" (*Truth and the Ethics of Criticism* 57). It is in this spirit that he praises Kristeva's recent "perception of the harms brought about by a rhetoric of cultural otherness, difference, or alterity that so easily translates into forms of ethnic hatred and racist paranoia" (104). Norris also points out that "otherness" can become a mere "rhetorical place-filler" if it confronts us with the false dilemma of choosing between the other as "an involuntary construction out of our own discourse" or "a locus of absolute alterity" before which we must refuse "any common ground of insight or mutual understanding" (73). Such is the case with the theories that remain tied to a descriptivist paradigm. This paradigm leaves only two options—either the other can be fit into our conceptual paradigm, or he/she cannot—and reduces the world to a textual field.

Although this either-or dilemma does perhaps plague both Lyotard's notion of the absolute alterity of the *differend* and historicist accounts that see the other as an ideological construction (Norris's targets), it is a false dilemma for both Coleridge and the theorists that I find most useful in illuminating Coleridge's ethics. Coleridge's foundational notion of the divine Person as "both transcendent and incarnate" (Perkins 146) is consistent with both his objections to the abstraction of the Kantian subject and his desire to make universal claims about ethical life. Norris's complaint is largely directed at Emmanuel Levinas's radical conception of absolute alterity, and to be fair, Levinas's work has too often been reduced to generalized statements about the untotalizable face of the other, ignoring the central fact that much of Levinas's work is devoted to constructing a theory of the subject.[7]

However, Levinas's notion of otherness does not, as Norris argues, require "the suspension of all preexistent concepts and categories (*Truth and the Ethics of Criticism* 47). Levinas's point is rather that such concepts and categories, to the extent that they stem from an instrumental rationality under the arbitrary control of a "free" autonomous subject, need to be grounded in the very real, "in your face" world of human contact: "the arbitrariness of freedom . . . is precisely what has to be grounded" (*TI* 85). This "grounding" acknowledges the messy arena in which Williams sees ethical life as operating (though Levinas sees it as operating in a very different way) as it interweaves public and private, absolute alterity and the everyday concerns that we approach through conceptual structures. In *Otherwise than Being,* Levinas distinguishes ethics, or the absolute, nonconceptualized proximity of the other, from justice, in which the presence of a third party generates "control, a search for justice, society and the State, comparison and possession, thought and science, commerce and philosophy, an outside of anarchy, the search for a principle" (161). However, he stresses the interdependence as well as the difference between these concepts: justice is a "betrayal" of ethical proximity, but also its necessary expression, and thus "[i]n no way is justice a degradation of obsession, a degeneration of the for-the-other" (159).

Gadamer's hermeneutics can be helpful in articulating the necessary ethical mediation between autonomous subjectivity and its other-oriented context partly because it escapes the "descriptivist" trap that Norris critiques.[8] One of Gadamer's main objects of critique in *Truth and Method* is the kind of binarism that informs the descriptivist aspect of the fact/value distinction, specifically the Enlightenment or twentieth-century view of language that sees meaning as constructed by systems of signs set in a representational opposition to the world.[9] According to Julius Kovesi's critique of the is/ought distinction, "moral notions and judgments," instead of being evaluations based on separable descriptions of the world, "are about our life insofar as our life is constituted by these very notions, judgments, concepts, and descriptions" (14). This is a hermeneutic point. According to Gadamer, "when we interpret the meaning of something," as opposed to when we indicate something semiotically, "we actually interpret an interpretation" (*The Relevance of the Beautiful* 68). As discussed in Chapter 2, "presence" for Gadamer is not a matter of the representational presence that the early Derrida finds at the heart of meaning, but rather the presence of one person to another in a "conversation" or "game" in which subjects put their prejudices at risk in pursuit of a truth that is more than the sum of the interlocutors' opinions.

As I argued in Chapter 2, Gadamer's notion of understanding is dependent on a modified version of the Levinasian ethical bond. Because self-understanding "encompasses all recognition of oneself in the other, which first opens up in dialogue," "self-understanding [*Selbstverständnis*] is, in all its forms, the extreme opposite of self-consciousness [*Selbstbewusstsein*] and self-possession [*Selbstbesitz*]" ("Letter to Dallmayr" 95). On the face of it, this dissociation between self-consciousness and self-understanding sounds very non-Coleridgean, but the difference is more terminological than conceptual. What Gadamer here calls "self-consciousness" resembles what Coleridge calls mere "consciousness of self," not to be confused with "self-consciousness" (*CM* 2:552). Coleridge's notion of self-consciousness resembles Gadamer's notion of self-understanding in being grounded in an orientation toward the other, as conscience grounds self-consciousness, which makes self-consciousness a hermeneutic and ethical foundation for subjectivity rather than an inward-directed self-knowledge. Even in perception, which for Coleridge is grounded in the imagination's finite repetition of divine self-consciousness, the gaze is directed outward, not inward. Objecting to Fichte's argument that seeing and hearing require a consciousness that one is seeing and hearing, Coleridge points out that this is the case only if the organs of perception are diseased: "No! I seem to myself to be conscious only [of] the object, not of my seeing: unless from its glitter or from Disease, it makes my eyes *feel*" (2:604).

Embracing the interpersonal implications of Heidegger's emphasis on human finitude, both Gadamer and Levinas shift the discussion of subjectivity from a problem of detached, conceptual, representational knowledge that starts with the subject to the scene of responsible human interaction. For Levinas, the proximity of the other in conversation overwhelms and thereby grounds subjective conceptuality: "to approach the Other in conversation is to welcome his expression, in which at each instant he overflows the idea a thought would carry away from it. It is therefore to *receive* from the Other beyond the capacity of the I, which means exactly: to have the idea of infinity" (*TI* 51). For Gadamer, it is the conversation, transcending either partner, rather than the other, that is foundational, but he and Levinas are discussing more or less the same kind of conversation. Ricoeur is right to note that Levinas's conception of otherness reduces it to the otherness of other people, excluding, for example, the otherness of one's own flesh and one's ancestors (*Oneself* 320, 352–53); Gadamer's expansion of otherness to the historical, and particularly the literary text is one answer, not without its own difficulties, to that objection. As I will argue below, Coleridge also expands the notion of otherness beyond the limits of Levinas's paradigm.

II. Christian Otherness

Coleridge, who resisted the exaltation of the autonomous self that worried Hegel, struggled to develop a concept of subjectivity that would succumb neither to the perceived solipsism of Fichte nor to the foundational polarity of Schelling while also avoiding the banality of materialism. Much of this struggle took the form of meditations on the nature of one's relation to the other. Lockridge argues that, despite his attraction to a formalist ethics, Coleridge not only expands Kant's directive to treat people as ends rather than means into an affective other-centered morality but also sees the relation to another as essential for self-consciousness: "to be conscious of oneself as a *self* requires a synchronous commitment to the reality of another" (*Coleridge the Moralist* 124–25).[10] However, there are two asymmetrical conceptions of ethical otherness at work in Coleridge. We might loosely call these a "Christian" (or, following Robbins, "Greek-Christian") and a "Hebraic" sense of otherness, already suggested by the notion of conversion discussed in Chapter 4. As Derrida says in "Violence and Metaphysics," his famous essay on Levinas, "We live in the difference between the Jew and the Greek, which is perhaps what is called history" (*Writing and Difference* 153).

The Christian sense is not unrelated to the logic of Christian conversion Robbins discusses, because it involves what Emmanuel Levinas would call a return to the Same: an otherness that is posited out of the self as a route back to self-authentication. This is in part the familiar Schellingesque "subject which becomes a subject by the act of constructing itself objectively to itself; but which never is an object except for itself, and only so far as by the very same act it becomes a subject" (*BL* 1: 273). Ethically, it is treating oneself as another, as in Coleridge's comment on Kant's *Metaphysik der Sitten:* "All morality presupposes in the Subject the faculty of regarding itself as an Object—i.e. of placing the first in the ranks of the third Persons, & acting to all as one rank, Me, thee, Him" (*CM* 3: 264). This notion of self-othering, which he found in Schelling and Fichte, was of course central to Coleridge's logos-philosophy as the basis of both God's relation to humans and the subject-object relation that was essential to human thought. It is broadly Christian in its emphasis on God as a divinity who become his human other in the incarnation.

In the effort to avoid the excesses of both idealism and materialism—the self is neither a collection of atoms as in the despised "Mechanico-Corpuscular Theory" of life (*C & S* 64) nor a self-sufficient ego as in the later Fichte[11]—Coleridge involves his notion of the self in what Ricoeur calls (following Wittgenstein) the "aporia of anchoring," or "the conjunction between the subject as the world-limit and the person as the object of identifying reference" (*Oneself* 53). The "I" is the limit of the world in being "a privileged point of perspective on the world and not one of its contents" (51)—a position which, for Coleridge, leads to the Scylla of Fichtean idealism if taken to the extreme—but that same "I" has a name, and thus appears as the object of an identifying reference *in* the world among other such unique "I"s: a position which, taken alone, leads to the Charybdis of atomism and determinism.

This is part of Ricoeur's overarching distinction between "ipse"-identity or "selfhood" and "*idem*"-identity or "sameness." *Idem*-identity is the "I" as an object of reference in the world, containing numerical identity, relations of resemblance, and permanence in time (*Oneself* 116–18). *Ipse*-identity, on the other hand, "implies no assertion concerning some unchanging core of the personality" (2), but instead engages "the dialectic of *self* and *other than self*" (3). These two versions of identity are reflected in the distinction, which Ricoeur sees as a historical confusion, "between the *self*, a phenomenological concept, and *man*, an anthropological concept" (313). While *idem* refers to the "mere permanence or perseverance of things," *ipse* strives, through promise and attestation, for "self-constancy through time" (267). The interaction of *idem* and *ipse* provides two models of "permanence in time" (118), or what Coleridge calls, in one of his discussions of conscience, a "*continuous* <& ever continuable> *Consciousness*." Attestation, or, in Coleridge's terms "a testifying state" is important to Coleridge's concept of conscience as that which illustrates the experiential character of conscience without reducing it to materialist sensation: "the conscience is neither a sensation or a sense; but a testifying state" (*LS* 67).

According to Ricoeur, the two categories overlap most completely in the notion of "permanence of character," or "the set of distinctive marks which permit the reidentification of a human individual as being the same" (*Oneself* 119), while they diverge in the notion of self-maintenance as "keeping one's word," which is where ethics comes into play. For the self-constancy of *ipse*, eschewing the objective permanence of *idem*-identity, to be more than Stoic rigidity or mere desire, it must be "permeated by the desire to respond to an expectation, even to a request coming from another" (267). For Ricoeur, the advantage of this dialectic between *ipse* and *idem*, which he sees as missing in discussions of the self from Descartes to Levinas, is that it presents "a self that will neither be exalted, as in the philosophies of the cogito, nor be humiliated, as in the philosophies of the anti-cogito" (318). In Coleridge studies, a general form of the distinction between *ipse* and *idem* has long been recognized, from McFarland's emphasis on Coleridge's vacillation between the "I am" and the "it is" to Modiano's discussion of Coleridge's desire for a distinction "between an 'accidental' or empirical 'I', a 'self-finding' that man has in common with animals, and a 'substantial personal I' that comes to man exclusively through participation in the divine Logos" (173, citing Notebook 36, ff. 172–73).

McFarland has argued for Coleridge's own recognition that a complete philosophical system will inevitably slight either the "it is" or the "I am" (253–55). McFarland is certainly correct that Coleridge's inability to reconcile the competing claims of the self and the world shows not a confusion or lack of resolve in his philosophy, but rather the "irreducible tensions" that constituted the "distinctive character" of "his total philosophical commitment" (254). However, he may paint too simple a picture by placing the "moral interest" completely on the "I am" side of the distinction, in antithetical opposition to the "pantheist" implications of the "it is" side, because of the ethical implications, for both Coleridge and recent thinkers, of the dialectic between the self as an acting agent ("I am") and as an object of reference in the world ("it is" expressed as "he/she is").

As Ricoeur's *Oneself as Another* demonstrates, the relationship between a "phenomenological" or first-person concept and an "anthropological" or third-person concept of the human remains an important issue in ethical thought. It is equally important for literary studies, asymmetrically torn between wanting to historicize the perceived Romantic exaltation of the self—a reduction of the "phenomenological" to the "anthropological" or "ideological"—and what could be called a reverse movement in some forms of feminism: the effort to critique the objective "anthropological" perspective of patriarchal discourse from a new phenomenology of the feminine.

Like Ricoeur, Coleridge gives a great deal of metaphysical and ethical authority to *ipse*-identity's first-person "attestation," which Ricoeur associates with "the unfolding of the dialectic between self and other" as opposed to the "certainty claimed by the [Cartesian] cogito" and "the criterion of verification of objective science" (*Oneself* 21). Coleridge similarly opposes his version of *ipse*-identity both to the subjective certainty of idealism and to the objective certainty of atomistic materialism. By grounding the continuity of self-consciousness in "conscience" defined as "my affections & duties toward others," Coleridge asserts the importance for him of what Ricoeur calls the *ipse*-identity of a selfhood dependent on a responsiveness to others, rather than the subsumption of *ipse*-selfhood under the permanence of "character." This self-othering is ultimately theological; in several places, including *The Constitution of the Church and State,* Coleridge comments on the fundamentality of the metaphor of "the *Word* (*Gosp. of John* I. 1.) for the Divine Alterity, the Deus Alter et idem of Philo" (84n). Using the same etymological evidence that Ricoeur uses, he sees God as engaged in a dialectic between "same" (idem) and "other" (alter) in his role as divine logos. This principle is an important part of Coleridge's ontology based on the primacy of the will. In an 1818 essay explicating the idea that "the Will is that which is causative of its own reality," which presents the divine Will as that which is causative of all reality, he argues that "reality" here is both one with the Will and necessarily other to it: "We are now to pass to those realities without the causation of which the Will could not be causative of its own reality but which realities . . . are . . . other than that of the Will though One with it—truly other and yet in a certain sense the same[,] at least thus only may we use if we use at all the phrase of Deus alter et idem" (*SW & F* 780–81). The example he gives is the relation between the Will and the intellect: intelligence is secondary to the will because "it is not per se causative," but it is one with the will in that "a Will without an Intelligence cannot be other than an absurdity." Intelligence must have reality separate from the will, as "the adequate Idea of the Will," or else it would be a mere "form," which would contradict the notion that the Will is causative of reality, not just unreal forms (781). This is a specific version of the "identity . . . of knowing and being in one and the same act," a relation which, though rather confidently placed into a Schellingesque dialectic in the *Biographia,* is later, according to an 1825 notebook entry, seen more problematically as "a memento of the inadequacy of words . . . to the expression of Ideas" (*CN* 4: 5288).

The interdependence of "community" and "diversity" (*SW & F* 780) in the relation between "idem" and "alter" is part of the ethics as well as the ontology of self-consciousness, and here Coleridge's phrasing (in Anthony Harding's translation of Coleridge's Latin) strongly resembles Ricoeur's: "To be conscious is to be aware of both myself and of another at the same time—therefore, self-consciousness is to be aware of myself *as if I were another*" (*CL* 4: 849).[12] In the *Opus Maximum,* this self-othering is defined according to the (for Coleridge) ethically foundational category of love: self-consciousness depends on the ability to constitute "the representative or objective Self (as distinguished from the primary originative Self) in whatever it wills to love" (*Opus Maximum* 3, fols. 49–51, qtd. Perkins 55). In his "Essay on Faith," he says that "there can be no *I* without a *Thou,* & . . . a Thou is only possible by an equation in which I is taken as <equal to> ~~a~~ Thou, & yet not the same." This equation becomes another definition of "conscience": "the equation of *Thou* with *I,* by means of a free Act, negativing the sameness in order to establish the equality is the true definition of *Conscience,*" and "the Conscience is the root of all Consciousness" (*SW & F* 837).[13] Thus self-consciousness depends not only on conscience defined as *relations* to others, as when the social human's "*idem* is modified by the *alter*" (842), but also on a Ricoeurean sense of the self *as* other. The ethical relation to another is grounded in a self-generated reciprocal equality that negates "sameness," preserving otherness.

Although his terminology is different (for Coleridge "idem" covers much of what Ricoeur would call "ipse"-identity), Coleridge often sees the distinction between what Ricoeur calls the first-person nature of *ipse-*

identity and the third-person nature of *idem*-identity in terms of the scholastic distinction between *natura naturans* (the active, living principle of "nature naturing") and *natura naturata* (the passive, reified principle of "nature natured"). His marginalia on Fichte demonstrate his alertness to the serious ethical consequences of confusing these terms as descriptions of the subject. In Fichte's argument in *Die Bestimmung des Menschen* that guilt is meaningful only "in respect to the external law," because "I do not act at all: nature acts in me," Coleridge detects (somewhat unfairly, according to the editor's notes) a slippage between *natura naturans* and *natura naturata:* "'I' hitherto has been used as Natura naturans individuata, per se determinata—but now it stands for the result & total effect of the former. In the first case it is ego contemplans—in the second, res contemplata" (*CM* 2: 602). Coleridge implicitly denies any incompatibility between the two states, suggesting the need to see the subject under both headings. One must avoid the error of the idealist in "conced[ing] a real existence to one of the two terms only—to the *natura naturans*" (*P Lects* 371), or the equal and opposite error of materialism, in which "all HERE is merged in the objective, as the former in the subjective" (372).[14]

Persons are thus both objects of reference and subjects of reflective utterance, both in the familiar dialectic of self-consciousness and ethically, in that "all morality presupposes in the Subject the faculty of regarding itself as an Object" (*CM* 3: 264). This is not a Kantian abstraction, as evidenced by Coleridge's equivocal relation to the categorical imperative, which, as Lockridge points out, was initially to call it an "empty generalization" (*CN* 1: 1711, qtd. Lockridge, *Coleridge the Moralist* 120). That view changed, and in *The Friend* Coleridge accepts the infallibility of Kant's internalization of ethical motivation: "the *object* of morality is not the outward act, but the internal maxim of our actions. And so far it is infallible" (1: 194). However, his defense of Kant against Christoph Friedrich Nicolai shows his particularist interpretation of Kant's ethics: "What vulgar Sophistry! When & where has Kant affirmed it to be a Man's Duty to discover principles of Legislation for all intelligent Be-ings? He announces a simple Truth, that A = A. Let *me* act on the same principle, as in the same circumstances I should be obliged by my own reason to demand of another" (*CM* 3: 958–59). Like Ricoeur, Coleridge reintroduces a concept of individual otherness in the categorical imperative by moving it from the sphere of universal humanity to that of real practical circumstances, and consequently rewriting Kant's imperative as a version of the Golden Rule.[15] Ricoeur sees the Golden Rule's practical "norm of reciprocity" as "the appropriate transitional formula between solicitude and the second Kantian imperative" (*Oneself* 219). ("Solicitude" is Ricoeur's name for the ethical relation to others promoted by dialogic *ipse*-identity.) Coleridge's similar expression glosses his distinction, in the definition of "conscience" quoted above, between the "sameness" that is "negative[d]" and the "equality" that preserves individual otherness in the ethical relation.

The need for exteriority—what Coleridge calls "outness"—is part of the self's desire for external certainty, and can thus be linked to his notion that morality presupposes seeing oneself anthropologically, as a third person character, in which, for Ricoeur, *idem* overlaps *ipse* most completely. However, for Ricoeur and for this side of Coleridge, the need for outness, the need to see oneself as having an external presence in the world, is a necessary activity of *ipse*-identity.[16] Coleridge thus joins Ricoeur in seeing reflection (the activity of *ipse*-identity) as needing the detour through analysis (the task of *idem*-identity): "the detour by way of objectification is the shortest path from the self to the self" (*Oneself* 313) because "the self is essentially an opening onto the world. Ricoeur finds Heidegger's attempt to replace this need for objectification with "the revelatory function recognized in Dasein" to be unsuccessful because that very function "appears to presuppose or to require" this "objectifying detour" (314). Because *ipse*-identity needs this "anthropological" detour, objectification does not detract from the "phenomenological" concept of the self any more than for Coleridge seeing the "I" as "res contemplata" detracts from its status as "ego contemplans." This self-objectification is of course best known in the dialectical formulation of that Coleridge borrowed from Schelling in chapter 12 of the *Biographia*, a formulation that Coleridge later found unsatisfactory. However, Ricoeur's terms, by preserving the distinction as well as the interdependence between the anthropological and the phenomenological versions of the self without resolving them dialectically, and by emphasizing the ethical role of this dual self, can, I hope, bring out some implications of Coleridge's thought that are somewhat hidden in that more familiar formulation.

The fundamental need for the objectifying detour is evident when Coleridge sees the need for outness as a product of the instinct for truth, rather than a ground for that instinct. He suggests that the *ipse*-self's desire for truth generates outness, while at the same time this process leads to the discovery of a "fixed cause" external to that self: "It is not the desire of attaching *Outness*, an *externality* to our representations which is at the bottom of this Instinct; on the contrary this very attachment of Outness originates in this Instinct—But it is to possess *a ground* to know a fixed Cause generating a certain reason" (*CN* 3: 3592). The Imagination's symbolizing activity is implicated in this need for outness: Coleridge describes the desire "for vividness of Symbol: which something that is *without,* that has the property of *Outness* . . . can alone fully gratify/even that indeed not fully" (3: 3325).[17]

The ethical implications of outness are suggested when Coleridge states that the impulse to record his guilt is motivated by "an effort to eloign and abalienate it from the dark Adyt of [his]own Being by a *visual* Outness—& not the wish for others to see it" (*CN* 3: 4166). The objective expression of guilt is an internal necessity of the subject, to be distinguished from the socially-generated exculpation that would be driven by "the wish for others to see it." For Coleridge, guilt is not driven by others' perception of oneself. However, the reality of outness—Coleridge's sense that the self is both "oneself and another"—also means that the will is not as autonomous as Kant's universal moral agent would suggest. In a comment on Kant's statement in the *Logic* that while the limitations of our understanding cause ignorance, "the fault of error we have to ascribe to ourselves," Coleridge notes that this is not the case, because judgment that is vulnerable to error is embedded in an experience of "outwardness" that we cannot control as the Kantian model says that we should be able to: "Nature compels us in numberless instances to judge according to our present perceptions modified by our past experience, and in these the limits and imperfection of our faculties are <sometimes> necessitating Causes of erroneous judgement—for this plain reason—that the sense of outwardness as a sense of reality, is a Law of our Nature, & no conclusion of our Judgement" (*CM* 3: 260). Thus we have to live in a world much more experiential than that of Kant's universal subject, but this redefines rather than reduces ethical responsibility. "Outwardness" or outness is "a Law of *our* Nature," not subject to the judgment of the will, but still very much part of our own existence. External limitations can cause error, but at the same time expressions of guilt are not reducible to a response to others' opinions, as they would be if wrong actions were dictated by external factors. As he says in the *Philosophical Lectures,* "[O]ur will is to a certain degree in our power . . . but the consequences of that will are not in our power" (364), a fact forcefully demonstrated in the *Rime*. As usual, Coleridge refuses to be trapped by materialism's alleviation of the individual's responsibility, arguing instead that the expression of guilt comes from within and is not simply a response to the outside world, or by idealism's reduction of ethics to subjective intention, arguing instead that error can be the result of factors beyond our subjective control.

The later Coleridge's attempt to retain the primacy of individual responsibility in the face of this lack of control is suggested by his insistent but problematic distinction between "regret" and "remorse," a distinction which for him proves the freedom of the will: "I have often remarked . . . that this essential *Heterogeneity* of Regret and Remorse is itself a sufficient and the best, *proof* of Free *Will,* and *Reason:* ~~on~~ the co-existence of which in man we call *Conscience*" (*CM* 4: 651–52). We feel "regret" when "we are distinctly conscious that our Will has had no share direct or indirect in the production of a given event or circumstance, that is painful or calamitous to ourselves or others" (*Lects 1808–1819* 1: 63). "Remorse," which proves "how deeply seated the conscience is in the human Soul," is "the *implicit* Creed of the Guilty" in that it makes the guilty man interpret "the calamities into *judgments,* Executions of a Sentence passed by an *invisible* Judge" (*AR* 127–28); the feeling of remorse is always accompanied by a conviction of individual responsibility. The reality of remorse provides an argument against what he perceives as Schelling's materialistic designation of freedom as the following of one's inner nature, which would deny the free choice that makes us moral beings. "Remor[se] and Self-Accusation" would be mere "Delusions" if freedom were only inner necessity (*CM* 4: 436–37).

One purpose of this distinction is to reinforce the agent's responsibility while preserving the knowledge that the will is, contra Kant, not always responsible for "error." The "facts" of regret and remorse "would be nonsense, . . . would not be facts, if there were not a free will. But <for> there being a free will, we should fall into an endless contradiction of nature" (*P Lects* 364). That is to say, without free will to distinguish the two, they would simply represent contradictory natural drives. According to the example in the *Philosophical Lectures* (whose final link back to the concept is unfortunately lost due to a hiatus in the manuscript), we have a natural demand for both "value," or "consequences with regard to our happiness," and a more intrinsic sense of "worth." He uses the example of a man who "in a moment of hatred or revenge stabs me with a dagger" and inadvertently "happens to have opened an imposthume and brings about my health." Such an action has "value" in its consequences, but the absence of "worth" makes us feel for the agent "nothing but detestation" (364).[18] Though the manuscript breaks here, the context suggests that Coleridge also gave a converse example, in which the absence of good consequences in a well-meant action presented "worth" without "value." If the felt distinction—like that between "regret" and "remorse"—did not stem from the agent's intention, it would not make sense. Where the conscience is concerned, even passivity is an act. According to the "Essay on Faith," "In the senses we find our *receptivity* and as far as our *personal* Being is concerned, we are passive; but in the facts of the Consci~~ous~~ence we are not only *agents,* but it is by these alone that we know ourselves to be such; nay, that ~~in~~ our very passiveness herein is an *act* of passiveness. . . . The result is the consciousness of *responsibil*[*ity*] and the proof is afforded by the inward experience of the *diversity* ~~of~~ between *Regret* simply and *Remorse*" (*SW & F* 836).

It is clear that "worth" and "remorse" have greater ethical weight than "value" or "regret," since the former are associated with will and intention, and since the purpose of the distinction itself is to carve out an ethical territory for the will. On the one hand, Coleridge's critique of Kant's subjective notion of error and his emphasis on outness suggest that he shares Bernard Williams's objection to a Kantian morality of obligation that "conceals the dimension in which ethical life lies outside the individual" (*Ethics and the Limits of Philosophy* 191). In the "Essay on Faith," this is suggested by the fact that "Fidelity under previous contract or particular moral Obligation" is a low order of faith, second in six ascending steps that culminate in the subservience of the individual will to the absolute Reason of God's will (*SW & F* 843–44). On the other hand, his practical distinction between remorse and regret places him within what Williams calls a restricted concept of morality based on individual guilt and responsibility. The problem with the modern conception of a morality of guilt, according to Williams, is that it irrationally attempts to make guilt both other-directed and strictly voluntary, insisting on "the primacy of guilt, its significance in turning us towards victims, and its rational restriction to the voluntary" (*Shame* 94).[19]

This combination of the voluntary and the other-directed is exactly the "irrationality" of the Coleridgean victim of remorse, who interprets calamities as "Executions of a Sentence passed by an *invisible* Judge," even though—according to Coleridge's very rational distinction—this experience is an exteriorization of remorse always connected with the will, *not* with factors outside of the will. The typically Coleridgean problem with the regret/remorse distinction is that, while it purports to demonstrate the ethical importance of the will, at the same time it demonstrates how much of life stands outside the will: we experience and are ethically affected by both regret and remorse, both worth and value.

Coleridge has difficulty maintaining the distinction itself between regret and remorse. The earliest articulation of the distinction I have been able to find is in Lecture 3 of the 1808 *Lectures on the Principles of*

Poetry (March 30, 1808). Several years earlier, however, in "The Pains of Sleep" (September 1803), Coleridge explored an experience that confuses the distinction. The poem describes the moral confusion of dreams characterized by a "remorse" that does *not* distinguish between the voluntary and the involuntary: "For all seemed guilt, remorse, or woe, / My own or others still the same" (31–32). While "[s]uch punishments . . . were due / To natures deepliest stained with sin" (43–44), it makes no sense for the speaker, who simply wants to love and be loved, to experience this strangely will-less remorse:

> Such griefs with such men well agree,
> But wherefore, wherefore fall on me?
> To be beloved is all I need,
> And whom I love, I love indeed.
> (49–52)

In the letter to Southey in which the first draft of "The Pains of Sleep" appears, he both distances himself from "these verses" as "doggerels" and affirms them as "a true portrait of my nights" (*CL* 2: 984). The poem was also included in an 1814 letter, which creates another kind of distance by attributing the state of mind expressed in the poem to the effects of opium, supposedly unrecognized at the time of composition (2: 984n). In the wake of the regret/remorse distinction, the state of mind depicted in the poem, which effectively denies that distinction, needs to be dismissed as aberrant.

But even in the 1808 lecture, while Coleridge is affirming the distinction, it starts to crumble. It is easy enough, he says, to distinguish regret from remorse in situations "not only independent of our will but out of ourselves," and it *should* be easy enough to make the distinction regarding ourselves. In the latter case "we do not indeed . . . confound . . . or lose the distinction," but it is not at all clear cut:

> in perhaps a majority of instances, however unconscious of Blame we may feel ourselves, yet a certain something more than Regret will mingle with the regret—a certain something will haunt and sadden the heart, which if not Remorse is however a phantom and Counterfeit of Remorse—~~is~~ may not this <be> a Fact, meant to make us sensible that however independent the calamity may be of any <moral> fault ~~of ourselves~~ as its proximate or immediate cause, it may nevertheless & often will be . . . yet a distant effect of something moraly wrong in our~~se own~~ past Actions—or—for

> why should I be ashamed of that which tho' Reason cannot comprehend nay even seems to start from, yet <of which> all nations of the Earth in one form or other have prostrated themselves before the mysterious reality—a distant effect of the guilt of ~~of our~~ ages past. (*Lects 1808–1819* 1:64)

In order to preserve the connection between remorse and the will, the will needs to be generalized into a past collective unconscious that the "Reason . . . seems to start from." The immediate cause of this digressive comment at the opening of Coleridge's lecture is his feeling of "regret" at Humphrey Davy's recent illness—clearly a situation out of the control of Coleridge's will, mixed, he says, with "a painful sense of impropriety at the thought, that *I* am now addressing you in the place, in which He has been so often" (*Lects 1808–1819* 1:63–64). Coleridge had been invited by Davy to give this series of lectures at the Royal Institution in London, and now Coleridge is standing in the very place where Davy himself had lectured. Clearly his "counterfeit" remorse is due to no fault of his own, but it still feels like remorse, not regret. Coleridge here comes up against the contradiction between his solicitude for Davy, both as a victim of illness and as his predecessor at the Royal Institution lectures, and his need for remorse to be restricted to his own will.

The recognition that a good portion of ethical life lies outside of the will can be reconciled with a morality based on the individual will only if regret can be distinguished from remorse, so that guilt can be tied firmly to the will, but Coleridge seems able to maintain this separation only with great difficulty, because experience presents us with something that looks very much like "remorse" rather than simply "regret" even when we have no consciousness of blame. He thus sees (or at least suggests by blatantly refusing to see) the difficulty that Williams notes: the morality of obligation and individual responsibility that Coleridge wants to assert tends to deny the forces that lie outside the will. Coleridge thus suggests, literally against his will, Williams's opinion that we do an injustice to our ethical life if we reduce it to restrictive notions of moral obligation. The problem with that restrictive notion of morality, as Williams sees it, is that, in "requir[ing] a voluntariness that will be total and will cut through character and psychological or social determination, and allocate blame and responsibility on the ultimately fair basis of the agents own contribution, no more and no less," morality neglects the surrounding context of "other practices of encouragement and discouragement, acceptance and rejection, which work on desire and character to shape them into the requirements and possibilities of ethical life" (*Ethics* 194).

In Coleridge's very effort to maintain that total voluntariness in ethical responsibility, we see his sensitivity to the "surrounding context" of practices that shape character: in order to maintain a completely voluntary ethical conception, he must generalize personal guilt to the level of the history of culture, implicitly expanding it to include those other cultural practices that are neglected by the restriction of responsibility to the individual will. Thus generalized, Coleridge's "guilt" approaches what Williams recovers from the ancient Greeks as "shame," a concept that "can transcend both an assertive egoism and a conventional concern for public opinion" (*Shame* 88) and that can free us, according to Williams, from the equally false ideas either that we are only responsible for what we intend or that the extra-subjective nature of ethical life reduces subjective ethical responsibility to an ideological fiction.

Like Ricoeur, and, I am arguing, Coleridge, Williams directs our attention here to both the phenomenological and the anthropological concepts of the person, the ways in which actions "stand between the inner world of disposition, feeling, and decision and an outer world of harm and wrong" (*Shame* 92), combining what Ricoeur discusses as "reflection" and "analysis." The restriction of ethics to a morality of the voluntary slights both self and other. It demands a "characterless" sense of the moral agent, a Christian or Kantian reduction of the agent to one who simply knows the moral law and needs "only the will to obey it" (94–95). Such a position slights the other by limiting the ethical role of other people to the function of "assisting reason or illumination" (95). The larger category of shame, by contrast, works according to a specific sense of "what I am" (93): we are ashamed not because we have violated a moral law, but because our actions or their results (potentially or actually, intended or not) have violated our sense of what we should be. However, that sense of "what I am" is not completely subjective; "the basic experience connected with shame is that of being seen, inappropriately, by the wrong people, in the wrong condition" (78). But this is not a matter of simply responding to public opinion, because the other can also internalized as an important and very specific part of the self who experiences "the imagined gaze of an imagined other"; we can be ashamed of doing, or even thinking, something stupid or wrong whether or not we are found out. But even if the other is imagined, it is not just a generalized other: "Shame need not be just a matter of being seen, but of being seen by an observer with a certain view" (82).

Williams's theory of shame echoes in some respects an ethical theory with which Coleridge may have had some acquaintance: Adam Smith's spectator theory of ethics in *The Theory of Moral Sentiments*. (Williams does not mention Smith.) Coleridge did know—and despise—Smith's laissez-faire economic theory presented in the later *Wealth of Nations*. He generally lumped Smith together with other rationalist economists, whose views he found objectionable because they denied the importance of both national political systems and religion. In a *Courier* article of 1814, for example, he objects to "the doctors and disciples of political economy, with whom 'The Wealth of Nations' is of higher authority than either the Bible or the Statute Book" (*EOT* 2: 394).[20] Although I have found no evidence that he actually read *The Theory of Moral Sentiments,* it would be unlikely that he was unfamiliar with this work, given its discussion by writers with whom he was very familiar, including Burke, Hume, and Kant, and the fact that it went through several editions during Coleridge's lifetime.[21] In the notes for an 1808 lecture he does refer positively to Smith's aesthetics, specifically "Of the Nature of the Imitation Which Takes Place in What Are Called the Imitative Arts" in *Essays on Philosophical Subjects,* which contributed to Coleridge's distinction between imitation and copy (*Lects 1808–1819* 1: 133, 133n).

For Smith ethical decisions revolve around the approval or disapproval of passions such as gratitude or resentment, and that approval or disapproval is determined by the sympathy of an "impartial spectator." Gratitude and resentment

> as well as all the other passions of human nature, seem proper and are approved of, when the heart of every impartial spectator entirely sympathizes with them, when every indifferent bystander entirely enters into, and goes along with them.
>
> He, therefore, appears to deserve reward, who, to some person or persons, is the natural object of a gratitude which every human heart is disposed to beat time to, and thereby applaud: and he, on the other hand, appears to deserve punishment, who in the same manner is to some person or persons the natural object of a resentment which the breast of every reasonable man is ready to adopt and sympathize with. (69–70)

The same goes for judgments of our own conduct; we must "remove ourself, as it were, from our own natural station," and view "our own sentiments and motives . . . with the eyes of other people, or as other people are likely to view them" (110).

Like Williams, Smith wants to replace an ethical judgment based on the individualized exercise of virtues such as benevolence or prudence with a socialized judgment conditioned by the gaze of another. For both, this other is an idealized version of other people, but one that involves, as Williams says, "intimations of a genuine social reality—in particular, of how it will be for one's life with others if one acts in one way rather than another" (*Shame* 102). For Smith, our ethical self-perception develops as our physical self-perception does: "we suppose ourselves the spectators of our own behaviour, and endeavor to imagine what effect it would, in this light, produce upon us" (112). Both prefer this view of ethical development, which gives a broad sense of "who I am," in Williams's phrase, within a complex network of social sympathy, to a narrower and more external one based on the consequences of actions. For Williams this narrower conception is "guilt," caused by "an act or omission of a sort that typically elicits from other people anger, resentment, or indignation" and is resolved by "reparation or punishment" (*Shame* 89). For Smith it is the realm of "justice," by which "men in this life are liable to punishment for their actions only, not for their designs and intentions" (105). Justice is for Smith a providential, socially useful, but ethically secondary response to the human inability to separate the effects of an action from the motivations behind it.

The major difference between Williams and Smith is that Smith, unlike the pre-Socratic Greeks to whom Williams turns, lives in a world in which, as Williams puts it, "the structure of human reason can, when properly understood, yield a pattern that makes sense of human life and human aspirations" (*Shame* 163). By universalizing the sympathetic spectator as "every indifferent spectator," Smith assumes that proper ethical judgments are always at least theoretically possible, and this allows him to find no real conflict between the moral law and the judgment of the impartial spectator. Smith distinguishes clearly between the unreliable judgments of actual spectators and what people should turn to as the "tribunal of their own consciences, to that of the supposed impartial and well-informed spectator, to that of the man within the breast, the great judge and arbiter of their conduct" (130). Because of the difficulty, stemming from self-deceit, that we have in following the dictates of the impartial spectator concerning our own conduct, we need general rules, but those rules stem from the same source: the "general rules of morality . . . are ultimately founded upon experience of what, in particular instances, our moral faculties, our natural sense of merit and propriety, approve, or disapprove of" (159). It is not hard to see why Kant approved of Smith, as the editors of *The Theory of Moral Sentiments* point out (31); the impartial spectator is able to issue what looks very much like the categorical imperative to which Williams objects, in which "the criticising self is simply the perspective of reason or morality" (*Shame* 159). Williams's spectator is idealized but not impartial; he "sees all of me and all through me" (89) on the analogy of my being exposed as naked to a potentially real human other. Smith presents an Enlightenment ability to distinguish clearly between individual motivation and the effects of fortune (while recognizing our tendency to confuse the two), tying both to a providential scheme that, like the free market economy, provides a system of checks and balances for human selfishness and its constraint. Williams turns to the Greeks for a sense of agency that allows for no such rational negotiation between an individual's motivation and the forces of luck or necessity, and that is, like the modern world, "not fully comprehensible and not under control" (165).

Coleridge's relation to both Williams's and Smith's versions of the internalized other is complex. Smith's version of the will is caught between self-love and the desire for approbation by the impartial spectator: "every man . . . is much more deeply interested in whatever immediately concerns himself, than in what concerns any other man," but every man also desires to "act so as that the impartial spectator may enter into the principles of his conduct" (82–83). However, Smith's complementary observation that every man is "the whole world to himself," while "to the rest of mankind he is a most insignificant part of it" (83), also suggests the thin notion of self, largely motivated by self-interest, that underlies the laissez-faire economic theory of *The Wealth of Nations* to which Coleridge objects.[22] Coleridge sees the willing self in a much larger context. The "will" is for him not a simple attribute of the self, as a power to be exercised in relation to a moral law, as in Kant, or in relation to the universality of the impartial spectator, as in Smith. Because self-consciousness, the defining characteristic of humans, is an *act*, the will, whether conscious or not, is in part closer to Williams's "what I am" than to a morality of the voluntary, even if the voluntary is, as in Smith, partly conditioned by a desire for the approbation of the impartial spectator. Furthermore, by grounding that self-consciousness in conscience, which involves seeing "oneself as another," and by reinterpreting the categorical imperative as the Golden Rule, Coleridge shows that ethical action should be considered in terms of real other humans, rather than in terms of an abstract concept, whether that concept comes from the Kantian imperative or the impartial spectator.

At the same time, Coleridge's combined emphasis on otherness and the individual will resembles Smith's model in several ways. On the one hand, Coleridge's definition of conscience in terms of a duty to others, as well as his sense that "[a]ll morality presupposes in the Subject the faculty of regarding itself as an Object—i.e. of placing the first in the ranks of the third Persons" (*CM* 3: 264), bears traces of Smith's directive to distance ourselves from our naturally selfish tendencies and adopt the third-person point of view held by the impartial spectator. On the other hand, in linking the distinction between regret and remorse, value and worth, to the will, Coleridge is attempting to maintain the kind of close link between ethics and individual motivation that Smith establishes. Smith maintains a distinction between the "propriety or impropriety" of a " sentiment . . . from which any action proceeds," which depends on motivation, or a relation to "the cause or object which excites it," and the "merit or demerit" of such a sentiment, which depends on "the beneficial or hurtful effects which the affection proposes or tends to produce" (67). This is very close to (and perhaps an indirect source for) Coleridge's distinction between the "value" of an action, determined by its effect, and the "worth" of an action, determined by its motivation. For Smith, as for Coleridge, our proper approbation or disapprobation of an action depends more on the motivation behind the action than its effect: "If in the conduct of the benefactor there appears to have been no propriety, how beneficial soever its effects," complete sympathy is impossible; the "beneficent tendency of the action" (Coleridge's "value") must be "joined to the propriety of the affection from which it proceeds" (Coleridge's "worth") (73).

This priority of worth to value also affects the nature of our response to unethical actions. An economy of retribution does not make sense in Coleridge's world any more than an economy of atonement makes sense theologically, because retribution deals only with effects of actions, not causes, "value" rather than "worth." This distinction drives the plot of Coleridge's play, *Remorse*. In the first scene the hero, Don Alvar, having returned to Spain from a six-year absence to set right the evil done to him by his brother Ordonio (as well as the evil he wrongly thinks has been done to him by his fiancée Teresa), is advised to seek revenge and "let the guilty meet the doom of guilt" (1.1.13). Alvar prefers the route of remorse: Ordonio's filial status increases his guilt, so Alvar says, "The more behoves it I should rouse within him / Remorse! That I should save him from himself" (1.1.18–19). The consequences of living within an economy of retribution are shown in Ordonio, whose "love" for his brother's betrothed Teresa is perversely conditioned by revenge: "by the deep feelings of revenge and hate / I will still love her—woo her—win her too!" (3.2.17–71).

For both Coleridge and Smith, the values of selfhood and otherness are complementary. The other's gaze is the determinant of moral judgment—both Coleridge and Smith direct us to view ourselves as others view us—but the individual will is what the other is looking at, as the major determinant in moral action. The terrors of remorse that Coleridge discusses, which include an overwhelming sense of being judged, show how this complementary relation between individual will and the perspective of the other can complicate the relationship between the motivations for and the effects of an action. Smith ties remorse more closely to the human need for sociality than Coleridge does, but like Coleridge he sees remorse as an extreme emotion: the guilty man "comes again into the presence of mankind, astonished to appear before them, loaded with shame and distracted with fear, in order to supplicate some little protection from the countenance of those very judges, who he knows have already all unanimously condemned him. Such is the nature of that sentiment, which is properly called remorse; of all the sentiments which can enter the human breast the most dreadful" (84–85). Smith is talking here about both the effects and the motivations of actions; remorse combines "shame for the impropriety of past conduct; or grief for the effects of it; or pity for those who suffer by it; and of the dread and terror of punishment from the consciously provoked resentment of all rational creatures" (85). Coleridge would agree that the consequences of an act are ethically connected to its motivation, even though the motivation is ethically prior: "To consider the proper consequences an Act or Course of Action is to consider the Act itself, and in no way inconsistent with the hatred of Sin for its own sake" (*CN* 4: 4846). Coleridge's "act" is part of a tripartite structure of will, act, and deed, moving from the internal to the external: "the sinful Will" is the source of the "*Act,*" which is "one with" that source in being "one with the Agent." It is self-deception to confuse the "act," which remains present "as long as the Will continues unregenerate," with the "*Deed,* which indeed is past" (*AR* 470).

Coleridge's concept of remorse, like Smith's, extends beyond guilt for intentional evil to the guilty man's interpretation of "sudden Calamities" as "*judgments,* Executions of a Sentence passed by an *invisible* Judge" (*AR* 127). But for Coleridge remorse extends beyond the individual will, despite its purported proof *of* free will, in a particularly Coleridgean way. Because, as an internal necessity, guilt requires outness, remorse achieves its own externality that, as Alvar's faithful Moorish attendant Zulimez reminds him in *Remorse,* "drops balmy dews / Of true repentance" or "is a poison-tree, that pierced to the inmost / Weeps only tears of poison" depending on the constitution of the "heart in which it grows" (1.1.20–24). Thus remorse can become "A fearful curse" that can "cling with poisonous tooth, inextricable / As the gored lion's bite" (1.2.311–12). Remorse is rooted in the will, but because it results from a denial of the inner voice of conscience, it becomes a frightening externalization of conscience, as in Alvar's concluding speech in *Remorse:*

> Conscience rules us e'en against our choice.
> Our inward Monitress to guide or warn,
> If listened to; but if repelled with scorn,
> At length as dire Remorse she reappears,
> Works in our guilty hopes, and selfish fears!
> (5.1.288–92)

Part of the effect of remorse's externalization of conscience is that it blurs the lines between the real and the imagined in a kind of perversion of poetic faith. According to a notebook entry from 1821–22, the "states of Morbid Sleep" with which Coleridge was familiar can produce "the Sensation that counterfeits Remorse," including, as demonstrated in "The Pains of Sleep," a confusion of moral agency. But real remorse can also do the same thing: "actual Remorse . . . when intense, ~~takes the~~ realizes all the horrors of Sleep & seems indeed the identity or co-inherence of Sleep & Wake, Reality and Imagination" (*CN* 4: 4846). Sleep and wake, reality and imagination are doubly confused: first, both real and counterfeit remorse produce the same kind of confusion between the real and unreal; second, counterfeit and real remorse, sleeping and waking, become indistinguishable. It is significant in this context that the victim of authentic remorse described in the *Aids to Reflection* is between sleep and wakefulness, "as one rudely awakend from a long sleep, bewildered with the new light, and half recollecting, half striving to recollect, a fearful something he knows not what, but which he will recognize as soon as he hears the name" (127).[23]

The connection between externalized remorse and poetic illusion is suggested by the use of illusion in *Remorse:* Alvar acts as the agent of Ordonio's remorse by staging a spectacular theatrical scene in which he impersonates a sorcerer and causes a portrait of his own attempted assassination to appear in a burst of fire (3.1.128–45). Paintings, like the externalization of remorse itself, have the ability to "call up past deeds, and make them live / On the blank canvas" (2.2.43–44). In terms of the tripartite structure of will, act, and deed, the outness of aesthetic illusion can share in the externalization of remorse by restoring the past "deed" to the presence of the "act." Just as for Teresa, whose hope in Alvar's survival turns out to be justified, the inner voice that speaks to her "though haply varied / By many a fancy, many a wishful hope, / Speaks yet the truth" (3.2. 29–31), so the illusion involved in aesthetic imitation can have true ethical effect. As suggested in the previous chapter, aesthetic illusion has for Coleridge a real ethical effect even as illusion; here that position is borne out by his link between the outness of remorse and that of art. There is an important difference in that poetic faith, as opposed to "delusion," depends on a clear distinction between illusion and reality, while remorse can confuse the two. But the successful effect of remorse also depends on reality and illusion being placed into their proper perspective; Alvar and Teresa are reunited in *Remorse* only after all illusions are recognized as such.

Like Smith, Coleridge wants to maintain a rational separation between the motivations of actions in the will and the forces that impinge on the will, and Coleridge is in some ways less comfortable than either Smith or Williams in granting ethical authority to the imagined other: the outness associated with guilt is an internal more than a social necessity. Poetic faith complicates the will's relation to external necessity, giving a real force to the willed illusion of supernatural necessity. More radically, remorse, although rooted in the will, spins out of control and blurs not only the boundary between individual will and external factors but also the very boundary between the real and the imagined. This pushes his thought in the direction of the uncontrollable universe that Williams finds in both pre-Socratic Greece and in the modern world. Thus, the "counterfeit" remorse that Coleridge describes in his 1808 lecture suggests the sort of "shame" that Williams discusses: despite his best efforts to define it in relation to the will, Coleridge is not feeling para-remorse because of his sense of voluntary moral obligation; he knows he not responsible for Davy's illness or previous lectures.[24] Rather, the feeling is the result of the sense of "who he is" in relation to an other—Davy—who is "an imagined other" as an idealized lecturer/thinker, and thus not too far removed from Smith's impartial spectator. But Davy is also a very real other as a recently sick friend, which suggests the thicker, less rationalistically universal sense of the imagined other that Williams describes. Coleridge often feels "shame" even writing privately (and sometimes in code), as in the notebook entry quoted above on the subjective impulse to give an outness to his guilt.

Though he calls it "guilt" there and stresses the subjectivity of the emotion, he is less concerned with the violation of a moral law than he is about his inadequacy to his own sense of himself.

Williams's internalized other need not be a Foucauldian panoptician or a Lacanian Other expressing the Law of the Father; this internal witness does not necessarily judge us, and most certainly does not judge us according to an abstract moral law; rather, the internalized other "is conceived as one whose reactions I would respect; equally, he is conceived as someone who would respect those same reactions if they were appropriately directed to him" (*Shame* 84). The notion of the other as judge is for Williams part of the psychology of guilt, not shame, which of course is exactly the psychology of remorse as "the *implicit* Creed of the Guilty" who experience "*judgments,* Executions of a Sentence passed by an *invisible* Judge." The complete internalization, as autonomous moral law, of the guilt-inducing "judge," is for Williams an "idealised picture" that "serves the false conception of total moral autonomy" (220). It is an "idealized picture" that Coleridge wants to preserve in the name of moral autonomy, but it is heavily qualified by his sense of an ethical world beyond the individual will, the instability of the regret/remorse distinction, and his sense of self-consciousness as a process of seeing the other in oneself as well as seeing oneself as another.

Just how closely ethics and hermeneutics are connected in Coleridge can be seen in the combination of ethics' positive demand to adopt a particular interpretive perspective (that of the third person) and remorse's negative effect of short-circuiting the interpretation of reality by confusing the imagined and the real. The ethical demand for a third-person perspective means that potential or actual others are also a foundational part of our ethical understanding, or, more accurately for Coleridge, our understanding that is always ethical. That understanding partakes of the hermeneutic and ethical circle by which subjective intention, both moral and interpretive, reaches back to self-consciousness only via the detour of the objectivity of analysis and the ethical orientation toward another. Since self-consciousness is grounded on "conscience," defined as duty toward others, without those others we lack even self-consciousness. This ethical definition of the self does not, as Williams argues modern morality does, lock the self into an "ethicised" entity that myopically reduces it to an autonomous, characterless, universal moral agent. The Coleridgean point is rather that without a full sense of a life lived with particular other people, neither self-consciousness (which depends on other-directed conscience) nor consciousness of others (which both grounds and results from self-consciousness), nor an ethical life in the large sense, would be possible. As Teresa says in *Remorse,* entering a dungeon alone, "O for one human face here—but to see / One human face here to sustain me!" (5.1.42–43).

The very need for the distinction between regret and remorse suggests the finitude of the human will, in the sense that if all of the consequences of our will were within the will's power, we would not acknowledge a difference between regret for that which we cannot control and remorse for that which we can. The fact that "the consequences of the will are not in our power" gives rise to "a moral interest that a Being should be assumed in whom is the only will, and the power that involves all consequences as one and the same" (*P Lects* 364); in other words, we experience the finitude of the human discrepancy between will and consequence in comparison with the divine will's unity of the two. This hierarchy does not simply reflect the Kantian principle that human freedom is regulative rather than constitutive. While Kant wants us to act *as if* freedom were universal, even though in the contingent world it is not, Coleridge's position suggests that this is a fiction that denies those aspects of life that are out of the will's control. At the same time, Coleridge wants us to see freedom as constitutive, rather than regulative, in the sense that human freedom, though limited, is a finite repetition of divine freedom. Thus we are constituted by a freedom that recognizes a limited horizon, a horizon that demands both an ethical consideration of otherness and a hermeneutic openness to that which is beyond, but accessible only through, our finite horizon.

III. The Problem of Sin

Self-consciousness requires an other-directed conscience, but it also, much more famously, requires a free will. Following Schelling, Coleridge argues that because self-consciousness is an act, it must be grounded in the freedom of the will: "intelligence or self-consciousness is impossible, except by and in a will. The self-conscious spirit therefore is a will; and freedom must be assumed as a *ground* of philosophy, and can never be deduced from it" (*BL* 1:280). The same principle is invoked in his discussion of the universality of the concept of original sin in *Aids to Reflection,* as a defense against materialism: "The Will is ultimately self-determined, or it is no longer a *Will* under the law of perfect Freedom, but a *Nature* under the mechanism of Cause and Effect" (285). Although this may seem to suggest the kind of Kantian or Christian morality of the characterless moral agent acting according to an abstract moral law, even here, where Coleridge has restricted his focus to the problem of moral evil in a theological context, rather than the larger arena (which is still within the ethical, broadly conceived) of considerations such as Kant's comments on "error," he finally resorts to calling original sin a "mystery" rather than accepting a Kantian morality that would reduce the moral agent to an abstract entity.

The unresolvable problem is that moral evil must, on the one hand, according to the law of freedom, originate in the individual will, rather than in an abstract violation of a universal law:

> We call an individual a *bad* Man, not because an action is contrary to the Law, but because it has led us to conclude from it some *Principle* opposed to the law, some private Maxim or By-law in the Will contrary to the universal Law of right Reason in the Conscience, as the *Ground* of the action. But this evil Principle again must be grounded in some other Principle which has been made determinant of the Will by the Will's own self-determination. For if not, it must have its ground in some necessity of Nature, in some instinct or propensity imposed, not acquired, another's work, not our own. Consequently, neither Act nor Principle could be imputed; and relatively to the Agent, not *original,* not *Sin*. (*AR* 286)

Sin must be "original" in the sense of originating with the individual agent, or else one must attribute its origin to a materialistic doctrine of necessity, or, as he states later, the even more unacceptable alternative of a divine origin: "this evil ground cannot originate in the Divine Will." On the other hand, evil is universal, both according to the doctrine of original sin and according to our experience, and "[a]n Evil common to all must have a ground common to all." Such a combination of universality and individuality in evil remains "a *Mystery,* that is, a Fact, which we see but cannot explain; and the doctrine a truth which we apprehend, but can neither comprehend nor communicate" (*AR* 288).[25]

The "universal Law of right Reason in the Conscience" is fairly Kantian in its transcendental subjectivity; earlier Coleridge defines the "Moral law" as "the Law of the Spirit, the Law of Freedom, the Divine Will" which "should, of itself, suffice to determine the Will to a free obedience of the Law," rather than working "*on* the Will" as "an extrinsic, alien force" (*AR*

286, 286n). But in order to see the potentially sinful will itself as universal, Coleridge must imagine a scenario easy for Kant but very difficult for Coleridge, in which "the subject stands in no relation whatever to Time," and in which the subject's temporal existence is as irrelevant to the question of sin "as the relations and attributes of Space (north or south, round or square, thick or thin) are to our Affections or Moral Feelings" (287). The difficulty of this thought-experiment demonstrates Coleridge's strong sense that our ethical life is as bound up in our individual temporal situation as it is independent of extrinsic determinations by the immediate contingencies of space.[26] In other words, a universal concept of evil must perform the impossible—or at least inevitably "mysterious"—task of acknowledging an originating human temporality (evil must originate from a will, and it cannot be the divine will) while acknowledging that evil as universal and therefore outside of time. This contradictory status of evil resembles the aporia that Derrida finds in Lévi-Strauss's admission that the universality of the incest taboo is a kind of "scandal," which for Derrida deconstructs the opposition between nature and culture: the incest taboo is a cultural phenomenon, but its universality in human culture makes it indistinguishable from a natural phenomenon (*Writing and Difference* 283–84). Similarly for Coleridge, original sin must be attributable to human will, not natural forces, but its universality is therefore a "mystery" within Coleridge's attempt to separate the "I am" of willed human subjectivity from the "it is" of natural determinism.

The case of evil thus institutes a different relationship between universal and particular from that which is assumed for ethical life in general, an ethical life oriented toward a concept of the good in which there is a built-in continuity between the divine Will and individual choice, an identity between moral law and freedom. The problem of evil opens up an area in which freedom is still universal, but it is a dangerous freedom that is no longer moored in the theological, ethical, and metaphysical concept of being that enables human repetition of the divine process of self-othering. At the same time, evil is not reducible to a simple subjective intentionality: the separation of evil intention from divinely-sanctioned freedom does not permit it to escape the fundamentally other-oriented context of all intention, because all intention, not just good intention, is grounded in the other-oriented self-consciousness. Coleridge's adherence to the Christian understanding of sin does, to be sure, ally him with what Williams critiques as the Christian and Enlightenment tendency to circumscribe ethical life within the narrow limits of an economy of "guilt" rather than "shame," which pits autonomous intention against moral laws. However, because, as I have tried to show, Coleridge's ethical thought goes beyond that economy, the effect of his explorations of "guilty" intentionality, particularly in the poetry, is to show precisely how problematic the notion of intention becomes when it operates, as it does in the context of sin, outside the Ricoeurean paradigm of "oneself as another."

Christabel provides a clear example of how murky intentionality can become in relation to evil. Christabel's prayer "[f]or the weal of her lover that's far away" (30) is not an evil intention, but it is also not an appropriate prayer. The problem is not that the prayer is a petition for divine favor; as Barth points out, Coleridge soon recanted his early (1794) view that "[o]f whose omniscient and all-spreading Love / Aught to *implore* were impotence of mind" ("To A Friend" 27–28, qtd. Barth, *Coleridge and Christian Doctrine* 182). The morning and evening prayers that Coleridge wrote in 1816 combine praise, thanksgiving, and petition. But these prayers petition God for the potential for right action (that "my faculties and affections" may be used "according to thy Will and Commandments"), protection by God ("the continuance of thy protecting providence thro' the coming night") and, most importantly, unity with God ("grant me a heart united in thy fear and love") (*SW & F* 418–19). The difficult ethical role of prayer is to enable moral action by imperfect beings for whom "[m]ere knowledge of the right . . . does not suffice to ensure the performance of the Right." "Prayer, & religious Intercommunion between Man & his Maker" address that imperfection by providing "a medium between mere conviction & resolve, & suitable *action*" (*CN* 3: 4017).[27] Christabel's prayer for her lover's weal, following a night of dreams about "her own betrothéd knight" (27), has none of the ethical force of appropriate prayer: her concern is that the knight will return and marry her, not that she will act rightly or unite with God.

Other prayers in the poem, such as the narrator's "Jesu Maria, shield her well" (54), participate in the economy of debt and repayment against which Coleridge argues all the way from the Unitarian *Lectures* of 1795, in which sacrificial atonement is not "a cause operating on Deity, but merely . . . the means of meliorating our own hearts" (202), to his explanation in the 1817 *Biographia* of his inability to reconcile redemption with "the vicarious payment of a debt" (1. 205), to the firmly Trinitarian *Aids To Reflection*, published in 1825.[28] Although the effect of Christ's redemptive act resembles the clearing of a debt, it is a mistake to assume "that the agonies suffered by Christ were equal in amount to . . . the infinite debt, which in an endless succession of instalments we should have been paying to the divine Justice, had it not been payed in full by the Son of God incarnate"

(*AR* 327), because the economy of debt and repayment applies only to things, not people. In Coleridge's example, a monetary debt incurred by one person can be satisfied by another's repayment of the debt, because it has to do with things, but a son's ingratitude to his mother cannot be atoned for by another who would take the place of the son, because that moral sphere follows the logic of persons, not things (328–31). After her night with Geraldine, Christabel prays "That He, who on the cross did groan, / Might wash away her sins unknown" (389–90). Here she not only invokes the illegitimate economy of Christ's death as an assumption of moral debt, but also admits no connection between prayer and moral action. In an 1816 notebook entry, Coleridge compares "[v]ain prayer to heaven," defined as "repentance with [a slip for "without"] amendment or abandonment of the Vice," to a "huge mass" of "ignited Rock flung perpendicular upward to an immense Height by the volcano, still falling back" (*CN* 3: 4278). By the same token, the prepaid forgiveness requested for "sins unknown" is "vain" in the sense that you cannot resolve to amend or abandon a vice you do not know you have. The "deed" must be present in the "act" for the mechanism of remorse to kick in.

The result of Christabel's prayer is Geraldine, who appears as a kind of answer to her prayer in the woods and who effects a literal shutting-down of ethical and interpretive discourse. Christabel is only permitted to rehearse a stock narrative of charitable rescue:

> "But vainly thou warrest,
> For this is alone in
> Thy power to declare,
> That in the dim forest
> Thou heard'st a low moaning,
> And found'st a bright lady, surpassingly fair;
> And didst bring her home with thee in love and charity,
> To shield her and shelter her from the damp air."
> (271–78)

There is a rift, in which Christabel can only struggle in vain, between her ethical knowledge of what Geraldine calls "'This mark of my shame, this seal of my sorrow'" (270) and her ability to talk about it. This is perhaps an extreme example of the human situation that for Coleridge necessitates prayer—the discrepancy between knowledge and right action—but it differs from the usual ethical situation in that the discrepancy is supernaturally enforced. Christabel is impelled by Geraldine's supernatural power, a distortion of poetic faith in which she can recognize the delusion being perpetrated by Geraldine but cannot escape from it or articulate a judgment upon it. In this evil world, intention is short-circuited and Geraldine's moral status is as inaccessible as her physical appearance that is "[a] sight to dream of, not to tell" (253).

The "Conclusion to Part II" (666–77) was grafted on to the poem from an 1801 letter to Southey, in which it is described as "[a] very metaphysical account of fathers calling their children rogues, rascals, & little varlets" (*CL* 2: 729). Anticipating the mysterious nature of sin that will be described in the *Aids to Reflection,* Coleridge suggests that "in a world of sin," the "giddiness of heart and brain" that causes fatherly affection to overflow into "words of unmeant bitterness" may be a result of "rage and pain." The intentional positions in the poem, including Christabel's prayer and the contradictory fatherly emotions of the Conclusion to Part II (not to mention Sir Leoline's contradictory stances toward his old friend Roland, Geraldine, Christabel, and Christabel's mother) bear out Coleridge's comment on Kant that error is not a simple result of intention. In a world of sin, intention can go haywire, and erroneous acts, for which we must nonetheless take responsibility, can result from intentions that are innocently wrong-headed, such as Christabel's prayer. She did not "intend" either her birth into an illegitimate pre-Reformation economy of prayer or the appearance of Geraldine. Even more seriously, "to be wroth with one we love / Doth work like madness in the brain" (412–13), and wrong can result from primitive emotions such as "rage and pain" that operate outside of the world of ethical responsibility, even though they must be called to account within that world. "O sorrow and shame should this be true!" (674), says the narrator parenthetically. Here Coleridge seems to be invoking the "shame" that Williams describes: it is not a matter of "guilt" that operates according to autonomous intention in the face of a moral law, but of "shame" not under the control of one's intention that goes to the heart of who one is, for example, a father with a specific and contradictory emotional response to one's child. "Value" (the effect of an action) and "worth" (the motivation for an action) are no longer easily divided, because that division depends on a clear sense of intention, and it is the notion of intention itself that is clouded in the ethically ambiguous world of *Christabel*.

In the famous 1803 notes on "the *streamy* Nature of Association," vice is associated with madness as a kind of diseased intentionality: "imperfect yet existing Volition, giving diseased Currents of association, because it yields on all sides & *yet* is—So think of Madness," which "Thinking = Reason curbs & rudders" only with great difficulty (*CN* 1: 1770). The notion that ethical thought occurs against the background of a sense of oneself that includes much that is not brought to consciousness is also an important part of the ethics that P. Christopher Smith derives from Gadamer: "ethical thinking . . . occurs against the background of what is not thought about at all. . . . Ethical understanding is . . . a function not just of mind but also of who we *are*" (*Hermeneutics and Human Finitude* 229–30). For Coleridge, "[t]rue Religion" consists not in external acts, and not even in specifically willed acts, but "in that habitual state of the whole moral Being, which manifests itself by these acts" (*CM* 4:625). Prior to the subjective intentionality of specific acts is the "whole moral Being," the "who we *are*" that cannot be reduced to intentional agency.

Although his later comments on sin give more responsibility to the will than do his "streamy association" notes, throughout his work he found it difficult, as those notes suggest, to isolate subjective intentionality from the larger and more complex category of who one is. Who one is is determined by neither intention, public opinion, nor material necessity, and fortunately, not solely by whether one is mad, but rather by one's relations to internal and external others. Both the *Rime* and *Christabel* press this sense of identity to the limit. Who the Mariner is can be answered only by the entire narrative of his encounter at sea, as the only possible answer to the Hermit's question, "What manner man art thou?" (623). The others who should sustain Christabel's identity are mostly absent: her lover is gone, her mother is dead, and her father is distant. In their place comes Geraldine, who as a supernatural being impersonating the living, is a cruel example of diseased volition, playing on Christabel's need for an other while parodying all the others in Christabel's life. She expels the mother's ghost and takes her place ("'Off, woman, off! This hour is mine'" [211]); she manufactures a link to Christabel's father by claiming to be the daughter of a long-lost friend; and she takes the place of Christabel's lover as the answer to her prayer and her bedroom companion.[29] Having no selfhood of her own, she is a perfect example of a will not realized in being, parodying the realization of the will and manipulating the realization of the wills of others.

"Frost at Midnight," a poem roughly contemporary with *Christabel* and similarly concerned with parent-child relationships, provides a good opportunity for summarizing both Coleridge's engagement in the "Christian" process of self-othering outlined by Ricoeur and the anxieties about that process manifested by the problem of sin. The child Hartley can be seen as a kind of internal and external other. On the one hand, he is within, as one

> Whose gentle breathings, heard in this deep calm,
> Fill up the interspersėd vacancies
> And momentary pauses of the thought!
>
> (45–47)

In this capacity, he provides a link to the deepest recesses of the poet's own past, the deeply phenomenological past self who lives in the temporal mode of anticipation, listening to the church bells "falling on [his] ear / Most like articulate sounds of things to come!" (32–33). The father, unlike Sir Leoline or the father described in the poem tacked on to the end of *Christabel,* feels an attachment to the child in the child's role as an alternative version of the father. The child is also an external other; as a projection of the self the narrator would like to have had, he will "learn far other lore" (50) and hear Nature's utterance of God's language. Ricoeur's otherness that belongs to "the ontological constitution of selfhood" (*Oneself* 317) is manifested in that the child, as the poet's other, becomes an occasion for promise and attestation. The poet promises the child a better life and attests to the child's potential relation to God and nature. This is attestation in Ricoeur's strong sense of "I believe in"—a faith in the other—rather than the merely doxic sense of "I believe that" (21), insofar as the poet expresses faith *in* the child, God, and nature, rather than simply a hope or opinion *that* the good things he describes will happen.

However, the child's status as an other is also a problem, because the difference between father and child forces the poet to look outside that relationship for the self's necessary self-objectification, Ricoeur's "detour by way of objectification" that "is the shortest path from the self to the self " (*Oneself* 313). At the beginning of the poem the child is separated from the narrator by enjoying the peaceful calm that the poet does share. The link to the past is therefore mediated by the negatively determined outness of the "film, which fluttered on the grate" (15) whose "[m]otion in this hush of nature," the narrator says,

> Gives it dim sympathies with me who live,
> Making it a companionable form,
> Whose puny flaps and freaks the idling Spirit
> By its own moods interprets, every where

Echo or mirror seeking of itself,
And makes a toy of Thought.

(18–23)

This objective detour, which provides the direct link to the past by reminding him of "that fluttering *stranger*" (26) seen at school, parodies the positive version of self-othering manifested in his relation to the child. The film's connection to the poet's self is structural and privative rather than positive; as the "sole unquiet thing" (16) it is connected to him not by a symbolic or even metaphorical resemblance, but by their common unquietness in opposition to the stillness around them. Without any anchoring in real human otherness, this shadowy other, or inhuman vehicle of objectification, becomes an "echo" or "mirror" subject to arbitrary interpretation by a will similarly lacking the anchoring that self-othering should provide.

Christabel, presenting "a world of sin," as opposed to the world of an internalized projection of one's best self, presents a full-blown version of the arbitrariness of the ungrounded will that is only suggested in "Frost at Midnight." In such a world, intention that is discontinuous with the self-othering logos—the evil will not realized in being—leads to a shutting-down of the hermeneutic and ethical principle of the logos. Or, in the terms of the "streamy association" passage, intention, cut off from its hermeneutic and ethical moorings, goes mad as "imperfect yet existing Volition." The ease with which subjectivity can go mad, tearing itself loose from the anchor of the Ricoeurean notion of oneself as another, suggests the inability of this model to give us a complete picture of the ethical and hermeneutic principles involved in Coleridgean subjectivity. Even "Frost at Midnight," which is one of Coleridge's most hopeful poetic presentations of oneself as another, suggests a paradox in Ricoeur's model: the self requires a detour through the objectification provided by the other, but the very difference of that other provides the potential for the self to detach itself from the process and pursue objectification in an arbitrary, self-demeaning rather than self-affirming way, as in the poet's identification with the film of ash on the grate.

IV. Levinasian Otherness

Levinas's more radical, "Hebraic" notion of otherness can help us address these complications of the Ricoeurean or "Christian" model in Coleridge's work. Otherness for Coleridge is not as easily reconcilable with subjectivity as his Logos-philosophy suggests, and it is not a problem only in the specific context of sin. As Geoffrey Hartman points out, "That Coleridge was deeply disturbed by the priority of others—and of the Other—is hardly in question" ("Reflections on an Evening Star" 167). The "ghostliness" that Hartman finds even in the ultimately false sublime of "Hymn Before Sun-rise, in the Vale of Chamouni" but also in the *Rime* "takes away the sense of easy personal presence while intensifying the presence of otherness. Emptied of personality he must stand on this very emptiness against impinging surreality" (173). Coleridge's theology and poetics posit a model of primary subjectivity that incorporates otherness in a way similar to Ricoeur's *ipse-idem* dialectic, but both his imaginative experience and what will later be resolved into a foundation for his mature theology make that subjectivity vulnerable to a more radical and overpowering notion of otherness. This vulnerability can be seen in the agonized penitent in "The Pains of Sleep," and even in the much happier speakers of "Lime-Tree Bower" and "Frost at Midnight," for whom primary experience happens mostly to other people, and of course in the Ancient Mariner, whose self is stolen by an experience of radical otherness that can be retold but not integrated into a life.

This kind of otherness resembles that described by Levinas in some important ways. It is not just a matter of the self becoming other as a gesture of ethical subjectivity, as in Ricoeur's terms, or even of the incorporation of an image of an external or internalized other, as in Williams's or Smith's model. Levinas's radical notion of otherness reworks the relationship between the particular and the absolute (a relationship of obvious importance to Coleridge, but one de-emphasized by both Ricoeur and Williams) by locating them in the same place: the face of the particular, unique, nontotalized other person *is* the command from the unconditioned. Thus for Levinas, "[t]he ipseity of the I consists in remaining outside the distinction between the individual and the general" (*TI* 118). As Ricoeur concisely (albeit critically) summarizes Levinas's position, "Each face is a Sinai that prohibits murder" (*Oneself* 336).

The two kinds of otherness are related to two ways in which humans think of the absolute: for Coleridge these are the two ways in which we think of God. To the extent that God exists as an active principle in the world, as Logos, he is thought of under the dialectical or polar logic by which the absolute can be thought of only in the context of the nonabsolute. In Coleridge's mature theology, this is God as "Ipsëity," the second stage in the theological pentad, or "[t]he eternally self-affirmant self-affirmed." The self-affirmation of God is necessary because "that which is essentially causative of *all* Being, must be causative of its own." Ipseity generates a dialectic with otherness, interacting with the "Alterity," or "the *essential* Infinite in the *form* of the Finite" which leads to creation, as well as to the actual synthesizing of the subjective and the objective in "Community" or "the eternal LIFE, which is LOVE . . . the Good in the ~~form~~ reality of the True, in the form of actual Life" (*SW & F* 1511–12). This process is repeated on the finite level in the dialectic of self-consciousness, the imaginative self-othering that leads to the "repetition in the finite mind of the eternal act of creation in the infinite I AM" (*BL* 1: 304). This is, as I have argued, the same theological and philosophical tradition that gives rise to Ricoeur's dialectic of *ipse-* and *idem-* identity. This sense of God as Logos implies a notion of the good not as a principle that is separate from life, but rather as a foundational principle of identity and diversity within life. It is thus something like the notion of the good as a "structure" rather than a transcendent principle outside of reality, that Gadamer finds in Plato, according to P. Christopher Smith: "the idea of the good we look to, far from being something transcendent and separate . . . is indeed the structure of unity in diversity, the structure of integrity we seek to effect *in* ourselves and others" (*Hermeneutics and Human Finitude* 236).

In the *Biographia,* under the influence of Schelling, Coleridge places that dialectical polarity at the origin of his theological and imaginative system. However, in a letter to J. H. Green of September 30, 1818, he recants his total allegiance to Schelling's dialectic in the *Biographia,* promising "steadily to deny and clearly to expose, the Polarity as existing or capable of existing in the unity of a perfect Will or in the Godhead as ens realissimum. *The divine Unity* is indeed the indispensable CONDITION of this Polarity; but both it's *formal* and it's immediate, *specific* CAUSE is the contradictory Will of the Apostasy" (*CL* 4: 874).[30] The polarity is grounded in God's absolute unity but is caused by the apostatic will contrary to God. God's own self-othering is a response to that apostacy, "a Spiritual Fall or Apostacy *antecedent* to the formation of Man." That apostacy is the locus of original sin, which is thus "the antecedent ground and occasion of Christianity" (*AR* 291).

Thus the human condition, and even the divine response to the human condition, are polar, but, according to Coleridge's later theology, we must embrace both that polarity and the sense of a nonpolar absolute behind it. God as "person" in this latter sense is separate from nature, and even from his own status as original nature; even "the divine Nature" or "Asëity" is "indivisibly distinguished from the divine Personëity" (*CM* 3: 944). In the 1833 "On the Trinity," this absolute unity that precedes the polarity or God's self-othering is called "identity" or the "prothesis." "Identity" is defined as "that which is essentially causative of *all* possible true Being—Ground and Cause. = The absolute WILL," to be distinguished from the beginnings of self-othering in the primordial self-consciousness of the "Ipsëity" (*SW & F* 1510–11). In an 1826 notebook entry, Coleridge distinguishes between the absolute Will as "Deus idem et ipse" ("God the same and himself") and the "Will eternally begotten" or "Eternal Word" as "Deus alter et idem" ("God other and the same") (*CN* 4: 5413).[31] The former is not simply an immanent structure of identity and diversity, but a truly transcendent principle of identity, manifested in an absolute Will that is not self-othering. Here, as the four- or five-part structure he elaborated in the 1830's[32] is presented more simply as a binary opposition, Coleridge's use of the phrase "idem et ipse" has a different force from Ricoeur's use of the same phrase, since for Coleridge it is to be distinguished from the self-othering function of "Deus alter et idem." In the more elaborate scheme, however, "Ipsëity" (as distinguished from the more primary "Identity") does incorporate the potential for self-othering that is present in Ricoeur's notion of ipse-identity.

"Taken *absolutely,*" the "identity or "prothesis" is the "Point which has no (real) Opposite or Counter-point" and "finds its application in the Supreme Being alone" (*AR* 181n). The polarity by which everything below the level of the absolute operates—the dialectical process that underlies Nature—is, like creation itself, a result of the original apostacy: "Nature itself is a peccant (I had almost said, an unnatural) State—or rather, no *State* at all, οὐ στασις, αλλα ἀπόστασις—['not a state (*stasis*) but a fall from a state (*apostasis*)']" (*CM* 2: 675).[33] But in this fallen world, the division is a philosophical, linguistic, and even mathematical fact as well as a theological one, because our fallen existence is inevitably dialectical, even as we can envisage a pre-dialectical unity. Thus, very much in the spirit of Kant's inaccessible noumena, which the "Christian" side of Coleridge tried to make more accessible, the absolute can be inferred, but cannot be manifested except as polarity:

> Absolute oneness in the manifestation may be known, indeed, or *inferred,* as Oneness; but cannot *appear* except in and by *the many,* or not-one, as the condition of the Distinct—an angle requires two lines to manifest it—&c. . . . Since then the ~~One~~ Monad or Indistinction can be made manifest only by *the Many* (*the Dyad* we will suppose;) and as each is distinct in relation to that from which it is

> distinguished; it follows, that all manifestation is by Opposition, each opposed to the other as Thesis and Antithesis, and both *as* both opposed to the Prothesis or that which is thus manifested, as ~~the~~ distinct Multeity to absolute Identity. (*CN* 4: 4513)[34]

Barth, following W. G. T. Shedd, sees this dual notion of God as theologically problematic: by positing "an aboriginal Unity . . . *before* a Trinity," Coleridge introduces into his notion of God "a process of development . . . which is incompatible with its immutable perfection" (qtd. *Coleridge and Christian Doctrine* 94).

It is tempting to argue, as Nicholas Reid does, that Coleridge's transition from Schelling's notion of a foundational polarity between subject and object to (after September 1818) a grounding of self-consciousness in a prior unity, is a move toward theological foundationalism (469–70). It is such a move, in the sense that Coleridge was reacting to the heterodox implications of Schelling's foundational polarity. However, the heterodoxy that Barth notes—the necessity of a unity prior to the dialectical constitution of the Trinity—has implications that are more radical philosophically than Schelling's foundational polarity. The theological mystery of the Trinity allows for a comfortable coexistence of the One and the Many in a God who is simultaneously one and three. Coleridge, however, stresses the fundamental aporia that the One must be expressed in the Many, even though the One, absolutely conceived, is the "Point which has no (real) Opposite or Counter-point" and is thus prior to the dialectic of the One and the Many. Absolute transcendence, then, is not reducible to the dialectic of even the self-othering logos, but must remain completely other to that dialectic, even though the logos is the (for us) necessary expression of the absolute.

In this sense, Coleridge's implicit critique of Trinitarian doctrine resembles Emmanuel Levinas's critique of traditional notions of transcendence. Levinas asks, "[W]ould not the bankruptcy of transcendence be but that of a theology that thematizes the *transcending* in the logos, assigns a term to the passing of transcendence, congeals it into a 'world behind the scenes,' and installs what it says in war and in matter, which are the inevitable modalities of the fate woven by being in its interest?" (*OB* 5). If Schelling's polarity, which can be seen in the divine logos and the human imagination, is at the foundation, it becomes a "world behind the scenes" that is not essentially different from what happens in the phenomenal world. Coleridge suggests that the human will must be self-othering, as in Ricoeur's notion of the self's ipse-identity, and on the model of God's own self-othering in relation to man, but at the same time the human will must acknowledge God, as well as the absolute in general, as an absolute other, prior to all subjectivity, prior to all nature, inassimilable to the self, and yet as that which must ground the self. Coleridge suggests these two notions of God in the distinction, posited speculatively in his marginalia on Eichhorn, between Elohim and Jehova: "What if Elohim expressed the Absolute Will, and the all-causative *Omnipotence*—/ and Jehova, or Jehova Elohim, the Godhead in its moral and spiritual relations to Man, as his Judge &c?" (*CM* 2: 389-90).[35] In a marginal note to the works of Jakob Böhme, Coleridge defines the former notion as "the abysmal Mystery, that there is in the causativeness or All-might of God more than God. ~~because~~ i.e. an xy that God did not realize in *himself*—for the Real containeth the Actual and the Potentiality—but in God as God there is no potentiality" (1: 693-94). The impossible thought of a God who is "more than God" is a transcendence that, in Levinas's terms, is not reducible to a "world behind the scenes." Levinas suggests Coleridge's absolute God in his assertion that "the God of the Bible signifies the beyond being, transcendence" a God who must be thought of as prior to the thematizing that "brings God into the course of being" ("God and Philosophy" 130). Coleridge's absolute God has this unthematizeable nature—"we must suppose an Absolute knowledge, incomprehensible and incommunicable"—which for him is complemented by God as logos: "But with the same evidence we must also assume a manifestative Knowledge, according to which ~~God~~ he revealeth himself to the Children of God" (*SW & F* 803-4).

Like Levinas, Coleridge objects to a theology that places the logos at the origin, because such a theology reduces the absolute to the human terms in which we *relate* to the absolute, granting the absolute the processual, dialectical character of the postlapsarian relation between God and humanity. For Levinas, this reduction of the absolutely transcendent to the logos "assigns a term to the passing of transcendence" and characterizes "the hold the *said* has over the *saying*" (*OB* 5). While the "saying" is "a foreword preceding languages" that "sets forth an order more grave than being and antecedent to being," the "said" designates the process by which "this pre-original saying does move into a language, in which saying and said are correlative of one another, and the saying is subordinated to its theme" (5-6). Levinas distinguishes the "betrayal" of the saying in the said (6) from "the fall from a higher order or disorder," because to characterize the relation thus would be to "fail to recognize being or treat it, ridiculously and pretentiously, with disdain" (16). Similarly for Coleridge, the apostacy that results in our dialectical existence and the necessary expression of the absolute in the language of polarity (which is to say, in language) is not a condition to be lamented because it is the necessary condition of our relation to the absolute.

Levinas makes much more, ethically and politically, of the distinction between the preontological "saying" and its betrayal in the "said" than Coleridge does of the distinction between the identity of the absolute and the dialectic of the logos. The difference in emphasis might be put this way: the cornerstone of Levinas's ethical philosophy is the need to move beyond the "said" in order to acknowledge the irreducible otherness of the "saying," as expressed in the encounter with the other person, whereas for Coleridge the otherness of the absolute is important as the ultimate ground for the self-othering of logos and dialectic, as suggested by the use of the "same evidence" to assert both an incomprehensible, incommunicable absolute and the "manifestative Knowledge" of God as logos. The latter is for Levinas the inevitable "betrayal" of the said and in Coleridge's Christian terms it is the divine response to human "apostacy"; this subtle difference suggests the difference between Levinas's fully Hebraic approach and Coleridge's heterodox combination of the Hebraic sense of God's absolute otherness with the Christian concept of an accessible, incarnated God who can provide a model for human behavior.

Both Coleridge and Levinas find this relationship embodied in language. For Levinas, the "one" of the "nominal form" of the subject "is irreducible to the verbal form" (*OB* 53). Similarly, but with a significant difference, for Coleridge (in a long notebook entry of March 1820), the absolute "prothesis" or "identity" is associated, not with the noun as such, so much as with the "verb substantive," ultimately the divine "I AM." Once that identity unfolds into a dialectic, noun and verb correspond to thesis and antithesis, respectively, suggesting Ricoeur's dialectic between subject and predicate in his antistructuralist theory of discourse: "the intertwining and interplay of the functions of identification and predication" (*Interpretation Theory* 11). Here Coleridge emphasizes the continuity rather than the distinction between the transcendence of "One" and the subsequent "polarity": the "One" is defined as "One containing the power of *two* as their radical *antecedent,* or as ~~the~~ a point *producing* itself into a bi-polar Line but contemplated as anterior to this production" (*CN* 4: 4644). Furthermore, the Identity, as a "verb-substantive" is an absolute *Will,* which is different, despite important connections, from the Levinasian "one" of the other human: "The subject as a term, as a noun, is someone" (*OB* 53).

Although Coleridge does not see ethics as "first philosophy" quite as explicitly as Levinas does, the priority of the ethical is always implicit.

Not only is "self-consciousness" grounded in "conscience," but the later Coleridge's emphasis on the "Identity" that precedes the dialectic of the logos is also ethical: the single attribute of "Identity" is "the GOOD" (*SW & F* 1510). Thus an instructive connection can be made between the absolute otherness of that "Identity" and the absolute otherness at the heart of the Levinasian ethical encounter. As Coleridge says in the *Theory of Life,* the polarity in all life is a polarity, not just within the Schellingesque dialectic of self-consciousness as presented in chapter 12 of the *Biographia,* but between first-person liberty and submission to an absolute: "As the liberty, so must be the reverence for law. As the independence, so must be the service and the submission to the Supreme Will!" (*Theory of Life, SW & F* 551).

Part of the connection between Coleridgean and Levinasian otherness can be made through the continued influence of Kant. The notion that the unconditioned is the source of an ethical command reverberates from Coleridge all the way to Derrida, whose indebtedness to Levinas is well known. Coleridge, in his rewriting of the Ten Commandments, equates the unconditioned command of Kant's Pure Reason with God's law: "it is a *command*—not an inducement. Do it—not for this reason or for that reason—but to fulfill the Law for the sake of the Law" (*CN* 3: 3293). Similarly, in the essays on method the commanding Law is an attribute of God: "We have thus assigned the first place in the science of Method to LAW; and first of the first, to *Law,* as the absolute *kind* which comprehending in itself the substance of every possible degree precludes from its conception all degree, not by generalization but by its own plenitude. As such, therefore, and as the sufficient cause of the reality correspondent thereto, we contemplate it as exclusively an attribute of the Supreme Being, inseparable from the idea of God" (*Friend* 1: 459).[36] We tend to think of the unconditioned in postmodern terms as the incommensurability of discourses—the "postmodern condition" of the *differend*—or the ungraspability of *differance* rather than in Coleridge's Christian terms as the infinite I AM. However, the unconditioned still sends us a commanding law, a "categorical imperative" to acknowledge the otherness of that which resides in the unconditioned. Derrida adopts, with sincere acknowledgment, the same Kantian terminology used by Coleridge in describing "unconditionality" as that which "intervenes in the determination of a context from its very inception, and from an injunction, a law, a responsibility that transcends this or that determination of a given context," and goes on to say that "this unconditionality also defines the injunction that prescribes deconstruction" (*Limited Inc* 152–53).[37] Vattimo finds a connection between the "'law' of religion," according to which "it is not by its own decision that the subject is committed to a process of ruin, for one finds oneself called to such a commitment by the 'thing itself'," and the hermeneutic experience of "the belonging of the interpreter to the 'thing' to be interpreted, or more generally to the game of interpretation" (*Beyond Interpretation* 53). The position of the subject as both a hermeneutic and an ethical entity determined by this command from the unconditioned, a position expressed in Coleridge's notion of the divine absolute, Derrida's deconstructive intervention, and Vattimo's radicalization of Gadamerian hermeneutics, thus give us a very different picture of the subject from that presented by the logos-philosophy that emphasizes the self-othering activity of the subject.

For Coleridge this absolute is as inaccessible as it is foundational, since it is ontologically prior to God's role as communicating logos. Coleridge here engages one of the central theological and ethical problems of German Idealism, in the wake of Kant's promotion of the rationally autonomous moral agent. As Emile Fackenheim frames the problem, summarizing Schelling's critique of Fichte in the period of the *System of Transcendental Idealism* (a book Coleridge owned and annotated both before and after writing the *Biographia*), "Sheer submission to an alien, external God, destructive as it is of freedom, is an immoral religion, and a true religion must spring from freedom, understood as autonomy." However, the problem here is that "moral freedom does not, immediately, imply belief in a moral order and hence religion, but on the contrary by itself implies absence of order and hence irreligion and atheism" (71). This suggests a conflict between the absolute, Levinasian God, functioning in his inaccessibility as a critique of autonomous human liberty, and the Christian God-as-logos who provides a model for creative human freedom. Coleridge wanted a concept of human autonomy based on a finite repetition of God's *ipse*-identity, but at the same time he refused the German humanization of the divine by retaining a concept of God's absolute otherness.

However, both his view of the problem and his attempted solution differ from Schelling's. For Schelling, a major obstacle to moral freedom was the otherness of nature. According to Fackenheim, "[T]he self's own absolute—unlimited moral freedom—clashes with another absolute—that nature, taken as a whole, is beyond its control" (71). This is not exactly the problem for Coleridge. Although, as Modiano points out, nature can become either a rival self as *natura naturans* or a problematic non-self as *natura naturata* (54–55), its status as an emanation of the logos-principle (as well its Wordsworthian familiarity) prevents it from taking on the philosophically absolute role assigned to it by Schelling. Coleridge explicitly prefers the Hebrew opposition between God and the world to Schelling's opposition between the world and the self, according to a marginal comment on Schelling's *Philosophische Schriften*. Schelling's notion "seems mere pot-valiant Nonsense, without the idea of a moral Power extrinsic to and above the World. . . . How much more sublime and, in other points of view, how infinitely more beautiful, even in respect of Taste, or aisthetic Judgement, is the Scriptural representation of the *World* as at enmity with *God*" (*CM* 4: 408).

In the "Hebraic" or Levinasian notion of otherness, otherness is not posited by the self as a route to self-knowledge but experienced by the self as an otherness that will always be transcendent, and that denies the priority of the self in a more extreme way than is suggested by the notion of "oneself as another." Perkins makes a strong case for the influence of kabalistic thought on Coleridge's logos-philosophy, and his interest, shared by his German sources, in Hebrew thought is well known.[38] Christianity synthesizes Greek ideality and Roman materiality, which are mediated by Hebrew culture, according to *The Friend:* "thus the Hebrews may be regarded as the fixed mid point of the living line, toward which the Greeks as the *ideal* pole, and the Romans as the *material,* were ever approximating; till the coincidence and final *synthesis* took place in Christianity, of which the Bible is the law, and Christendom the phaenomenon" (1: 505–6). In Coleridge's dialectic, synthesis does not, as in Hegel, negate its previous terms,[39] and Hebrew culture is already a mediation between, although not a synthesis of, Greek and Roman culture, so Coleridge's interpretation of Hebrew thought is still very much a part of his Christian theology. Earlier in this *Friend* essay he finds a progression from the Hebrew notion of ideas as spirit without image—"[t]he common and ultimate object of the will and of the reason was purely *spiritual,* and to be present in the mind of the disciple . . . in the idea alone, and never as an image or imagination" (1: 501)—to Greek attention to ideas and Roman materialization of those ideas (1: 505), synthesized by Christianity.

Without the mediation of imagination, which of course for Coleridge is a function of the Christian Logos, imageless Hebrew spirituality is completely other to the imagining self. The Hebrew tradition itself also presents for Coleridge what Prickett calls the "unresolvable contradiction between the past as a living source of legitimation and the past as history," in which the continuity with the past is seen simultaneously in terms of similarity and difference (*The Origins of Narrative* 161). Within this contradiction, Coleridge asserts the contemporary relevance of Hebrew political thought—"the inspired poets, historians and sententiaries of the Jews, are the clearest teachers of political economy: in short . . . their writings are the STATESMAN'S BEST MANUAL" (*LS* 128)—while also arguing for the primitiveness of Hebrew narrative as "an accommodation to the then childhood of the human race" ("On the Prometheus of Aeschylus," *SW & F* 2: 1267). As noted in Chapter 5, the ontological, moral and theological priority of Christian inwardness is paired with the necessary temporal priority of the external, as the shell precedes the kernal, legality precedes morality, and Judaism precedes Christianity (*CN* 3: 4003).

Both as a tradition of divine otherness and as a tradition whose contradictory relation to the present gives it the status of an historical other, resisting any simple assimilation to a unified "present" concept, this "Hebraic" side of Coleridge provides a context for a Levinasian sense of otherness that differs sharply from the Ricoeurean self-othering of the logos-philosophy. For Levinas, "[t]he ethical is the field outlined by the paradox of an Infinite in relationship with the finite without being belied in this relationship" (*OB* 148). The copresence for Coleridge, in his theology as well his ethical thought (not that the two are really separable) of both a Ricoeurean dialectic of "oneself as another" and a more radical Levinasian sense of absolute otherness demonstrates how forcefully he pressed this paradox: as self-othering logos, the infinite is in a relationship with the finite but risks being "belied"; as absolute Identity the infinite retains its full infinity at the price of a relationship with the finite.

The copresence of these two kinds of otherness is perhaps most visible in the poetry. For example, just as the Mariner's "conversion" suggests but also denies the closure of the Augustinian conversion narrative, the ethics of his situation and narrative suggest both a Greco-Christian self-generated otherness, like Ricoeur's notion of "oneself as another," and a Hebraic sense of absolute otherness, like Levinas's notion of an otherness that transcends the self's conceptual categories. As Adam Newton says in his Levinasian reading of the *Rime*, "beyond the moral thematics of Coleridge's poem is a realm of ethical confrontation" (4). The Mariner's journey is somewhere between an Odysseus-like return and an Abramic exile, to invoke Levinas's comparison: "To the myth of Ulysses returning to Ithaca, we would like to oppose the story of Abraham leaving his homeland forever for a still unknown land and even forbidding his son to be brought back to its point of departure" ("The Trace of the Other" 348). Like Odysseus the Mariner returns, and like the Christian Augustine he has a conversion story to tell. However, instead of basking in the retrospection of permanent conversion or triumphant return, he must, like

Abraham, "pass, like night, from land to land" (632), and like a Hebrew prophet he is an outsider, with a message that is both immediately confrontational and mediated, as discussed in Chapter 4, by the demands of narrative, a genre associated by Coleridge with the Hebrew Bible.[40] In 1832 Coleridge himself pictured the Mariner as "the everlasting wandering Jew" who had, at the time of the encounter with the Wedding Guest, "told this story ten thousand times since the voyage which was in early youth and fifty years before" (*TT* 1: 274). The Mariner experiences what Barth appropriately calls "the terror of the infinite" (*Coleridge and the Power of Love* 67), which I am suggesting is also the Levinasian experience "in which the nucleus of the ego is cored out" (*OB* 64) by absolute otherness, and in turn he gives the Wedding Guest an experience of being confronted by the absolutely other in human form.

As I argued in Chapter 4, the Mariner's role as "example" suggests something very different from the exemplary Christian conversion as described by Robbins, the psychoanalytic conversion described by Harpham, and even the moral imitation of God advocated by the later Coleridge. The Mariner teaches the "love and reverence" he advocates "by his own example," the Christianizing marginal gloss tells us, and one might hope that the Wedding Guest will somehow imitate that love and reverence, but no sane Wedding Guest would really want to imitate the Mariner in either his terrifying experience at sea or his compulsive, nomadic life at home. The Christian conversion narrative holds up a spiritually fulfilled life as an incentive to imitate the process of conversion; the Mariner's story does no such thing. The Wedding Guest does not even learn a coherent lesson:

> He went like one that hath been stunn'd,
> And is of sense forlorn:
> A sadder and a wiser man
> He rose the morrow morn.
>
> (668–71)

Here the "Hebraic" side of Coleridge's ethics is in strong evidence, because the Mariner "teaches" not by offering a concept, but by effecting a confrontation that, as Newton argues, resembles in many respects Emmanuel Levinas's preconceptual, foundationally ethical, absolute otherness experienced in the particularity of another human face. The Mariner's confrontation suggests the approach of the "infinite" in the Levinasian sense of the face that exceeds the subject's conceptual categories; the Mariner presents an "infinity" that is "present" only "in its refusal to be contained," remaining "infinitely transcendent, infinitely foreign" (*TI* 194).

One of the ethical paradoxes of the notion of God as a model for the polarity of human subjectivity (Coleridge's logos-principle) and as an absolute will prior to that polarity (Coleridge's notion of the absolute) is that "will" considered as a separate phenomenon is both the definition of the absolute God and the definition of human evil. God considered absolutely is "The Absolute WILL, essentially immanifestable in itself" (*CM* 2: 423). On the human level, however, as noted above in connection with Geraldine's role in *Christabel*, the unactualized will is the source of evil: "For pure Evil what is it but Will that would manifest itself as Will, not in Being (Ετερότης) [otherness]), not in Intelligence (therefore *form*less), not in Union or Communion, the contrary therefore of Life, even eternal Death" (*CN* 4: 5076).[41] This makes theological sense, since man's greatest sin is to pretend to Godhood, "to will no potential, in itself, but to be as ~~the~~ God, the Universal Will" (4: 4998), attempting to usurp the place of the absolute other instead of accepting the other's claim, or, in Coleridge's words, "striving to be the one instead of striving after & toward the One" (4: 5076).

Perhaps the most extreme theological example of evil as will actualized only as will rather than in Being can be found in "The Wanderings of Cain." Wandering in a desolate dream-landscape, Cain's only interaction is with a ghostly "Shape" taking the form of, but thereby negating, the one other with whom Cain should have interacted: his murdered brother Abel. He is accompanied by his son Enos, who is already learning "far other lore" by recognizing life in nature but, who (unlike the imagined Hartley in "Frost at Midnight") finds himself unable to interact with it, and for whom Cain shows little paternal concern. This is a world grounded on the will's inability to interact with either natural or human otherness. The Shape, presumably conjured out of Cain's guilty psyche and sinfully ungrounded will, is himself wandering in agony and posits a heretically dualistic inversion of the Judeo-Christian universe:

> But Cain said, 'Didst thou not find favour in the sight of the Lord thy God?' The Shape answered, 'The Lord is God of the living only, the dead have another God.' Then the child Enos lifted up his eyes and prayed; but Cain rejoiced secretly in his heart. 'Wretched shall they be all the days of their mortal life,' exclaimed the Shape, 'who sacrifice worthy and acceptable sacrifices to the God of the dead; but after their death their toil ceaseth. Woe is me, for I was well

> beloved by the God of the living, and cruel wert thou, O my brother, who didst snatch me away from his power and dominion.' (138–48)

In his solitary wandering, Cain is persuaded to follow a god that is literally the "contrary of life," whose perverse theology takes Cain's murderous action out of the ethical context of sin into the realm of "power and dominion": his cruelty consists in moving "Abel" from the jurisdiction of one arbitrary power to that of another. In such a universe, ethics can have nothing to do with the development of ethical self-consciousness through a process of self-othering, but becomes a simple matter of which arbitrary power structure one allies oneself with. Cain secretly rejoices to think that he in fact is following the right god—the god of the dead—for his future welfare, which introduces a complete disparity between the cruelty of Cain's actions and the matter of his relation to "god."

The notion of evil as will operating on its own, without actualization in being, without the form granted by intelligence, without union or communion, coupled with the suggestion of "The Wanderings of Cain" that the evil will of Cain produces a solipsistic universe of arbitrary power, suggests what Levinas calls "the arbitrariness of freedom." For Levinas, freedom, which by itself is arbitrary and violent, needs to "put itself in question, in penetrating beneath its own condition" in order to ground "the arbitrariness of freedom" in the welcoming of the "Other": "To welcome the Other is to put in question my freedom" (*TI* 84–85). Coleridge cannot directly mount such a critique of freedom, of course, because human freedom is ultimately grounded on the free, divine act of self-othering, which enables a process that retains the priority of a free self-consciousness. Coleridge is also enough of a rationalist to say that the will's actualization in the forms of intelligence is part of its ethical actualization, while Levinas sees such conceptual "thematization" as part of freedom's potentially violent (albeit unavoidable) arbitrariness. However, the ease with which freedom can go wrong and reveal itself as unactualized will in Coleridge's text, instituting a universe of arbitrary power, suggests the extent to which the subjective, free will needs to remain grounded both in the lives of others—in "Union or Communion"—and in the recognition of humanity's Levinasian dependence on absolute otherness, in Coleridge's case the absolute otherness of God insofar as he is *not* actualized in Being, and therefore *not* imitable.

The *Rime,* despite (or perhaps because of) the fact that it was written before Coleridge's theology had matured, presents a particularly complex case study of the relations among evil, freedom, and otherness. The shooting of the albatross is an act of violent, arbitrary will according to either Coleridgean or Levinasian standards, an act of "Will that would manifest itself as Will, not in Being," which certainly demonstrates the arbitrariness and violence of the "freedom" that, as Levinas says, "discovers itself murderous in its very exercise" (*TI* 84).[42] As the 1817 gloss to lines 78-82 attempts to place the event into an economy of hospitality, the shipmates' equal and opposite interpretations of the act—that it was wrong "the Bird to slay / That made the breeze to blow!" ([1817] 95-96), and then (once the breeze resumes) "right . . . such birds to slay, / That bring the fog and mist" ([1817] 101-2)—portray the arbitrariness of the conceptual economy within which freedom, "the very movement of representation and its evidence" (*TI* 85), works. In the process of expiation the Mariner learns some Christian principles of love, but through an experience of absolute otherness more comparable to Job's or Jonah's ego-annihilating experiences than to Augustine's ego-reconstructing experiences. Though he desires "[t]o walk together to the Kirk / With a goodly company" (649-50), the Mariner's repentant will is not exactly actualized in being, intelligence, union, or communion, as Coleridge says the nonapostatic will should be, and he is not able to find peace in the Levinasian acceptance of the other's priority. Instead, he can only expiate his excess of will by giving that will over to the forced repetition of the story of that excess. This perhaps reflects the Mariner's entrapment in a situation not easily covered by Levinas's paradigm: the Mariner is caught between his own ego-robbing experience of otherness on his journey and his status as an absolute other fulfilling a similar role for the Wedding-Guest.

As the critical history of the *Rime* attests, there is no question of understanding the Mariner under a "concept," as the ego attempts to do, according to Levinas, when "every relation between the same and the other . . . reduces itself to an impersonal relation within a universal order" (*TI* 87-88). The Hermit, however, attempts exactly this: with apparent faith in the is/ought derivation, he asks "What manner man art thou?" (623) before he can consider the possibility of "shriev[ing]" (559) the Mariner. The response is not a self-concept, but rather the first convulsive tale-telling: an unstable narrative of an incomprehensible experience.[43] In laying out his argument for a Levinasian "narrative ethics," Newton presents the Mariner's tale-telling situation as a paradigmatic instance of Levinas's ethically performative "Saying" (as opposed to the "Said" of moral propositions). The Mariner's response "not only returns him to death-in-life, but similarly sentences every person whose ear (and destiny) he bends" (6). Like Coleridge, Levinas sees "conscience" as foundational, and the Mariner's tale can be seen as inducing just such a Levinasian experience of conscience: "in conscience I have an experience that is not commensurate with any a priori framework—a conceptless experience" (*TI* 100–101).

For Levinas, it is precisely the breakup of the unified surface of the thematized ego by an accusing other that produces the first-person "I" engaged in life's ethical dimension: the "obsession by the other, my neighbor . . . reduces the ego to a self on the hither side of my identity, prior to all self-consciousness, and denudes me absolutely" (*OB* 92). Something like this seems to happen when the Mariner "holds" the wedding Guest with "his skinny hand" (13) and his "glittering eye" (17), reducing the Wedding Guest to a pre-self-conscious form of attention: he "listens like a three year's child" (19). The face of the other in Levinas is not "seen," which would be to reduce it to a representation, a subjectively controlled visual concept, "an adequation of exteriority with interiority" (*TI* 295). We have a few visual details for the Mariner—the skinny hand, the glittering eye, the grey beard, the appearance of being "long and lank and brown, / As is the ribb'd Sea-sand" (228–29)—but they function more as arresting manifestations of the Mariner's otherness than as representations. The sea-sand comparison (for which Coleridge thanks Wordsworth) is in effect an antirepresentation, reducing human form to the shifting. unintelligible patterns traced by ocean waves. According to Levinas, "the face with which the Other turns to me is not reabsorbed in a representation of the face. To hear his destitution which cries out for justice is not to represent an image to oneself, but is to posit oneself as responsible" (215). The Mariner presents just such a motivation for responsibility rather than an image for representation.

The Wedding Guest does not use his status as a free subject to choose to hear the Mariner's story. "He cannot choose but hear"; his involuntary response in effect precedes the understanding of any command. Levinas emphasizes the priority of the ethical command that is not chosen: "the Good is not presented to freedom; it has chosen me before I have chosen it" (*OB* 11). Levinas describes this unrepresentable "proximity" of the other as a combination of transcendence and destitution: "the being that presents himself in the face comes from a dimension of height, a dimension of transcendence whereby he can present himself as a stranger without opposing me as an obstacle or enemy," but at the same time "my position as *I* consists in being able to respond to this essential destitution of the Other. . . . The Other who dominates me in his transcendence is thus the stranger, the widow, and the orphan, to whom I am obligated" (*TI* 215). The Mariner comes from the "height" of his authority to interrupt the Wedding Guest's life, but, as he successively destroys the Wedding Guest's attempts to represent him as a "grey-beard Loon" (15) or a "spirit" ([1817] gloss to 228–31), the Mariner calls to the Wedding Guest's responsibility for his destitution, eliciting the exclamation, "'God save thee, ancyent Marinere! / From the fiends, that plague thee thus!'" (77–78), and finally enabling the Wedding Guest's turn "from the bridegroom's door" (667). The Wedding Guest thus rejects what Levinas would call the symmetrical conceptuality of, in this case, nuptial reciprocity, even though he is "next of kin" (*Rime* 6), for the asymmetry and "irreversibility" (*TI* 101) of the sadness and wisdom resulting from the encounter with the Mariner as a nonreciprocal other.

These two forms of otherness—the Ricoeurean "oneself as another," suggested by Coleridge's philosophy of the logos, and the Levinasian absolute other, suggested by Coleridge's principle of the absolute will—are admittedly modern interpretive categories that do not match Coleridge's explicit theological history. I hope to have shown that there is an informative connection between Coleridge's own interest in Hebrew thought and the link I have proposed between Levinas's Hebraic sense of otherness and Coleridge's notion of God as absolute. However, Coleridge argues that the principle of God as absolute rather than self-othering is not a Judaic principle, but one present throughout the Judeo-Christian tradition and revealed only in Christianity. Following Count Zinzendorf, he suggests that this absolute notion of God was in fact not brought to consciousness in the Old Testament, but was made known only through the Christian incarnation: "In short, the Fathers under the Law knew only Jehova God, the Lord, and the Spirit of the Lord. The Absolute WILL, essentially immanifestable in itself but eternally begetting the Supreme Reason, or Absolute Being as its manifestation, ~~or~~ person, or essential Form, Deus Alter et Idem, was indeed from the beginning manifest *in* the co-eternal ~~I~~ Word, but first declared or made known *by* the word Incarnate" (*CM* 2: 423).

This history suggests the hermeneutic interdependence of the two concepts of otherness. Precisely because the absolute will is "essentially immanifestable in itself" (*CM* 2: 423), it can be approached only through the Christian logos. Thus a version of Ricoeur's detour through objectification is present even on the Levinasian side of the picture: we need the secondary, communicative structure of the logos—God's self-othering as the founding principle of human conceptuality—in order to approach the primary, incommunicable notion of the absolute. Jill Robbins sees a similar interdependence as an important part of Levinas's relation to Judaism: "to approach the Judaic in its specificity *requires* the detour through the Christian conceptuality" (*Altered Reading* 43). On the one hand, just as for Coleridge the "Absolute WILL" is "eternally begetting the Supreme Reason," the paradigm for human self-consciousness, for Levinas the inaccessible saying of ethical otherness is what gives meaning to the said of consciousness and thematization: "in the anarchical provocation which ordains me to the other, is imposed the way which leads to thematization, and to an act of consciousness" (*OB* 16). On the other hand, just as for Coleridge the divine absolute is revealed only through the logos, for Levinas the saying requires the articulation of the said: this "Judaic" ethics of the saying is accessible only through the "Christian" conceptuality of the said: "this astonishing saying . . . must spread out and assemble itself into essence, posit itself, be hypostasized, become an eon in consciousness and knowledge, let itself be seen, undergo the ascendancy of Being. Ethics itself, in its saying which is a responsibility, requires this hold" (44). Saying is experienced as an interruption of the said; it "approaches the other by breaking through the noema involved in intentionality" (48). Although Coleridge's theology attempts to hold both the absolutely other and the incarnationally self-othering senses of God together, poems such as *Christabel* and the *Rime,* as well as his speculations on the mystery of original sin and the origins of evil, move toward this Levinasian perspective. They generate a sense of absolute otherness out of the inadequacies of a philosophy based on the self-othering of the logos, even as the very adequacies of the logos-philosophy must be grounded in a prior sense of God as absolutely other.

7

Love, Otherness, and the Absolute Self

I. The Ethical Status of Love

Coleridge's speculations on love, which, as Lockridge, Modiano, and Wendling have shown, influenced and gave ethical content to his theory of the symbol,[1] demonstrate the importance of both a Ricoeurean *ipse/idem* dialectic and a more radical, Levinasian notion of otherness. In an important sense, love entails reciprocity that *overcomes* otherness; Lockridge argues that Coleridgean love attempts to "transcend human alienation by denying that the 'thou' is unconditionally 'other'" (*Coleridge the Moralist* 192), and the final lines of "The Pains of Sleep" plead for reciprocity in love: "To be beloved is all I need, / And whom I love, I love indeed" (51–52). However, the reciprocity in the Coleridgean I-Thou relationship—a relationship epitomized by love—is grounded in the otherness of a third party, ultimately the divine command from the unconditioned: "No I without a Thou: no Thou without a Law from *Him,* to whom I and Thou stand in the same relation. Distinct Self-knowledge begins with the sense of Duty toward my Neighbor; and Duty felt *to,* and claimed from my Equal supposes & implies the Right of a Third, superior to both because imposing it on both" (Notebook 26, fol. 41, qtd. Perkins 75). Similarly, Levinas, in *Totality and Infinity,* grounds human fraternity in the approach of the Other as a third party: "the stranger . . . presents himself as an equal. His equality . . . consists in referring to the *third party,* thus present at the encounter. . . . Society must be a fraternal community. . . . Monotheism signifies this human kinship, this idea of a human race that refers back to the approach of the Other in the face, in a dimension of height, in responsibility for oneself and for the Other" (*TI* 213–14).

If, as both passages suggest, human relationships are grounded in a command from the unconditioned, then the reciprocity of the love relationship within the human community may be theoretically compatible with the need for a grounding of the self in absolute otherness,[2] which is of course part of the Judeo-Christian marriage tradition. However, for Coleridge the love-relationship becomes problematic when the otherness of the beloved, rather than the otherness that guarantees the relationship for both parties, is taken into account, because the beloved (for him the unattainable Sara Hutchinson) functions both as one who would complete the self in its excursion into "oneself as another" and one who approaches the self as an absolute other. This situation points up the conflict, explicitly addressed by Ricoeur, between his concept of the ethical subject as self-othering and Levinas's grounding of the subject in absolute otherness.

Coleridge sets himself a difficult task by giving love a primary ethical status. With important exceptions such as Julia Kristeva's *Tales of Love* and Martha Nussbaum's *Love's Knowledge,* and to a certain extent Ricoeur's *Oneself as Another,* love has not usually been seen as a paradigm for human ethical relations in a secular ethical tradition that rejects sentiment as a foundational ethical source. After Kant's exclusion of the affective realm from rational ethics[3] and Freud's assertion of a conflict (if also an interdependence) between love and "the interests of civilization" (745) philosophy has found it difficult to use human love as a paradigm for ethical relations. The tradition begun by Hegel, as Cyrus Hamlin notes, substitutes "an awareness of difference" for "the model of love in Romantic aesthetics" as "the basis for mutual self-understanding" (47). Altieri points out the methodological difficulty for modern philosophy of basing ethical theory on the directness of relations such as love, which provide no terms for comparison. He distinguishes between our responsiveness "to people and situations that are the direct objects of our attention" and our responsiveness "towards those with whom we feel ourselves in the kind of dialogues producing senses of identity" (*Subjective Agency* 218). The first area of direct responsiveness has "no stopping point, no site where different modes of responsiveness can be compared" (218–19), and thus, he says, is of limited value for ethical discussion even though it is essential "for any discussion of love or care" (219).

Love, as a synthesis of *eros* and *agape,* plays a central role in the Augustinian tradition of Christian ethics,[4] which is of course an important source for Coleridge, whose ambivalence toward this synthesis is seen in his assertion that love is both "the only Perpetuator" and "the strongest antagonist" of "desire" ("Love and Desire," *SW & F* 284). When they coexist, desire can function as love's "outward Symbol & Declaration" (*SW & F* 291), and love can call forth and purify desire as sunlight calls forth and purifies "the dank Vapor of the Earth" (*CN* 4: 5463).[5] Coleridge's complex attitude toward "feeling," discussed in Chapter 5, manifests a divided relation to the eighteenth-century tradition, from Shaftesbury to Wordsworth, that would link ethical life to sentiment and sympathy. While feelings, in which Coleridge includes "all that goes by the names of *Sentiment,* Sensibility, &c, &c." can be "a part of the *instruments* of Action," they "never can without serious injury be perverted into the *principles* of Action" (*SW & F* 570).

Coleridge furthers the eighteenth-century tradition of the sympathetic imagination, the tradition that led to Keats's concept of negative capability and elevated Shakespeare as a "Proteus" who "darts himself forth, and passes into all the forms of human character and passion" (*BL* 2: 27). However, there is an important difference between the essentially aesthetic virtue of sympathy, which refers to "H[umanitas] aesthetica," as in the thought, "My friend is forced to live in a garret—it really made me *weep* to *think* of it" and the practical virtue of participation in suffering, which refers to "Humanitas *practica,*" as in the act of visiting that friend and improving his situation (*CN* 3: 3561).[6] Coleridge implicitly objects to placing sympathy at the ethically foundational level granted by the tradition of Shaftesbury and Adam Smith. According to Smith, the word "sympathy" "may now . . . be made use of to denote our fellow-feeling with any passion whatever" (10). For Coleridge, this emphasis on and connection between "fellow-feeling" and "passion" would not only grant feeling the status of principle, but it would also approach a materialism that would deny the all-important progress of life as "an ascension toward Mind" (*SW & F* 1427). His ambivalence toward the importance of empirical "sensation" on which philosophies of sentiment are based is evident in his comment on "conscience" as "neither reason, religion, or will, but an *experience* . . . of the coincidence of the human will with reason and religion. It might, perhaps, be called a *spiritual sensation;* but that there lurks a contradiction in the terms" (*LS* 66–67). He needs the experiential vocabulary of sensation but also needs to sever that vocabulary from its materialist basis.

For Coleridge, love's ethical value depends on its being separated from a psychology of the affections: if love were not "an act of will—and that too one of the *primary* & therefore unbewusst [unknown], & ineffable Acts," it would be no more than "a romantic Hum"; inconstancy would have no moral effect as an object of "Blame & Immorality" if it were "confined to the Affections" (*CN* 3: 3562). Love mediates between the vexed categories of the "interest" associated with the ethical and the "disinterestedness" of the sense of beauty, in Coleridge's adaptation of Kant: "Love = Beauty + Interest," the result of which is "to reveal the close analogy of Love and Beaut~~iful~~y, and thus at once to present the likeness and the distinction of the Lovely and the Beautiful" ("On Love," *SW & F* 422). To combine Coleridge's somewhat cryptic argument here with that in "The Principles of Genial Criticism," love combines the immediacy of an actually existent being demanded by "interest" with the intuition of wholeness, the Pythagorean "REDUCTION OF MANY TO ONE" (*SW & F* 377) associated with the disinterested contemplation of beauty.

Despite his rejection of sentiment, sympathy, desire, and feeling as ethically foundational, the importance he grants to the affections as an instrument of action shows that Coleridge is closer to a world that did not divide emotional from moral life to the extent that the modern world does, at least in the United States, where we tend to entrust our emotional life to nonjudgmental therapists, leaving ethics to moral systems in which feelings operate not as instruments or determinants of moral action, but only in the context of individual rights, as that which we have a right to express, if not always act upon.[7] However, both Williams and Ricoeur depart from this modern separation of the ethical and the affective by giving philosophical reasons for assigning ethical importance to the affective. Williams points out that "[d]esiring to do something is of course a reason for doing it," and desire is thus involved in the ethical question of what one "should" do (*Ethics* 19). Ricoeur points out that desire is not necessarily egoistic: "the good man's own being is desirable to him; given this, the being of his friend is then equally desirable to him" (*Oneself* 186). Levinas is ambivalent on the ethical status of love. He says that "the metaphysical event of transcendence—the welcome of the Other . . . is not accomplished as love." However, according to Levinas, love "brings into relief the ambiguity of an event situated at the limit of immanence and transcendence" (*TI* 254), and is thus not simply a reduction of the Other to the Same. In *Otherwise than Being,* he clearly distinguishes his ethics, including "an assignation to a non-erotic proximity" (123) from "the moral philosophies of feeling" (197n27) that Coleridge both distances himself from and implicates himself in.

By granting ethical authority to love, Coleridge complicates the Levinasian model, because in his complex notion of love otherness is not easily isolated from reciprocity: love combines a recognition of human finitude standing before an (ultimately divine) infinite other with the symbolic hope that love will enable a reciprocal completion of the incomplete individual. Here again we see Coleridge's uneasy combination of a self-generated and a self-denying notion of otherness: love will complete the self, but love will also expose the finitude of the self. Coleridge differs sharply from Kant in elevating love above desire, and from the later Fichte, in whom Coleridge finds "O woeful Love whose first act and offspring is *Self!*" (*CM* 2: 596). Human love is directly involved in the symbolic relation to God: "The best, the truly lovely, in each & all is God. Therefore the truly Beloved is the symbol of God to whomever it is truly beloved by" (*CN* 2: 2540). Love is a human necessity and a function of human finitude and imperfection, but just as the symbol provides a link between the finite and the infinite, love provides a completion of the incomplete self. In a long digression on love in his 1811 lecture on *Romeo and Juliet,* Coleridge argues that love compensates for the "inevitable" feeling that the human being is "of itself imperfect and insufficient, not as an animal merely but altogether as a moral being." Love provides a human necessity that is also "a step of that exaltation to a higher and nobler state" as "*a perfect desire of the whole being to be united to some thing or some being which is felt necessary to its perfection by the most perfect means that nature permits & reason dictates*" (*Lects 1808–1819* 1: 314).

Love is an "element" rather than a "compound" (*CM* 3: 265) and demonstrates a noumenal act of will at the foundationally ethical level of "conscience" though it is below "consciousness: "What Kant affirms of Man in the state of Adam, an ineffable act of the will choosing evil and which is underneath or within the *consciousness* tho' incarnate in the *conscience,* inasmuch as it must be conceived as taking place in the Homo Νουμενον [noumenal man] not the Homo Φαινομενον [phenomenal man]—something like this I conceive of *Love*—in that highest sense of the Word, which Petrarch understood" (3: 265).[8] In its highest form, love is, with wisdom, one of the two ways the foundational Will manifests itself: "In its state of immanence (or indwelling) in reason and religion, the WILL appears indifferently, as wisdom or as love: two names of the same power" (*LS* 65). The task of granting love a foundational status cannot be made easier by qualitative distinctions between kinds of love: according to an 1826 notebook entry, "Love is always the same in *essence;* tho' it will receive a different shade according to its object. . . . *Love is Love*—essentially the same, whether the Object be a helpless Infant, our Wife or Husband, or God himself" (*CN* 4: 5463).

Theologically, love is the principle of the Holy Spirit or community—the synthesis of subjective and objective in the pentad of operative Christianity. If love is the spirit of community and the synthesis of the subjective and the objective, its ethical priority is indistinguishable from its hermeneutic priority, which is partly why it is such a fundamental concept for Coleridge. Ellison points out in her reading of the late poem/dialogue "The Improvisatore" that love is distinguished by its "powers of self-expression . . . and receptive understanding. . . . Love, then, is communicated understanding" (114). As Modiano explains, love shares and supports the symbol's unifying function: "In a sense, the symbol represents the means by which the phenomenal world can be redeemed of its otherness and its forbidding physicality and brought into closer communication with the self" (67). Most concepts that underlie ethical theories, such as utility, conscience, duty, responsibility, or (especially) contractual relations, involve some communicative aspect, but for Coleridge love *is* reciprocal understanding, and that same hermeneutic reciprocity is ethically foundational; love is the one concept in which ethics and understanding join seamlessly.

However, to realize this reciprocity is not an easy task, because love involves a return to the self only via a particularly difficult version of Ricoeur's "detour by way of objectification" (*Oneself* 313). According to an 1807 notebook entry, Love is "a sense of Substance/Being seeking to be self-conscious, I. of itself in a Symbol. 2. of the Symbol as not being itself. 3. of the Symbol as being nothing but in relation to itself—& necessitating a return to the first state, Scienta absoluta" (*CN* 2: 3026). This dialectical path between subject and object is familiar, but it leads in an unfamiliar direction when love, rather than simply self-consciousness, is at issue. The price one pays for love's external verification of the self (stage I) involves the sense of the "Symbol's" absolute difference from oneself as well as its existence only in relation to oneself (stages 2 and 3), heightening both the subjective and the objective in a way that makes love a difficult foundation for ethics.

Love is the "Mysterium finale," because, like the synthesis of *natura naturans* and *natura naturata* it is a "Synthesis . . . of Action and Passion," or "Εγω + Ουχ εγω" ["I" + "Not-I"], by which, even though "Εγω

= Εγω" ["I = I"] and "Ουχ εγω = ουχ εγω" ["Not-I = Not-I"], it is also true that "Ουχ εγω = Εγω" ["not I = I"] and vice versa (*CM* 3: 266). That is, in Ricoeur's terms, the third-person *idem*-identity (not-I) is able to equal the first-person *ipse*-identity (I) despite their opposition.[9] Love is a mystery because it finds an equal reciprocity in the midst of an obvious dissymmetry. However, in a notebook entry of 1808 (*CN* 3: 3308) that was expanded in 1812, Coleridge performs an act of demystification, illustrating "Love's compound triangles" geometrically by depicting a nest of triangles that incorporates the lovers' common basis in "human nature," the lovers' common qualities that distinguish them from others, and the "*opposites in correspondency*" of gender (*SW & F* 285–87). This attempt to reduce love from a mystery to a geometric figure, although it accounts for the otherness of the beloved in one way, conspicuously omits one factor essential to Coleridge's experience of love: the beloved's unique otherness that is not reducible to the symmetrical opposition of gender.

Of course Coleridge's ideal of love was personally unattainable; a notebook entry from sometime during the dark years of 1808–10, while Coleridge was feeling rejected by both Wordsworth and Sara Hutchinson, laments the failure of love's geometry: "I loved, I trusted, in whom my Soul had full faith as its Counterpart, the a + c that was to blend with and complete the a + b—blend by the identity of the a a, complete by the ~~necessity~~ difference of b and c, and the necessity of c to b" (*CN* 3:3303).

The geometry fails even in the case of the idealized Sara Hutchinson, who, as Barth notes, could be Coleridge's "true ideal 'other'" because he had "no familial responsibilities toward her" (*Coleridge and the Power of Love* 36). Love should produce self-completion, but it often confronts us with a mystery. As in *Christabel*'s worst-case scenario, the prayer for the arrival of one's beloved can produce instead the monstrous Geraldine, who usurps and silences Christabel. Thus it is not surprising that in Coleridge's tormented thoughts about Sara Hutchinson, we find a confrontation between the Ricoeurean notion of otherness as supporting selfhood and Levinas's opposite emphasis, that there can be no authentic subjectivity without an other who cannot be comprehended by the self, but who instead calls one to responsibility by "coring out" the autonomous ego.

In diverging from Kant by giving love a primary ethical status, in connecting love to the symbol as that which can remove otherness by embracing it, and in thus using love rather than ethical responsibility in general as the test case for the self-other relation, Coleridge is forced toward an ideal but problematic reciprocity that is much too fragile to withstand the onslaught of radical otherness. The moral other is always there to accept our solicitude, and thus one can perhaps feel fairly confident in grounding subjectivity, as Ricoeur does, on ethical solicitude in general, but there is no guarantee that the beloved will always be there, which means the subject depends on the beloved much more, and in a different way, than on the more generally defined ethical other.

Coleridge tries hard to bring his notion of love close to a general notion of moral solicitude. For example, the difference between love and hunger is that while "the hungry savage is a mere animal thinking of nothing but the satisfaction of the appetite," love is "an associative quality," generalizable, somewhat like moral solicitude, in its transformative effect on all objects, at least initially: "What was the first effect of love, but to associate the feeling with every object in nature" (*Lects 1808–1819* 1: 316). Along the same lines, the incest prohibition—"dividing the sisterly & fraternal from the conjugal affections"—allows "the affections in general" to urge us "to leave the parental nest" and "invite us to enter into the world" (1: 332); conjugal love has an important socializing function that goes beyond the two lovers. He would not say, with Pope, "[t]hat true SELF-LOVE and SOCIAL are the same" (*An Essay on Man* 4.396), but love is the fundamental mediating force that makes other-oriented "duty" compatible with subjective "inclination": the "height of Love" is to effect "that Incarnation & Transfiguration of Duty as Inclination" (*CN* 2: 3026), ideally mediating between the demands of self and other so important for both his ethics and his dialectic of self-consciousness.

However, the fact that love's ideality is involved in the attachment to one ideal person pulls it away from general moral solicitude. Love is more valuable than friendship, which, like moral solicitude in general, is directed toward everyone: "Love which includes Friendship" is of more value than friendship alone because "we cannot love many persons, all *equally* dearly. There will be *differences,* there will be *gradations.* . . . It is with the affections in Love, as with Reason in Religion—we cannot *diffuse* and equalize—we must have a SUPREME—a *One the highest.*" However, that same ideality also demands a reciprocity that is not always forthcoming: "in order that a person should *continue* to love another, better than all others, it seems necessary that this feeling should be reciprocal. For if it be not so, Sympathy is broken off at the highest <point>" (*CM* 1: 752).

We have seen in several Coleridgean contexts both the hermeneutic and the ethical importance of the concrete application of the universal—neither the universal nor the particular, the ideal nor the real, is to be slighted—but in love, as illustrated in Coleridge's discussion of *Romeo and Juliet,* the human need to concretize the ideal, coupled with the self-consciousness of human imperfection, can be a cause of error. For "men of genius" (implicitly including, according to the context, Shakespeare, Romeo, and Coleridge), the problem is that "they have formed an ideal in their minds & they want to see it realized," while "their own consciousness of imperfection makes it impossible for them to attach it to themselves." The result is that the ideal is erroneously concretized in the love of undeserving others: "they fall down and adore almost one greatly inferior to themselves" (*Lects 1808–1819* 1:335).

There are other ways in which, although love's link to the symbol connects it to the hermeneutic process of understanding, such understanding is not always reliable. For example, if the beloved does not want to be loved, what the lover might view as "moral solicitude" can become what we now call the selfishness of harassment. This is in fact the situation that Coleridge found himself in the winter of 1806–7: while he continued to insist on the moral efficacy of his love for Sara—that she was the source of his best self—the Wordsworths worried about the one-sided possessiveness of his feelings for her (Moorman, *Wordsworth: The Later Years* 92–93). And as Harding points out, although Coleridge opted to view love as "a real reaching out, a self-transcending act which can be free of all taint of egotism," he remained plagued by the fear that love may be egotistical, "the refuge of the selfish and self-fearing man" (*Coleridge and the Idea of Love* 38).

Coleridge's desire to make the difficult link between love and moral solicitude is clearly illustrated in his "Letter" to Sara Hutchinson, revised into the "Dejection" ode, where the poet attempts to turn the "dark, distressful Dream" (185) of his agony over Sara into a narrative of moral solicitude: "Be happy, and I need thee not in sight" (144). Moral knowledge offers a conceptual permanence missing in the actual encounter with the beloved:

> To all things I prefer the Permanent;
> And better seems it for a Heart like mine,
> Always to *know* than sometimes to *behold*
> Their happiness and thine.
>
> ("A Letter to—" 150–53)

As Martha Nussbaum, who shares Coleridge's desire to grant an ethical force to love, points out, there is an inevitable hermeneutic conflict between the blind "exclusivity and intensity of personal love" and the "equilibrium of perception" demanded by a "fine-tuned vision of the complete life" (*Love's Knowledge* 189), a conflict that points up the limits both of love and of ethical perception. Coleridge here seems to opt for the equilibrium of "to *know*" rather than the partial blindness of "to *behold*" that happens only "sometimes," but in fact the poem traces a version of the conflict that Nussbaum describes. Like Ricoeur, Coleridge sees moral solicitude as part of a theory of subjectively-generated exchange—"we receive but what we give" ("A Letter to—" 295)—but it becomes for Coleridge the shrill paean to a "joy" (312–39) that Sara, not he, will experience. Thus the narrative of a subjective joy that will give us a new and improved aesthetic and moral life, "A new earth and a new Heaven, / Undreamt of by the Sensual and the Proud!" (316–17), contains a painful irony. This new world will come about through the agency of "the Spirit and the Power / That wedding Nature to us gives in dower / A new Earth and new Heaven" (314–16), but that wedding remains strictly metaphorical, since it is predicated on Sara's absence and contrasts sharply with Coleridge's own unhappily married state. Yoking the permanence of moral solicitude to the changeability and necessary absence involved (at least for Coleridge) in love leaves the subject in the one place he does not want to be as a lover *or* a moral agent: alone.

II. Love and Otherness

The 1805 "Blossoming of the Solitary Date Tree," one of several poems from Coleridge's Malta period emphasizing the horrors of solitude, suggests, in terms of a mother's love for her child, a Ricoeurean structure of seeing oneself reflected and supported by solicitude for another that, temporarily, finds no discrepancy between love and moral solicitude: as the child prepares to repeat the mother's sounds, "She hears her own voice with a new delight" (70).[10] But the final stanza makes it clear that this only works as long as the other is there, which suggests that the self is dependent on the other, rather than just its own solicitude toward the other. If the child should die, "What then avail those songs, which sweet of yore, / Were only sweet for their sweet echo's sake" (74–75).[11] Similarly, and more autobiographically, love's ideal of reciprocity becomes the pathetic plea for reciprocal love at the end of "The Pains of Sleep," suggesting that that fallibility of reciprocal love leads to a sense of the other that is precisely not a reciprocal completion of the self.

At the divine end of the spectrum, and in Coleridge's more hopeful moments, love is a manifestation of God's self-othering, but at the human, experiential end it becomes a desired reciprocity vulnerable to the experience of an otherness that is prior to, rather than an emanation from, subjectivity. This is not necessarily inconsistent; if God's self-othering is the result of an original apostacy, it fits that another, less benevolent but perhaps more human kind of otherness would result from the necessary apostacy of a human fallen from an ideal of reciprocal love. This is a hermeneutic as well as an ethical problem. The symbol must ideally efface itself before that which it symbolizes, which paradoxically points up the difference between symbol and symbolized: "Hard to express that sense of the analogy or likeness of a Thing which enables a Symbol to represent it, so that we think of the Thing itself—& yet knowing that the Thing is not present to us" (*CN* 2: 2274).[12] In the symbolism of love, "the Lover worships in his Beloved that final consummation <of itself which is> produced in his own soul by the action of the Soul of the Beloved upon it, and that final perfection of the Soul of the Beloved, <which is in part> the consequence of the reaction of his (so ammeliorated & regenerated) Soul upon the Soul of his Beloved" (2:2540). This reciprocity combines "self-oblivion" with the preservation of "outness": "each contemplates the Soul of the other as involving his own, both in its givings and its receivings, ~~in a mood that~~ and thus still keeping alive its *outness,* its *self-oblivion* united with *Self-warmth,* & still approximates to God!" (2: 2540). Here Coleridge engages the need for language to work according to an "incarnational" rhetoric. In line with God's self-expression in the logos, and in his incarnation as a human, words are incarnated as living things in the world. Coleridge wrote to Godwin that he "would endeavor to destroy the old antithesis of *Words* and *Things,* elevating, as it were, words into Things, and living Things too" (*CL* 1: 625–26). Like all living things, however, words are ultimately effaced and reabsorbed into a larger process. For Wordsworth, this combination of incarnation and effacement is worked out in relation to the experience of death,[13] and in a Kantian theory of the sublime, as expressed in the "Imagination" passage in the *Prelude,* Book 6, that sees the overwhelming of the self as a route to self-sufficiency. For Coleridge, in whose notion of the sublime "the self grows out of any determinate form and is swallowed up by an indefinite 'allness'" (Modiano 122), the absorption of the finite in the infinite remains as a divine mystery, an example of what Coleridge, speaking of the difficulty of prayer, calls "the transcendency of religious Intuitions over Language, which only by balancing of contradictions can represent or rather suggest them" (*CN* 3: 4183).

That this unity of self-oblivion and outness, which can be admired as a divine paradox in the abstract, is painful in experience, is shown in this passage about Sara in which the process of thoughts becoming symbols results not in a happy consummation, but in an emptying out of the self into a shadowy, insubstantial symbolism: "Every single thought, every image, every perception, was no sooner itself, than it became *you* by some wish that you saw it & felt it or had—or by some recollection that it suggested—some way or other it always became a symbol of *you*—I played with them, as with *your shadow*—as Shakespere has so profoundly expressed it in his Sonnet" (*CN* 3: 3303). The self, defined as self-consciousness, is effaced as thought, image and perception disappear into symbols of Sara, which, according to the logic of the symbol's effacement, means that those symbols disappear into the inaccessible "thing itself" of the beloved. The emptied self is thereby left playing with shadows.

Love, as a primary ethical force for Coleridge, can ideally engage in a process of self-othering like that which Ricoeur describes, but its potential for both egoism and separation from the other can isolate the self, and love's participation in a process of symbolic self-effacement can be a painful loss of self as well as a para-divine consummation.[14] As the self is thus both posited and effaced in love, Coleridge engages the Levinasian tension between the ethical relation to another and the separated ego, a tension according to which the ethical can be reached only by an annihilation of that separated ego. "The Pains of Sleep," a version of which Coleridge sent to Southey the autumn before his departure for Malta, describing it as "a true portrait of my nights" (*CL* 2: 984), dramatizes this tension. The poet's nocturnal anguish is framed by two versions of "love." The first is a complete submission to the unknowable "Eternal Strength and Wisdom" that are "in me, round me, every where" (11–12). This formulation rests squarely within Coleridge's theologized Kantian epistemology: "Eternal Strength and Wisdom" form the ground of the self, but exist in the inaccessible realm of Pure Reason. He emphasizes the inaccessibility of this realm to language, ritual, desire, and expressed thought. He does not pray with the "moving lips" of speech or the "bended knees" of ritual prayer (3); instead he composes his spirit to "Love" with "no wish conceived, no thought expressed" (8), suppressing both desire and thought, and allowing the symbolic to be effaced before its object. The negatives within which this "sense of supplication" must be couched (as well as the obvious fact that the account of this state requires language) already suggests the difficulty of the escape from language even as it posits what, for Levinas, is a "passivity" that is on the way to the ethical because it releases the egoistic grip that would encase the logos in a narrative: "a pure surrender to the logos, without regard for the propositions that will make of the thing a narrative to which the logos belongs" (*OB* 110). For the earlier Coleridge this is the fifth and final stage of prayer, which Coleridge describes in a note as "self-annihilation—the Soul enters the Holy of Holies" (*CN* 1: 257).[15] Levinas's notion of a nonegoistic "obsession" by the other is suggested by a later (1808) Coleridgean characterization of the properly praying self as being "possessed by another—without the wish to rob that other of it or any part of it" (3: 3355).

The Levinasian problem, already hinted at in the first verse-paragraph of "The Pains of Sleep," is that, because we are trapped in speaking egos, the authentic ethical position demands that the ego be "accused." Passivity before the absolutely other—a passivity that would ground human freedom—can only occur if the ego is stripped of the thoughts we express with moving lips, the wishes we conceive, and the bended knees of ritual—all the things that define us as self-conscious beings, and that cannot for long be simply suspended in wordless prayer. According to Levinas, this accusation entails an expulsion of the ego that, by denying the self a "conditioned" foundation, links it to the "unconditioned" and therefore the ethical: "it strips the ego of its pride and the dominating imperialism characteristic of it. The subject is in the accusative, without recourse in being, expelled from being, outside of being . . . without a foundation, reduced to itself, and thus without condition" (*OB* 110).

The second verse paragraph presents exactly this: the "unconditioned" of Coleridge's Kantian God—"Eternal Strength and Wisdom"—becomes the unconditioned that accuses the ego, stripping it of its foundations in self-consciousness and conceptual systems. This state is tied to speech: the poet experienced "anguish and agony" when he "prayed aloud" (14–15). But the anguish is not *caused* by the intentionality of speech; it is precisely that intentionality that is being put in question: he prayed aloud as he was "Up-starting from the fiendish crowd / Of shapes and thoughts that tortured me" (16–17). The accusation, the "torture," precedes willed speech in what Levinas calls an "anarchic" temporality; it is "like the echo of a sound that would precede the resonance of this sound" (*OB* 111). Outside the logic of cause and effect, the speaking ego's determinations are totally dissolved in what Levinas calls "a deafening trauma, cutting the thread of consciousness which should have welcomed it in its present, the passivity of being persecuted" (111). This agonized use of language, whose absence in the first verse-paragraph brought peace, reveals the confrontation between the ego's need for what Levinas calls the "said" of a totalized language-system manipulated by separated egos and the "saying" of the ego-dissolving "proximity of one to the other" that is "antecedent to the verbal signs it conjugates" (5).

In experiencing "a trampling throng," the poet finds "whom I scorned, those only strong!" (20). "Strength" here is not part of "Eternal Strength and Wisdom," but instead resides in those who are "scorned": precisely those to whom the ego would not want to grant strength, which shows how the ego's determinations are "baffled." The now "powerless will" is "still baffled, and yet burning still": as the ego is dissolved, it "burns" (21–22), a precisely ambivalent metaphor suggesting a fire that consumes the ego but that at the same time heightens the desire that is brought into this painful conflict with the unconditioned. The resulting "shame and terror" (26) is not simply a shame experienced *by* the ego but is a shame that goes to the heart of the ego's existence; hence the confusion regarding "deeds" which he "could not know / Whether [he] suffered or [he] did" (29).

Guilt is unmotivated and agency is confused because in this aspect of Coleridge we have left the realm of thematized "egos" operating more or less according to organized principles. Instead, this guilt resembles Levinas's general "shame that freedom feels for itself" (*TI* 86) as the self recognizes the problematic nature of its status as a putatively "free" subject. Agency is confused because we are not simply talking about guilty agents, but about a generalized guilt—"all seemed guilt, remorse, or woe, / My own or others still the same" (30–31)—that puts agency itself into question, blurring the boundary between self and other that Coleridge sees as essential for dialectical self-definition. Coleridge's notion of evil as unactualized will suggests the Levinasian point that the evil for which we really should be guilty is not some particular act which, bad as it may be, would still be, in Coleridge's terms, an actualization of the will in Being. We are more foundationally guilty of the pure freedom of the ego as it separates itself into an autonomous agent and thus denies or attempts to assimilate the proximity of the other. This is what Levinas calls the "egoism" that is "arbitrary and unjustified, and in this sense detestable" (*TI* 88). The guilty "I" cannot simply attach guilt *to* the separated ego, for that would be to maintain the ego in the very separateness for which it needs to be guilty; to confuse the agency of guilt, as in the lines quoted above, is to approach a recognition of the ego's very separateness as the proper locus of guilt. Coleridge would thus agree in an important sense with Levinas that the self-interest of the separated ego may lead to conflict; he recognizes the danger in the fact that "each man will universalize his notions, & yet each is variously finite" (*CN* 2: 2208). Similarly for Levinas, "Being's interest takes dramatic forms in egoisms struggling with one another" (*OB* 4).

The first two sections of the poem present equally problematic alternatives: the unsustainable state of a complete—and therefore wordless and thoughtless—self-effacement before the absolutely other, or the agony of the speaking ego being stripped of its freedom. In the third verse-paragraph, some resolution is achieved when the poet says that, having been awakened by "my own loud scream . . . I wept as I had been a child" (37, 40). The child is often for Coleridge the passive self prior to self-consciousness, as in the "Dear Babe" (44) of "Frost at Midnight" or the Wordsworthian lost child "Upon a lonesome wild" ([1802] 116) in the "Dejection" ode. However, this passivity is very different from the passive prayer of the opening verse-paragraph. He has awakened, like the Wedding Guest, "A sadder and a wiser man" (*Rime* 670), because he must now live within the contradiction of the guilt he has experienced. In a world of self-conscious egos, guilt only makes sense within a logic of sin and punishment that can be attached to those egos: "Such punishments, I said, were due / To natures deepliest stained with sin" (43–44). Within the Levinasian "said" of the ego using a coherent system of language—that is, as long as we can say, as the poet does, "I said"—the guilt that dissolves the ego can only be viewed as a contradiction.

The poem's conclusion, in pursuing that contradiction, presents a striking example of the confrontation between Ricoeurean and Levinasian notions of the self-other relation and the consequences of placing those notions in the context of love. Separating himself from the "natures deepliest stained with sin," he says,

> Such griefs with such men well agree,
> But wherefore, wherefore fall on me?
> To be beloved is all I need,
> And whom I love, I love indeed.
> (49–52)

The reciprocity of love, framed in the self's solicitude for and acceptance of the beloved other, should protect him from the anguish of guilt. If ethical life can be understood in Ricoeurean terms as a self-othering grounded in the self, then it does not makes sense that the attesting *ipse*-identity should suffer the guilt of sinful natures. If, however, as in Levinas's paradigm, the guilt one feels is the guilt of the separated ego itself, then no amount of attestation will remove that guilt. In fact, self-originating attestation—perhaps even attesting to one's capacity for mutual love—is precisely what the ego is necessarily guilty for. The final plea for reciprocal love as a "need" of the self invokes Coleridge's ethical ideal of love, but also hints at love's fragility and potential selfishness.

One of Coleridge's most intense experiences of a Levinasian dissolution of the ego, as well as his problematic faith in love as a source of authentic ethical life, is documented in the notebooks he kept on his journey to Malta in 1804, a journey commenced shortly after he sent "The Pains of Sleep" to Southey. Before and during his voyage, Coleridge thematizes himself as his own Ancient Mariner, journeying beyond the limits of the known into an ethically ambivalent geography. Just as the Mariner crosses from the known world into the "silent Sea" (*Rime* 102) which he and his crew are the first to enter, Coleridge finds himself in a new and empty world, "alone on the wide wide Sea" (235). Both seek comfort in inadequate analogies between the unknown present vista and the known scenes of the past: the Mariner seeks respite in the noise of sails "like of a hidden brook / In the leafy month of June" (367–68), and Coleridge, "a Traveller, with his Heart at Home" (*CN* 2: 2064), sought temporary consolation in scenes reminiscent of home and a quotation from Wordsworth's praise of the binding power of natural piety: "While I was thus musing, I turned to the Larboard side of the Vessel, & my Heart did indeed leap up/—Was it the Placefell Bank of Ulswater?" As reality returns in the form of a squall, he ironically notes the inadequacy of this analogy: "What a sweet Image to precede a Ship-wreck!" (2: 2013).[16]

In the notes made on this journey, Coleridge documents his experience of what Levinas presents as the paradox in which authentic subjectivity—the first-person "I" beyond the masks of "ego"—is glimpsed through a process by which the ego's existence as a separated, thematized self-consciousness is destroyed, so that the self can emerge as "for another" (*OB* 52). Levinas describes the "ultimate secret of the incarnation of the [authentically ethical] subject as "a recurrence in which the expulsion of self outside of itself is its substitution for the other" (110–11). As Coleridge separates himself from England, he experiences the negative side of the process Levinas describes, the dissolution of the self-conscious ego. In a dream associated with death at sea, the freedom of the self is followed immediately by crushing despair and passivity. He describes "these frightful Dreams of Despair when the sense of individual Existence is full and lively only <for one> to feel oneself powerless, crushed *in* by every power—a stifled boding, one abject miserable Wretch/yet hope less, yet struggling, removed from all touch of Life, deprived of all notion of Death/ strange mixture of Fear and Despair—& that passio purissima, that mere

Passiveness with Pain (the essence of which is perhaps Passivity—& which our word—mere Suffering—well comprizes)" (*CN* 2: 2078). Passivity is here not simply the principle of ***natura naturata,*** as it will be presented later in the ***Philosophical Lectures;*** it is the experience of suffering. This state resembles the Levinasian dissolution of the ego, the movement from self-conscious activity to a passivity that threatens consciousness. This passivity of suffering, unrepresentable within the structures of either life or death, presents another version of what was suggested in "The Pains of Sleep." It is what Levinas calls "the passivity of a trauma, but one that prevents its own representation" (*OB* 111). Coleridge, of course, sees no room for hope in this experience, whereas Levinas sees it as the condition for welcoming otherness, but it nevertheless forces Coleridge into the uncharted ethical territory that Levinas explores.

This process of "the expulsion of self" is literalized as a nausea that "prevents its own representation": for Coleridge, the solidity of visual representation, one of the ego's main protections, is destroyed. According to Levinas, "vision is essentially an adequation of exteriority with interiority" (*TI* 295); as such it is an epistemological, representational system to be broken up in the "expulsion of the self." The expulsion of Coleridge's dinner on April 25, 1804, occasions just such an experience of the breakup of visual representation, as the ship's bilge-water, which is at least metaphorically, and probably literally mingled with the vomit that "burst[s] forth" from Coleridge, changes the colors in his visual field: "I was ill after dinner which I did not retain/the Mephitis of the Bilge burst forth, like a Fury/horrid stench that turned the gold red, & silver black, bemudded whatever part of the paint had been before soiled, & covered the rest of it with <quick->silvery grease drops. Hepatic Gas?" (*CN* 2: 2051).[17] The physical boundaries of the self dissolve as internal and external fluids are mingled, and even the sensory categories are confused: syntactically it is the "stench" that changes the colors. That this phenomenon is of more than passing importance is suggested when, on May 3, he makes a note to ask Humphrey Davy about the "Bilge Water . . . its hideous Stench . . . its Red'ning of Gold, black'ning of Silver not without a tinge of red-brown, and its turning the red paint of the letters on the Sacks into lead or dove-color" (2: 2070). He hopes that the scientist Davy will be able to put this chaotic experience of self-expulsion, associated with the ship's own obnoxious bilge-water, back into the safe thematization of an epistemological system.

This entry is followed shortly by a grotesque description which, though based on a fellow-passenger,[18] is at least partly interpretable as a self-description. The destructive effects of over-indulgence turn the face into an undifferentiated mass and transform the eyes from subjective organs of vision into objects of fear: "By purpler Pimples ~~gem~~ gemm 'd the Face one purple Blotch . . . where two black shining Eyes for ever shine and shine/—And shine and shine, and as they shine for ever will shine on, Till what with Brandy, what with Rum, the Liver's fairly gone! Eyes that like watch *lights* shine, as if they were there not for themselves to see with, but as a *sight* For others to avoid" (*CN* 2: 2072). In a negative version of the demon-poet at the end of "Kubla Khan," the ego disintegrates—through alcohol, not inspiration—into an inhuman object to be avoided. The dissolving ego becomes "a *sight* For others to avoid"; the ego feels its shame as it recognizes itself as an undesirable object. This dissolution of the ego bears little resemblance to the dialectical dissolution of the subject-object split in the service of self-consciousness described later in the *Biographia:* "The spirit (originally the identity of subject and object) must in some sense dissolve this identity, in order to be conscious of it" (1: 279). The breakup of the highly privileged category of self-consciousness itself, suggested by the strange objectification and undifferentiation that he observes in his shipmate's face, as well as by his own experience of nausea, is not simply the negative stage of a dialectic; rather, it is the breakup of that which is fundamentally implicated in both understanding and ethical interaction, which brings Coleridge's thought face to face with the Levinasian sense of the self as accused and dissolved.

For Levinas, the purportedly "free" ego must recognize the other as a persecuting force, so that it will be ashamed of its freedom, as Coleridge experienced in "The Pains of Sleep." That Coleridge felt persecuted needs no documentation. However, I would like to suggest that behind his well-known paranoia lies at least the potential for the ethical experience of persecution as the putting into question of the ego, which allows subjectivity to reestablish itself as responsibility for the very other who is the source of persecution, instead of as egoism. Levinas describes the "trauma of persecution" as follows: "In the trauma of persecution it is to pass from the outrage undergone to the responsibility for the persecutor, and, in this sense from suffering to expiation for the other. Persecution is not something added to the subjectivity of the subject and his vulnerability; it is the very movement of recurrence. The subjectivity as *the other in the same,* as an inspiration, is the putting into question of all affirmation for-oneself, all egoism born again in this very recurrence" (*OB* 111). Seen in this way, the very other who persecutes and destroys my ego is also welcomed in a gesture of responsibility: "the face of the neighbor in its persecuting hatred can by this very malice obsess as something pitiful" (111).

On the way to Malta, Coleridge drafts a letter to James Webb Tobin in which Tobin is a source of both persecution and "integrity." Complaining about Tobin's tendency to substitute accusations for sympathy, he writes, "I confess to you, that being exceedingly low & heart-fallen, I should have almost sunk under the Operation of Reproof and Admonition . . . at the moment I was quitting, perhaps for ever! my dear Country, and all that makes it so dear" (*CN* 2: 2032). His feeling of persecution is intimately tied to his sense of himself as a separated ego adrift at sea. Continuing the marine analogy in which his sense of separation and guilt had been couched, Coleridge sees Tobin's "Integrity" as a wind that "blows upon [him] refreshingly, as the Sea Breeze ~~and~~ on the tropic Islander." "Integrity" is a strong word for Coleridge, which he defines in *The Friend* etymologically as "the *integral* character" of one's "moral Being." For one who intends to communicate truth, integrity involves both a general and a specific relation to the other: "the reverence which he owes to the presence of Humanity in the person of his neighbor; the reverential upholding of the faith of man in man" and "gratitude for the particular act of confidence" (*Friend* 1: 45). There is no denying that Coleridge's letter to Tobin is a typically ambivalent combination of complaint and suspiciously overstated praise. However, that very ambivalence (which will reach its peak in Coleridge's already strained relation to Wordsworth) suggests what appears to be an almost necessary connection between a friend's persecution of the Coleridgean ego—uncomfortably adrift at this point—and the possibility of authentic ethical existence in proximity to the friend. To put it in terms of this letter, the "wind" from the other can both sink the ego and be an authenticating breeze of integrity.

In Coleridge's thoughts about Sara Hutchinson, we find a connection between the dissolution of the ego and the approach of the other in which the guilt and shame that the ego feels for its freedom enables a potentially nonegoistic ethical existence. In this context the difficulties turn on the problem of the other's "presence." As he is tortured psychologically and physically, Coleridge speculates on both the desire for and the impossibility of Sara Hutchinson's presence as both an other to be known and a ground for his moral life. On April 30, he moves directly from another experience of nausea associated with bilge-water—he "retained not a morsel of [his] Saturday Dinner" and "the Bilge-fury broke loose again"—to speculation on whether it is from an excess of sympathy or "a cause common to all men" that "we abstract the pleasant or the painful Sensations of others & so contemplate & sympathize with them as pure pain, or pure pleasure" (*CN* 2: 2057). The painful "expulsion of self" is thus directly related to the problem of experiencing others. However, our tendency to "abstract" the experience of the other into a particular form or represented sensation, as in the ethical systems grounded on sympathy to which Coleridge objects, prevents an authentic experience of the other *as* other, as what Levinas calls the "infinity" of the nontotalized face that is "present" only "in its refusal to be contained," remaining "infinitely transcendent, infinitely foreign" (*TI* 194). According to Levinas, as the "I" reduces itself to the category of "ego," it also reduces the other to an element in a system: "every relation between the same and the other . . . reduces itself to an impersonal relation within a universal order" (87–88).

To make something or someone representationally "present" is the act of an ego that has separated itself in a thematization and that thereby thematizes the other in what Coleridge calls an "abstraction," which prevents one from experiencing "the whole contexture" of the other, as he puts it in a note from 1808–9: "If you *feel* the whole contexture when with the person, try to imagine it when thinking of any one action, & remember that this *oneness,* this separation, exists only in your mind by virtue of Abstraction; but in the man himself is only a bason full of the Billow rolling on/& even this character of individuality—a bason full—is derived from the Bason that scoops it out" (*CN* 3: 3419). Even the metaphors within which we characterize the other's nontotalized existence as a "Billow rolling on" are efforts by the ego to "scoop out" and, to use Levinas's term, "contain" his otherness in a "separation" that "exists only in your mind by virtue of an Abstraction." Levinas argues that this distance of abstraction, when the other is contained in an image, denies the unmediated ethical proximity of the other: "the neighbor reveals himself and delivers himself in his image, but it is precisely in his image that he is no longer near" (*OB* 89). In Coleridge's terms, the ego that demands this kind of presence is equivalent to the finite will that illegitimately "universalize[s] its notions," and thus misses the "whole contexture" of the other. In one of Coleridge's definitions of conscience, the conscience-dependent self is defined by the boundary that separates and relates it to others: "Self is Definition; but all Boundary implies Neighbourhood—& is knowable only by Neighbourhood, or Relations" (*CN* 2: 3231). In the abstraction of making someone representationally present, the very boundary around the self that enables self-definition in relation to the other (as in Ricoeur's model) turns the self into a separated ego which treats the other as an abstraction, demanding his or her presence as an "image," and (in Levinas's terms) preventing the welcoming of the other as truly other.

Coleridge continues his Malta note on abstracting sensations, "I have felt as if it were impossible that I could sustain the *presence* of Sara, or

Mary & Dorothy, on board a vessel for Malta—<suffering only what I suffer—>" (*CN* 2: 2057). Though the later interpolation (marked by the *Notebooks* editors with angled brackets) of "suffering only what I suffer" suggests a simple altruism (he wouldn't want them to endure what he is experiencing), as well as Ricoeur's notion, explicitly opposed to Levinas, of "sympathy for the suffering other, where the initiative comes from the loving self" (*Oneself* 192), the original note corresponds to his earlier and later speculations on the difficult nature of Sara's "presence" to him. He perhaps recognizes that her "presence" as an image or form thematized within the context of the Wordsworth network—what Coleridge would have to face if Sara came on board the ship in the company of Wordsworth's wife and sister—would in fact be distance, or at least a grim reminder of the impossibility of a more intimate connection. Thus her presence is an object of both desire and fear, both of which are presented a few months later in a plan for a poem: "Why are you not here? + O no! O no! I dare not wish you were here.—A poem in 2 parts" (*CN* 2: 2118).

But Coleridge struggles to transcend the limits of the ego toward a more authentic experience of Sara as other. She is seen, not as an object to be "known" by her form, but as a "conscience" that transcends her "form." The epistemological limit of knowledge as knowledge of forms (a limit set by Kant even in the realm of pure Reason) is transgressed in the direction of an ethical contact, but that contact is still desired as an impossible "presence": Sara as loved by Coleridge is, in a note made after his return from Malta, "herself & the Conscience of that self, beyond the bounds of that form which her eyes behold when she looks ~~down~~ up on herself/O there is a form which seems irrelative to imprisonment of Space!" (*CN* 2: 3146). This transgression of the bounds of spatial form results in the idealization of Sara, and it also could be seen as a serious version of the game of mountain echoes that Coleridge played in 1802,[19] shouting out his friends' names in a sheepfold, of which Keith Thomas says, "Coleridge evidently recognizes that the game is forgery of presence by means of counterfeit signs" ("Coleridge, Wordsworth, and New Historicism" 96). However, Sara's presence as "conscience" also grants her a Levinasian proximity that is not reducible to, and is in fact an interruption of, the epistemological/psychological notion of presence that informs Keith's argument. Even in Coleridge's theology, conscience is "an *experience,*" rather than a conceptualization, "of the coincidence of the human will with reason and religion" (*LS* 66). In the much more personal context of his experience of Sara, her existence as "Conscience"—the ethical ground of self-consciousness—beyond the bounds even of her own formal self-consciousness, suggests her authentic, though unrepresentable, otherness: the hermeneutic and ethical presence in Gadamer and Levinas that is a function of human proximity rather than representation.

"Conscience" is for Levinas as well as Coleridge "a conceptless experience" (*TI* 101). The other's ethical "presence" is incommensurate with the "presence" at which conceptual representation aims. En route to Malta, Coleridge makes a related distinction, which he then generalizes, between the "feeling" of Sara and her form or image; after a dream in which Sara was not present but which "seems to have been *Her-She*" even though it had "no form no ~~image~~ place, no incident, any way connected with her," he concludes, "Does this not establish the existence of *a Feeling* of a Person quite distinct at all times, & at certain times *perfectly separable* from, the Image of that Person?" (*CN* 2: 2061). Here Coleridge struggles with the irreconcilability of two forms of presence: on the one hand a desire for the conceptual, visual, representational presence that Levinas critiques as imperialistically egocentric, and on the other hand Levinas's notion of the ethical experience of the Other's "proximity," the very different kind of hermeneutic and ethical "presence" by which the immediate presence of the other person, (even though here it is only an imagined presence) exceeds and destroys subjectively controlled categories of representational presence.

III. The Absolute Self

The very impossibility of Sara's presence being "sustained" suggests to Coleridge that there is an "intimate Synthesis" between "*Ego*" and "the principle of Co-adunation" (*CN* 2: 2057); for better and for worse, the self is constituted by the approach of the other, however impossible or fear- and guilt-laden that approach may be. (That he treats this observation as an insight for Wordsworth's poetic use may suggest the difficulty Coleridge feels in applying it to himself.) In the depths of his anguish over Sara in 1807, Coleridge suggests that her existence as an other *and* as a version of the self is the ground of his own moral subjectivity. His other "must be one who is & who is not myself—not myself, & yet so much more my Sense of Being <(The very Breath owes its power moral feeling)> than myself that myself is therefore only not a feeling for reckless Despair, because she is its object/Self in me derives its sense of Being from having this one absolute Object" (2: 3148). This note not only suggests a subjectivity defined in relation to an other, as Ricoeur would have it, and as

Coleridge's ideal love-dialectic posits, but it also suggests the Levinasian subjectivity whose authenticity depends on accepting responsibility for the other, beyond any coherent image or form of self-consciousness. Sara is not manifested as an objectification to be dialectically synthesized with the "I" in Schellingean terms like those in chapter 12 of the *Biographia;* instead, she throws the "ego," or here the accusative "myself" into paradox, breaking up the unity of "myself" by being both "not myself" and more essential than "myself."

This view of the self complicates Ricoeur's "aporia of anchoring." It is not just that the speaking subject is both "the limit of the world" in its first-person "singular perspective" and also, as evidenced by that subject's externally verifiable proper name and by the notion of his speech as an "event," a part of the world. For Coleridge, the I "both [is] and [is] not the limit of the world" (*Oneself* 51) in a different sense. The very subjectivity of Coleridge's definition of all life (that is, the equation of the world's creation with God's subjectivity as "the eternal act of creation in the infinite I AM" [*BL* 1:304]) means that the first-person speaking subject is the limit of the world only insofar as he cannot see beyond his own consciousness. This is the sense in which self-consciousness involves "the two Activities, the one positive, the other negative, the one *fills,* the other bounds, a Sphere." But that very limitation suggests a subjectivity beyond that limit, a subjectivity by definition inaccessible to consciousness—Coleridge's version of Kant's Unconditioned—according to which "in [the self] subsists the primary Union of Finity and Infinity" (*CN* 3:4186).

This sense of an inaccessible subjectivity is suggested by the lines, "What is Life?" dated near the end of his stay in Malta (August 16, 1805) though later dismissed as juvenilia:

> RESEMBLES life what once was deem'd of light,
> Too ample in itself for human sight?
> An absolute self—an element ungrounded—
> All that we see, all colours of all shade
> By encroach of darkness made?—
> Is very life by consciousness unbounded?
> And all the thoughts, pains, joys of mortal breath,
> A war-embrace of wrestling life and death?

In this modernization of Milton's metaphorics of divine light,[20] the notion of an "absolute self—an element ungrounded" looks forward to Coleridge's later theological emphasis on an absolute unity that precedes the polarity in God's relation to man.[21] Here, however, the notion that subjective life transcends consciousness, that the problem with life is "her largeness, and her overflow / Which being incomplete, disquieteth me so! ("The Blossoming of the Solitary Date Tree" 56–57), emphasizes the self's vulnerability to its own transcendent potential. This threatening transcendence is what Coleridge identified in Wordsworth's *Prelude* as "the dread watch-tower of man's absolute self" ("To William Wordsworth" 40).[22] Conscious life is a darkening of the light that is too strong for us, which opens the possibility that conscious experience—"all the thoughts, pains, joys of mortal breath"—is, viewed from this perspective, "a war-embrace of wrestling life and death," since the dark bounding of consciousness is in conflict with the boundlessness of the light of the absolute self.

Coleridge here offers something different from both Levinas and Ricoeur, though it shares the problematics of both. Unlike Ricoeur, Coleridge sees the first-person self as possibly *not* the limit of its subjective world, and thus vulnerable not only to the approach of the other but also to the excessive brightness of the absolute self. If this is subjective idealism, it carries a high price, because the conscious ego is attacked on two flanks. The ego is on the one hand potentially too subjective, and therefore it must suffer the dissolution traced in the Malta notebooks and the Levinasian accusation of the self. On the other hand, in terms of the expanded notion of subjectivity in the concept of the "absolute self," the conscious ego may not be subjective enough, if consciousness is a mere darkening of the "absolute self" instead of its "bound." Thus he cannot enjoy Ricoeur's confidence that solicitude for others, expressed in the dialectic of *ipse* and *idem,* is an essential and supportive structure of the self, because the *idem* beyond the *ipse* is not only the objective continuity of character, but also unconditioned transcendence, whose absolute otherness to the conscious self threatens the ego. But neither can he enjoy Levinas's confidence that peace can be achieved through a dissolution of the ego and a responsible welcoming of the other person's proximity because, as a consequence of the conscious ego's incompleteness relative to the "absolute self," transcendent otherness assaults one from within as well as from without. Here Coleridge approaches Heidegger's notion that "[*i*]*n conscience Dasein calls itself. . . .* The call comes *from* me and yet *from beyond me and over me*" (*Being and Time* 320), and perhaps Kristeva's sense that "the foreigner lives within us" as "the hidden face of our identity" (*Strangers to Ourselves* 1).[23]

Coleridge's internalization of otherness implicitly answers one of Ricoeur's criticisms of Levinas: that the Levinasian concept of "otherness" is restricted to the encounter with another person and thus to a hyperbolic separation between self and other that "renders unthinkable . . . the distinction between self and I [*idem* and *ipse*], and the formation of a concept of selfhood defined by its openness and its capacity for discovery" (*Oneself* 339). This criticism of Levinas is also a challenge to Coleridge, however, because Ricoeur's point is based on an objection to grounding ethics in "conscience," as both Coleridge and Levinas do. Ricoeur objects to an ethics grounded in "conscience" partly because its "metaphor of the voice and the call" moves ethics from "the attestation of our powers-to-be" to the essentially nonmoral idea of "debt," and consequently to a restriction of otherness to the other person (341). Coleridge takes up this challenge by uncoupling conscience's activity of atonement from debt and by including the internal other of the absolute self in his concept of conscience. As in his theory of Christian redemption, duty is not a matter of payment of a debt: although he admits the falseness of the etymology, "atonement" is understood by Coleridge as "At-one-ment," not the payment of a debt (*LS* 55). And if the command of conscience can come not only from one's duty to other people, but also from the "other" of one's own transcendent self, conscience is not *reduced* to the otherness of the other person, although the other is its main source, as in the definition of conscience as "my affections & duties toward others" (*CN* 2: 3231).

Coleridge retains a subject-oriented concept of otherness: that is to say, as Nicholas Reid argues, the existence even of objects is the result of a subjective act of predication: "It would be absurd, then, to assert that buses and beefsteaks are possessed of egoity, but the argument is that in so far as they *exist* it is as subjects and not objects" ("Coleridge and Schelling" 471). This is consistent with the process-oriented theory of "individuation" in *The Theory of Life* that includes everything from minerals to humans in the process. By grounding all otherness in subjectivity, both Coleridge and Ricoeur paradoxically *expand* the category of otherness. If all otherness, whether of people or of objects, is within the category of subjectivity, then one can have a self-other relation with just about anything, from people to watersnakes to mountains one has never seen, as when Coleridge turns Mont Blanc into an echoing emanation of God in "Hymn before Sun-rise." This is because nature in the world has no necessity of its own, but acquires it only through the interposition of an "idea":

> eine Voraussetzung *relativ* der *sinnlichen* Natur, oder der Natur in der *Welt,* kann *nicht* ihre Nothwendigkeit in sich selbst tragen—kann gar keine absolute *Nothwendigkeit* haben. [A presupposition

> relative to material nature, or to nature in the world, can not carry its necessity in itself—can have no absolute necessity.] It is an *Anticipation* that *acquires* necessity by becoming an IDEA; but it becomes an IDEA in the moment of it's coincidence with an objective LAW: and vice versa, a *constant Phaenomenon* first becomes a LAW in the moment of its coincidence with an IDEA. (*CL* 4:875–76)

If materiality requires a subjective "idea" to achieve the necessity that can give it the status of an other, the converse of this logic is that, by its participation in this expanded concept of subjectivity, the material can really be an other. This applies most obviously to the familiar notion of nature as other, but one's own flesh can also become other, as when the Mariner bites into his own arm in order to announce the approach of the spectre-ship that will continue his persecution, and when Coleridge refers to his own body as "that more troublesome Luggage, my poor crazy whimsical Carcase" in a letter written shortly before his departure for Malta (*CL* 2: 1089), a phrase repeated with variations in two other letters from that time (2: 1090, 1105). In one of his many objections to Schelling's conflation of the sensory with the intellectual, Coleridge affirms the otherness of his body: "I [do] not, & seem to myself never to have [r]egarded my Body as identical with [my]self—my Brain no more than my [n]ails or [h]air—or [mo]re than [a p]air of [sp]ectacles" (*CM* 4:461). Although this separation of self from body testifies to his idealism, Coleridge's framing of his own suffering in terms of his body as an alienated other also bears out Ricoeur's point that "the passivity belonging to the metacategory of one's own body overlaps with the passivity belonging to the category of other people; the passivity of the suffering self becomes indistinguishable from the passivity of being the victim of the other than self" (*Oneself* 320). The self is for Coleridge a victim of his own body in addition to being "accused" by both the absolute self and other selves such as Sara Hutchinson.

If, however, as in Levinas, the goal of otherness is to annihilate the ego, then otherness obviously cannot be validated by its connection to subjectivity; rather, subjectivity must be grounded in otherness. In that situation, the other with which the self can interact must contain its own principle of necessity, which for Levinas (but not for Coleridge, who grants such a principle to all of nature) narrows the category to human or divine others. Coleridge combines both positions: the centrality of subjectivity expands the category of admissible others, all under the umbrella of the subject, but the importance of ego-annihilation means that this is at the same time an expansion of the forces to which the ego is vulnerable. This vulnerability is mitigated by the notion that the others that really matter are other people, similarly vulnerable selves in relation to whom the self grounds its conscience and consciousness. Whereas for Ricoeur the modulation of otherness into areas such as one's own flesh ultimately confirms the originary status of the self (even if it is the suffering self), the experience of the Mariner and poems such as "What is Life?" suggest that locating otherness within the self does not necessarily remove the ego-annihilating force of that otherness.[24]

Coleridge's sense that the absolute, unconditioned self can be a source of absolute otherness is consoling as well as terrifying, just as his notion of a God that is absolutely other, a pure will prior to its self-othering realization in the Logos, provides both theological stability and the "deeply disturbing" sense of absolute otherness that Hartman finds. The unimaginability of transcendence, according to the familiar logic of the sublime, can be a source of both positive awe and negative terror, forces which Coleridge could not simply reconcile in either Burke's "delight" (*A Philosophical Enquiry* 53) or Kant's conclusion that "the mind has a power surpassing any standard of sense" (*Critique of Judgment* 106). His self-absorbing rather than self-absorbed sublime meant that he would have been unable to accept Wordsworth's version of this self-generated transcendent otherness, which occurs in the *Fourteen-Book Prelude* (6: 593–617), when the "Imagination" rises

> from the Mind's abyss
> Like an unfathered vapour that enwraps,
> At once some lonely Traveller.
>
> (595–97)

Unlike Coleridge, Wordsworth is able, within a few lines, to perform the Kantian gesture of allowing this sublime experience to attest to the self's glorious association with the "infinitude" (606) of "something evermore about to be" (609).

In Coleridge's theological writings, a version of the transcendence of the self that is so feared in "What is Life?" has a theologically positive function that shares Levinas's call for an annihilation of the separated ego, or what Coleridge calls the finite self, but this annihilation is accomplished through the agency of his expanded notion of self rather than through the agency of the other.[25] In the 1795 "Religious Musings," when he was still a Hartlean and a Unitarian, and thus relatively untroubled by the problems of the will and the personal triune God that would later dominate his thought, self-annihilation was a relatively unproblematic result of faith; the soul "by exclusive consciousness of God / All self-annihilated it shall make / God its Identity" (41-43); Coleridge's footnote to these lines points to Hartley's demonstration of this point. Rather than making one's "own low self the whole," one should "make / the whole one Self" (151-54). Later, the issue becomes much more problematic. For Coleridge self-interest can be "*the essential cause of fiendish guilt*" (*Friend* 1:427n), partly because "each man will universalize his notions, & yet each is variously finite" (*CN* 2: 2208), and, as Modiano says, "In Coleridge's personal experience a retreat into subjectivity often meant not a purifying ascent to a spiritual ideal, but a descent into 'the unfathomable hell within' that led to progressive isolation and artistic sterility" (66). However, self-interest can also be "the condition of all moral good" because of its link, via self-consciousness, to the infinite will (*Friend* 1:427n).

Even without that theological link, self-interest can rise to the ethically productive disinterestedness of appropriate "self-love": "that which makes us capable of vicious self-interestedness capacitates us for disinterestedness." We have "the power of comparing the notion of *him* & *me* objectively," seeing ourselves in third-person terms. This same power enables us both to prefer "a smaller advantage of my own to a far greater good of another man's" and to prefer "a greater good of another's to a lesser good of my own." This objectification of the self allows love to return to the self: the fact that, Coleridge says, "I am capable of loving my neighbor as myself, empowers me to love myself *as* my neighbor" (*CN* 3:4007). This sense of the self that transcends self-interest operates very differently from the ungrounded absolute self in "What is Life" in that the *idem* beyond the *ipse* depends on a Ricoeurean sense of *idem* as objective continuity of character. But the Levinasian side of the picture appears in Coleridge's notion that this self love annihilates the finite self. The "Freedom of moral Being" to which proper self-love aspires is a thought that "tends to annihilate self" by removing the distinctions between individual selves: "That Selfishness, which includes of necessity the Selves of all my fellow-creatures is assuredly a social & generous Self," because it "annihilates Self, as a notion of diversity."[26] This is a self-love directed toward the "unindividual nature of the idea, Self or Soul"; consideration of the "course of action" that "will purchase heaven for *me,* for my Soul, involves the thought, all men who pursue that course" (3:4007).

While Levinas might call this a return to the Same, a totalization of self, because it negates the absolute finitude of the other person by negating diversity,[27] it shares Levinas's goal of annihilating the self that practices what Coleridge calls "self*ish*," as opposed to "self" love, which "depends on our transferring our present passion or appetite or rather diluting & stretching it out in imagination, as the covetous man does" (*CN* 3: 4007). This selfishness is what Levinas calls the "dominating imperialism" of the ego that assimilates the Other to the ego's concepts. Proper self-love, according to Coleridge, requires "as great an effort if not far greater of disinterestedness than to give up a present enjoyment to another person who is present to one" (3: 4007), because the "freedom of moral being" of the transcendent self is at a further degree of alienation from our present, finite self than is the other person in front of us. The self contemplated in eternity "differs unimaginably from my present self" (3: 4007), acquiring something of the absolute, unthematizeable otherness that Levinas assigns to the face of the other person.

Like Adam Smith's impartial spectator, who combines the perspectives of all informed and rational minds, this eternal self rises above the partiality of the individual self, "involv[ing] the thought, all men who pursue that course." However, Coleridge's sense of the self as so much more than simply an agent exercising passions of sympathy or egoism, as well as his sense of the subjective rather than the social origins of this higher sense of self, means that this absolute self is much more a participant than a spectator in the life of the self. Coleridge calls for what Levinas terms an "ontological indifference" and "disinterestedness" (*OB* 178) that avoids "that aspiration to the other which still stays in the midst of essence, and is complacent in aspiring" (177). However, this is not to be confused with emotional detachment; for Levinas, this indifference to the self is "non-indifference to another, to the other" (178). As Kathleen Coburn points out, Coleridge saw in Shakespeare such a combination of indifferent impartiality with a nonindifference to the specific other; the achievement of "great impersonality in probing a character while still feeling intensely the agony or the ecstasy in every fibre of it" (97). Coleridge's version of the higher self is "Christian" in the sense that it is based on the potential divinity of the self rather than the otherness of God, and Ricoeur echoes Coleridge's defense of self-love as rising to disinterestedness: "What one loves in oneself is not the desiring part that motivates friendship for the sake of utility or pleasure but the best part of oneself" (*Oneself* 184). The difference in Coleridge is that the individual, attesting self is also annihilated by the absolute self, both in the frightening sense described in "What is Life?" and in the positive sense in his speculations on self-love. In different ways, both scenarios allow a transcendent version of self to function as an other whose threat to the finite self is both devastating and productive of the highest form of moral freedom.

IV. Coleridge and Romantic Autonomy

This way in which the self can generate a Ricoeurean self-othering and also be a Levinasian other that both threatens and consoles provides an important insight into how Coleridge both is and is not vulnerable to the charge of promoting an ethics of idealistic autonomy, the charge that has informed so much recent criticism under the banner of the "Romantic Ideology." By concluding with this point, I hope to suggest how the hermeneutical and ethical conversation I have staged between Coleridge and some twentieth-century descendents of the Romantic union of ethics and hermeneutics might enrich our understanding of the inseparable ethical and hermeneutic implications of Coleridgean subjectivity. McGann is certainly correct in his characterization of "Coleridge's cherished belief that the realm of ideas provides a ground for reality" (*The Romantic Ideology* 106). As I hope to have shown, McGann is not correct, or only partially correct, in attributing to Coleridge the "belief that poetical works can transcend historical divisions by virtue of their links with Imagination" on the grounds that "poetic vision is the . . . final ground on which all other conceptual formations depend, at least so far as human perceptions are concerned" (100–101). Coleridge's faith in imagination is not simply at odds with, but is part of, a deep appreciation for the historicity of language, poetry, and religion, and he was aware, even more than Wordsworth, of the conflicted relationship between aesthetic ideas and cultural reality. And while ideas are *ontologically* prior to cultural reality (in Coleridge's terminology, Idea is prior to Law), this is balanced by the *historical* priority of cultural reality to ideas. From Gadamer's hermeneutic perspective, it is the historical character of language as event that reveals the historicity of "the *process of concept formation*" (*TM* 427–28).

It is therefore not sufficient to divide the "Truth-content of ideas"—their "ideological" function—from "the human commitment with which they have been invested—their "critical" function (*The Romantic Ideology* 104) as McGann does in seeing Coleridge's poetry, particularly his later poetry, as a critical undercutting of his ideological position, because the historicity of human commitment is more complexly intertwined with truth-content all the way down in both the concepts and their poetic embodiment. This is not to deny that there is a tension between what happens to concepts in Coleridge's poetry and his philosophical prose, as should be clear from the tensions I have tried to elucidate. But it is a tension between the genres (informed by but not identical to Coleridge's own theories about generic differences), not simply a tension between the truth value of concepts and their status as symptoms of human commitment.

The autonomy of the aesthetic, the idea, and the imagination is not simply translatable into moral autonomy, and McGann himself does not make that translation. As I tried to show in Chapter 2, there is a sense in which the autonomy of the art-object works specifically against the autonomy of the moral agent by presenting an engagement with otherness. However, there is a deep historical link between the two concepts, which Eagleton traces back to Shaftesbury, in that "the morally virtuous individual" is expected to live "with the grace and symmetry of an artefact" (*The Ideology of the Aesthetic* 35). Therefore it seems appropriate to conclude by discussing Coleridgean subjectivity in the context of the fate of the morally autonomous subject, a topic of vital concern to both Romantic and contemporary thought.

Ricoeur, like Williams, sees the need for moral norms of obligation, based on a Kantian sense of autonomy, to be grounded in a larger ethical perspective; we must "doubt the autonomy of autonomy" (*Oneself* 215) (though unlike Williams he finds this doubt implicit in Kant's own notion of "respect" [213]). Coleridge also, as noted in Chapter 4, sees the freedom of Kantian moral autonomy as confusing juridical law and its grounding context of moral law; the latter excludes the freedom to release one from obligation because "the law of Conscience," stemming from the divine unconditioned, is immutably binding. However, for Coleridge the unconditional obedience demanded by moral law does not conflict with the "moral freedom" to which the self-annihilating activity of the transcendent self can lead, because individual choice is grounded in a higher "freedom" that both annihilates and grows out of the choices of the individual self. Commenting on Fichte's *Die Bestimmung des Menschen,* and invoking Schelling's distinction between *Wille,* or will, and *Willkühr,* or choice, Coleridge says, "But Willkühr ist nicht der Wille; and the highest Object of the Latter is to soar above the former—to leave it behind. Else, every perfect Habit of Virtue would be a Loss of Freedom" (*CM* 2: 603).

The annihilation of self by proper self-love, or the annihilation of *Willkühr* by *Wille,* is a movement toward a freedom that transcends the caprice of individual choice, even though "that wavering Choice" is what "we learn our freedom from" (*CM* 2:603). Were this not the case, virtuous habits would lead to a decrease in freedom. Coleridge is here arguing against Fichte's statement that if the self is determined "by the inexorable power of strict necessity," then that power would also determine whether one became a "foolish and vicious person" or "a wise and good person" (qtd. 2:603). For Coleridge, this statement misunderstands both necessity and the relation between will and choice. "[E]very perfect habit of virtue" must be seen as leading from the caprice of individual choice to the higher will associated with God, not towards the loss of freedom that would be implied if the habitual nature of virtue simply reflected our determination by internal or external forces. "Perfect habits of virtue" are higher than individually chosen acts of virtue because they rise above the caprice of single choices that may be made for any of a number of reasons, good bad or indifferent, and thus such habits represent the potential transcendence of *Willkühr* by *Wille,* or a movement toward a higher form of freedom. Such "habits" exhibit a higher, not a lower order of freedom, because they represent the internalization of virtue not necessarily present in specific acts, and thus engage "the whole moral being": "True *Religion* does not subsist *quoad essentiam* [in essence]" in "acts" of ceremonial observance, "but in that habitual state of the whole moral Being, which manifests itself by these acts" (4:625). Individually chosen or even culturally legislated "acts" are merely the specific externalization of a kind of freedom that is higher than mere choice.

Just as freedom in this higher sense is not to be confused with choice, necessity is not to be confused with compulsion (*CM* 2:641). Coleridge's running complaint about both Fichte and Schelling is that they tend to confuse metaphysical and sensory concepts in this way.[28] In an absolute sense, "Necessity and absolute Freedom are one" (2: 641). Coleridge's "Foretaste and Analogon" to this identity is "the Assent of the Mind to a Mathematical Demonstration"(2: 642); that is to say, we freely assent to the necessary truth of a mathematical proof, and the necessity of the truth in no way impinges on the freedom of our assent. The theoretical possibility of uniting freedom and necessity in this way demonstrates that the perceived conflict between Romantic notions of autonomy and modern notions of ideological determinism is a false dichotomy, or at least one that Coleridge attacked with a good deal of sophistication. Coleridge's union of freedom and necessity is ultimately a theological idea, but as the mathematical example demonstrates, it is also a philosophical principle that stands on his own. It resembles Gadamer's objections to the false dichotomy of independent reason and submission to authority, which, in his view, the Enlightenment mistakenly took to be mutually exclusive. Authority "rests on acknowledgement and hence on an act of reason itself which, aware of its own limitations, trusts to the better insights of others. . . . [A]uthority has not to do with obedience but rather with knowledge" (*TM* 279). The free, rational decision to accept an authority detracts from neither the freedom of that decision nor the legitimacy of the authority accepted; in fact the authority is legitimized only by such acts. Similarly, for Coleridge the free assent to a necessary principle detracts from neither the freedom of the assent nor the necessity of the principle, and on the theological level, the more we rise from a freedom based on individual choice to one based on a free assent to necessary truths, the freer we are.

Only in God are freedom and necessity united "from the Beginning." Coleridge objects to Schelling's implication that there is a conflict between divine freedom and the necessity implied by God's knowledge of the future, and his objection stands even if one grant's Schelling's inappropriate ascription of sensory qualities such as temporality to God: "[?Even] admitting the incongruous Predicate TIME, in the Deity, says Coleridge, "I cannot see an[y] absolute incompossibility of Foresight with Freedom" (*CM* 4:421). For man, however, the unity is arrived at only through "a succession of acts" (4:445). This statement demonstrates the ethical value of individual choices—the "wavering Choice" from which "we learn our freedom"— even though the goal of those choices should to be arrive at the "absolutely permanent" state in which "Self becomes evanescent, or transfigured" in "the work of the Free Will aided by Grace i.e. a Will ~~more~~ perfectly free" (2: 642). Thus the lower order of freedom expressed in individual choice is not simply negated in a Hegelian dialectic that would replace it with a higher order of freedom; the individual choosing self is both extended and annihilated as it assents to the aid of grace.

There is a good deal of Kant in Coleridge's translation of free will into a universal principle of necessary freedom, but in Coleridge's version we arrive at the union of freedom and necessity by annihilating, as well as extending, the autonomous freedom of the individual. For Kant, "a free will and a will under moral laws are the same" because the particularly human causality of individual freedom is universalized into the categorical imperative: "'Will is in all its actions a law to itself' expresses . . . only the principle of acting on no maxim other than one which can have for its object itself as at the same time a universal law" (*Groundwork of the Metaphysic of Morals* 114). Coleridge recognizes a more problematic relationship between individual autonomy and absolute freedom, because the self is both embraced in a Ricoeurean dialectic of self-othering and "cored out" in a Levinasian annihilation of the ego.

Coleridge's association of the "juridical" with subjective freedom and moral law with absolute obligation in his criticism of Kant suggests Levinas's distinction, developed in *Otherwise than Being,* between "ethics" and "justice." Justice begins with the entrance of a third party, and the ethical relationship of absolute otherness is brought into the sphere of representation and comparison:

> the relationship with the third party is an incessant correction of the asymmetry of proximity in which the face is looked at. There is weighing, thought, objectification, and thus a decree in which my anarchic relationship with illeity is betrayed, but in which it is conveyed before us. . . . Out of representation is produced the order of justice moderating or measuring the substitution of me for the other, and giving the self over to calculus. . . . The extraordinary commitment of the other to the third party calls for control, a search for justice, society and the State, comparison and possession, thought and science, commerce and philosophy, an outside of anarchy, the search for a principle. (158–61)

This sphere of justice is thus a return to the order of the comparing, possessing subject, who manipulates the instrumental reason of "representation" and "calculus." Ricoeur, as might be expected, objects to "the extreme—even scandalous—hypothesis that the Other is no longer the master of justice" (*OB* 338) in the later Levinas, and wants to preserve the possibility of "an authentic reciprocity in exchange" (191) that informs, rather than betrays and expresses at a secondary level, the ethical.[29]

For Coleridge and Levinas, the autonomy of "juridical" law needs to be grounded in a prior sense of the ethical, which it both betrays and conveys, and Coleridge shares Levinas's sense that that prior ethicity is a command from the unconditioned. This is part of Coleridge's defense of the English Constitution, which he calls, quoting "an old writer," "a law not to be derived from Alured, or Alfred, or Canute, or other elder or later promulgators or particular laws, but which might say of itself—When reason and the laws of God first came, then came I with them" (*C & S* 22). English law (unlike, of course, the kind of law based on instrumental reason invoked by revolutionaries-become-tyrants in France), must answer to the higher context of the moral law of the unconditioned rather than simply the "juridical" law that can be manipulated by individuals. But that higher context includes the category of the "absolute self," which thus provides a route to "moral freedom" that is not based on individual autonomy, but that in fact annihilates it, even as individual "choice" can be both a training ground for and an external manifestation of the higher freedom. At the same time, the logos-philosophy allows for a Ricoeurean crossing of the gap between the other and the self, between the external manifestation and the internal principle, enabling the individual mind to internalize the otherness of that trans-individual "law" as "idea": "That which, contemplated *objectively* (i.e. as existing externally to the mind) we call a LAW; the same contemplated *subjectively* (i.e as existing in a subject or mind), is an idea" (13). There is thus a continuity between an "ethical" notion of law—what Coleridge calls the "moral law" and what Levinas calls the approach of the other—and the reciprocity of individuals that Ricoeur wants to maintain as foundational in "juridical" law, or Levinas's "justice," because Coleridge maintains both the transcendent self's participation in the Levinasian "ethical" and a Ricoeurean accessibility of the other (whether human, objective, or divine) to the self. This version of the Romantic self is thus "autonomous" only within a complex network of reciprocal and nonreciprocal, self-generated and self-annihilating otherness, and within a concept of freedom that has only a limited relation to the autonomous moral agent.

There is nothing essential about my positioning of Coleridgean subjectivity between Ricoeur and Levinas; other contemporary voices in philosophy would produce an equally fruitful dialogue with Coleridge. My choice of these two as partners in this hermeneutical conversation is more a reflection of my own interest in their approaches to the modern problems of ethical subjectivity than a suggestion that they provide any kind of master key that will unlock the thought of Coleridge. Conversely, although I have argued that Coleridge's thought can shed light on the modern ethical problems investigated by Ricoeur, Levinas, Williams, and others, I hope this book will not be taken as suggesting that Coleridge provides the answers to these modern problems. As has often been observed, Coleridge failed brilliantly in his attempt to develop a unified theory of human ethical life. To suggest otherwise would be to substitute, and anachronistically defend, a new version of Romantic ideology. Paul de Man has taught us that blindness and insight are closely intertwined, and Coleridge's blindnesses are often as illuminating as his insights. But blindness and insight can not be simply opposed on either the Romantic or the modern side of the conversation.

In Gadamer's terms, these modern philosophers have helped define the horizon of my interpretive prejudice, to be put at risk in a conversation, sometimes agreeable, sometimes confrontational, and usually more complicated than either, with the multiple and shifting horizons of Coleridge. The point is not to catalogue either the blindness or the insight on either side of the conversation, which would suggest the hubristic possibility of rising above the conversation itself. The point is rather to *have* the conversation and reflect on it, for two important reasons that, for me, provide the only reasonable justification for the practice of literary criticism. First, the interpretive conversation with the past, at least since the origin of hermeneutics, is as foundational a part of human life as is the creation of art. The dynamics of this conversation, which needs no justification beyond itself, are too often taken for granted, even given the valuable but often short-sighted recent emphasis on the historical and cultural contexts of literature. Second, a conversation with someone who thought as deeply as Coleridge did about the imagination's complex relation to ethical life can help to illuminate the close connection between the hermeneutic adventure of an interpretive engagement with the other and the ethical adventure of living with the other. Coleridge was not any better at either adventure than most of us are, but both the differences and the continuities between his efforts and our own may help us learn and teach how interpretative and ethical action, while not identical, are connected in ways important to both reading and living.

Notes

Preface

1. See, for example, Shaun Gallagher, *Hermeneutics and Education;* Timothy W. Crusius, *A Teacher's Introduction to Philosophical Hermeneutics;* Brenda Deen Schildgen, "Reconnecting Rhetoric and Philosophy in the Composition Classroom"; and Richard Rorty, *Richard Rorty on Hermeneutics, General Studies, and Teaching*.

2. Clifford Siskin, for instance, compares poems in terms of "the technology they share: combinations of practices used in different ways at different times." This is the technology of "writing": "by calling it *technology* I am acknowledging it as something other, something to which people must adapt, something that can, in a sense, be done to them" (31).

Chapter 1: Hermeneutics, Ethics, and Historicism

1. See Smith's explication of this notion in *Hermeneutics and Human Finitude* 86–87, 169, 190, 279–81.

2. Gadamer keeps ethics in the background in *Truth and Method,* but he shows an "underlying and pervasive concern with ethics and politics" (Bernstein, "From Hermeneutics to Praxis" 281) in his other writings. Fred Dallmayr has written extensively on the ethical and political implications of Gadamer's thought, particularly as a model for cross-cultural understanding; see, for example, *Critical Encounters* 130–58, 165–82, and *Beyond Orientalism* 39–62.

3. For an interesting exchange on the advantages and disadvantages of accepting Coleridge's own biases, see Anthony John Harding's review of Wendling's book and Wendling's response in *The Wordsworth Circle*.

4. De Man, *Romanticism and Contemporary Criticism* 98; Hartman, "On Traumatic Knowledge and Literary Studies" passim; Christensen, "The Romantic Movement at the End of History" 454–56, 475–76.

5. "Order, peace, and fecundity depend on cultural distinctions; it is not these distinctions but the loss of them that gives birth to fierce rivalries and sets members of the same family or social group at one another's throats" (49).

6. See Gerald Bruns's response to Eagleton's dismissal of Gadamer's notion of tradition (*Hermeneutics Ancient and Modern* 195–212). The accusation of an overdependence on tradition came first from Habermas, in his "A Review of Gadamer's *Truth and Method,*" to which Gadamer responds that Habermas has taken his views in "a particularly one-sided way." In fact, Gadamer explicitly criticizes theories of objectively defined traditions that ignore their own historical situatedness, "the conceptions of world history, those constantly outstripped conceptions, in which one unconsciously always behaves like the latest historian" (*Philosophical*

Hermeneutics 36). For a defense of Gadamer's "conservatism" see P. Christopher Smith 267–82. Smith applauds Gadamer's emphasis on tradition and allies him with Edmund Burke, but carefully distinguishes Gadamer's conservatism from a "reactionary" position, and points out that Gadamer's "tradition" is not simply accepted social practice, because some common practices—such as those that arise out of self-interest—are exactly what need to be "superseded" by an ethically defined notion of tradition (269).

7. Unfortunately, Hamlin's recent book will do little to encourage dialogue between hermeneutics and new historicism, because the majority of the essays in *Hermeneutics of Form* were originally written in the 1970s, before the advent of the major new-historical studies.

8. See *Contingency, Irony, and Solidarity*, esp. 73–95.

9. One finds the same inconsistency on both sides of the debate over academic tenure. Many on the right argue against this guarantor of academic freedom while arguing for the freedom of consumer choice and the play of market forces. Many on the left (especially those with tenure) argue for tenure in the name of academic freedom and autonomy while critiquing the ideology of the autonomous self on which that freedom must rest.

10. See *Sources of the Self* 121–23, 211–18.

11. In his ecological study of Romanticism, Jonathan Bate suggests that the specific Romantic relation to nature also provides an "ideology" more complex than the oppositional politics of left and right: "An 'ideology' based on a harmonious relationship with nature goes beyond, in many ways goes deeper than, the political model we have become used to thinking with" (*Romantic Ecology* 19–20).

12. "[U]nder the name of Theology, or Divinity, were contained the interpretation of languages; the conservation and tradition of past events; the momentous epochs, and revolutions of the race and nation; the continuation of the records; logic, ethics, and the determinations of ethical science, in application to the rights and duties of men in all their various relations, social and civil; and lastly, the ground-knowledge, the prima scientia as it was named,—PHILOSOPHY, or the doctrine and discipline of *ideas*" (*C & S* 46–47).

13. In her introduction to a volume of *Romantic Praxis* on "Irony and Clerisy," Deborah Elise White points out that "[t]he irony of Coleridgean clerisy lies in the thoroughly secular nature of its defense of theology. It also lies in the thoroughly theological ground of its secular ideals. More precisely, it lies in the impossibility and the necessity of bringing these together" (10). White's introduction and the other essays in this volume suggest the philosophical, theological, and political complexity of Coleridge's concept of the clerisy.

14. In "A Philosophical View of Reform," Shelley distinguishes between the aristocracy of "great land proprietors and merchants" and that of the new paper-money economy: "an aristocracy of attorneys and excisement and directors and government pensioners, usurers, stock jobbers, country bankers, with their dependents and descendents." Although any aristocracy is "a prodigious anomaly in the social system" and "at the bottom it is all trick," the former is preferable: "There is something frank and magnificent in the chivalrous disdain of infamy connected with a gentleman" and "it is difficult for the imagination to refuse its respect in the faithful and direct dealings of the substantial merchant" (*Shelley's Prose* 245).

15. In discussing the Enlightenment "conquest of mythos by logos," Gadamer argues that "precisely because romanticism disparages this development, it takes over the schema itself as a self-evident truth. It shares the presupposition of the Enlightenment and only reverses its values" (*TM* 273).

16. For a detailed and subtle effort to provide a "thick" history of recent historicism, see James Chandler's *England in 1819*, especially 51–93. Chandler traces usefully Frederic Jameson's "structuralist genealogy of the so-called return to history" (93) back to the debate between Sartre's promulgation of a narrative "sense of history" and Lévi-Strauss's insistence on the arbitrary character of the "historian's code" (70–71), as well as to related debates in the early nineteenth century.

17. This history, as well its antecedents in the Reformation and in Classical thought is traced in *Truth and Method*. See also Maurizio Ferraris, Gerald Bruns, *Hermeneutics Ancient and Modern*, and Jean Grondin.

18. In discussing Derrida's reading of Levinas, Critchley argues that "ingratitude is the only mode in which one can write a text *for* Levinas if that text is going to maintain the ethical structure that Levinas's work sets to work"; Derrida "must be cautious to avoid rendering to Levinas what is Levinas's, for in so doing, he would make the ethical relation correspond to the time of the 'rendez-vous' ('"that common time of clocks"' [a Levinasian phrase quoted by Derrida]), where the Other would render itself up and return to the Same" (*The Ethics of Deconstruction* 111). See also Jill Robbins's discussion of the necessary "ingratitude" in Levinas's notion of the "gift": "The asymmetrical structure of the gift necessitates an ingratitude so radical that it approaches ambivalence and persecution" (*Altered Reading* 14).

19. In emphasizing "the centrality of hermeneutics for education," Cyrus Hamlin argues similarly that "[w]e need to recognize that a sense of difference and limit, not only in the study of literature, is an essential aspect of that dialogical form of experience which, since Plato and even since Homer, has constituted education and has been the prerequisite to self-knowledge" (*Hermeneutics of Form* 58).

20. See *TM* 120n for Gadamer's critique of Jauss. Gadamer's own literary criticism will be addressed in Chapter 2.

21. Quotations from "A Letter to ———" and the 1802 and 1817 versions of "Dejection" are from the "Reading Texts" in Parrish's edition (*Coleridge's Dejection*).

22. Including, as Rajan notes, important shifts and double perspectives on the "authority" of the poet: "Obliged by the poet's authority to concur in his idealization of Sara, we are also compelled by that authority to sympathize with Coleridge and to read the margins of his self-effacement" (*The Supplement of Reading* 124).

23. I discuss the crossing of public/private boundaries in Wordsworth's 1802 experiences in "Nuptial Interruption."

24. Stephen Prickett complicates usefully the notion of "appropriation," with specific reference to the Romantic appropriation of the Bible, by finding in it an inevitably contradictory combination of "theft" and legitimacy that goes all the way back to the Biblical account of Jacob's appropriation of Esau's birthright: "there is in the very idea of 'appropriation' *both* a quality of thinly disguised theft *and* a recognition that such a takeover is a necessary part of the way in which any person, or even a society, makes an idea its own" (*The Origins of Narrative* 32).

Chapter 2: Ethics and Art: Problems of *Phronesis* and *Techne*

1. Romanticism has often been accused of furthering Kant's separation of the aesthetic from the ethical, as when Charles Taylor, using the example of Schiller, notes that the aesthetic provides a sense of "wholeness" that "engages us totally in a way that morality cannot" (*The Ethics of Authenticity* 65), but it is Arnold who rightly points out in the essay just quoted that the situation was different in England: Wordsworth differs from Schiller, Lessing, and others in his ability to recombine the aesthetic with the ethical: "he deals with more of *life* than they do" ("Wordsworth" 340).

2. See Ricoeur's discussion of the tension between the "ethical aim" and the "moral norm" (*Oneself* 203–39), Williams's radical objections to the systematic "purity of morality" (*Ethics* 195) to which he opposes "thick ethical concepts" (200), and Adam Newton's distinction—with specific reference to Coleridge's *Rime*—between "moral propositionality" and "ethical performance" (*Narrative Ethics* 5).

3. The union of poetry and philosophy is also for Coleridge part of the prehistory of both in Greek and Hebrew myth, "while yet poetry remained the union of the sensuous and the philosophic mind" ("On the Prometheus of Aeschylus," *SW & F* 1267).

4. Quotations from the *Rime* are taken from Wallen's edition (*Coleridge's Ancient Mariner*). Unless otherwise indicated, the 1798 version is quoted.

5. Heidegger's essay dates from 1955; computer technology provides an even clearer illustration of his concept of standing-reserve: my computer is less important as an "object"—it is relatively unimportant whether it is an original IBM or a clone, and it will be obsolete in a few years—than as a repository for the switchable, regulated energy that resides increasingly on the internet, standing in reserve to be called on anytime.

6. See James Chandler's discussion of this issue and this passage in *England in 1819* 87–92.

7. For a discussion of the influence on American liberal arts education of the European universities founded in the early nineteenth century, particularly the University of Berlin, see Oakley, *Community of Learning*. On the overall importance of the University of Berlin for setting a new protocol for university work, see McClelland, *State, Society, and University*. On Humboldt's importance in the history of hermeneutics, see Gadamer, *TM* 439–43.

8. Even recent work by a sophisticated new historicist such as Alan Liu, while it revises cultural *techne*, asking it to account for the production of "service," retains the model of production: "[t]o prove that the practice of language is labor, perhaps, is a hollow victory without also proving that the labor of words provides a service" ("The New Historicism and the Work of Mourning" 558). Stephen Greenblatt, while criticizing Frederic Jameson's reduction of the differences between the aesthetic and the social to a capitalist ploy, still sees the interaction between art and other forms of culture as a matter of *techne*, calling attention to "the whole structure of production and consumption" and claiming that the work of art "is itself the product of a series of manipulations" ("Towards a Poetics of Culture" 8, 12)

9. In related examples, the aesthetic is seen as what Alan Liu calls an "aesthetics of closure," which acknowledges "history" in the act of denying it (*Wordsworth* 400); or as an impossible project, as in Richard Bourke's analysis of the doomed tradition of Arnoldian "aestheticization" (*Romantic Discourse* 77); or, more subtly, as what Terry Eagleton traces as the both disabling and enabling "self-referentiality" of the aesthetic (*The Ideology of the Aesthetic* 9).

10. To be fair, Booth qualifies heavily this initial emphasis on *techne* later in the book by expanding his criteria beyond the aesthetic, explicitly "rebut[ting] the claim that the only moral demand we can make of a work of art is that it be good *as* art—meaning 'as craft'" (217), and combining the ethics of artistic technique with "the patterns desire, the figurings of metaphor" and "the cosmic myths of happiness and misery" (377).

11. Rorty eschews the traditional "moral-aesthetic contrast," not by reconciling the differences between art and life but by seeing the distinction as tied to belief in separate faculties: "we treat both 'conscience' and 'taste' as bundles of idiosyncratic beliefs and desires rather than as 'faculties' which have determinate objects" (*Contingency* 142). This is an odd way to mix philosophical and psychological questions, since there is no necessary connection between whether or not there are conflicts between aesthetic and moral judgment and whether or not one subscribes to a psychology of "faculties" or of "idiosyncratic beliefs and desires."

12. See Cyrus Hamlin's discussion of this poem in terms of the paradox of Romantic self-creation (132–34). I would suggest a different emphasis: by calling this kind of self-making a "trade," Coleridge seems to distinguish it from the dialectical development of self-consciousness and reduce it to the level of an impossible *techne*.

13. Altieri's own emphasis in *Canons and Consequences* on the performative intentionalism of individual agents tends to reduce ethics to a learned set of technical skills, or the manipulation of a "grammar": "As we exercise a cultural grammar to grasp the force of complex performative implicatures, we grow more adept at the combinatorial possibilities of that grammar

and more aware of the range of attitudes that have been constructed out of those possibilities" (16). In *"Subjective Agency,"* he suggests more subtly, following Wittgenstein, that the "impersonal 'mastery of a technique'" can lead beyond *techne:* "the mastery itself leads beyond the technique to a sense of how one's own power manages a fit with the world so that will and imagination . . . prove nonetheless anchored within what can yield descriptions and organize practices"(46-47). And if "persons" are reduced to technical "methods" that ignore the importance of first-person expressivity, the consequences are ethically restrictive: "Once we have reduced persons to methods, we have the means to deny the importance of anything method cannot handle"(225).

14. See also Gadamer's discussion of how Aristotelian *phronesis* is linked to rhetoric and jurisprudence in *Reason in the Age of Science* 120-37. For a thorough discussion of Gadamer's use of Aristotelian *phronesis,* see Foster (*Gadamer and Practical Philosophy* 45-78).

15. Here Gadamer echoes and departs from Heidegger's argument that Greek *techne* originally "belongs to bringing-forth, to *poiesis"* ("The Question Concerning Technology" 13).

16. Wayne Booth builds on this tradition in *The Company We Keep* (10, 169-96). For him, however, the conversation is ultimately with the "implied author," a concept that obscures some of the tension between *phronesis* and *techne,* as valuable as it has been for our understanding of narrative. Newton raises a similar objection to Booth (*Narrative Ethics* 64-65) and suggests that we understand the "material self-sufficiency" of a text's otherness "on the analogy with a person" (45).

17. Gary Aylesworth notes that Gadamer's dialogic model of the relation to a text, which assumes that "whatever says something to us speaks, and whatever speaks is ontologically the same as we ourselves" is the object of Ricoeur's critique, insofar as Ricoeur sees the need for "a moment of textual objectification" ("Dialogue, Text, Narrative" 64). Ricoeur in effect extends Gadamer's claim for the autonomy of the aesthetic text to all texts, which "decontextualize" themselves in relation to "the intention of the author[,] . . . the cultural situation and all the sociological conditions of the production of the text[,] . . . and . . . with respect to the original addressee," but this removes them from the dialogical situation: "the mediation of the text cannot be treated as an extension of the dialogical situation" (*Hermeneutics and the Human Sciences* 91).

18. As Joel Weinsheimer points out, Gadamer's notion of the sign comes from Plato, Kant, Humboldt, and Cassirer rather than from figures more familiar to contemporary literary theory such as Saussure and Peirce (*Philosophical Hermeneutics and Literary Theory* 88-89). This accounts for his tendency to discuss the sign in its direct relation to the world, rather than in the more familiar Saussurean terms of a material signifier's relation to a signified concept. For a thorough discussion of Gadamer's relation to modern semiotics, see Weinsheimer's chapter, "A Word is Not a Sign" 87-123.

19. I discuss language as incarnational event in *William Wordsworth* 13-44, 113-27.

20. In his introduction to *Gadamer on Celan,* Gerald Bruns links Gadamer's aesthetics to Levinas's notion of ethical alterity by way of their mutual appreciation of Celan's poetry, concluding that "it is correct to think of the poem in terms of an ethical relation" because "it is an instance of attentiveness, as if to another human being" ("The Remembrance of Language" 25-26). However, he also sees Gadamer's perspective as "requir[ing] neither ethics nor ontology" (26), implicitly reflecting Gadamer's insistence that that the aesthetic/hermeneutic relation is not necessarily or even primarily ethical.

21. See also Taylor's *The Ethics of Authenticity* 63.

22. See Booth's discussion of this point in *The Company We Keep* 230-35.

23. See Warren 210-11, 214. As Irving Massey notes, "at least since Coleridge . . . even perception is either ethical or unethical" (184).

24. See *Wordsworth's Great Period Poems* 14-57.

25. Coleridge was careful to distinguish (as well as compare) poetic and religious faith, as will be discussed below in Chapter 5, but in terms of reading the experience is the same; in fact

the universality of this hermeneutic experience *increases* scriptural authority: "the more . . . tranquilly an Enquirer takes up the Bible as he would any other Body of Ancient Writings, the livelier and steadier will be his impressions of its superiority to all other books" (*SW & F* 1164).

26. There is an obvious connection between the "overwhelming" character of the work of art and both Romantic and postmodern discourses on the sublime, where the relationship between the aesthetic and the ethical is similarly complex. Kant specifically discriminates between aesthetic and ethical judgment, but an aesthetic judgment about the sublime "has its foundation in . . . the predisposition to the feeling for (practical) ideas, i.e., to moral feeling" (*Critique of Judgment* 125). Schiller equates the sublime with moral freedom, but only by making the moral subject an aesthetic subject ("On the Sublime" 200). Despite his restriction of the sublime to the aesthetic, Lyotard suggests that the sublime is dependent on the ethical: "there is no sublime . . . without the development of the speculative and ethical capacities of the mind" (*Peregrinations* 41). Gary Shapiro concludes his discussion of the political and moral implications of the sublime with the hope that a reconsideration of Kant might provide an "antidote to those currents in contemporary aesthetic theory and practice which deliberately seek to repress the moral and political aspects of the artistic" ("From the Sublime to the Political" 233). I discuss the Romantic sublime in the context of Levinasian ethics in "Wordsworth and Levinas."

27. Quotations from "Resolution and Independence" are from *Poems, in Two Volumes, and Other Poems, 1800–1807*, 123–29.

28. Clifford Siskin uses this poem to outline a change in the role of writing's *techne* from Pope to Wordsworth in which "concern has shifted . . . from the potentially disruptive power of the technology of writing to the possibly disrupted personalities of people who wrote" as the "work" of writing linked "individual development" to "disciplinary concentration and professionalization" for "We Poets" (*The Work of Writing* 34, 36). Siskin's analysis highlights the way in which the evolution of individuals' ability to manipulate *techne* goes hand in hand with the power of *techne* to control the individual, as Gadamer argues.

29. See *Lects 1808–1819* 2: 193. This issue will be discussed in more detail in Chapter 5.

30. Claire Miller Colombo points to a similar tension in the necessity for the "poet" in many of Coleridge's poems to function both as "an internal 'reader' of his own poem . . . and as a structural device, a rhetorical trope." In the latter function, "the allegorizer is allegorized," which brings up the danger that "allegory is, potentially, a seduction to power and autonomy, an extraction of self from context and an attempt to self-create" ("Reading Scripture" 39), a danger closely linked to poetic *techne*.

31. This unity is not the autonomy of the New Critical autotelic art object, despite the fact that the irreducible iconicity of the poem described by Ransom, Wellek, Warren, and others, like the Levinasian otherness I am describing, is often identified as that which cannot be contained by interpretation. Alan Liu explains the New Critical position, quoting from Ransom's *The New Criticism:* "'The icon is a particular,' Ransom stresses, and 'a particular has too many properties, and too many values,' to be restricted to precise significance" (Ransom 291; Liu, *Wordsworth: The Sense of History* 312). The difference is that the ambiguity, tension, paradox, irony, and other qualities found by the New Critics produced, in Liu's words, "the illusion that humanity can be a timeless personality spanning without difference from Romanticism to our own century" (312), while the autonomy I am describing makes a claim comparable to that of the Levinasian other, with whom we have highly temporalized, specific, historically various, and changing relation in an encounter that denies the possibility of anything like a "timeless personality."

32. "[T]he confrontation between 'truth' and 'method' should not have misled Gadamer to oppose hermeneutic experience abstractly to methodic knowledge as a whole" ("A Review of Gadamer's *Truth and Method*" 267).

33. In both capacities—as an irreducible "other," confronting us with the autonomy that Gadamer grants to the work of art, and as a performance of its own existence as *techne,* art's ethical force has one distinct advantage over moral philosophy, in that it escapes the circularity of

the "ethicised self" that Bernard Williams finds in both Plato and Aristotle, for whom the naturalness of virtue —"the view that the functions of the mind . . . are defined . . . in terms of categories that get their significance from ethics" (*Shame* 160)—guarantees that the world will make sense in human ethical terms, and places us in a circularly argued illusion. Although the work of art's status as an "other" allies it with the process of *phronesis,* this is not a question of "making sense" in ethical or any other terms, and in its self-acknowledgment as *techne* art admits that it does not make ethical "sense."

34. See *TM* 147-51. For accounts of Levinas's complex relation to art, see Eaglestone, *Ethical Criticism* 98-128, 152-63, and Robbins, *Altered Reading* 39-54, 75-154. For an attempt to mitigate the antiaesthetic character of Levinas's thought via Kierkegaard, see Edith Wyschogrod, "The Art in Ethics."

35. Jill Robbins discusses this paradox in *Altered Reading* 39-54.

36. See *TM* 101-34 for Gadamer's full explanation of his concept of play. Gadamer's word, translated here as "structure," is *Gebilde,* not *Struktur. Gebilde* includes meanings of "creation" and "formation" not found in the English word "structure," and it is etymologically related to *Bildung* or cultural formation, a prominent word in Gadamer's theory of the historicity of culture. Therefore "transformation into structure" should not be interpreted as a move toward the ahistorical or "structural" in the sense associated with structuralism or formalism.

37. Gadamer specifically differentiates his concept of "play" from "the subjective meaning that it has in Kant and Schiller" (*TM* 101). However, Altieri's adaptation of Kant's "purposiveness without a purpose" (*Critique of Judgment* 73) in the service of an expressivism that is subjective, but without a subjective *content,* ends up in the same general area as Gadamer's concept of play. Wittgenstein is an important link here; Gadamer connects his concept of play to Wittgenstein's language games in the "Afterword" to *Truth and Method* (557) and Altieri uses Wittgenstein to offer "a minimalist Kant" *sans* categorical imperative and idealized self (*"Subjective Agency"* 151). Altieri's expressive agent is more subjective than Gadamer's *Spiel*-player, but nonetheless shares the Gadamerian engagement with a practice that is not dependent on subjective concepts. For Altieri, "[T]he aim of our efforts at expression is less to express a latent self that to intensify our expressiveness as agents working through relationships to specific contexts" (122). The result is a practical reason for which "intelligibility lies not in making reason actual but in the specific predicates linking the action to the contexts that the agent brings to bear on it" (204). Despite the much stronger sense of subjective agency, this resembles the Gadamerian play that bonds thought "to the work's own possibilities of being" rather than to determinate concepts associated with subjects.

38. Although Gadamer treats this notion of structure in ways that suggest Levinas's association of "otherness" with "proximity," as when he argues that "the openness toward the spectator is part of the closedness of the play" (*TM* 109), it should be noted that Levinas's antiaesthetic tendency directly opposes what he sees as poetry's dionysiac promotion of an artist's transformation into his work of art or into a "role"; he prefers the prosaic "language that at each instant dispels the charm of rhythm and prevents the initiative from becoming a role" (*TI* 203).

39. Echoing the primitivist theories of language espoused by Rousseau and Herder, this passage also recalls Wordsworth's account, in the Appendix to the Preface to the *Lyrical Ballads,* of poetic language's decline from the figurative language of the "earliest poets," who "wrote from passion excited by real events," to "the mechanical adoption of these figures of speech" (*Prose Works* 1: 160). The difference, as might be expected, is that Coleridge is interested in the history of poetry for its own sake, and Wordsworth is interested in the relative distance between poetic language and "the real language of men" (1: 160).

40. This mechanism is for Jerome Christensen the repressed heritage of Hartley, returning in contemporary literature and criticism (*Coleridge's Blessed Machine of Language* 147, 177-78, 182-85); for Julie Ellison it is an aggressively male "threat to authorial peace" (*Delicate Subjects* 156n). The barrel-organ, patented in 1772, which could mechanically reproduce music by means

of a revolving cylinder studded with pegs that activated a system of bellows, valves, and pipes, had apparently become a standard contrast to the efforts of creative genius by 1796. The *Oxford English Dictionary* cites a review of William Mason's *Essays, Historical and Critical, on English Church Music* (1795), in which the anonymous reviewer complains that Mason's strict rules for the playing of a voluntary, eliminating creative improvisation, would turn organ-paying into a technical exercise: "If his notions of a voluntary were to be established into a law, there would be an end to all attempts of masterly and good organ-playing, by students on that instrument. A *barrel-organ,* with fit pieces, in simple counterpoint, would do the business much more to his satisfaction, than the fingers of a man of genius" (400). What would Coleridge have said about digital sampling?

41. For the distinction between "idea" and "conception" see *C & S* 20.

42. The distinction is as much a theological as a metaphysical one and is rooted in the Protestant distinction between the written letter of the law and the inner presence of the spirit, as in Luther's commentary on Rom. 1: 17: "This Spirit . . . cannot be contained in any letter, it cannot be written with ink, on stone, as the law can be, but is written only in the heart [of one who reads], a living writing of the Holy Spirit" (qtd. Bruns *Hermeneutics Ancient and Modern* 144). See also Prickett's explanation of Coleridge's notion of "idea" as something that "can be neither generalized nor abstracted from particular concrete examples" and that "may ever recede before us even as we seek it" (*Romanticism and Religion* 28).

43. Harpham is quoting, with slight revision, what he says in *Getting it Right* 52.

44. The classic discussion of Coleridge's attraction to both the pantheist and the monotheistic tradition, the "it is" of pantheism and the "I AM" of the Judeo-Christian tradition, is Thomas McFarland's *Coleridge and the Pantheist Tradition*.

Chapter 3: Knowledge, Being, and Hermeneutics

1. On Coleridge's adaptation of this fundamental relationship explored by German *Naturphilosophie,* see Modiano, *Coleridge and the Concept of Nature* 138–206.

2. P. Christopher Smith sees Burke's emphasis on a nonrationalist ethics based on authority and tradition as an important antecedent to Gadamer's views (210–11, 216–17).

3. Sabina Lovibond summarizes this history (*Realism and Imagination in Ethics* 1–17), defining noncognitivism as the thesis that, in the absence of an "objective moral reality," "there is no such thing as moral cognition or knowledge" (1).

4. See Chandler, *Wordsworth's Second Nature,* which argues for the pervasive influence of Burke on the early as well as the later Wordsworth, and Simpson, *Romanticism, Nationalism, and the Revolt Against Theory,* which traces our own problematic relation to "theory" back to the Burkean response to French rationalism.

5. Coleridge suggests that Schelling's principle, if it is in fact different from the traditional veiw of God, lessens his power: "This Ground to God's existence either lessens, or does not lessen, his Power—in the first, it is in effect a co-existent God, evil because the ground of all evil—in the second, it leaves us as before. With that '*before*' my understanding is perfectly satisfied" (*CM* 4: 443).

6. See, for example, *CN* 4: 5280.

7. Not satisfied with either a deontological or a teleological approach, "Coleridge proposes instead a mixture of criteria—the intrinsic character of a particular act, the worthiness of the agent, the general rule, the circumstances, the consequences—as all having bearing on the judgment of right. Neither the general rule nor the consequences alone suffice" (*The Ethics of Romanticism* 148)

8. See Nussbaum, *The Fragility of Goodness* 290–317, *The Therapy of Desire* 48–101; MacIntyre, *After Virtue* 27–31, 146–64; Taylor, *Sources of the Self* 3–24.

9. For other statements on the grounding force of conscience, see *CM* 2: 663 and "The Statesman's Manual," *LS* 66–68. See also Lockridge's discussion of the complex relation between "conscience" and "consciousness" in *Coleridge the Moralist* 120–30.

10. See Elinor Shaffer's discussion of the hermeneutics of "friend" in Schleiermacher and Coleridge ("The Hermeneutic Community" 205–14).

11. This resembles McGann's call, discussed in Chapter 1, for a shift in critical criteria from conceptual structures to admittedly falsifiable, but empirically successful investigative practices.

12. James McKusick discusses Coleridge's belief that "the mere fact of signification is not what makes language distinctively human" (*Coleridge's Philosophy of Language* 125).

13. This is not a proto-Darwinian view of evolution, because Coleridge's theory emphasizes a consistently operating inner force, not a contingent process of environmental adaptation. On Coleridge's anticipation and rejection of the Darwinian position, see Gatti, "Coleridge's Reading of Giordano Bruno" 139–40.

14. As Elinor Shaffer argues in her discussion of Coleridge's reply to Lessing's worries about the role of historical "fact," "Coleridge . . . argues that there is no such specially privileged class of witnessed 'fact'. *Vernunftswahrheiten* [truths of reason] cannot be separated out in this way from *Geschichtswahrheiten* [historical truths] because what we see or experience depends on expectations formed by what we accept as *Vernunftswahrheiten*" (*"Kubla Khan" and* The Fall of Jerusalem 46).

15. Cyrus Hamlin, following J. Hillis Miller, points out that the word "form" presents a related ambiguity that goes all the way back to the Greek *typos* if one attempts a neat division between the conceptual and the material, because "form" refers both to "an abstract principle of origin or priority" and "the external shape" or "outward appearance" (*Hermeneutics of Form* 202).

16. See *LS* 114 for another suggestion that the constitutive staus of ideas stems from their participation in God's word as expressed in the opening of John's Gospel. This aspect of Coleridge is given a full treatment in James McKusick's *Coleridge's Philosophy of Language*.

17. For example, in "Keats, Gadamer and Historicity" and *William Wordsworth*.

18. Julie Ellison associates this phrase with the feminine side of Coleridge's model of understanding (*Delicate Subjects* 151), the other side being the Kantian concept of understanding as the lower-order term in the pair reason/understanding.

19. See Jean Grondin's discussion of the problems generated by Luther's radical (but not original) doctrine of *sola scriptura* (*Introduction to Philosophical Hermeneutics* 41).

20. For a detailed account of Coleridge's relationship with Eichhorn, see Shaffer, *"Kubla Khan" and* The Fall of Jerusalem 17–33.

21. "Neologism" is a general term usually applied to the rationalist biblical interpreters who followed Selmer and Michaelis. See Baird 116–17 and the editor's note to *CN* 3: 4401.

22. Coleridge's neologism for "mere (or shallow) wisdom" "from the Greek *psilos* (slender) and Sophia Wisdom, in opposition to Philosophy, The Love of Wisdom and the Wisdom of Love" (*CL* 4: 922).

23. See *Beyond Interpretation* 47–50. Vattimo is radicalizing Gadamer's notion that the Christian incarnation introduces historicity into human existence (*TM* 418–19). Charles Taylor also finds Christianity linked to secularization in the increasing celebration of ordinary life (*Sources of the Self* 215–18).

Chapter 4: Is and Ought in Literature and Life

1. In arguing that moral distinctions cannot be derived from reason, Hume expresses his surprise that "instead of the usual copulation of propositions, *is*, and *is not*, I meet with no proposition that is not connected with an *ought*, or an *ought not*" (*A Treatise of Human Nature* 469).

2. This history is traced in Barbara Herrnstein Smith's chapter "Fact and Value in the Academy" in *Contingincies of Value* (17–29).

3. This is of course a central part of MacIntyre's argument in *After Virtue*. In discussing the loss of moral teleology—the theological teleology in which an opposition between "ought" and "is" made sense—MacIntyre traces part of the failure of the Enlightenment project to the resulting incoherence: "they did indeed attempt to find a rational basis for their moral beliefs in a particular understanding of human nature, while inheriting a set of moral injunctions on the one hand and a conception of human nature on the other which had been expressly designed to be discrepant with each other" (55).

4. This priority of dialogue to description has some common ground with Altieri's effort to ground "third-person procedures in first-person efforts to secure identities from second persons," such that "we not only place value in a discursive framework, we also find a plausible way to finesse traditional fact-value dichotomies" (*Subjective Agency* 213). Altieri would not, of course, share the emphasis on either the "ought" or the theology in Coleridge's position.

5. See Perkins's discussion of this relationship (*Coleridge's Philosophy* 91–140).

6. Coleridge defines the distinction between these terms as follows: ***natura naturata*** is "nature in the passive sense," while ***natura naturans*** is "THE SUM OR AGGREGATE OF THE POWERS INFERRED AS THE SUfficient causes of THE former," or "nature in the active sense" (*P Lects* 370). See Modiano's discussion of these terms in relation to the shifting priority of self and nature in Coleridge (*Coleridge and the Concept of Nature* 54–65).

7. This sense of "example" resembles Charles Altieri's notion of the example as ethically "performative," as opposed to Adam Newton's assimilation of the Mariner's "exemplary" status to the realm of general moral rules (Newton, *Narrative Ethics* 66–67). According to Altieri, "the demonstrative use of representational instances" enable "the arts to speak of presentational strategies that in Wordsworth's terms, actually produce 'truth that is its own testimony'" (*Canons and Consequences* 246).

8. As Mileur points out, the necessary imposition of interpretive narratives defines Coleridge's "revisionary interpretation": "what defines the text is the imposition of a language on a language (that is, the imposition of one system of meanings on another), and where textualizing consciousness finds no language, it must create one as an attribute of its object" (*Vision and Revision* 160).

9. Lockridge uses this notebook entry as evidence for Coleridge's protoexistentialism (*Coleridge the Moralist* 196–97).

10. See Benveniste, *Problems in General Linguistics* 206–9. I discuss these terms' relevance to Wordsworthian autobiography in "The Emergence of the Autobiographical Figure."

11. Jerome McGann distinguishes "four clear layers of development" by the time of the 1817 text, which form successive layers of interpretation: "(a) an original mariner's tale; (b) the ballad narrative of that story; (c) the editorial gloss added when the ballad was, we are to suppose, first printed; and (d) Coleridge's own point of view on his invented materials" ("The Meaning of the Ancient Mariner" 221). On the poem's interpretive layering, see also Martin Wallen, "Return and Representation"; Frances Ferguson, "Coleridge and the Deluded Reader"; and Homer Brown, "The Art of Theology" (esp. 254–55 on the double repetition of the usurping crime and its narrative in the Mariner's retelling).

12. As Nancy Easterlin points out, the Romantic experience of conversion is itself problematic because "there is nothing definite to be converted to" (*Wordsworth and the Question of "Romantic Religion"* 40).

13. Michael Macovski's analysis of Coleridge's "agonistic" dialogue provides further evidence for why the *Rime* lacks the completion of a Christian conversion narrative. He points out that the Mariner's "failed confession" to the Hermit sets up a strangely nonreciprocal dialogue, characterized by the Guest's misinterpretations and the Mariner's nonexplanations, that depends on "what is 'noumenal,' 'hidden,' and 'secret'" remaining that way: Coleridge "recognizes that, in order

to effect such dialogue, his interlocutors must continue to come up against this noumenal object, that they must remain agons" (*Dialogue and Literature* 73, 96).

14. Although his model differs from Ricoeur's, Altieri sees these two perspectives as the modern version of Kant's effort to base the fusion of "will and objective substance" on "a bond between mind and the empirical world, and hence between values and facts." The appropriate modern effort is not to correlate fact and value, but instead "to correlate two basic dispositions, the first-person stance that sees itself conferring values or complying in established valuations and the third-person stance that can impersonally assess what such claims involve and work out shareable criteria" (*Subjective Agency* 127).

15. Macovski suggests that "the Mariner's recursive narration" is "*itself a potential origin of 'moral evil'*" (90), according to Coleridge's 1803 definition of evil as stemming from the "imperfect yet existing Volition" of "the *streamy* Nature of Association" (*CN* 1: 1770). Although he does not mention Levinas in this context, Macovski makes the very Levinasian point that the only rescue for this associatively evil narration—a kind of arbitrary narrative freedom—is exposure "to another in the form of dialogue" (91).

16. See Haney, "'Rents and openings in the ideal world'".

Chapter 5: Literary Criticism and Moral Philosophy

1. For a critique of this commonly accepted view of artistic freedom, see Arthur C. Danto, "The Naked Truth." Danto argues for the recognition of the very real cruelty in photographs—such as those of Richard Avedon—that degrade their subjects by manipulating the very different capabilities of the camera and the unaided human eye.

2. "It is true that an intelligible world in which everything would be actual just because it is (both good and) possible—and, along with this world, even freedom, its formal condition—is for us a transcendent concept that is inadequate for a constitutive principle for determining an object and its objective reality. Yet [the concept of] freedom serves us as a universal *regulative* principle because of the (in part sensible) character of our nature and ability" (*Critique of Judgment* 287).

3. See, for example, Coleridge's statement, following Schelling and other post-Kantian idealists, that "In spite therefore of his own declarations, I could never believe, it was possible for him to have meant no more by his *Noumenon,* or THING IN ITSELF, than his mere words express" (*BL* 1: 155). The famous definition of "Imagination" as "a repetition in the finite mind of the eternal act of creation in the infinite I AM" (1: 304), as well as the "tautegorical" definition of the symbol as implying a continuity between divine and human concepts (*LS* 30) assert a continuity between the realms Kant divided.

4. As Burwick points out, the chief difference between Coleridge and Schlegel, despite Coleridge's many borrowings in the lectures of 1811–12 and after, is Coleridge's insistence on the active participation of the will both in Shakespeare's act of "imitation" and in "the spectator's act of will in accepting the illusion" (*Illusion and the Drama* 210).

5. An example of such "dissociation" might be Carlson's effort to demystify Coleridge's dramatic theory as symptomatic of his gendered and historical situation, in the argument that Coleridge's mature theatrical theory and practice (especially in *Remorse*) is a compensatory expression of "remorse over his revolutionary past" that "allows him to relive and relieve that past" (*In the Theatre of Romanticism* 209). Carlson's claim tells us a good deal about the possible psychological genesis of Coleridge's theory, but at the same time denies the positive knowledge-value of Coleridge's aesthetic "testimony" by reducing it to the context of psychological history.

6. A discrediting Gadamer sees Romanticism as attempting: see *TM* 272–77, 280–91.

7. An assumption held by followers of Descartes, but that was of course discredited by the skeptical tradition of the English Enlightenment. As in his characterization of Romanticism,

Gadamer's sweeping statements fail to do justice to the complex considerations of the necessity of prejudice in eighteenth century English thought. For a Gadamerian reading of this English tradition see Joel Weinsheimer, *Eighteenth-Century Hermeneutics*.

8. Some extreme forms of postmodern ethical thought provide a good example of this potential for destruction in reflection. If, as might be argued is the case with Lyotard, reflection leads us to a position of ontological relativism, and then we invoke the abstract formula of the is/ought transition, the absence at the heart of the "is" leads to an ethical "ought" that can only be expressed in relativistic terms such as the "differend," which is a very "thin" piece of ethical knowledge that destroys "thicker" forms of ethical knowledge, such as how individual and communities in fact interact in ways that cannot be accounted for within a monolithic paradigm of incommensurability.

9. See also *CN* 4: 5421.

10. Building on the "theatricality" of the French Revolution and associating Romantic "antitheatricality" with Burkean conservatism, Carlson casts the "commanding genius" of the male Romantic in "a role that sympathizes with male but not female criminality and that pits theater against poetry" ("Remorse for Jacobin Youth" 131) by promoting a "drama of self-divided men" (*In the Theatre of Romanticism* 211) that prefers quiescent imaginative life to theatrical revolutionary activity.

11. Gadamer may not be fair to Schleiermacher here, as Shaffer points out ("The Hermeneutic Community" 202). Gadamer's critique of Schleiermacher resembles the new-historicist critique of Coleridge: in both cases Romanticism is seen as substituting an ahistorical, subjectively-oriented aesthetic concept of understanding for a more authentically historical concept of understanding. Ellison astutely comments that Gadamer's critique of Schleiermacher masks Gadamer's own Romantic impulses: "Gadamer's failure to remember the complex impulses which produced Schleiermacher's hermeneutic formula dooms him to repeat the gestures he wishes to avoid" (*Delicate Subjects* 93).

12. The *Collected Coleridge* prints "from," not "form" without comment, but it must be a slip for "form," as the passage would not make sense otherwise.

13. As Burwick points out, Coleridge exploits this principle in *Remorse* when, in the climactic scene in the third act, Teresa, the intended victim of Ordonio's attempted "delusion," rejects this "staged" trickery even as Coleridge exploits the spectacle "that many in the audience had paid their money to see" (*Illusion and the Drama* 268).

14. See, for example, William Galperin's *The Return of the Visible*. Although Galperin reads the visible in this way, he rightly sees Coleridge as "more willing—even driven in a way—to accommodate" the visible than, for example, Charles Lamb (160).

15. On the role of spectacle in late eighteenth-century theater, particularly in reference to "the stereotypes and nervous prejudices against the masses" (220), see Backscheider, *Spectacular Politics*, 220–33.

16. See Haney, "'Rents and openings in the ideal world'," from which some of the following discussion is adapted.

17. See Charles Taylor's discussion of the ethical implications of this aestheticization of ethics in *The Ethics of Authenticity* 64–66.

18. I discuss the role of "interest" and "disinterest" in the relation between aesthetics and ethics in Wordsworth, with attention to the question of how genres are "interested," in "Poetry as Super-Genre."

19. For other histories of the complex connections among feeling, thought and aesthetics, see Eagleton, *The Ideology of the Aesthetic* 31–66 and Taylor, *Sources of the Self* 371–74.

20. See Tilottama Rajan's discussion of Coleridge's vacillation between authorial and readerly authority in *The Supplement of Reading* 101–35.

21. That this Coleridgean principle is still at work can be seen in the appeal of Thomas Harris's novel and Jonathan Demme's film, *The Silence of the Lambs*, in which both the audience and

FBI investigator Clarice Starling are torn between horror at Hannibal Lecter's complete amorality and the seductiveness of his intellectual power and psychological insight.

22. This may be the sort of process that Rajan analyzes in Kristevan psychoanalytic terms as the "introjection" of what she calls the "textual abject" in Coleridge. The "abject" is "that which does not fit, and therefore produces a sense of disease in the Kantian or Cartesian subject." While the "normal" course is to expel the abject, the melancholic or Coleridgean approach is to "introject" it textually: "the speaker submerges in some trauma or affect from which he will not separate by constructing an objective correlative for it in what Lacan calls the 'symbolic' order" ("Coleridge, Wordsworth, and the Textual Abject" 62).

23. Booth backs off from this position late in his book, suggesting that, as in the case of Rabelais's sexism, there comes a point at which "we have a duty to articulate our differences with whatever others we encounter" (*The Company We Keep* 415). Coleridge would certainly agree, as when he says of Matthew Lewis in his early (1797) review of *The Monk*, "The sufferings he describes are so frightful and intolerable, that we break with abruptness from the delusion, and indignantly suspect the man of a species of brutality, who could find a pleasure in wantonly imagining them" (*SW & F* 1: 59). Even here, however, the ethical objection is at least partly made on imaginative grounds: Lewis's sin is to break the imaginative "delusion" (what Coleridge would later call "illusion," though he will also see the novel as a poor vehicle for authentic illusion; see *Lects 1808–1819* 2: 193).

24. See Burwick's discussion of the anticipatory nature of imagination in poetic faith (*Illusion and the Drama* 215).

25. This kind of reading contrast sharply with the explicitly Hegelian sacrificial sublation called for by Cyrus Hamlin's "hermeneutics of form," developed around a positive reading of Coleridge's hermeneutic practice, by which "all particularity of the self is dissi-pated and a true spiritual subjectivity is achieved" (*Hermeneutics of Form* 198).

26. See *William Wordsworth* 222–34.

27. That the theatrical adoption of roles, particularly by women, is important to an understanding of early nineteenth-century views of theater and gender has been stressed in recent feminist accounts of the period. In *Romantic Theatricality*, for example, Judith Pascoe shows in detail how the "theatrical stance" adopted by many women writers in the early nineteenth century was both "empowering" and dangerous (94), as it provided a liberating medium for women's voices even as it fed the evolving Romantic ethos that pitted "theatrical," feminine "surface" against "natural" male "depth." See also Amy Muse's study of female portrayals of Hamlet in the eighteenth and nineteenth centuries.

28. For an account of Coleridge's evolution toward a concept of willed illusion, and the relationship between Coleridge and Schlegel on this issue, see Burwick, *Illusion and the Drama* 191–229. My discussion of Coleridge's dramatic theory is generally indebted to Burwick's clarification of Coleridge's terms.

29. Percy Shelley radicalizes this notion of the historical contingency of the manners of any given period, which constitute a necessary but secondary "veil" for more permanent truths. He argues in "A Defense of Poetry" that "every epoch, under names more or less specious, has deified its particular errors," so that "a poet considers the vices of his contemporaries as the temporary dress in which his creations must be arrayed and which cover without concealing the eternal proportions of their beauty" (*Shelley's Prose* 282). This contingency applies to the poet himself: he says in his preface to *The Cenci*, "I . . . have sought to avoid the error of making [the characters] actuated by my own conceptions of right or wrong, false or true, thus under a thin veil converting names and actions of the sixteenth century into cold impersonations of my own mind" (*Shelley's Prose* 323).

30. Of course, Coleridge might react to *Natural Born Killers* as he did to *The Monk* (see footnote 23 above). There is for Coleridge a fine line between drama in which the actor "takes us by storm" (*Lects 1808–1819* 1: 429), in which the audience productively suspends disbelief in

characters whose qualities, however different from our own, are still "the natural growth of the human mind" (*BL* 2: 185), and drama in which the "soul" is "stupefied into mere sensations, by a worthless sympathy with our own ordinary sufferings, or an empty curiosity for the surprising" (2: 184-85), which perhaps explains why, despite his objections to the gothic trappings of contemporary drama, his own successful *Remorse* has gothic elements in many ways indistinguishable from such drama. For a subtle argument that Coleridge both utilizes and undercuts popular generic conventions, see Karen Swann, "'Christabel': The Wandering Mother and the Enigma of Form."

31. A cultural condition brilliantly satirized in *South Park: Bigger, Longer and Uncut*. As the audience is aware that this is exactly the kind of film to which parents object, the children sing, on their way to the highly "inappropriate" Terrance and Philip movie, "Off to the movies we will go / Where we learn everything that we know / 'Cause the movies teach us what our parents don't have time to say."

32. For a detailed account of how Coleridge's generic distinctions reflect his own hermeneutic anxieties about poetry, politics, and gender, see Ellison, *Delicate Subjects* 103-213. Although my purpose is different—I am interested in the positive force of Coleridge's thought where Ellison is interested in its psychological and historical genesis from a feminist perspective—the following discussion is indebted to Ellison's insights even more than the specific references suggest.

33. For a thorough feminist analysis of the implications of Coleridge's bias against fiction's femininity, particularly in relation to philosophical prose and biography, see Ellison 185-96.

34. Coleridge is also suspicious of the irony that is so much a part of modern discourse on the novel. He dismisses Scott's juxtaposition of supernatural events and an ironic recognition of their falsehood as an unnecessary anxiety "to let his Readers know, that he himself is far too enlightened not to be assured of the folly & falsehood of all" (*CM* 4: 605).

35. As Altieri points out in his discussion of Charles Taylor's emphasis on narrative, narrative can limit the options for understanding human agency because it forces us "to imagine expression as necessarily a discursive process of self-interpretation" and "we correspondingly blind ourselves to the various ways that second-order investments can become evident within the expressive activity, without requiring our narratives" (*Subjective Agency* 109-10). Even if one does not subscribe to Altieri's "expressivist" theory, this comment clarifies the fact that ethical expression is not inextricably tied to narrative.

36. Wayne Booth, who is squarely within the modern tradition of "novelistic" ethical reading, is nonetheless attuned to the kind of warning Coleridge gives against the seduction of novelistic delusion: the danger of succumbing to, for example, Jane Austen's presentation of Knightley as Emma's means of fulfillment in *Emma*, is that the novel's extended scope causes us to "love heroes and heroines with an intensity and depth of acquaintance that cannot be matched by shorter forms," while at the same time the conventional novel's demand for a romantic happy ending tempts the reader to "succumb morally to what was simply required formally" (*The Company We Keep* 431).

37. See *William Wordsworth* (esp. 36-44, 100-102, 115-17, 138-39); "Poetry and Super-Genre in Wordsworth" (83-86), and "'Rents and openings in the real world'" (188-96).

38. P. Christopher Smith, who is competent to address this issue, sees no discrepancy between the two accounts of aesthetic consciousness in his annotations to "Plato and the Poets" (Gadamer, *Dialogue and Dialectic* 65).

39. One argument against the interpretation of at least English Romanticism as such a retreat can be made in terms of the Romantic use of the ode form. According to Gadamer, Plato's admission of songs of public praise into his ideal Republic as the only appropriate form of poetry represents an antidote to the alienated subjectivity—the "aesthetic consciousness"—of imitative art: "the song of praise in the form of poetic play is shared language, the language of our common concern" (*Dialogue and Dialectic* 66). The closely related and highly public forms of the hymn and the ode were of course central to the Romantic aesthetic—Wordsworth's "Immortality" ode

is the most obvious example—and even if the Romantics made the ode a more "private" discourse, as in the variation on the ode form that became known as the "conversation" poem, a private conversation is still the shared language of conversation. Even one of the most self-consciously "private" of the Romantic odes, Keats's "Ode to Psyche," in which the poet offers to compensate for the absence of a public temple by building one "in some untrodden region of [his] mind" (51), ends by leaving the window open for shared experience, "a casement ope at night / To let the warm Love in" (66-67).

Chapter 6: Oneself as Another: Coleridgean Subjectivity

1. See Paul de Man, "The Rhetoric of Temporality," *Blindness and Insight* 187-98; Thomas McFarland, *Coleridge and the Pantheist Tradition* passim; Raimonda Modiano, *Coleridge and the Concept of Nature* 28-100; Jean-Pierre Mileur, *Vision and Revision* 101-34; Jerome Christensen, *Coleridge's Blessed Machine of Language*, esp. 17-27; Stephen Bygrave, *Coleridge and the Self*, esp. 30-42; Laurence Lockridge, *The Ethics of Romanticism* 147-48; David Vallins, "Production and Existence: Coleridge's Unification of Nature" 109-10; Nigel Leask, *The Politics of Imagination in Coleridge's Thought* 13; Paul Magnuson, *Coleridge and Wordsworth* passim.

2. Louis F. Caton argues that Romanticism in general and Coleridge's speculations on subjectivity and otherness in particular can help provide an antidote to the "rigidly ideological" form that much postcolonial theory has taken, a form in which "the crucial Romantic underpinnings of agency, identity, and reason have been eclipsed" as these philosophical issues are ignored or reduced to the objects of a one-sided ideological critique ("Feeling Romantic" 23).

3. See Taylor, *Sources of the Self* 379-81, 420, 430. An important exception to this trend is Cavell's *In Quest of the Ordinary*, which argues that the interpretation of Romanticism as self-consciousness closes off the more complex question of the relationship between self-consciousness and skepticism (45).

4. See Bernard Williams's analysis of this conflict in "Persons, Character, and Morality" and in *Ethics and the Limits of Philosophy* 114-15. As Donald Wehrs argues, cultural studies scholars are often caught in the bind of wanting to acknowledge the particularity of persons while making universal (and ultimately Eurocentric) claims about personhood, as when African novelists are praised for articulating a "postmodern" view of the person.

5. Harding treats "the recognition of personality, rather than conduct, as the starting point of morality" as one of the main points of Coleridge's account of human relationships (*Coleridge and the Idea of Love* 5). See also 139-44. McFarland sees Coleridge's emphasis on the divine Person in his acceptance of Trinitarianism as analogous to Buber's "conception of God, not as a final 'it,' but as an eternal 'Thou'" (237).

6. As Lockridge points out, "More often than not, 'philosophy' or even 'metaphysics' means moral philosophy for the Romantics" (*The Ethics of Romanticism* 13).

7. For example, Levinas says "*The individual and the personal are necessary for Infinity to be able to be produced as infinite*" (*TI* 218; Levinas's emphasis). See also his discussion of the "incarnate" subject in *OB* 77-81.

8. Norris himself has little patience with "the profoundly conservative implications" of the "ontological priority of linguistic tradition" in Gadamer (*Uncritical Theory* 143).

9. See *TM* 413-18.

10. See also Harding's discussion of Coleridge's other-centered ethics in *Coleridge and the Idea of Love* 121, 144-46, 188-92.

11. See, for example, this note on Fichte's *Die Anweisung zum seeligen Leben* (1806), written between 1815 and 1820: "O woeful Love whose first act and offspring is *Self*? 'I!' and this not a present 'I AM' but a poor *reflection* thereof!—In his better Days F. taught a nobler dogma—viz.

the generation of the I from the Thou in all finite Minds" (*CM* 2: 596). Lectures 12 and 13 of the *Philosophical Lectures* are devoted to the equal and opposite errors of materialism and idealism, by which "'OBJECTIVE' ACQUIRED TWO MEANINGS, THE FIRST BEING THE REALITY OF ANY THING, OUTWARDLY CORRESPONDENT TO OUR PERCEPTION OR NOTION thereof, independent of the perception itself, and the second, meaning the universality of the perception as arising out of inherent laws of human nature" (*P Lects* 373).

12. See Harding's discussion of this passage in *Coleridge and the Idea of Love* 144–45.

13. See Lockridge's discussion of how these and other passages demonstrate that the other-oriented "conscience" becomes "a means of self-definition" rather than, as in Kant, "a divisive faculty of self-incrimination" (*The Ethics of Romanticism* 115).

14. The practical stakes of Coleridge's position are high: he sees the twin errors of idealism and materialism as the results of an extrapolation of Locke's position resulting from his association with a developing commercial society and political freedom: "the same great revolution was to go on in mind that had been going on in state affairs, and . . . as King William had completely done away with all the despotism of the Stuarts, so Mr. Locke had done away altogether with the nonsense of the Schoolmen and the universalists" (*P Lects* 376). Contrary to arguments portraying Coleridge as championing "an idealization of culture severed from history and society" (Leask 13), Coleridge here shows a deep understanding of the relationship between political/economic events and intellectual history, implicitly arguing for a greater cultural self-consciousness about that relationship, *because* of, not in denial of, the ethical and political implications of metaphysical positions.

15. See also this similar comment in the *Philosophical Lectures:* "We believe it, because it is not a mere idea but a fact, that our conscience bids us to do unto others as we would be done by, and in all things to make that a maxim of conduct, which we can conceive without contradiction as being the law of all rational being" (364).

16. On the role of outness in Coleridge's theories of the relationship between mind and nature, see Barfield 59–68. William Macovski connects Coleridge's need for a semiotic outness—the production of symbols that grant a necessary exteriority—to dialogue: "When he addresses a dialogic presence . . . Coleridge focuses on a 'system of symbols' that renders his inmost thoughts 'visual' to the other. The dialogic address allows him to express these thoughts externally, to turn his mind outward, as he would have to do if he were actually communicating with another" (83).

17. Pierre Mileur makes a related point, seeing the Coleridgean symbol as "a revision of poetic practice" by which "[t]his objectivity and discipline of otherness which it implies intercepts desire and reassures us of the role of truth in the poetic act" (*Vision and Revision* 22).

18. For other instances of the distinction between "worth" and "value," see *AR* 6, *Friend* 2: 350–51, *EOT* 2: 320, *LS* 74, 189, 211, and *C & S* 168.

19. For somewhat different reasons, Ricoeur also sees morality as a restrictive concept that needs the larger context of an ethical orientation, though he sees this sense of morality as necessary, while Williams sees it as expendable. See *Oneself* 203–39.

20. For other disparaging comments about Smith's economic theory, see *TT* 1: 383, 490; *EOT* 2: 346, *CN* 3: 3565, 3590.

21. On the reception of *The Theory of Moral Sentiments* in England and on the Continent, see the editor's introduction, 25–34.

22. The question of the consistency between Smith's views in *The Theory of Moral Sentiments* and in *The Wealth of Nations* has long been debated as "the Adam Smith problem." See the editor's introduction to *The Theory of Moral Sentiments* 20–25 for a survey of the debate and an argument for reconciling the views presented in the two works.

23. As Ordonio begins to feel (and tries to hide) the effects of remorse in *Remorse,* he describes himself in similar terms as a child "that too abruptly / Roused by a glare of light from deepest sleep / Starts up bewildered and talks idly" (3.2.144–46)

24. Coleridge does, however, take responsibility for his own failings as a lecturer (*Lects 1808-1819* 1:64-65).

25. Anthony Harding suggests that in his late notebooks Coleridge connects the imagination to intimations in the pre-Mosaic patriarchal culture—obviously heretical in both Jewish and Christian traditions—"that good and evil have a common and primordial origin in the division of light and darkness" ("Imagination, Patriarchy, and Evil" 19).

26. In a comment on Fichte, Coleridge expresses his antipathy to generalizing on matters of subjectivity: "Mem. to state the use and utility of generalizing, or making some one name the representative of a group—& thence to shew its inapplicability & uselessness to inward & indescribable experiences, except insofar as nature herself has generalized them for us" (*CM* 2:639).

27. On the difficulty of prayer, see also *CN* 3:4183 and Barth, *Coleridge and Christian Doctrine* 183.

28. On the development of Coleridge's attitudes toward the doctrine of atonement, see Wendling, *Coleridge's Progress to Christianity* 103, 112, 196.

29. In one of Coleridge's accounts of how the poem might have ended, Geraldine takes her parody of sustaining others one step further, impersonating the lover directly. Christabel feels an inexplicable aversion to the false knight; Geraldine's presence as the faux lover makes him even more absent, *qua* lover, than before. (Gillman 301-2).

30. See also this marginal note from Feb. 27, 1817: "Schelling makes separati[on] in God—and not distinction only" (*CM* 4:366)

31. See also *CN* 4:5256.

32. Barth lists other examples between 1830 and 1834 in *Coleridge and Christian Doctrine* 94n.

33. For a full explication of Coleridge's relation to Schelling on this issue, see Modiano 168-73 and Perkins 163-68.

34. For similar statements of the priority of the absolute to polarity, see *CN* 4:4538, *SW & F* 783-85, *AR* 168.

35. Coleridge's discussion of these two versions of the Hebrew God reflects the tension Ricoeur sees in the Hebrew prophetic tradition between "the absolute, but formless, demand, and the finite law, which breaks the demand into crumbs," a tension "essential to the consciousness of sin: one cannot just feel oneself guilty in general" (*The Symbolism of Evil* 59).

36. Elsewhere in *The Friend* Coleridge is careful to give this command an appropriately Protestant inwardness to distinguish it from the legalism of ethical systems such as Paley's. Paley's consequentialist doctrine "draws away the attention from the *will*, that is, from the inward motives and impulses which constitute the essence of *morality*, to the outward act: and thus changes the virtue commanded by the gospel into the mere legality, which was to be enlivened by it" (1:314). "Law" is also subordinated to "Idea" in some contexts, as noted in Chapter 2.

37. See Simon Critchley's discussion of Derrida, Levinas, and unconditionality, with specific reference to this passage from *Limited Inc*, in *The Ethics of Deconstruction* 32-44. Lyotard also uses the Kantian notion of law as a means of articulating ethical obligation in *Peregrinations* 35-36.

38. See Perkins 31-32. For other explanations of the influence of Jewish thought on Coleridge, see Perkins 17, 30-32, 62-63. In Coleridge's work, see, for example, the "Rabbinical Tales" of *The Friend*, Essay IV (1:370-73), which begin with Schelling's complaint about contemporary neglect of Hebrew sources. That these are specifically moral tales suggests the depth of Coleridge's interest in Judaic ethics.

39. See Perkins 65, 245-47, 285 for a discussion of this issue.

40. Ian Balfour describes the prophetic tradition inherited by the Romantics as a tradition in which "the immediacy of prophetic revelation" occurs only "in the mediated mode of citation" (124-25). A connection between Romantic poetry, particularly Wordsworth, and the Hebrew

prophetic tradition has often been noted by Geoffrey Hartman, in essays such as "The Poetics of Prophecy."

41. On this point, see Lockridge, *Coleridge the Moralist* 65.

42. As Robert Penn Warren notes, Coleridge's notion of evil as "the will in abstraction" helps to explain the nature of the Mariner's sin in shooting the albatross: it is evil *because* it is motiveless (228), or, as Lockridge puts it, the Mariner "attempts to establish a base in what is baseless, his own will" (*Coleridge the Moralist* 70)

43. On the instability of the narrator's response to the Hermit's question, see Wallen, "Return and Representation" 148–49.

Chapter 7: Love, Otherness, and the Absolute Self

1. See Modiano 67–76, Lockridge, *Coleridge the Moralist* 187–89, and Wendling, *Coleridge's Progress to Christianity* 146. On the ethical primacy of love in Coleridge, see also Harding, *Coleridge and the Idea of Love* and Barth, *Coleridge and the Power of Love*.

2. This "equality" before a third party is the relation that Levinas later, in an important revision (at least in emphasis) of his earlier views, puts under the heading of "justice." In *Otherwise than Being*, "justice" is more sharply differentiated from the asymmetry of the ethical encounter than in the earlier *Totality and Infinity*, as I will discuss below.

3. See, for example, Kant's critique of moral "feeling" in *Groundwork of the Metaphysic of Morals* 110.

4. See Tillich's discussion of this synthesis in *A History of Christian Thought* 115–16, and Augustine's discussion of good and bad love in *City of God* Book 14, section 7 (4: 287–93). On Coleridge's relationship to the Augustinian tradition, see Barth, *Coleridge and the Power of Love* 19–21.

5. Irving Massey similarly acknowledges the antiethical force of desire while granting a strong, if provisional and ambivalent ethical force to sexual and familial love: "If it is desire that helps to undermine the categories of the ethical, any moment of harmony in the relation between the sexes will tend to the restoration of those categories and of the social order" (185). On the relationship between love and sensuality in Coleridge, see Wendling, *Coleridge's Progress to Christianity* 148–49.

6. This distinction also informs Coleridge's qualified praise of Wordsworth as having "the sympathy indeed of a contemplator, rather than a fellow-sufferer or co-mate" (*BL* 2: 150).

7. I discuss this historical difference in terms of Wordsworth's relation to the tradition of sentiment in "Wordsworth and Levinas."

8. See Harding's discussion of this passage in *Coleridge and the Idea of Love* 129–30. See also Coleridge's comment in an 1811 lecture on *Romeo and Juliet* that "love was an act of the will," as opposed to what he saw as "the sickly nonsense of Sterne and his imitators, French and English, who maintained that it was an involuntary emotion" (*Lects 1808–1819* 1: 338).

9. Like Coleridge, Ricoeur also defines the phenomenological experience of otherness in terms of passivity and activity, as "the variety of experiences of passivity, intertwined in multiple ways in human action" (*Oneself* 318).

10. The mother-child relationship is Coleridge's best example of love, according to this 1826 note: "what *is* Love? I answer—Ask the Mother!" (*CN* 4: 5463).

11. See also the 1796 sonnet on his son Hartley beginning "Charles! my slow heart was only sad, when first / I scann'd that face of feeble infancy," in which what the poet calls a "dark remembrance and presageful fear" (10) regarding "[a]ll I had been, and all my child might be" (4) is dispelled only by the mother-child reciprocity: "So for the mother's sake the child was dear, / And dearer was the mother for the child" (13–14).

12. See Modiano's discussion of this issue (79–81).

13. I discuss this issue in *William Wordsworth*, esp. 76–102.

14. That "outness" is intimately connected to the alienation of the self is suggested by Peter Hühn, who in "Outwitting Self-consciousness" argues that "Kubla Khan" enacts a process of "*self-alienation* and *self-externalization*" (237). Hühn emphasizes this as an aesthetic strategy rather than an ethical dilemma, but the process is similar.

15. This undated note from the Gutch notebook that Coleridge used between 1795 and 1800 implies a Unitarian attitude toward prayer that he would later revise, but although that revision changed the context of "self-annihilation," the concept itself remained important.

16. Coleridge makes similar comparisons to Lake District landscapes throughout his journey: see, for example, *CL* 2: 1126 and *CN* 2: 2029. Kathleen Coburn traces his identification with the Mariner in her notes to entries 2078, 2086, 2090, 2557, and 2610 in volume 2 of *CN*.

17. Though both Kathleen Coburn (in her note to *CN* 2: 2070) and Donald Sultana (129) see these comments as applying primarily to the ship's bilge-water, the context clearly mingles bilge-water and vomit. For example, since "hepatic Gas" comes from the liver, it is clear that Coleridge has his own as well as the ship's effluence in mind. The connection is made even closer by the fact that "belly" and "bilge" are etymologically related, according to the *Oxford English Dictionary*. Both "belly" and "bulge," the original form of "bilge," come from words meaning "bag." Coleridge himself is quoted in the OED as using "bulge" for the verb form of "bilge," in the sense of damaging a ship's bilge (see entry 2 under the verb "bulge").

18. Identified by Donald Sultana on the authority of one of Coleridge's letters as "a half-pay lieutenant turned small merchant, whose yellow-purple face betrayed that half his liver was gone or going" (116).

19. Described in *CL* 2: 844.

20. Coleridge appears to be thinking of Milton's celestial hymn to God the Father, the "[f]ountain of light" who is himself "invisible" and "[t]hroned inaccessible" to even angelic eyes, but who becomes visible (albeit "dark with excessive bright") only "through a cloud / Drawn round about [him]" (*Paradise Lost* 3: 375–80)

21. In chapter 12 of *Biographia Literaria*, when Coleridge still accepted Schelling's notion of a polarity at the heart of the concept of God, the term "absolute self" is equated with "the great eternal I AM" (1: 275). In opposition to Fichte, Coleridge sharply distinguishes the absolute self from divinity itself, stating the relation thus, commenting on Fichte, *Grundlage der Wissenschaftslehre:* "Im absolute~~m~~n Ich erkennt man Gott—nicht—im Gotte erkennt man das absolute Ich" [In the absolute I one recognizes God—no—in God one recognizes the absolute I] (*CM* 2: 623).

22. Wordsworth expresses a similar insight in the "Prospectus" to the *Recluse*, first published as part of the Preface to the *Excursion*, although for him the absolute self is generalized to the individual and collective "mind." In a passage that Blake found comparable to Solomon's apostacy (Blake 666), the poet claims to be able to "pass . . . unalarmed" the traditional sources of personified awe and terror in both the Hebraic and the Greek traditions— "All strength—all terror, single or in bands, / That ever was put forth in personal form"—including Jehovah, Chaos, and Erebus, but none of this "can breed such fear and awe / As fall upon us when we look / Into our Minds, into the Mind of Man" (31–40). This is of course the fear of the autonomous imagination that Hartman analyzes in *Wordsworth's Poetry*.

23. Gadamer acknowledges the theological origins of this historical-hermeneutic notion of the necessary incompleteness of self-understanding: "The statement 'I don't understand myself' expresses a primal religious experience within Christianity. Indeed, human life is a matter of the continuity of one's self-understanding, but this continuity consists in constantly putting oneself into question and a constant being-other" ("Hermeneutics and Logocentrism" 119).

24. It can be argued, as Mileur has done, that this annihilation of the self is something of a Coleridgean sleight-of-hand—"it is by creating an absence of self that Coleridge is able to posit

imagination as that which unifies the discrete faculties into 'self'" (*Vision and Revision* 156)—that in fact avoids the problems faced by Ricoeur's analysis. Mileur notes (in his discussion of the *Rime*) Coleridge's "inability to accept the fundamental strangeness of self to itself" (73), suggesting that Coleridge in fact avoids the implications of the continuous presence of the self-as-other that Ricoeur discusses.

25. See Bygrave, *Coleridge and the Self*, for an extended discussion of Coleridge's vacillation between egotistical (Miltonic) and protean (Shakespearean) notions of the self.

26. A similar point is made in the fragment on "Self-Love, Fame, and Reputation," probably from 1808: "Strange & generous Self, that can only be such a Self, by a compleat divesting of all that men call Self, of all that can make it either practically to others, or consciously to the Being himself, different from the Human Race in its Ideal. Such Self is but a perpetual Religion, an inalienable acknowledgement of God, the Sole Basis & Ground of Being—In this sense, how can I love God & not love my self, as far as it is God" (*SW & F* 215–16).

27. This also raises the question, for Levinas, of whether, even in his philosophy of otherness, which certainly encourages diversity, self-annihilation does not in fact necessarily also annihilate the diversity among selves.

28. Hence his preference for Kant's proof of free will over Schelling's. Kant separated the determined realm of the phenomenal from the free realm of the noumenal, "demonstrating that Time and Space were Laws of the former only . . . and irrelative to the latter, to which Class the Will must belong" (*CM* 4:436).

29. This combination of difference and interdependence in the relation between the one-to-one realm of ethics and the political realm of justice is tied up with Levinas's controversial defense of Zionism: "I think there's a direct contradiction between ethics and politics, if both these demands are taken to the extreme," he says in an interview, but "[i]t's a contradiction that is usually an abstract problem," and for him "[t]he Zionist idea . . . is nevertheless a political idea which has an ethical justification" ("Ethics and Politics" 292).

Works Cited

Abrams, M. H. "Coleridge and the Romantic Vision of the World." In *Coleridge's Variety: Bicentenary Studies*, edited by John Beer, 101–33. Pittsburgh: University of Pittsburgh Press, 1975.

———. *Natural Supernaturalism: Tradition and Revolution in Romantic Literature*. New York: W. W. Norton, 1971.

Altieri, Charles. *Canons and Consequences: Reflections on the Ethical Force of Imaginative Ideals*. Evanston, Ill.: Northwestern University Press, 1990.

———. *Subjective Agency: A Theory of First-person Expressivity and its Social Implications*. Cambridge, Mass.: Blackwell, 1994.

———. "The Values of Articulation: Aesthetics After the Aesthetic Ideology." In *Beyond Representation: Philosophy and Poetic Imagination*, edited by Richard Eldridge, 66–68. Cambridge Studies in Philosophy and the Arts. New York: Cambridge University Press, 1996.

Ameriks, Karl, and Dieter Sturma. Introduction to *The Modern Subject: Conceptions of the Self in Classical German Philosophy*, edited by Ameriks and Sturma, 1–9. SUNY Series in Contemporary Continental Philosophy. Albany: State University of New York Press, 1995.

Anscombe, G. E. M. "Modern Moral Philosophy." In *The Is-Ought Question: A Collection of Papers on the Central Problem in Moral Philosophy*, edited by W. D. Hudson, 175–95. New York: Macmillan, 1969.

The Arabian Nights Entertainments: A New Translation. Translated by Edward Forster from a French edition translated by Antoine Galland. 4 vols. New York: David Huntington, 1815.

Aristotle. *Nicomachean Ethics*. Translated by Terence Irwin. Indianapolis: Hackett Publishing Co., 1985.

Arnold, Matthew. "Wordsworth." In *Poetry and Criticism of Matthew Arnold*, edited by A. Dwight Culler, 331–46. Boston: Houghton Mifflin, 1961.

Augustine, Saint. *City of God*. Translated by Philip Levine. 7 vols. Loeb Classical Library. Cambridge, Mass.: Harvard University Press, 1966.

Aylesworth, Gary E. "Dialogue, Text, Narrative: Confronting Gadamer and Ricoeur." In *Gadamer and Hermeneutics*, edited by Hugh J. Silverman, 63–81. Continental Philosophy 4. New York: Routledge, 1991.

Backscheider, Paula A. *Spectacular Politics*. Baltimore: The Johns Hopkins University Press, 1993.

Baird, William. *History of New Testament Research*. Minneapolis: Fortress Press, 1992.

Balfour, Ian. "The Future of Citation: Blake, Wordsworth, and the Rhetoric of Romantic Prophecy." In *Writing the Future*, edited by David Wood, 115–28. Warwick Studies in Philosophy and Literature. New York: Routledge, 1990.

Barfield, Owen. *What Coleridge Thought*. Middletown, Conn.: Wesleyan University Press, 1971.

Barth, Robert, S. J. *Coleridge and the Power of Love*. Columbia: University of Missouri Press, 1988.

———. *Coleridge and Christian Doctrine*. Cambridge, Mass.: Harvard University Press, 1969.

Bate, Jonathan. *Romantic Ecology: Wordsworth and the Environmental Tradition*. New York: Routledge, 1991.

Benjamin, Walter. "The Work of Art in the Age of Mechanical Reproduction." In *Illuminations*. Translated by Harry Zohn, 217–51. New York: Schocken Books, 1969.

Benveniste, Émile. *Problems in General Linguistics*. Translated by Mary Elizabeth Meek. Coral Gables: University of Miami Press, 1971.

Bernasconi, Robert. "'Failure of Communication' as a Surplus: Dialogue and Lack of Dialogue Between Buber and Levinas." In *The Provocation of Levinas: Rethinking the Other*, edited by Robert Bernasconi and David Wood, 100–135. New York: Routledge, 1988.

Bernstein, J. M. *The Fate of Art: Aesthetic Alienation from Kant to Derrida and Adorno*. Literature and Philosopy. University Park: The Pennsylvania State University Press, 1992.

Bernstein, Richard J. "From Hermeneutics to Praxis." In *Hermeneutics and Praxis*, edited by Robert Hollinger, 272–96. Revisions: A Series of Books on Ethics. Notre Dame: University of Notre Dame Press, 1985.

Blake, William. *The Complete Poetry and Prose of William Blake*. Edited by David Erdman. Newly Rev. ed. New York: Anchor, 1988.

Booth, Wayne C. *The Company We Keep: An Ethics of Fiction*. Berkeley and Los Angeles: University of California Press, 1988.

———. *Modern Dogma and the Rhetoric of Assent*. Chicago: University of Chicago Press, 1974.

Bourke, Richard. *Romantic Discourse and Political Modernity: Wordsworth, the Intellectual and Cultural Critique*. New York: St. Martin's Press, 1993.

Bretzius, Stephen. "Dr. Jacques L. and Martin Hide-a Guerre: The Subject of New Historicism." *Diacritics* 27, 1 (spring 1997): 73–90.

Brown, Homer Obed. "The Art of Theology and the Theology of Art: Robert Penn Warren's Reading of Coleridge's *The Rime of the Ancient Mariner*." In *The Question of Textuality: Strategies of Reading in Contemporary American Criticism*, edited by William V. Spanos et al., 237–60. Bloomington: Indiana University Press, 1982.

Browning, Elizabeth Barrett. *Aurora Leigh*. Edited by Margaret Reynolds. Norton Critical Editions. New York: W. W. Norton, 1996.

Bruns, Gerald. *Hermeneutics Ancient and Modern*. New Haven: Yale University Press, 1992.

———. "The Remembrance of Language: An Introduction to Gadamer's Poetics." Introduction to *Gadamer on Celan: "Who Am I and Who Are You" and Other Essays*, 1-51. State University of New York Press, 1997.

Burke, Edmund. *A Philosophical Enquiry into the Origin of our Ideas of the Sublime and Beautiful*. 1757. Edited by Adam Phillips. New York: Oxford University Press, 1990.

———. *Reflections on the Revolution in France*. 1790. Edited by Thomas H. D. Mahoney. The Library of Liberal Arts. New York: Bobbs-Merrill, 1955.

Burwick, Frederick. *Illusion and the Drama: Critical Theory of the Enlightenment and Romantic Era*. University Park: The Pennsylvania State University Press, 1991.

Bygrave, Stephen. *Coleridge and the Self: Romantic Egoism*. London: Macmillan Press, 1986.

Carlson, Julie. "Remorse for Jacobin Youth." *The Wordsworth Circle* 24 (summer 1993): 130-33.

———. *In the Theatre of Romanticism: Coleridge, Nationalism, Women*. New York: Cambridge University Press, 1994.

———. "Command Performances: Burke, Coleridge, and Schiller's Dramatic Reflections on the Revolution in France." *The Wordsworth Circle* 23 (spring 1992): 117-34.

Carlyle, Thomas. "Signs of the Times." 1829. *Critical and Miscellaneous Essays*, 56-82 (page citations are to the reprint edition). Vol. 2. London: Chapman and Hall, 1899. Reprint. 5 vols. New York: AMS Press, 1980.

Cascardi, Anthony J. Introduction to *Literature and the Question of Philosophy*, edited by Cascardi, ix-xvii. Baltimore: The Johns Hopkins University Press, 1987.

Caton, Louis F. "Feeling Romantic, Thinking Postmodern: Notes on Postcolonial Identity." *Post Identity* 2 (1999): 22-44.

Cavell, Stanley. *In Quest of the Ordinary: Lines of Skepticism and Romanticism*. Chicago: University of Chicago Press, 1988.

Chandler, James K. *England in 1819: The Politics of Literary Culture and the Case of Romantic Historicism*. Chicago: University of Chicago Press, 1998.

———. *Wordsworth's Second Nature: A Study of the Poetry and Politics*. Chicago: University of Chicago Press, 1984.

Christensen, Jerome. "The Romantic Movement at the End of History." *Critical Inquiry* 20 (spring 1994): 453-76.

———. *Coleridge's Blessed Machine of Language*. Ithaca: Cornell University Press, 1981.

Coburn, Kathleen. "Coleridge: A Bridge Between Science and Poetry." In *Coleridge's Variety*, edited by John Beer, 81-100. New York: MacMillan, 1974.

Coleridge, Samuel Taylor. *Aids to Reflection*. Edited by John Beer. Vol. 9 of *The Collected Works of Samuel Taylor Coleridge*. Bollingen Series 75. Princeton: Princeton University Press, 1993.

———. *Biographia Literaria*. Edited by James Engell and W. Jackson Bate. 2 vols. Vol. 7 of *The Collected Works of Samuel Taylor Coleridge*. Bollingen Series 75. Princeton: Princeton University Press, 1983.

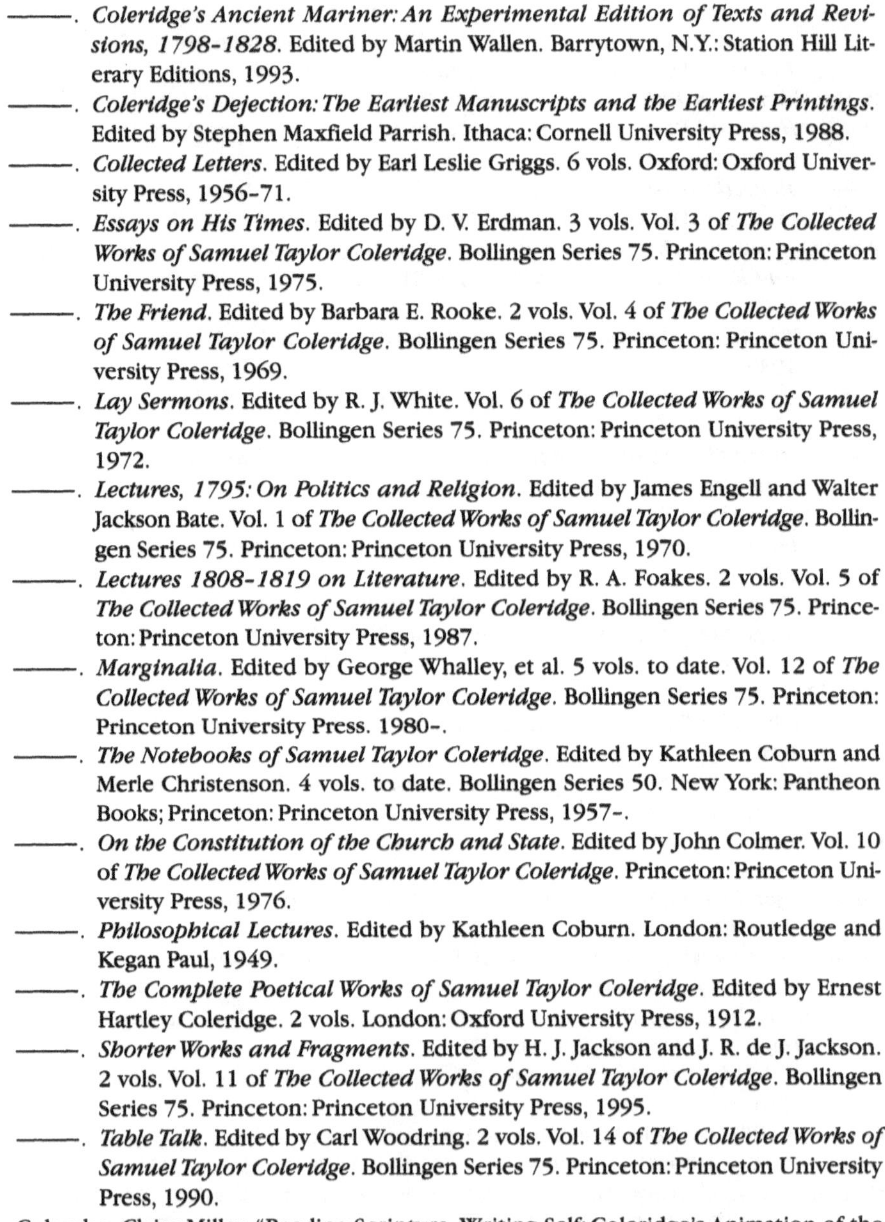

———. *Coleridge's Ancient Mariner: An Experimental Edition of Texts and Revisions, 1798–1828*. Edited by Martin Wallen. Barrytown, N.Y.: Station Hill Literary Editions, 1993.

———. *Coleridge's Dejection: The Earliest Manuscripts and the Earliest Printings*. Edited by Stephen Maxfield Parrish. Ithaca: Cornell University Press, 1988.

———. *Collected Letters*. Edited by Earl Leslie Griggs. 6 vols. Oxford: Oxford University Press, 1956–71.

———. *Essays on His Times*. Edited by D. V. Erdman. 3 vols. Vol. 3 of *The Collected Works of Samuel Taylor Coleridge*. Bollingen Series 75. Princeton: Princeton University Press, 1975.

———. *The Friend*. Edited by Barbara E. Rooke. 2 vols. Vol. 4 of *The Collected Works of Samuel Taylor Coleridge*. Bollingen Series 75. Princeton: Princeton University Press, 1969.

———. *Lay Sermons*. Edited by R. J. White. Vol. 6 of *The Collected Works of Samuel Taylor Coleridge*. Bollingen Series 75. Princeton: Princeton University Press, 1972.

———. *Lectures, 1795: On Politics and Religion*. Edited by James Engell and Walter Jackson Bate. Vol. 1 of *The Collected Works of Samuel Taylor Coleridge*. Bollingen Series 75. Princeton: Princeton University Press, 1970.

———. *Lectures 1808–1819 on Literature*. Edited by R. A. Foakes. 2 vols. Vol. 5 of *The Collected Works of Samuel Taylor Coleridge*. Bollingen Series 75. Princeton: Princeton University Press, 1987.

———. *Marginalia*. Edited by George Whalley, et al. 5 vols. to date. Vol. 12 of *The Collected Works of Samuel Taylor Coleridge*. Bollingen Series 75. Princeton: Princeton University Press. 1980–.

———. *The Notebooks of Samuel Taylor Coleridge*. Edited by Kathleen Coburn and Merle Christenson. 4 vols. to date. Bollingen Series 50. New York: Pantheon Books; Princeton: Princeton University Press, 1957–.

———. *On the Constitution of the Church and State*. Edited by John Colmer. Vol. 10 of *The Collected Works of Samuel Taylor Coleridge*. Princeton: Princeton University Press, 1976.

———. *Philosophical Lectures*. Edited by Kathleen Coburn. London: Routledge and Kegan Paul, 1949.

———. *The Complete Poetical Works of Samuel Taylor Coleridge*. Edited by Ernest Hartley Coleridge. 2 vols. London: Oxford University Press, 1912.

———. *Shorter Works and Fragments*. Edited by H. J. Jackson and J. R. de J. Jackson. 2 vols. Vol. 11 of *The Collected Works of Samuel Taylor Coleridge*. Bollingen Series 75. Princeton: Princeton University Press, 1995.

———. *Table Talk*. Edited by Carl Woodring. 2 vols. Vol. 14 of *The Collected Works of Samuel Taylor Coleridge*. Bollingen Series 75. Princeton: Princeton University Press, 1990.

Colombo, Claire Miller. "Reading Scripture, Writing Self: Coleridge's Animation of the 'Dead Letter.'" *Studies in Romanticism* 35 (spring 1996): 27–53.

Connolly, John M. and Thomas Keutner, trans. and ed. *Hermeneutics Versus Science? Three German Views*. Notre Dame: Notre Dame University Press, 1988.

Critchley, Simon. *The Ethics of Deconstruction: Derrida and Levinas*. Oxford: Blackwell, 1992.

Crusius, Timothy W. *A Teacher's Introduction to Philosophical Hermeneutics*. NCTE Teacher's Introduction Series. Urbana, Ill.: National Council of Teachers of English, 1991.

Curran, Stuart. "The I Altered." *Romanticism and Feminism*. Edited by Anne K. Mellor, 185–207. Bloomington: Indiana University Press, 1988.

Dallmayr, Fred. *Beyond Orientalism: Essays on Cross-Cultural Encounter*. Albany: State University of New York Press, 1996.

———. *Critical Encounters: Between Philosophy and Politics*. Notre Dame: University of Notre Dame Press, 1987.

Danto, Arthur C. "The Naked Truth." In *Aesthetics and Ethics: Essays at the Intersection*, edited by Jerrold Levinson, 257–82. Cambridge Studies in Philosophy and the Arts. Cambridge: Cambridge University Press, 1998.

De Man, Paul. *Blindness and Insight*. 2d ed. Theory and History of Literature 7. Minneapolis: University of Minnesota Press, 1983.

———. *Romanticism and Contemporary Criticism: The Gauss Seminar and Other Papers*. Edited by E. S. Burt, et al. Baltimore: The Johns Hopkins University Press, 1993.

Deleuze, Gilles, and Félix Guattari. *Anti-Oedipus: Capitalism and Schizophrenia*. Translated by Robert Hurley, et al. Minneapolis: University of Minnesota Press, 1983.

Derrida, Jacques. *Limited Inc*. Translated by Samuel Weber, et al. Evanston, Ill.: Northwestern University Press, 1988.

———. *"Speech and Phenomena" and Other Essays on Husserl's Theory of Signs*. Translated by David B. Allison. Northwestern University Studies in Phenomenology and Existential Philosophy. Evanston, Ill.: Northwestern University Press, 1973.

———. *Writing and Difference*. Translated by Alan Bass. Chicago: University of Chicago Press, 1978.

Eaglestone, Robert. *Ethical Criticism: Reading After Levinas*. Edinburgh: Edinburgh University Press, 1997.

Eagleton, Terry. *The Ideology of the Aesthetic*. Cambridge, Mass.: Blackwell, 1990.

———. *Literary Theory: An Introduction*. Minneapolis: University of Minnesota Press, 1983.

Easterlin, Nancy. *Wordsworth and the Question of "Romantic Religion."* Lewisburg, Pa.: Bucknell University Press; London: Associated University Presses, 1996.

Eilenberg, Susan. *Strange Power of Speech: Wordsworth, Coleridge, and Literary Possession*. New York: Oxford University Press, 1992.

Ellison, Julie. *Delicate Subjects: Romanticism, Gender, and the Ethics of Understanding*. Ithaca: Cornell University Press, 1990.

Fackenheim, Emile. *The God Within: Kant, Schelling, and Historicity*. Edited by John Burbidge. Toronto: University of Toronto Press, 1996.

Farraris, Maurizio. *The History of Hermeneutics*. Translated by Luca Somigli. Atlantic Highlands, N.J.: Humanities Press, 1996.

Ferguson, Frances. "Coleridge and the Deluded Reader: 'The Rime of the Ancient Mariner.'" In *Post-structuralist Readings of English Poetry*, edited by Richard Machin and Christopher Norris, 248–63. New York: Cambridge University Press, 1987.

———. *Solitude and the Sublime: Romanticism and the Aesthetics of Individuation*. New York: Routledge, 1992.

Feuerbach, Ludwig. *The Essence of Christianity*. Translated by George Eliot. Buffalo, N.Y.: Prometheus Books, 1989.

Figal, Günter. "Phronesis as Understanding." In *The Specter of Relativism: Truth, Dialogue and Phronesis in Philosophical Hermeneutics*, edited by Lawrence K. Schmidt, 236–47. Northwestern University Studies in Phenomenology and Existential Philosophy. Evanston, Ill.: Northwestern University Press, 1995.

Foster, Matthew. *Gadamer and Practical Philosophy: The Hermeneutics of Moral Confidence*. American Academy of Religion Studies in Religion 64. Atlanta, Ga.: Scholars Press, 1991.

Frank, Manfred. "Is Subjectivity a Non-Thing, an Absurdity (*Unding*)? On Some Difficulties in Naturalistic Reductions of Self-Consciousness." In *The Modern Subject: Conceptions of the Self in Classical German Philosophy*, edited by Karl Ameriks and Dieter Sturma, 177–97. SUNY Series in Contemporary Continental Philosophy. Albany: State University of New York Press, 1995.

Freud, Sigmund. "Civilization and Its Discontents." In *The Freud Reader*, edited by Peter Gay, 722–72. New York: W. W. Norton, 1989.

Gadamer, Hans-Georg. *Dialogue and Dialectic: Eight Hermeneutical Studies on Plato*. Translated by P. Christopher Smith. New Haven: Yale University Press, 1981.

———. *Gadamer on Celan: "Who Am I and Who Are You" and Other Essays*. Translated by Richard Heinemann and Bruce Krajewski. SUNY Series in Contemporary Continental Philosophy. Albany: State University of New York Press, 1997.

———. "Hermeneutics and Logocentrism." *Dialogue and Deconstruction: The Gadamer-Derrida Encounter*. Edited by Diane P. Michelfelder and Richard E. Palmer, 114–25. SUNY Series in Contemporary Continental Philosophy. Albany: State University of New York Press, 1989.

———. "Hermeneutics and Social Science." *Cultural Hermeneutics 2*, 307–16. Dordrecht, Holland: D. Reidel, 1975.

———. *The Idea of the Good in Platonic-Aristotelian Philosophy*. Translated by P. Christopher Smith. New Haven: Yale University Press, 1986.

———. "Letter to Dallmayr." *Dialogue and Deconstruction*, 93–101.

———. *Literature and Philosophy in Dialogue: Essays in German Literary Theory*. Translated by Robert H. Paslick. SUNY Series in Contemporary Continental Philosophy. Albany: State University of New York Press, 1994.

———. *On Education, Poetry, and History: Applied Hermeneutics*. Edited by Dieter Misgeld and Graeme Nicholson. Translated by Lawrence Schmidt and Monica Reuss. SUNY series in Contemporary Continental Philosophy. Albany: State University of New York Press, 1992.

———. "On the Truth of the Word." In *The Specter of Relativism: Truth, Dialogue, and Phronesis in Philosophical Hermeneutics*. Translated by Lawrence K. Schmidt and Monika Reuss. Edited by Lawrence K. Schmidt, 135–55. Northwestern University Studies in Phenomenology and Existential Philosophy. Evanston, Ill.: Northwestern University Press, 1995.

———. *Philosophical Hermeneutics*. Translated and edited by David E. Linge. Berkeley: University of California Press, 1976.

———. *Praise of Theory: Speeches and Essays*. Translated by Chris Dawson. Edited by Joel Weinsheimer. Yale Studies in Hermeneutics. New Haven: Yale University Press, 1998.

———. *Reason in the Age of Science*. Translated by Frederick G. Lawrence. Cambridge, Mass.: The MIT Press, 1981.

———. *The Relevance of the Beautiful and Other Essays*. Edited by Robert Bernasconi. Translated by Nicholas Walker. Cambridge: Cambridge University Press, 1986.

———. "Reply to Jacques Derrida." *Dialogue and Deconstruction*, 55–57.

———. "Text and Interpretation." *Dialogue and Deconstruction*, 21–51.

———. *Truth and Method*. 2d rev. ed. Translation revised by Joel Weinsheimer and Donald G. Marshall. New York: Crossroad, 1990.

Gallagher, Shaun. *Hermeneutics and Education*. SUNY Series in Contemporary Continental Philosophy. Albany: State University of New York Press, 1992.

Galperin, William. *The Return of the Visible in British Romanticism*. Baltimore: The Johns Hopkins University Press, 1993.

Gasché, Rodolphe. Foreword to Friedrich Schlegel's *Philosophical Fragments*. Minneapolis and Oxford: University of Minnesota Press, 1991. vii-xxxii.

Gatti, Hilary. "Coleridge's Reading of Giordano Bruno." *The Wordsworth Circle*. 27, 3 (summer 1996): 136–45.

Gillman, James. *The Life of Samuel Taylor Coleridge*. London: W. Pickering, 1838.

Girard, René. *Violence and the Sacred*. Translated by Patrick Gregory. Baltimore: The Johns Hopkins University Press, 1977.

Goodhart, Sandor. *Sacrificing Commentary*. Baltimore: The Johns Hopkins University Press, 1996.

Greenblatt, Stephen. "Towards a Poetics of Culture." In *The New Historicism*, edited by H. Aram Veeser, 1–14. New York: Routledge, 1989

Grondin, Jean. *Introduction to Philosophical Hermeneutics*. Translated by Joel Weinsheimer. Yale Studies in Hermeneutics. New Haven: Yale University Press, 1994.

Habermas, Jürgen. *The Philosophical Discourse of Modernity: Twelve Lectures*. Translated by Frederick Lawrence. Cambridge, Mass.: The MIT Press, 1987.

———. "A Review of Gadamer's *Truth and Method*." In *Hermeneutics and Modern Philosophy*, edited by Brice R. Wachterhauser, translated by Fred Dallmayr and Thomas McCarthy, 243–76. Albany: State University of New York Press, 1986.

Hamlin, Cyrus. *Hermeneutics of Form: Romantic Poetics in Theory and Practice*. New Haven, Conn.: Henry R. Schwab, 1998.

Haney, David P. "The Emergence of the Autobiographical Figure in *The Prelude*, Book I." *Studies in Romanticism* 20 (1981): 33–63.

———. "Nuptial Interruption: Marriage and Autobiography in Wordsworth's 'A Farewell.'" In *Autobiography and Post-Modernism*, edited by Leigh Gilmore, et al, 240–65. Amherst: University of Massachusetts Press, 1994.

———. "Poetry as Super-Genre in Wordsworth: Presentation and Ethics." *European Romantic Review* 5 (1994): 73–89.

———. "'Rents and openings in the ideal world': Eye and Ear in Wordsworth." *Studies in Romanticism* 36 (1997): 173–99.

———. "Viewing 'the Viewless Wings of Poesy': Gadamer, Keats and Historicity." *Clio* 18 (1989): 103–22.

———. *William Wordsworth and the Hermeneutics of Incarnation*. Literature and Philosophy Series. University Park,: The Pennsylvania State University Press, 1993.

———. "Wordsworth and Levinas: Making a Habit of the Sublime." In *In Proximity: Levinas and the Eighteenth Century*. Edited by Melvyn New. Lubbock: Texas Tech University Press. Forthcoming.

Harding, Anthony John. *Coleridge and the Idea of Love: Aspects of Relationship in Coleridge's Thought and Writing*. London: Cambridge University Press, 1974.

———. "Imagination, Patriarchy, and Evil in Coleridge and Heidegger." *Studies in Romanticism* 35, 1 (spring 1996): 3–26.

———. Review of Morton D. Paley, *Coleridge's Later Poetry* and Ronald C. Wendling, *Coleridge's Progress to Christianity: Experience and Authority in Religious Faith*. *The Wordsworth Circle* 27 (autumn 1966): 197–99.

Harpham, Geoffrey Galt. "Ethics." *Critical Terms for Literary Study*, edited by Frank Lentricchia and Thomas McLaughlin, 387–405. 2d ed. Chicago: University of Chicago Press, 1995.

———. *Getting it Right: Language, Literature, and Ethics*. Chicago: University of Chicago Press, 1992.

Harris, Thomas. *The Silence of the Lambs*. New York: St. Martin's Press, 1988.

Hartman, Geoffrey. "On Traumatic Knowledge and Literary Studies." *New Literary History* 26, 3 (summer 1995): 537–63.

———. "The Poetics of Prophecy." In *The Unremarkable Wordsworth*, 163–81. Minneapolis: University of Minnesota Press, 1987.

———. "Reflections on an Evening Star: Akenside to Coleridge." In *New Perspectives on Coleridge and Wordsworth: Selected Essays From the English Institute*, edited by Geoffrey Hartman, 85–131. New York: Columbia University Press, 1972.

———. *Wordsworth's Poetry 1787–1814*. New Haven: Yale University Press, 1964.

Heidegger, Martin. *Being and Time*. Translated by John Macquarrie and Edward Robinson. New York: Harper and Row, 1962.

———. "Building Dwelling Thinking." In *Poetry, Language, Thought*, translated by Albert Hofstadter, 145–61. New York: Harper and Row, 1971.

———. *"The Question Concerning Technology" and Other Essays*. Translated by William Lovitt. New York: Garland, 1977.

Hiley, David R. *Philosophy in Question: Essays on a Pyrrhonian Theme*. Chicago: University of Chicago Press, 1988.

Hoagwood, Terence Allan. *Politics, Philosophy, and the Production of Romantic Texts*. DeKalb, Ill.: Northern Illinois University Press, 1996.

———. "Prolegomenon for a Theory of Romantic Drama." *The Wordsworth Circle* 23 (spring 1992): 49–64.

Hudson, W. D., ed. *The Is-Ought Question: A Collection of Papers on the Central Problem in Moral Philosophy*. New York: Macmillan, 1969.

Hühn, Peter. "Outwitting Self-Consciousness: Self-Reference and Paradox in Three Romantic Poems." *English Studies* 72, 3 (June 1991): 230–45.

Hume, David. *Hume's Ethical Writings*. Edited by Alasdair MacIntyre. Notre Dame: University of Notre Dame Press, 1965.

———. *A Treatise of Human Nature*. Edited by L. A. Selby-Bigge. 2d ed. rev. P. H. Nidditch. Oxford: Oxford University Press, 1978.

Independence Day. Directed by Roland Emmerich. 20th-Century Fox/Centropolis Entertainment, 1996.

Jameson, Frederic. *The Political Unconscious: Narrative as a Socially Symbolic Act*. Ithaca: Cornell University Press, 1981.

Kant, Immanuel. *Critique of Judgment*. Translated by Werner S. Pluhar. Indianapolis: Hackett Publishing, 1987.

———. *Groundwork of the Metaphysic of Morals*. Translated by H. J. Paton. New York: Harper and Row, 1964.

Keats, John. *Complete Poems*. Edited by Jack Stillinger. Cambridge, Mass.: Harvard University Press, 1982.

Knapp, Steven. *Personification and the Sublime: Milton to Coleridge*. Cambridge, Mass.: Harvard University Press, 1985.

Kovesi, Julius. "Against the Ritual of 'Is' and 'Ought'," 5–16. In *Studies in Ethical Theory*. Vol. 3 of *Midwest Studies in Philosophy*, edited by Peter E. French, et al. Morris, Minn.: University of Minnesota at Morris, 1978. Revised reissue, Minneapolis: University of Minnesota Press, 1980.

Kristeva, Julia. *Tales of Love*. Translated by Leon S. Roudiez. New York: Columbia University Press, 1987.

———. *Strangers to Ourselves*. Translated by Leon S. Roudiez. New York: Columbia University Press, 1991.

Kroeber, Karl. *Ecological Literary Criticism: Romantic Imagining and the Biology of Mind*. New York: Columbia University Press, 1994.

Kucich, Greg. "Romanticism and Feminist Historiography." *The Wordsworth Circle* 24, 3 (summer 1993): 133–43.

Leask, Nigel. *The Politics of Imagination in Coleridge's Thought*. London: Macmillan Press, 1988.

Levinas, Emmanuel. "Ethics and Politics." In *The Levinas Reader*. Edited by Seán Hand, 289-97. Cambridge, Mass.: Basil Blackwell, 1989.

———. "God and Philosophy." In *Basic Philosophical Writings*. Edited by Adrian T. Peperzak, Simon Critchley, and Robert Bernasconi, 129–48. Bloomington: Indiana University Press, 1996.

———. *Nine Talmudic Readings*. Translated by Annette Aronowicz. Bloomington: Indiana University Press, 1990.

———. *Otherwise than Being or Beyond Essence*. Translated by Alphonso Lingis. The Hague: Martinus Nijhoff, 1981.

———. "Reality and its Shadow." In *The Levinas Reader*, 129–43.

———. *Totality and Infinity: An Essay on Exteriority*. Translated by Alphonso Lingis. Duquesne Studies Philosophical Series 24. Pittsburgh: Duquesne University Press, 1969.

———. "The Trace of the Other." In *Deconstruction in Context*, edited by Mark C. Taylor, translated by Alphonso Lingis, 345–59. Chicago: University of Chicago Press, 1986.

———. "The Transcendence of Words." *The Levinas Reader*, 144–49.

Levinson, Marjorie. "The New Historicism: Back to the Future." In *Rethinking Historicism: Critical Readings in Romantic History*, edited by Levinson, et al., 18–63. Oxford: Basil Blackwell, 1989.

———. "Romantic Criticism: The State of the Art." In *At the Limits of Romanticism: Essays in Cultural, Feminist, and Materialist Criticism*. Edited by Mary A. Favret and Nicola J. Watson, 269–81. Bloomington: Indiana University Press, 1994.

———. *Wordsworth's Great Period Poems: Four Essays*. New York: Cambridge University Press, 1986.

Liu, Alan, "Formal vs. Historical Value." North American Society for the Study of Romanticism [online posting 29 July 1997; cited 29 July 1997]. Available from http://www.arts.uwaterloo.ca/~jmwright/nassr.html.

———. "The New Historicism and the Work of Mourning." *Studies in Romanticism* 35: 4 (1996): 553–62

———. *Wordsworth: The Sense of History*. Stanford: Stanford University Press, 1989.

Lockridge, Laurence S. *Coleridge the Moralist*. Ithaca: Cornell University Press, 1977.

———. *The Ethics of Romanticism*. New York: Cambridge University Press, 1989.

Lovibond, Sabina. *Realism and Imagination in Ethics*. Minneapolis: University of Minnesota Press, 1983.

Lyotard, Jean-François. *The Differend: Phrases in Dispute*. Translated by Georges Van Den Abbeele. Theory and History of Literature 46. Minneapolis: University of Minnesota Press, 1988.

———. "Levinas's Logic." In *The Lyotard Reader*, edited by Andrew Benjamin, translated by Ian McLeod, 275–313. Cambridge, Mass.: Basil Blackwell, 1989.

———. *Peregrinations: Law, Form, Event*. New York: Columbia University Press, 1988.

MacIntyre, Alasdair. *After Virtue: A Study in Moral Theory*. 2d ed. Notre Dame: University of Notre Dame Press, 1984.

———. "Moral Philosophy: What Next?" In *Revisions: Changing Perspectives in Moral Philosophy*, edited by Stanley Hauerwas and Alasdair MacIntyre, 1–15. Notre Dame: University of Notre Dame Press, 1983.

Macovski, Michael. *Dialogue and Literature: Apostrophe, Auditors, and the Collapse of Romantic Discourse*. New York: Oxford University Press, 1994.

Magnuson, Paul. *Coleridge and Wordsworth: A Lyrical Dialogue*. Princeton: Princeton University Press, 1988.

Marshall, Donald G. "Dialogue and Écriture." *Dialogue and Deconstruction*, 206–14.

Massey, Irving. *Find You the Virtue: Ethics, Image, and Desire in Literature*. Fairfax, Va.: George Mason University Press, 1987.

McClelland, Charles E. *State, Society, and University in Germany 1700–1914*. New York: Cambridge University Press, 1980.

McFarland, Thomas. *Coleridge and the Pantheist Tradition*. Oxford: Clarendon Press, 1969.

McGann, Jerome J. "Keats and the Historical Method in Literary Criticism." In *Romantic Poetry: Recent Revisionary Criticism*, edited by Karl Kroeber and Gene W. Ruoff, 439–64. New Brunswick, N.J.: Rutgers University Press, 1993.

———. "The Meaning of the Ancient Mariner." In *Spirits of Fire: English Romantic*

Writers and Contemporary Historical Methods, edited by G. A Rosso and Daniel P. Watkins, 208–39. Rutherford, N.J.: Fairleigh Dickinson University Press, 1990.

———. *The Poetics of Sensibility: A Revolution in Literary Style*. Oxford: Clarendon Press, 1996.

———. "Reconstructing Sensibility Again." North American Society For the Study of Romanticism [online posting 25 July 1997; cited 25 July 1997]. Available from http://www.rc.umd.edu/reference/anthologies/hemans2.htm.

———. "Rethinking Romanticism." *ELH* 59 (1992): 735–54.

———. *The Romantic Ideology: A Critical Investigation*. Chicago: University of Chicago Press, 1983.

———. "The Third World of Criticism." In *Rethinking Historicism: Critical Readings in Romantic History*, edited by Levinson, Marjorie, et al., 85–107. Oxford: Basil Blackwell, 1989.

McKusick, James. *Coleridge's Philosophy of Language*. New Haven and London: Yale University Press, 1986.

Mileur, Jean-Pierre. *The Critical Romance: The Critic as Reader, Writer, Hero*. Madison: University of Wisconsin Press, 1990.

———. *Vision and Revision: Coleridge's Art of Immanence*. Berkeley: University of California Press, 1982.

Miller, J. Hillis. *The Ethics of Reading*. New York: Columbia University Press, 1987.

Milton, John. *Paradise Lost*. Edited by Scott Elledge. Norton Critical Edition. New York: W. W. Norton, 1975.

Modiano, Raimonda. *Coleridge and the Concept of Nature*. Tallahassee: Florida State University Press, 1985.

Montrose, Louis. "The Elizabethan Subject and the Spenserian Text." In *Literary Theory/ Renaissance Texts*, edited by Particia Parker and David Quint, 303–40. Baltimore: The Johns Hopkins University Press, 1986.

Moorman, Mary. *William Wordsworth: A Biography. The Early Years 1770–1803*. Oxford: Oxford University Press, 1957.

———. *William Wordsworth: A Biography. The Later Years 1803–1850*. Oxford: Oxford University Press, 1965.

Muse, Amy M. 1999. They All Want to Play Hamlet: Actresses, Performance, and Identity. Ph.D. diss., Auburn University.

Nancy, Jean-Luc. "The Unsacrificeable." *Yale French Studies* 79 (1991): 20–38.

Natural Born Killers. Directed by Oliver Stone. Warner Bros., 1994.

Newton, Adam Zachary. *Narrative Ethics*. Cambridge, Mass.: Harvard University Press, 1995.

Norris, Christopher. *New Idols of the Cave: On the Limits of Anti-Realism*. Manchester: Manchester University Press, 1997.

———. *Truth and the Ethics of Criticism*. Manchester: Manchester University Press: 1994.

———. *Uncritical Theory: Postmodernism, Intellectuals, and the Gulf War*. Amherst, Mass.: University of Massachusetts Press, 1992.

———. *What's Wrong With Postmodernism: Critical Theory and the Ends of Philosophy*. Baltimore: The Johns Hopkins University Press, 1990.

Nussbaum, Martha C. *The Fragility of Goodness: Luck and Ethics in Greek Tragedy and Philosophy*. New York: Cambridge University Press, 1986.

———. *Love's Knowledge: Essays on Literature and Philosophy*. New York: Oxford University Press, 1990.

———. *The Therapy of Desire: Theory and Practice in Hellenistic Ethics*. Princeton: Princeton University Press, 1994.

Oakley, Francis. *Community of Learning: The American College and the Liberal Arts Tradition*. New York: Oxford University Press, 1992.

Orsini, G. N. G. *Coleridge and German Idealism: A Study in the History of Philosophy with Unpublished Materials from Coleridge's Manuscripts*. Carbondale: Southern Illinois University Press, 1969.

Pascoe, Judith. *Romantic Theatricality: Gender, Poetry, and Spectatorship*. Ithaca: Cornell University Press, 1997.

Perkins, Mary Ann. *Coleridge's Philosophy: The Logos As Unifying Principle*. Oxford: Oxford University Press, 1994.

Plato. *The Collected Dialogues of Plato, Including the Letters*. Edited by Edith Hamilton and Huntington Cairns. Bollingen Series 71. Princeton: Princeton University Press, 1961.

Pope, Alexander. *An Essay on Man*. In *Poems of Alexander Pope*. 10 volumes. Edited by John Butt. London: Methuen, 1950.

Prickett, Stephen. *Romanticism and Religion: The Tradition of Coleridge and Wordsworth in the Victorian Church*. Cambridge, Mass.: Cambridge University Press, 1976.

———. *The Origins of Narrative: The Romantic Appropriation of the Bible*. Cambridge: Cambridge University Press, 1996.

Rajan, Tilottama. "Coleridge, Wordsworth, and the Textual Abject." *The Wordsworth Circle* 24 (spring 1993): 61–68.

———. *The Supplement of Reading: Figures of Understanding in Romantic Theories and Practice*. Ithaca: Cornell University Press, 1990.

Ransom, John Crowe. *The New Criticism*. Norfolk, Conn.: New Directions, 1941.

Rawls, John. "Justice as Fairness: Political Not Metaphysical." *Philosophy and Public Affairs* 14 (1985): 223–51.

Reid, Nicholas. "Coleridge and Schelling: The Missing Transcendental Deduction." *Studies in Romanticism* 33: 3 (fall 1994): 451–79.

Rev. of *Essays, Historical and Critical, on English Church* Music, by William Mason. *Monthly Review* 20 (Aug. 1796): 398–408.

Ricoeur, Paul. "Hermeneutics and the Critique of Ideology." In *Hermeneutics and Modern Philosophy*. Edited by Brice R. Wachterhauser, 300–339. Albany: State University of New York Press, 1986.

———. *Hermeneutics and the Human Sciences: Essays on Language, Action, and Interpretation*. Edited and translated by John B. Thompson. Cambridge: Cambridge University Press, 1981.

———. *Interpretation Theory: Discourse and the Surplus of Meaning*. Fort Worth, Tex.: Texas Christian University Press, 1976.

———. *Oneself as Another*. Translated by Kathleen Blamey. Chicago: University of Chicago Press, 1992.

———. *The Symbolism of Evil*. Translated by Emerson Buchanan. Boston: Beacon

Press, 1967.

Risser, James. *Hermeneutics and the Voice of the Other: Re-Reading Gadamer's Philosophical Hermeneutics*. SUNY Series in Contemporary Continental Philosophy. Albany: State University of New York Press, 1997.

Robbins, Jill. *Altered Reading: Levinas and Literature*. Chicago: University of Chicago Press, 1999.

———. *Prodigal Son/Elder Brother: Interpretation and Alterity in Augustine, Petrarch, Kafka, Levinas*. Chicago: University of Chicago Press, 1991.

Rorty, Richard. *Contingency, Irony, and Solidarity*. Cambridge: Cambridge University Press, 1989.

———. *Richard Rorty on Hermeneutics, General Studies, and Teaching*. Selected Papers From the Synergos Seminars. Vol. 2. Fairfax, Va.: George Mason University, 1982.

Ruoff, Gene, ed. *The Romantics and Us: Essays on Literature and Culture*. New Brunswick: Rutgers University Press, 1990.

Schelling, Friedrich Wilhelm Joseph von. "Treatise Explicatory of the Idealism in the *Science of Knowledge*" (1797). In *Idealism and the Endgame of Theory: Three Essays by F. W. J. Schelling*, translated and edited by Thomas Pfau, 61–138. Intersections: Philosophy and Critical Theory. Albany: State University of New York Press, 1994.

Schildgen, Brenda Deen. "Reconnecting Rhetoric and Philosophy in the Composition Classroom." In *Into the Field: Sites of Composition Studies*, edited by Anne Ruggles Gere, 30–43. New York: The Modern Language Association, 1993.

Schiller, Friedrich von. "On the Sublime." In *Naive and Sentimental Poetry and On the Sublime: Two Essays*, translated by Julias A. Elias, 193–212. Milestones of Thought. New York: Frederick Ungar, 1966.

Shaffer, E. S. "The Hermeneutic Community: Coleridge and Schleiermacher." In *The Coleridge Connection: Essays for Thomas McFarland*, edited by Richard Gravil and Molly Lefebure, 200–229. New York: St. Martin's Press, 1990.

———. *"Kubla Khan" and* The Fall of Jerusalem*: The Mythical School in Biblical Criticism and Secular Literature, 1770–1880*. Cambridge: Cambridge University Press, 1975.

Shapiro, Gary. "From the Sublime to the Political: Some Historical Notes." *New Literary History* 16: 2 (winter 1985): 213–35.

Shelley, Percy Bysshe. *Shelley's Prose or the Trumpet of a Prophecy*. Edited by David Lee Clark. New York: New Amsterdam Books, 1988.

Siebers, Tobin. *The Ethics of Criticism*. Ithaca: Cornell University Press, 1988.

The Silence of the Lambs. Directed by Jonathan Demme. Orion Pictures, 1990.

Simpson, David. *Romanticism, Nationalism, and the Revolt Against Theory*. Chicago: University of Chicago Press, 1993.

Siskin, Clifford. *The Work of Writing: Literature and Social Change in Britain, 1700–1830*. Baltimore: The Johns Hopkins University Press, 1998.

Smith, Adam. *The Theory of Moral Sentiments*. Edited by D. D. Raphael and A. L. MacFie. Oxford: Oxford University Press, 1976.

Smith, Barbara Herrnstein. *Contingencies of Value: Alternative Perspectives for Critical Theory*. Cambridge, Mass.: Harvard University Press, 1988.

Smith, P. Christopher. *Hermeneutics and Human Finitude: Toward a Theory of Eth-*

ical Understanding. New York: Fordham University Press, 1991.

South Park: Bigger, Longer and Uncut. Directed by Trey Parker. Paramount/Warner Bros., 1999.

Sultana, Donald. *Samuel Taylor Coleridge in Malta and Italy*. Oxford: Basil Blackwell, 1969.

Swann, Karen. "'Christabel': The Wandering Mother and the Enigma of Form." *Studies in Romanticism* 23 (winter 1984): 533–53.

Taylor, Charles. *The Ethics of Authenticity*. Cambridge: Harvard University Press, 1992.

———. *Sources of the Self: The Making of the Modern Identity*. Cambridge, Mass.: Harvard University Press 1989.

Thomas, Keith G. "Coleridge, Wordsworth and the New Historicism: 'Chamouny, The Hour before Sun-Rise. A Hymn' and Book 6 of *The Prelude*." *Studies in Romanticism* 33: 1 (spring 1994): 81–117.

———. *Wordsworth and Philosophy: Empiricism and Transcendentalism in the Poetry*. Ann Arbor: UMI Research Press, 1989.

Tillich, Paul. *A History of Christian Thought: From Its Judaic and Hellenistic Origins to Existentialism*. Edited by Carl E. Braaten. New York: Simon and Schuster, 1967.

Vallins, David. "Production and Existence: Coleridge's Unification of Nature." *Journal of the History of Ideas* 56: 1 (Jan. 1995): 107–24.

Vattimo, Gianni. *Beyond Interpretation: The Meaning of Hermeneutics for Philosophy*. Translated by David Webb. Stanford: Stanford University Press, 1997.

Wallen, Martin. "Return and Representation: The Revisions of 'The Ancient Mariner.'" *The Wordsworth Circle* 17 (1986): 148–56.

Warren, Robert Penn. "A Poem of Pure Imagination: an Experiment in Reading." In *Selected Essays*, 198–305. New York: Random House, 1958.

Wehrs, Donald. *African Feminist Fiction, Western Theory, and the Politics of Close Reading*. Gainesville: University of Florida Press. Forthcoming.

Weinsheimer, Joel. *Eighteenth-Century Hermeneutics: Philosophy of Interpretation in England from Locke to Burke*. New Haven: Yale University Press, 1993.

———. *Philosophical Hermeneutics and Literary Theory*. New Haven: Yale University Press, 1991.

Wendling, Ronald C. *Coleridge's Progress to Christianity: Experience and Authority in Religious Faith*. Lewisburg: Bucknell University Press; London: Associated University Presses, 1995.

———. "Reply to Professor Harding." *The Wordsworth Circle* 27, 4 (autumn 1996): 199.

White, Deborah Elise. "Introduction: Irony and Clerisy." In *Romantic Praxis: A Hypertext Collection of Theory and Criticism* [online posting August 1999; 11 paragraphs; cited 26 Aug. 1999]. Available from http:www.rc.umd.edu/praxis/irony.

Wilde, Oscar. *The Picture of Dorian Gray*. 1891. *The First Collected Edition of the Works of Oscar Wilde*. Edited by Robert Ross. 15 vols. London: Dawsons, 1969.

Williams, Bernard. *Ethics and the Limits of Philosophy*. Cambridge, Mass.: Harvard University Press, 1985.

———. "Persons, Character and Morality." In *The Identities of Persons*, edited by

Amélie Oksenberg Rorty, 197–216. Berkeley: University of California Press, 1976.

———. *Shame and Necessity*. Sather Classical Lectures 57. Berkeley: University of California Press, 1993.

Wordsworth, William. *The Fourteen-Book Prelude*. Edited by W. J. B. Owen. Ithaca: Cornell University Press, 1985.

———. *Lyrical Ballads, and Other Poems, 1797–1800*. Edited by James Butler and Karen Green. Ithaca: Cornell University Press, 1992.

———. *Poems, in Two Volumes, and Other Poems, 1800–1807*. Edited by Jared Curtis. The Cornell Wordsworth. Ithaca: Cornell University Press, 1983.

———. *The Poetical Works of William Wordsworth*. Edited by Ernest de Selincourt. 2d ed. 5 vols. Oxford: Clarendon Press, 1963–66.

———. *The Prose Works of William Wordsworth*. Edited by W. J. B. Owen and J. W. Smyser. 3 vols. Oxford: Oxford University Press, 1974.

———. *The Thirteen-Book Prelude*. Edited by Mark L. Reed. 2 vols. Ithaca: Cornell University Press, 1991.

Wyschogrod, Edith. "The Art in Ethics: Aesthetics, Objectivity, and Alterity in the Philosophy of Emmanuel Levinas." In *Ethics as First Philosophy: The Significance of Emmanuel Levinas for Philosophy, Literature, and Religion*, edited by Adrian T. Peperzak, 137–48. New York and London: Routledge, 1995.

Zengotita, Thomas de. "The Gunfire Dialogues: Notes on the Reality of Virtuality." *Harper's* (July 1999): 55–58.

Index

www.ingramcontent.com/pod-product-compliance
Lightning Source LLC
Chambersburg PA
CBHW031544300426
44111CB00006BA/175

* 9 7 8 0 2 7 1 0 2 7 8 6 9 *